Registered Representative

Stockbroker

ARCO

Registered Representative

—

Stockbroker

NASD Series 7 Exam

PHILIP MEYERS ● PETER SOLOMON

Prentice Hall

NEW YORK   LONDON   TORONTO   SYDNEY   TOKYO   SINGAPORE

This edition is a revised edition of the Work entitled
HOW TO PASS THE REGISTERED REPRESENTATIVE/STOCKBROKER EXAM

Prentice Hall General Reference
15 Columbus Circle
New York, NY 10023

An Arco Book

Prentice Hall and colophons are registered
trademarks of Simon & Schuster, Inc.

Manufactured in the United States of America

1 2 3 4 5 6 7 8 9 10

Library of Congress Cataloging-in-Publication Data

Meyers, Philip.
    Registered representative/stockbroker : NASD Series 7 exam /
Philip Meyers, Peter Solomon.
        p.   cm.
    Rev. ed. of: How to pass the registered representative
stockbroker's exam. c1988.
    Includes index.
    ISBN 0-13-770702-9
    1. Stocks—United States—Examinations, questions, etc.
2. Stockbrokers—United States—Examinations, questions, etc.
I. Solomon, Peter.   II. Meyers, Philip. How to pass the registered
representative stockbroker's exam.   III. Title.
HG4910.M39   1991
332.63′22′076—dc20
                                                    91-33590
                                                    CIP

FOREWORD

This second edition of Arco's *Registered Representative / Stockbroker* should prove just as successful as the first, due to two important factors. The first is the clear, precise way that the authors explain the complex subjects that prospective stockbrokers must master in order to pass the Series 7 Exam. In all of the twenty-four subject areas covered on the test, this book is right on target both with the information test-takers need to know and with the way that information is addressed on the exam.

The second factor that will surely contribute to the book's success is its low price. In a market where some study materials can cost up to $150, this information-packed book is, quite simply, a great value. Because its price is so economical, it makes not only an ideal single-volume guide to the test, but also a natural supplement to a larger-scale preparation program. In addition, for readers who are not necessarily preparing for the Series 7 Exam but who are interested in the securities industry in general, this book makes an excellent, concise introduction to the day-to-day workings of Wall Street.

For this new edition, Philip Meyers and Peter Solomon have judiciously expanded the original text, providing the reader with additional information in those areas that now receive more emphasis on the Series 7 Exam. They have also updated all of the instructional and review sections to reflect the most recent industry regulations—and today's most popular investment instruments and strategies. Furthermore, the practice tests have been similarly updated so that the amount of coverage given to each topic accurately reflects the actual makeup of today's Series 7 Exam.

To derive the most benefit from this book, the reader will need to be both diligent and conscientious. Just as the authors have taken no shortcuts in presenting the information, the reader should take no shortcuts in studying the material. Furthermore, it pays to remember that the Series 7 Exam is not static. The pool of several thousand questions is constantly being revised and updated, and most recently there has been a decreasing emphasis on simply memorizing facts—and an increasing emphasis on understanding basic principles. For the prospective stockbroker, this means a more difficult examination. This book is a good place to begin not only your preparation for the Series 7 Exam, but also your career in the securities industry.

Alvin D. Hall
Faculty Member
New York Institute of Finance

William A. Rini
Senior Vice President
New York Institute of Finance

CONTENTS

Registered Representative

—

Stockbroker

PART ONE

About the Series 7 Examination

Introduction

GENERAL EXAMINATION INFORMATION AND PREPARATION FOR THE SERIES 7 TEST

This book is intended for those people who plan to become stockbrokers—licensed registered representatives or account executives employed by brokerage firms. These professionals must be able to call on an extraordinary amount of knowledge in their day-to-day dealings with the investing public and with colleagues in the investment industry. To ensure that they have command of the needed information, they must pass the Qualification Examination for General Securities Registered Representative ("Test Series 7"). This comprehensive test consists of 250 questions on every aspect of the industry and is formulated and administered by the National Association of Securities Dealers (NASD).

Anyone who masters the material in these pages should be able to pass the test.

The comprehensive focus should also make this book useful to the serious investor or to anyone who is considering becoming an investor—in fact, to anyone curious about just what a stockbroker knows. Because it contains so much information in such a clearly organized fashion, it can also be a convenient general reference source for anyone who needs to know (or be reminded) of details about various facets of the investment industry.

In short, while our principal audience is the potential registered representative, this is not simply a test preparation manual. Although some knowledge of general business practice and terminology is helpful, every effort has been made to present the material in a way that is accessible to any reader. All technical terms are thoroughly defined; industry practices, rules, and regulations are not simply described but explained in terms of their rationale in the context of actual operations. Wherever possible, we provide illustrations and examples and avoid long lists of facts.

This approach should also serve those whose main interest is in taking the examination, as many of the questions require more than recalling the pertinent term or formula. Rather, candidates are asked to apply their understanding of the industry in making judgments and comprehending and analyzing unfamiliar material.

Note that these pages contain more information than any single test will cover; we have tried to be as complete as space allows, offering more detail than strictly necessary. At the same time, it is not possible to cover every item on every test in any one book. The work of the registered representative is not based on a fixed code; products, practices, laws, and regulations are all subject to change, and the test along with them.

Plan of the book

We begin the book with five chapters of basic information on the "products" that a registered representative can offer a customer, the basic elements of the securities industry: common and preferred stocks, bonds and other debt instruments, mutual funds, and investments designed to present tax advantages.

In the following four chapters we examine the operation and role of the various securities markets, tracing the steps involved in a new issue of each of several types of instruments and describing in detail the workings of over-the-counter markets, the national exchanges, and options markets.

In Chapters 10 and 11 we describe the procedures followed in handling customer accounts and orders, both regular brokerage office practices and the special treatment required in dealing with margin accounts and short sales.

Chapter 12 presents an extended review of the elements involved in analyzing and selecting investments or investment strategies for a particular individual. There are separate sections on broad economic analysis, the "technical" and "fundamental" approaches, ways to assess a particular firm and its securities, and mathematical techniques.

Chapter 13 sketches out the tax consequences of investment moves and positions. This has become a volatile area in recent years, with major changes in thinking about taxation on investments, but we provide the essential general information needed to guide registered representatives and their customers.

Chapter 14 follows with a guide to reading published financial news.

Chapters 15 and 16 cover the rules that affect all securities transactions: federal and state laws, regulations imposed by the National Association of Securities Dealers, rules of the national exchanges, and the special rules governing municipal issues.

Special features of the book

In addition to the text, with its many examples and clearly defined subsections, each chapter is followed by a brief glossary of key terms. These, along with the index, should serve as a helpful "refresher" both while studying for the test and in years to come.

Review questions at the end of each chapter are designed to help strengthen your comprehension of the material in that chapter. These questions should be approached not so much as a challenge, but as a way of highlighting and reinforcing information. In effect, they help teach the material: many of the questions describe a fact or condition that is not explicit in the text but must be inferred, so becoming thoroughly familiar with the answers is essential to mastering the material.

Practice Tests

Finally, there are two complete tests, chances for a trial run. It is impossible to overemphasize their importance. The Series 7 Exam includes 250 questions; this means, on average, you will have less than a minute and a half to choose the correct answer. As each question offers four possible answers, it is essential that you become thoroughly familiar with the *form* of the questions. With 1000 answers to choose from, there is no time during the test to do more than remember the correct information.

These practice tests simulate the actual exam in length, form, and content (that is, in the mix of questions). It cannot simulate the presentation precisely, as the test is now offered on the PLATO™ system. This involves a video terminal which displays questions much as they are on these pages, but to answer, one touches an indicated point on the screen. PLATO draws questions randomly from a central question bank.

Although randomly selected, the questions are chosen in the proportions shown below. The questions are distributed so that more difficult ones occur in the middle of the test with easier ones at the beginning and end of the exam. The system allows individual testing and immediate grading.

Distribution of Questions

TOPIC	NO. OF QUESTIONS	PCT. OF EXAM
Corporate and Government Securities	30	12%
Municipal Securities	50	20%
Packaged Securities and Direct Participation Programs	35	14%
Exchanges and Regulation	50	20%
Options	50	20%
Margin	10	4%
Retirement and Taxation	10	4%
Economic and Securities Analysis	15	6%

The best possible preparation involves working within the real time limits imposed by the examiners. Try to complete the practice exam in two three-hour sessions, with a one-hour break.

In grading yourself, remember that the exam is designed only to gauge your knowledge of the duties of a registered representative. You are not competing with others taking the test; anyone who correctly answers 70 percent (175) of the 250 questions is considered qualified.

Question Format

All questions asked, on the test and in this book, are in one of six formats:

1. *A simple question.*
   Which of the following is true of T-bonds?

   (A) They have little inflation risk.
   (B) They have little interest rate risk.
   (C) They have little credit risk.
   (D) They are not widely available.

2. *An incomplete statement; you must find the answer which logically completes it.*
   A trade between an investment company and a bank is a:

   (A) first market trade
   (B) second market trade
   (C) third market trade
   (D) fourth market trade

3. *An incomplete statement; you must find the answer which is incorrect. To differentiate this sort of question, the word "EXCEPT" is always used in capitals.*
   All of the following are acceptable investments for an IRA EXCEPT:

   (A) unlisted stocks
   (B) non-investment grade bonds
   (C) diamonds
   (D) junk bond funds

4. *Multiple-answer questions; here, two or more (sometimes all) responses are correct. The possible responses are identified by Roman numerals.*
   Option allocation assignments notices to customers may use which of the following methods?

   I. random selection
   II. FIFO
   III. LIFO
   IV. equitable allocation

       (A) I, II and IV only
       (B) II, III and IV only
       (C) I and II only
       (D) II and IV only

5. *Matching one or more offered answers with its appropriate description, usually offered in a series of questions. Note that more than one, or none, of the choices may apply.*
   Questions 37-39 refer to the following choices:

   (A) Spread
   (B) Takedown Concession
   (C) Reallowance
   (D) Manager's Expense

   Which choice is described in the following questions?

   37. The portion of municipal bond offering which is the difference between the public offering price and what the issuer receives.

   38. The amount that a member of the syndicate receives.

   39. The amount that a member of the selling group receives.

6. *Questions based on an exhibit, such as a tombstone ad, a stock table, or a rule; the questions themselves are usually of the type described in (1) or (2) above.*

PART TWO

Subject Review

CHAPTER ONE

Stocks

T he predominant form of business in the United States today is the corporation. All corporations must issue common stock; each share of stock represents a unit of ownership in (a "share of") the corporation.

All U.S. corporations must be chartered in some state under the laws of this state. This charter, filed with the secretary of state, is also called the Articles of Incorporation. It includes the:

- □ name, purpose, and nature of the business
- □ number and type of shares of stock being offered ("authorized stock")
- □ duties of corporate officers
- □ names and addresses of the corporation's original directors

Those who hold common stock have certain rights (enumerated below), but only a limited liability. That is, they are liable only for the amount they paid for their stock, not for any of the debt of the corporation.

Before going further, let us define some terms used in connection with stocks.

STOCK TERMS

Authorized stock

As noted above, a corporation's charter limits the number of shares it may issue. This amount allowed is referred to as "authorized stock."

Unissued stock

This is stock authorized but not yet issued by the corporation. Most firms issue less stock than has been authorized and hold the remainder for future use.

Issued stock

Issued stock can be divided into:

Outstanding stock Issued shares currently in public hands.

Treasury stock Outstanding stock that has been reacquired by the corporation. Treasury stock can be held, reissued or retired. It carries no right to vote or to collect dividends and, in general, is not part of the capitalization of the company.

Par value

An arbitrary value assigned when the stock is issued and printed on the stock certificate. Historically, par value has been used as a corporate bookkeeping entry. It has been traditionally set at a low price, partly because some states' taxes are based on it. This value has no relationship to any other valuation of the stock.

For stock issued at a price above par value, the difference is carried on the books as paid-in surplus. Sometimes stock is issued with no par value.

Book value

Unlike par value, the book value of a share reflects the net worth of the corporation, as determined by generally accepted accounting principles, divided by the number of shares outstanding.

Market value

This is simply the value assigned to the stock in the marketplace, for example, the currently quoted price of a share.

OWNERSHIP

The stock certificate

This document provides evidence of ownership of stock. The stock certificate is negotiable. It shows:

- name of the corporation
- number of shares represented by the certificate
- name or names of the registered owner(s)
- name of the transfer agent
- name of the registrar
- signatures of authorized corporate officers.

Transfer of ownership

A stockholder has the right to transfer ownership of his or her shares, except in the case of certain "restricted stocks" where this right is specifi-

Figure 1.1 Stock Certificate (front)

cally withheld. The issuing corporation must record the name of any purchaser of its stock. When stock changes hands, the new owner is entitled to stockholder's rights only after a record of the transfer of ownership is made.

To transfer a stock, the stockholder endorses the back of the certificate.

Such a transfer involves two vital steps:

Transfer Agents A transfer agent records the name, address, social security number, and number of shares held by each registered shareholder. The transfer agent also assures that properly endorsed old certificates are cancelled and that new certificates in the name(s) of the new owner(s) are signed (by the responsible corporate officer), sealed (with the corporate seal), and delivered (to the new shareholder(s)).

This transfer agent is typically independent of the corporation.

Registrars The registrar must always be independent of the corporation. The registrar gets both old and new certificates, determines that the corporation has not issued more stock than authorized under its charter, and that all outstanding shares are accounted for (as to ownership) on the corporation's books.

Assignment

Stocks may also be "assigned." This requires a form called a "stock power." Assigned changes of ownership are not recorded on a corporation's books.

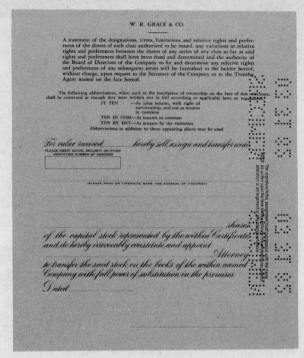

Figure 1.2 Stock Certificate (back)

RIGHTS OF OWNERSHIP—VOTING

The principal rights of ownership are voting rights and the right to share in the profits of the corporation by receiving dividends.

Voting rights

Most common stock entitles the owner to attend annual meetings and to vote on all important matters affecting shareholders. These include:

□ alterations to the corporate charter

□ mergers and acquisitions

□ recapitalization (an exchange of one form of security—stock, preferred stock or bond—for another)

□ financial reorganization

□ election of the board of directors of the corporation (the choice shareholders face most frequently)

Voting for directors follows one of two procedures:

Regulatory (Statutory) voting Each share has one vote for each position on the board of directors. For example, if there are seven positions to be filled on the board of directors, a shareholder owning 100 shares may cast up to 100 votes for each of seven different candidates. Under this system, a majority of the shareholders can determine the composition of the board.

Cumulative voting Each share controls as many votes as there are members of the board. For example, if there are seven positions to be filled, a shareholder with 100 shares can cast 700 votes and may cast them all for a single board member if he or she so desires. This method of voting allows a minority—by cumulating votes for one candidate—to assure itself representation on the board.

Proxies

As it is not possible for most shareholders to actually attend corporate meetings, corporations are required to send all shareholders a "proxy" or power of attorney, authorizing the holder to vote on the shareholder's behalf either according to specific instructions or at the proxyholder's discretion.

The proxy form also includes all pertinent information on matters to be voted on at the meeting. Organized exchanges like the NYSE are required to de-list firms that fail to provide the proxy form.

RIGHTS OF OWNERSHIP— DIVIDENDS

The principal financial rewards of owning common stock are the opportunity for capital appreciation—the chance that the price of the stock will rise—and dividend income. Dividends are paid to common shareholders at the discretion of the company's directors (that is, if they choose to do so). Common stock dividends may only be paid after all taxes, interest on bonds and preferred stock dividends (if any) have been paid. *They must come from current earnings or retained earnings from prior years.*

When a cash dividend is declared, it is recorded immediately on the corporation's books as a current liability. Actual payment of the dividend causes a reduction in the working capital of the company.

Directors must officially declare the dividend, including the size, date of record, and the date payable. Thus the stockholder has a right to the dividend "when, as and if declared." Shareholders have rights to dividends in proportion to their holdings of the outstanding stock. Someone holding 5% of the outstanding stock is entitled to 5% of the total declared dividend, whether paid in cash or in stock.

Owners of the stock before the date determined by the board of directors as the "record date" for dividends are entitled to the dividends. This is true until four business days before the record date (since the transactions are settled in five business days). From then on the stock sells "ex-dividend" and the market price declines to reflect that loss of dividend.

■ EXAMPLE

Amalgamated Consolidated Inc. is selling at $50 and a $2.50 dividend is declared for owners of record date of Friday, March 15th. Assuming no other changes we can expect the stock to have an opening price on the 11th at $47.50.

Cash dividends

Most often, dividends are paid in cash and declared as dollars per share rather than total dollars of dividend. If XYZ Corp. declares a dividend of $2.40 per share, a person owning 200 shares of XYZ would receive a check for $480.

Stock dividends

Corporations sometimes declare "stock dividends" as opposed to cash dividends. These are expressed in percentage terms. For example, if XYZ Corp. declares a 5% stock dividend, a holder of 200 shares would receive a stock certificate for 10 additional shares.

This can sometimes lead to the creation of fractional shares. A 5% stock dividend on 50 shares would generate $.05 \times 50$ or 2.5 additional shares. Most often, firms redeem fractional shares for cash or allow them to be bought and sold through a broker at no commission. Increases beyond 25% are generally called stock splits.

Property dividends

A corporation may declare a property dividend. This is often in the form of securities. For instance, a corporation wishing to divest itself of a subsidiary might do so by distributing stock in that subsidiary to its own shareholders.

Stock splits

A firm will sometimes declare a stock split, i.e., a declaration that each old share is now equal to some number of new shares. This does not change the value of the underlying corporation and so the other values are changed proportionately. Stock splits that do increase the number of authorized shares or change the par value must be approved by the shareholders.

■ EXAMPLE

A stock with a par value of $1.00 and a market value of $20.00 which had a 2-for-1 stock split would now have twice as many authorized shares, each with a par value of $.50. Each outstanding share would now have a market value of $10.00.

Reverse splits

A reverse split declares that each old share is now equal to some fraction of a new share.

■ EXAMPLE

In a 1-for-3 reverse split, 300 shares of old stock would now be 100 shares of the new stock. Both the par and market values would be tripled.

OTHER RIGHTS

Pre-emptive right

The right of a shareholder to maintain a proportionate share of ownership of the corporation. When this right exists, a current shareholder has the right to purchase any newly-issued stock in proportion to his or her original holdings in the company.

■ EXAMPLE

A person owning 10% of the outstanding shares of a particular stock would have the right to purchase 10% of any new issue of this stock. If

50,000 new shares are issued this person would have the right to purchase 10% of 50,000 or 5,000 of the shares.

Value of rights The subscription price of a new issue is usually lower than the market price of already-issued stock. Hence, the right to purchase this new issue has some value and may be traded in the marketplace.

As with dividends, those who buy the stock before the date determined by the board of directors as the "record date" for "subscription rights," get the rights as well. The stock is said to sell "cum rights" or "with rights."

Again, this holds until four business days before the record date. From then on the stock sells "ex-rights" and the market price declines to reflect that loss of rights.

One can compute the theoretical value of a right as follows:

For stock selling "cum rights" the value is given by the formula:

$$\frac{\text{Market Price} - \text{Subscription Price}}{\text{Number of Rights required} + 1} \text{ or } \frac{M - S}{N + 1} = \text{Value}$$

Note that the market price of the stock M includes the value of the right in this case.

■ **EXAMPLE**

If a stock is selling for $60 and two (2) rights are required to purchase a single share at the subscription price of $51, the value of a single right would be:

$$\frac{\$60 - \$51}{2 + 1} = \frac{\$9}{3} = \$3$$

For a stock selling "ex-rights" the theoretical value for a right is given by the formula:

$$\frac{\text{Market Value} - \text{Subscription Value}}{\text{Number of Rights required}} = \frac{M - S}{N} = \text{Value}$$

■ **EXAMPLE**

If the stock in the example above is now "ex-rights" its market value should reflect that and be $60 - $3 or $57. Thus we have

$$\frac{\$57 - \$51}{2} = \frac{\$6}{2} = \$3$$

Note that both formulae give the same theoretical value for the right.

Rights to inspection

Shareholders have the right to inspect certain corporate records, for example, the list of shareholders, minutes of shareholders' meetings and certain corporate books.

Rights in liquidation or dissolution

When a company is liquidated or dissolved, the shareholders have residual rights to the assets of the company after bonds, other liabilities and preferred stockholders are satisfied.

PREFERRED STOCK

Like common stock, preferred stock is an equity security, representing ownership in the company. It differs from common stock in the following ways:

- the dividend for preferred stock is fixed at some rate
- par value is usually set at $100 and the dividend is quoted, for example, "7% preferred" or, especially if the stock has no par value, as some dollar amount, *e.g.* $6.50 "preferred"
- the preferred dividend must be paid before any common stock dividend can be paid
- preferred stock has prior claim in the event of liquidation
- in general, preferred stock holders do not have preemptive rights

Types of preferred stocks

There are several varieties of preferred stock, each differing in the method of payment and privileges.

Cumulative Any dividend due that is not declared accumulates and must be paid before any common stock dividend can be declared.

Non-cumulative By contrast, holders of non-cumulative preferred lose their dividend for any period when directors do not declare one.

Participating Here an additional dividend is paid over and above the stated dividend if the common stock dividend exceeds a stated amount.

Convertible These shares can be exchanged for (converted into) a designated number of shares of common stock at a specified rate. For obvious reasons, the value of these shares tends to rise and fall with the price of the common stock.

The term "parity price" applies to common stock delivered in exchange for convertible preferred. It is the price at which the shares of common are equal in value to the preferred. Given a preferred convertible into two shares of common, the parity price of the common is ½ the price of the preferred. In general, the parity price of common is equal to the market price of the preferred divided by the conversion rate of preferred to common.

Callable These are shares that the corporation reserves the right to "call," *i.e.*, to buy back at some (premium to the issued) price.

These features can be combined. For example, one might have a convertible, cumulative, participating preferred.

If a company issues several classes of preferred, they would be called Class A and Class B preferred, with the A having precedence as to dividends and at liquidation.

ADRs AND WARRANTS

Two other equity securities deserve brief mention here.

ADRs An American Depository Receipt (ADR) is a security which represents shares of a foreign company. It is issued and traded in the United States. By issuing ADRs, foreign companies gain access to American investors.

The ADRs are usually issued by large commercial banks which have the underlying stock in their vaults. ADRs are registered on the bank's books, and any dividends, as well as proceeds from other rights sold overseas, are passed through to the ADR holders. While foreign stocks themselves are not subject to SEC regulation, ADRs are covered; in particular, they are subject to the rules on disclosure of the 1934 Securities Act.

Warrants Warrants are securities which are sometimes attached to issues of bonds or preferred stock. They are also sometimes attached to speculative stock offerings and awarded to underwriters of these offerings as incentives. A warrant gives its owner the right to buy a share of common stock at some fixed price, called the exercise price. Warrants are considered an attractive feature since they provide the investor with the opportunity to participate in appreciation of the common stock. Some can be detached and traded; these have an intrinsic value equal to the difference between the market price of the stock and the exercise price. The warrant may be detachable immediately on issue, or at some later date; if the warrant is not detachable, it has no market value of its own.

The warrant and the right to buy typically expire after a number of years. When a warrant is exercised, its owner relinquishes it and pays the exercise price in return for the share of common stock.

TERMS

Stock Units of ownership in a corporation

Authorized stock Number of shares a corporation may issue

Issued stock Shares of authorized stock actually issued

Outstanding stock Stock issued to the public

Treasury stock Stock issued but reacquired

Par value Arbitrarily assigned at issue; not book value or market value

Stock certificate Documentary proof of ownership

Transfers Owners have right to transfer ownership; transfers involve transfer agent and registrar; must be recorded on the issuing corporation's books

Assignment Owners may assign stock without transferring ownership through a stock power

Rights of ownership
Voting:

Statutory method Each share = one vote for each position on the board of directors

Cumulative method Each share = as many votes as there are directors

Proxies Authorize holder to vote for shareholder; corporations must send proxies to all shareholders

Dividend rights Dividends declared at directors' discretion; must come from earnings; must be paid in proportion to holdings; can be in cash or in stock

Splits Corporation may declare that each share is now split into several shares, e.g., a 3-for-1 split with each old share equal to 3 new shares

Pre-emptive rights Shareholders keep their proportion of outstanding shares if new shares are issued; rights have value and may be traded

Theoretical Value for stock selling with rights

$$\frac{\text{Market Price} - \text{Subscription Price}}{\text{Number of Rights Required} + 1} = \text{Value}$$

for a stock selling "ex-rights"

$$\frac{\text{Market Price} - \text{Subscription Price}}{\text{Number of Rights Required}} = \text{Value}$$

Other rights Right to inspect corporate records; right to assets of a firm in liquidation (after bondholders, other creditors, preferred shareholders)

Preferred stock Represents ownership, pays fixed dollar or percentage dividend; par usually at $100; preferential treatment when dividends declared or in liquidation

Kinds of preferred

Cumulative Undeclared dividends accumulate

Non-cumulative Undeclared dividends not payable

Participating Can pay more than the stated dividend

Convertible Can be exchanged for common stock at stated rate

Callable Must be sold back to issuer at its request (several features may be combined in one type of preferred)

Other equity securities

ADRs American Depository Receipts, represent shares of a foreign company; usually issued by banks; subject to SEC regulation

Warrants Attached to some bonds or preferred; carry right to buy common at fixed price ("exercise price"). If detachable, can be traded; typically expire after a number of years

REVIEW QUESTIONS

1. The record and payable dates for stock dividends are chosen by:

   (A) the SEC
   (B) the corporation's transfer agent
   (C) the corporation's board of directors
   (D) a majority of the stockholders

2. If a $.20 dividend is declared with a record date of Monday, June 12, the stock goes "ex-dividend" on:

   (A) June 5
   (B) June 6
   (C) June 8
   (D) June 12

3. In the event of a corporate liquidation, which of the following would be last in claiming assets?

   (A) common stock
   (B) preferred stock
   (C) Internal Revenue Service
   (D) convertible debentures

4. If ACI has a 7% participating preferred, then 7% represents the:

   (A) maximum dividend
   (B) minimum dividend
   (C) maximum dividend but not the minimum
   (D) minimum dividend but not the maximum

Questions 5-7 are based on the following information: The XYZ Corp. has authorized 10,000,000 shares of stock. It has issued 9,500,000 shares and has since repurchased 300,000 shares.

5. The number of unissued shares is:

   (A) 200,000
   (B) 500,000
   (C) 700,000
   (D) 800,000

6. The number of outstanding shares is:

   (A) 10,000,000
   (B) 9,800,000
   (C) 9,500,000
   (D) 9,200,000

7. The amount of treasury stock is:

   (A) 200,000
   (B) 300,000
   (C) 700,000
   (D) 800,000

8. Voting stock is the same as:

   (A) treasury stock
   (B) outstanding stock
   (C) authorized stock
   (D) issued stock

9. If three directors are to be elected under statutory voting rules, which of the following is permitted to an owner of 200 shares of common stock?

   (A) 200 votes for each of three candidates
   (B) 300 votes for one candidate
   (C) 600 votes for each of two candidates
   (D) all are permitted

10. Under cumulative voting rules, an owner of 200 shares voting for three directors could cast:

    (A) 300 votes for each of two directors
    (B) 600 votes for one director
    (C) 200 votes for each of three directors
    (D) all of the above

11. A woman owning 3,000 shares of common of a firm with 300,000 shares outstanding would be entitled to what portion of a $100,000 total declared dividend?

    (A) 1% of the dividend
    (B) $1,000
    (C) $.33⅓ per share
    (D) all of the above

12. If the company in question 11 subsequently declared a 5% stock dividend, she would receive:

    (A) 150 shares
    (B) 500 shares
    (C) 750 shares
    (D) 15,000 shares

13. The pre-emptive rights of stockholders include the right to:

    (A) continue proportionate ownership
    (B) vote on stock dividends

(C) treasury stock
(D) inspect records

14. A corporation offers a new issue of stock at $55. The market price of existing common is $60. If four rights are required to purchase each share of new stock, the theoretical value of a right is:

(A) $1.00
(B) $1.25
(C) $5.00
(D) $20.00

15. Amalgamated Consolidated, Inc., has not paid dividends for the past three years. Before a common stock dividend could be paid, dividends for the past three years must be paid to:

(A) all common stockholders
(B) all preferred stockholders
(C) all cumulative preferred stockholders
(D) all of the above

16. A firm with 1,000,000 shares outstanding is to issue 200,000 new shares. A shareholder owning 1,000 shares would receive how many rights?

(A) 40
(B) 200
(C) 5,000
(D) 1,000

17. In this case, how many rights would be needed to buy 100 shares?

(A) 100
(B) 200
(C) 500
(D) 1,000

18. A 5.5% preferred stock with par value of $100 would pay someone owning 300 shares:

(A) 5.5% of $300
(B) 16.5 shares
(C) $550
(D) $1,650

19. If a preferred stock is convertible into 2 shares of common for each share of preferred, the parity price for the common on a preferred selling at $105 is:

(A) $50
(B) $52.50
(C) $100
(D) $105

20. Election of the board of directors is the responsibility of:

(A) common stock holders
(B) preferred stock holders
(C) officers of the corporation
(D) all of the above

21. If a firm is liquidated, which is the correct order for claimants?

I.   common stockholders
II. bond holders
III. unpaid employees
IV. preferred stockholders

(A) I, II, III, and IV
(B) III, II, I, and IV
(C) III, II, IV, and I
(D) IV, III, II, and I

22. Every U.S. corporation has a charter filed with the:

(A) Securities and Exchange Commission
(B) US Attorney General's office
(C) attorney general of its charter state
(D) secretary of state of its charter state

23. The registrar for the stock of XYZ Corp.:

(A) must be independent of the corporation
(B) is the same as the transfer agent
(C) cancels old stock certificates
(D) all of the above

24. The transfer agent for XYZ Corp:

(A) may be from part of XYZ
(B) records vital data on shareholders
(C) assures that properly endorsed stock is cancelled
(D) all of the above

25. CAI declares a dividend of $1.75. The stock is selling at $40 and goes "ex-dividend" tomorrow. Assuming no other changes, we can expect tomorrow's opening price to be:

(A) $38.25
(B) $40.00
(C) $41.75
(D) Cannot be determined

ANSWERS TO REVIEW QUESTIONS

1. (C) These are all part of the board's responsibility when they vote to declare a dividend.

2. (B) Since settlement is in five business days, the stock goes "ex-dividend" four business days before the record date.

3. (A) The common stock holder is the residual owner after all of the other claims have be...

presents the payable divi-
... since it is participating pre-
... participate in additional
..., it is the minimum but

... thorized − 9,500,000
... nissued.

... ed − 300,000 repur-
... outstanding.

... stock issued and re-

... stock can be voted.
... y stock cannot be

... g, votes may not be
... no more than 200
... stock) can be cast

... ive voting is pre-
... ation of votes for
... ors.

... 150.

... y pre-emptive

14. (A) The formula is (market price − subscription price) ÷ (number of rights required + 1). Here ($60 − $55) ÷ (4 + 1) = $1.

15. (C) The right to unpaid dividends belongs to those holding cumulative preferred. Those dividends accumulate and must be paid before any common stock dividend can be paid.

16. (D) Each original share is entitled to one right.

17. (C) Since 1,000,000 rights are issued to purchase 200,000 shares, each share requires 5 rights.

18. (D) 5.5% of $100 × 300 shares.

19. (B) For parity to exist, 2 shares of common must be worth $105. Therefore, each share is worth $105 ÷ 2.

20. (A) The common stockholders elect the board of directors.

21. (C) The important idea is that bonds come before preferred stock which come before common stock.

22. (D) The charter, called the Articles of Incorporation, must be filed under the laws of that state. The filing is with the Secretary of State.

23. (A) Choices (B) and (C) are the responsibility of the transfer agent.

24. (D) By definition.

25. (A) When it goes "ex-dividend" it loses the value of the dividend. So with no further changes we have $40 − $1.75 = $38.25.

CHAPTER TWO

Bonds

Bonds are long-term fixed interest debt obligations. There are three major categories of bonds: corporate, federal government, and municipal. Each will be covered in a separate section of this chapter, though much of the information about corporate bonds applies to all bonds.

Part One will describe and discuss corporate bonds: the forms and the types of bonds available, methods of retiring bonded debt and, finally, how these instruments are traded and priced.

PART ONE   CORPORATES

Corporations issue bonds to obtain capital for relatively long-term use. They represent debts of the corporation. Like stocks they are securities, but "debt securities," not equity securities. Bondholders are creditors, not owners. They have no voting rights or other say in the management of the issuing company.

Bondholders have rights as creditors that are not accorded to shareholders. In particular, the issuing company is bound to pay interest on bonds, whereas with stock, even preferred, there is no comparable obligation with respect to dividends. Interest on bonds must be paid before stock dividends are considered. Similarly, at liquidation, bondholders' claims are honored before shareholders'. For this reason, bonds are sometimes called "senior securities."

The bond is a contract between the issuing firm and the investor. Under this contract, the corporation promises to repay the amount it has borrowed on a given date, the "maturity date," and to pay interest at a stated rate for the life of the bond.

Corporate bonds are usually issued in $1,000 denominations though they can be in smaller amounts, called "small pieces" or "baby bonds" (this increases handling and other costs and is generally discouraged), or in larger amounts.

Interest is customarily paid semi-annually on the 1st or 15th of the month (so particular issues can be described as "J-J 1" for January-July paying interest on the 1st and "F-A 15" for February-August paying interest on the 15th, and so forth). Bonds typically mature in 20 to 30 years, though some shorter- and longer-term bonds are issued.

Failure to pay interest when due or to repay the principal at maturity can lead to bankruptcy. Payment must be in "legal tender," though with some bonds issued abroad, payment can be in U.S. and/or one or more foreign currencies. These are called multiple currency bonds.

The bond certificate shows the name of the issuing firm, the face value of the bond, and the rate of interest, and gives the name of a "paying agent" for both interest and principal. This can be the issuing corporation itself or an outside agent like a bank. The certificate also shows the interest dates, the maturity date, and any call features.

FORMS OF BONDS

Coupon or Bearer bonds

These bonds have actual coupons attached to them that must be clipped twice a year and mailed or presented to the paying agent for interest payments. The coupon is, in effect, a promissory note to the bearer.

Such bonds are negotiable and should be kept in a secure place, such as a safe deposit box. The coupon and the certificate are proof of ownership; the corporation keeps no record of ownership. Bearer bonds are no longer issued though there are still many in circulation. As transactions in these bonds require no registration, the registered representative should exercise due diligence and request a copy of the record of any transaction from the customer.

Registered bonds

Most corporate bonds are registered in the owner's name on corporate books. Such bonds are usually "fully registered," that is, registered as to both principal and interest. (Bonds registered as to principal only have coupons attached which the owner "clips" and forwards to the paying agent. Because of the additional work required to process these instruments, they are now virtually non-existent.)

The certificates carry no coupons. Interest payments are mailed on schedule by the paying agent. When registered bonds are sold or otherwise exchanged, the certificate goes to a transfer agent, who cancels the old certificate and issues a new one.

As with stocks, to effect a transfer the seller must endorse the certificate or fill out a "bond power." The transfer is complete only when the new name is recorded. At maturity, the certificate is surrendered to the transfer agent, who issues payment to the registered holder.

Book-Entry bonds

With this type of bond, no certificate is issued, but a computerized record of ownership is kept. As this avoids the costs of printing and handling documents, these are becoming more common.

TRUST INDENTURE

An essential part of every bond issue is the "trust indenture," also called a "deed of trust." This contract supplements the bond contract itself and is required under the Trust Indenture Act of 1939 for all issues registered under the Securities Act of 1933 (which exempts issues of under $5,000,000, government and municipal bonds, and those issued by foreign governments). A copy must be filed with the SEC.

While designed to protect bondholders' rights, the trust indenture is really an agreement between the issuer and the trustee who is acting as a fiduciary administering the property and funds. Basically, it sets forth the terms between corporation and creditors. It describes both bondholders' rights and issuer's obligations, and appoints a trustee—usually a commercial bank or trust company with expertise in this area—to see that these obligations are carried out.

Typical provisions not only oblige the issuer to pay interest and repay principal when due, but also stipulate locations where coupons or bonds can be presented for payment. Other items may cover protecting properties pledged as security for the bond (for example, requiring the trustee to hold adequate insurance; in case of loss, the trustee is paid and pays for repairs). Still others may call for keeping equipment in good repair and, more generally, pledge that the issuer continue doing business, etc. These and many other promises are called "protective covenants."

If the trust indenture is abrogated, the corporation can be considered in default and compelled to immediately repay the principal amount of the bonds. Thus, the indenture can give the trustee the right to take over the business and operate it for the bondholders' benefit, or sell pledged property to the highest bidder, etc. The rationale underlying many of these rights is the attempt to preserve the seniority of bondholders when a corporation faces reorganization, liquidation, or bankruptcy.

Changes in the trust indenture require the consent of the bondholders. Typically, bondholders will give their consent by depositing their bonds with a committee appointed to oversee the changes. Usually, the changes are made only if a sufficient number of bonds—at least a majority—are deposited. In some circumstances, changes are made only on those bonds voting their consent; these bonds are duly stamped and trade separately.

SECURED BONDS

Bonds can be considered in two broad groups: "secured," those backed by real assets; and "unsecured," where backing is less tangible. There are several types in each group.

First Mortgage bonds or Senior Lien bonds

These give the bondholder claim against the corporation's fixed assets, that is, assets secured by real property. In fact, these issues involve two instruments: the bond itself and a mortgage. First mortgage bondholders have priority of claim in reorganization or liquidation. This is the most secure type of corporate bond available.

Second Mortgage bonds or General, Consolidated or Refunding bonds or Junior Liens

These bonds are also backed by real property, but are second in priority.

Mortgage bonds of any class may be "open-end" or "closed-end" issues.

Open-end The corporation may issue more bonds of the same class under the same indenture. There are usually restrictions in the indenture of an open-end issue to protect creditors. For example, the value of the property pledged must provide adequate collateral for the new bonds.

Some open-end issues are limited with a maximum dollar amount set for bonds issued under this priority.

Closed-end No additional bonds may be issued beyond a maximum number authorized in the indenture as first mortgage bonds; all others are second, or third, etc.

Collateral Trust bonds

These bonds are backed by marketable securities deposited with the trustees. These must be securities in a company other than the issuing company (it can be a subsidiary). Rarely they are intangible assets, like a patent. In case of default, the trustees have the right to sell these securities.

The collateral pledged can be stocks or bonds, but not real estate. Either the trustee or the debtor can hold actual title, but the trustee always has the power to transfer property in a default.

Equipment Trust Certificates or Equipment Trusts, notes or bonds

These are issued generally by corporations engaged in transportation, like railroads or airlines, with a specific piece of equipment pledged as collateral. The trustee holds title to the equipment—say an airplane or locomotive—until the certificate is paid.

ETCs are considered a high-grade security, since transportation equipment is generally saleable in case of default. Such issues have a good record and pay relatively low yields.

UNSECURED BONDS

These bonds are not backed by any specific assets. If default should occur, bondholders have no direct claim on any real property.

Debentures

These are backed by the issuing corporation's "good faith and credit," in other words, by its promise to pay. For investors, these are inferior to secured instruments, but they are superior to stocks in liquidation because debentures must be honored first before any payment to holders of equity securities.

Because they are unsecured, the protective covenants of the trust indenture are particularly important with debentures, as is the credit-worthiness of the issuing corporation. Debentures usually pay higher interest than secured bonds and are often "convertible" (see below).

Subordinated debentures

The issuer is obliged to pay principal and interest on these instruments, but they are "subordinate" in the sense that they are honored after debentures in the case of liquidation or reorganization (though still before stocks). Subordinated debentures tend to pay relatively high interest, to be relatively short-term, and to be convertible.

Other Types of Bonds

Income or Adjustment bonds

These may be secured issues or debentures. They include a promise to repay the principal at maturity but no interest is guaranteed in the trust indenture. Interest is contingent on the company's earnings, must be declared by the board of directors, and can be skipped entirely.

These bonds are usually issued when a company is in reorganization or receivership. Again, they are less safe, but pay relatively high interest when they do pay interest. Income bonds are traded "flat," that is without interest (see page 32).

Guaranteed bonds

These are guaranteed by a corporation or corporations other than the issuer. Most often, the guarantor is the stronger of the two, and the issue thus enjoys a lower rate. These bonds are usually unsecured, though collateral may be pledged. Indeed, they are often used when the issuing firm leases property to the guarantor. As the name implies, the guarantor pays in case of default. The guarantee may cover interest only or both interest and principal.

Zero-coupon bonds

These pay no regular interest. Instead, the bonds are purchased at a discount and paid off at par on maturity. The difference between the purchase and redemption price is equivalent to a specified annual return.

Convertibility

Many debentures and some other types of issues include the right to "convert" holdings into common or preferred stock. The trust indenture usually spells out the conditions and terms of conversions. This feature merits a separate discussion.

Advantages and disadvantages of convertibility

Offering convertibility presents a number of advantages to the issuer:

□ Convertible issues can usually be offered at a somewhat lower interest rate, as buyers expect the issue to grow in value as the common stock rises.

□ These issues do not dilute ownership immediately as a stock issue would and they offer the potential for reducing debt when conversion occurs.

□ As bondholders only convert when stock has risen in value, the issuer in effect gets a good price for stock purchased through conversion. Thus the bond offering does not tend to depress the stock's market price as a new stock issue does.

There are also disadvantages:

□ When conversion does take place, existing stockholders' equity is diluted. In addition, the total declared dividend is now divided by a larger number of shares so dividends per share can go down, making the stock less attractive. This is why convertible issues are often offered to current shareholders, like stock rights on a new issue.

□ Conversion on a significant scale could lead to a change in the controlling interest in the company.

□ Since bond interest is tax-deductible for the issuer but stock dividend payments are not, issuing debt securities can result in greater retained earnings for the company than issuing stocks and any such advantage is lost when investors convert their bonds to stock.

□ Finally, issuing convertible instruments can cause doubts about the corporation's financial structure, as there is no way to know how many bonds will be converted.

For investors, too, convertible issues have both advantages and disadvantages.

Chief among the advantages is that they offer, in theory, both the safety associated with bonds and the possibility of rising in value like stocks. A convertible debenture will tend to hold its value more firmly than a stock because it pays fixed interest and may rise in price as the stock price rises, giving the investor a profit even without conversion if he or she trades the debenture.

Investors or institutions barred by law from owning significant amounts of common stock often turn to convertibles to try to capture some of the advantages of common stocks.

Among the disadvantages to investors are the fact that convertibles tend to offer lower rates than non-convertible issues, that convertibles are sometimes issued when a company is in a relatively weak financial position or when the market is not strong, and that a large outstanding convertible issue can depress stock prices.

Mechanics of conversion

The terms of conversion stated in the indenture can include:

Conversion rate and conversion price The conversion rate (or ratio) indicates the number of shares of (usually) common stock that one would receive in exchange for a bond. For example, a conversion rate of 20:1 would mean that one receives 20 shares of common when converting a bond. If the bond was selling at par ($1,000) this would imply a "conversion price" of $50 since $20 \times \$50 = \$1,000$. Conversely, if a $1,000 par value bond had a conversion price of $40 this would imply a conversion ratio of 25:1.

Owners of the convertible debentures must decide whether to convert to common stock. Since the number of shares of common stock per debenture, the conversion rate, is fixed, the decision is based on comparing the price of the bond with the price of the common stock. When the bond's market price is equal to the market value of the equivalent number of common shares, bond and stock are said to be at parity. In practice, the stock usually trades at somewhat less than parity to reflect the fact that the bond has investment value in its own right.

■ **EXAMPLE**

If a bond has a conversion rate of 25:1 to a stock trading at 35, the parity price for the bond would be $87.50 ($25 \times \$35$), but the bond would usually trade at a premium.

At the time of issue, the conversion price is usually set above parity in order to discourage quick conversion.

Duration In most cases, conversion is allowed over the life of the bond, but often at terms that become less favorable as time goes on. With some issues, convertibility is not allowed for a certain time after issue, or for a short period before maturity.

Rights As noted, stockholders can have pre-emptive rights to purchase convertible shares and these have value like pre-emptive rights with stocks (see page 14).

Other safeguards A number of protections are included in the indenture for holders of convertible issues. These cover such matters as stock splits and stock dividends, both of which increase the number of shares outstanding, so the conversion rate must be adjusted accordingly. Similar non-dilutive provisions limit the number of shares the corporation can issue.

CALLABILITY

Corporations sometimes desire to redeem outstanding bonds, "retire" them, before they reach maturity. They may do so by buying the bonds in the marketplace, by refunding (that is, by offering a new bond issue and using the proceeds to retire the old issue), or, where possible, by calling the bond. Many bonds and debentures can be "called" at the option of the issuing company, at par or at a slight premium, generally declining at a given percent for each year since issue. When a call is issued, bondholders must return their bonds except in very rare instances of an "optional call."

Reasons for calling

Issuers may call a bond for many reasons. The most obvious occurs when interest rates drop significantly below what they were when the bond was issued. A call then allows the corporation to replace a high-interest obligation with a low-interest one. Another is to change the date of maturity of the debt by calling one bond and issuing another one with a different (usually longer) maturity date. These are both examples of "refunding."

Another reason for calling a bond is to get out of an indenture agreement that has proved unfavorable.

Call procedures

These are spelled out in the indenture, and usually include "call protection" for investors, prohibiting any call for an initial period. The agreement also often stipulates a higher call premium if the call comes early in the term of the bond.

The recalling firm must notify bondholders before the actual call date. Owners of registered securities are usually contacted directly; others are notified through a newspaper announcement. It is the investor's responsibility to know about the call and, since no interest is paid on the bond beyond the call date, there is a need to respond quickly.

A call may involve an entire issue, only part of one, or a given portion each year. In partial calls, the actual bonds to be recalled are chosen by lot.

Sometimes a firm "calls" a convertible bond when the conversion value of the stock to which it can be converted is higher than the redemption price of the debt issue, thereby "forcing conversion."

PUTABILITY

Just as callability gives the issuer the right to redeem a bond before maturity, so putability gives the investor the right to "put" or have the issuer redeem a bond before maturity. This gives the investor some insurance during the life of the bond.

Typically this right is combined with the right of the issuer to change the nominal rate of the bond. The effect is to give the investor a choice—accepting the new rate or getting his money back. This choice is usually available once a year beginning some years after the issuance of the bond.

Put procedures

These are spelled out in the indenture and usually include some initial period during which puts are prohibited. The agreement usually specifies redemption at some premium over par. This premium declines during the term of the bond.

The issuer announces a new nominal rate effective some 30 to 60 days in the future. For some period after the effective date, typically 30 days, the investor then has the right to put the bond back to the issuer at the announced price. If he doesn't exercise that right he is assumed to have agreed to accept the new rate.

OTHER BOND TYPES AND TERMS

Serial bonds

Most municipal and some corporate bonds are issued in this fashion. With serial bonds, one offering is made with maturity coming over a period of years: for example, 2,000 bonds issued in 1987 with 500 coming due each year from 2007 to 2010.

Serial bonds can be issued at one rate for the early-maturing bonds with a higher rate for the later-maturing bonds, or with the longer-term bonds sold at a discount.

If the issuing company defaults at any time, the entire issue is considered in default. Serial bonds can be callable, but normally are not. They are quoted on yield rather than price (see below).

Series bonds

Securities of the same class issued over a period of years but with the same maturity date.

Sinking fund

As part of the trust indenture, the issuing corporation may be required to set money aside regularly into a "sinking fund" to assure it will be able to redeem the bonds at maturity. This is the most usual method of retiring issues (it can be used to buy bonds in the market), and allows the issuer to avoid the burden of having to raise a large sum at one time.

Balloon maturity

These are serial bonds, but where most mature in one year. For example, a corporation might issue $20 million of bonds with $1 million maturing every year from years 15 to 19 and the remaining $15 million maturing in the 20th year.

BOND TRADING, PRICING AND YIELDS

Bonds are negotiable. They can be bought and sold. Some are traded on the NYSE Bond Division but most transactions are over the counter. Trading is usually far less active than with stocks.

Pricing

Like stocks, bonds have both a par value which is fixed, and a market value that fluctuates. Since par value represents an actual future payment, bond prices are always quoted as a percentage of par, which is assumed to be $1,000. Thus a $1,000 bond selling "at 97" sells for 97% of par or $970.

Fractions are quoted in ⅛ths, the minimum movement up or down, and again, this indicates a percentage. A bond selling at 97⅛ will cost $971.25. (If the bond matures in less than one year, increments of ¹⁄₁₆ can be quoted.)

Changes in bond prices are often described in "points." Each point is 1% of par, so, for a bond with a par value of $1,000, a change from 95 to 97 is a change of two points or $20.

Yields

A basic consideration in discussing any investment is its return. For bonds this return is called the yield and we speak of three different types of yields:

Nominal yield (or the coupon rate) This is the rate proclaimed on the bond. It is the interest rate that one receives when the bond is selling at par. For example, a $1,000 par value bond with a stated rate of 10% would return $100 per year. We say its nominal yield is 10%.

Current yield This is the actual rate of return based on the current price of the bond.

■ **EXAMPLE**

If a bond with 10% nominal yield is selling at $1,250, the actual interest payment of $100 represents a return of 8% on the purchase price of $1,250. This would be the current yield of the bond. If it were selling for $800, the current yield would be 12.5%.

This example also demonstrates the potentially confusing inverse relationship between bond prices and bond yields. That is, bond prices rise when yields go down and vice versa. If comparable bonds being issued currently carry a nominal yield of 12.5%, those who purchase older bonds with a nominal yield of 10% will demand a discount to $800 so they can receive the 12.5% available on new issues.

Yield to maturity This is the return on a bond if it is held to maturity. If the bond is selling at par, this is the same as the nominal yield (and the current yield); however, if it is selling at a discount, at maturity the investor will receive, in addition, the difference between the discount and par. Similarly, if it is currently at a premium, the investor loses the difference between the premium and par at redemption.

■ **EXAMPLE**

If the $1,000, 10% bond of the previous examples is selling at $800 and matures in 5 years, then, at maturity, the investor will receive $200 in addition to the $100 per year for the five years, a total of $700.

An exact computation of the yield to maturity is complex and is usually left to bond tables or to specially designed calculators. However, a useful and fairly accurate approximation can be computed as follows:

1 Compute the average annual increase in price between the purchase price and par: $1,000 − $800 ÷ 5 = $40

2 Find the return as the sum of this and the annual return: $100 + $40 = $140

3 Find the average cost of the bond as the average of the first and last prices: $800 + $1,000 ÷ 2 = $900

4 Find the yield to maturity as the return divided by the average cost: $140 ÷ $900 = 15.55%.

In summary, this bond with a nominal yield of 10%, if selling for $800, has a current yield of 12.5% and a yield to maturity (approximate) of 15.55%. If this bond were currently selling for $1,250, the yield to maturity would be approximately

1 ($1,000 − $1,250) ÷ 5 = −$50

2 $100 − $50 = $50

3 ($1,000 + $1,250) ÷ 2 = $1,125

4 $50 ÷ $1,125 = 4.44%

Yield to maturity is a way of accounting for the money received over the cost of the bond. It considers both the purchase price of the bond and also the gain to a bond bought at a discount (or the loss on one bought at a premium) when redeemed at par at maturity.

Yield to call is calculated like yield to maturity, with the call date substituted for the maturity date, and the call price for the maturity price. One general rule is that for bonds at a discount, yield to call is higher than yield to maturity; for bonds at a premium the reverse is true. These yields are discussed again in the section on municipal bonds.

Formulae for these two yields are

$$YTM = \frac{\text{Coupon} + (\text{Net Change in Price})/(\text{Years to Maturity})}{(\text{Purchase Price} + \text{Market Price})/2}$$

$$YTC = \frac{\text{Coupon} + (\text{Net Change in Price})/(\text{Years to Call})}{(\text{Purchase Price} + \text{Market Price})/2}$$

Accrued interest

Almost all bonds trade "with interest" or "and interest." Any transaction completed between the regular semi-annual payment dates must include interest accrued and the buyer must pay this amount to the seller.

The rules for calculating this are very specific. Each month is considered to have 30 days (except for U.S. government bonds); the year has 360 days. Accrued interest is found by multiplying:

principal × rate × time = interest

Time is calculated to begin on the morning of the last interest payment and extending to, *but not including*, the settlement date. That date is usually 5 business days after trade, but can vary. (The only exception to the accrued interest rule is with bonds where interest is in default, on income bonds or on zero-coupon bonds; such bonds trade "flat," *i.e.*, without accrued interest.)

■ **EXAMPLE**

If the 10% bonds cited above were purchased at par on July 10 for settlement on July 17, and the payable dates are February 15 and August 15, accrued interest up to but not including the settlement date would be:

February 15–30 [sic]	16 days
March	30 days
April	30 days
May	30 days
June	30 days
July	16 days
	152 days

Thus the accrued interest would be:

$$\$1,000 \times 10\% \times (152/360) = \$42.22$$

Types of transactions

A bond trade can be completed in one of several ways:

Regular way Almost all transactions fall into this category. Settlement is on the 5th business day after the day of the trade, which is also called the "settlement date."

Seller's or buyer's option When either party wishes to postpone delivery, the date can be delayed. Under NYSE rules, such transactions can take no less than 6 business days nor more than 60 calendar days. Most often, if the delay is at the seller's request the bond goes at a discount; if at the buyer's request, at a premium.

Cash transactions If cash or the bond certificate are needed urgently, or if either party has failed to satisfactorily complete a transaction in the past, cash terms can be agreed to. Under these terms, the security must be delivered "same day," which is defined as no later than 2:30 p.m. Eastern Time. If the trade takes place after 2:00 p.m., then delivery must take place within 30 minutes.

When issued Some new issues are traded on the NYSE (or, if unlisted, through NASD) for delivery when the corporation schedules delivery of the actual certificates. As soon as the physical bond appears, when-issued transactions must be reconfirmed.

BOND RATINGS

Most corporate bonds carry "ratings" made by an independent firm, usually Standard & Poor's, Moody's, or Fitches Investors' Service.

ILLUSTRATION OF RATINGS

S & P	MOODY'S
AAA	Aaa
AA	Aa
A	A
BBB	Baa
BB	Ba
B	B
CCC	Caa
CC	Ca
C	C
D	

Ratings of BBB to AAA for S & P (Baa to Aaa for Moody's) are called "investment grade." Those below these ratings are considered speculative with increasing risk of default as the rating goes down. Additional refinements in these ratings are (+) and (-) for S & P (*e.g.*, A, A +, AA-, AA are increasingly higher ratings); and 1 for Moody's (*e.g.*, A, A1, Aa are increasing ratings).

These ratings reflect the rater's best judgment of the issuing corporation's ability to pay both interest and principal. In making this assessment, they use a number of standardized approaches to examine the corporation's earnings potential with particular attention to income stability and predictability, as well as gauging the value of corporate assets.

In general, the higher the rating the lower the yield.

PART TWO   UNITED STATES GOVERNMENT ISSUES

Because it borrows more money than any organization or institution in the world, the U.S. government must seek funds regularly and often. To do this, it issues a variety of debt instruments, most of them marketable, with maturities ranging from 3 months to 35 years.

These securities—called "government obligations," "government issues," or just "governments"—are considered the safest offered in any market. There has never been a default and these issues are backed by the full faith and credit of the U.S. government and by its power to tax its citizens.

This section will discuss both negotiable and non-negotiable securities issued directly by the government, and instruments issued by government agencies or government-sponsored agencies. Material on trading will focus on the differences between government and corporate issues.

NEGOTIABLE SECURITIES

These securities are traded continuously. There is a vigorous market with relatively narrow changes in price. Among the reasons for this high level of activity is the fact that these are the most liquid issues traded on any market, are extremely safe, have some tax advantages (returns are not usually subject to state or local taxes), and can be used as loan collateral.

Treasury bills

These are short-term instruments; sold at auction, that is, by competitive bidding. They are sold at a discount and mature at their face value. *For tax purposes the difference between selling price and face is considered interest income, not a capital gain.*

"T-bills" are book-entry instruments; no certificates are issued. Instead, banks that are members of the Federal Reserve System hold securities accounts at the Federal Reserve, which maintains a computerized record.

They are issued with maturities of 3 months (91 days), 6 months (182 days) or one year although they are sold in the secondary over-the-counter market with all maturities from 1 day to 1 year. Minimum denomination is $10,000, with larger bills usually in increments of $5,000. T-bills are highly liquid and essentially risk-free.

Auctions for the 3- and 6-month issues are held weekly; those for 12-month issues take place monthly. Individual investors can participate directly in these auctions though most prefer to buy through a bank or broker, usually paying a service charge.

Because these are discounted notes, the winners of the auction are the bidders who offer the highest dollar prices. This is equivalent to the lowest interest cost for the U.S. government since the difference between the dollar price and the face value is the cost to the U.S. Some bidders enter noncompetitive bids. The amount of these bids is subtracted from the total offering and the remainder of the offering is awarded competitively. The noncompetitive bidders are then awarded their T-bills at the average price of the winning competitive bid.

Return on T-bills To calculate the current return—called "bond equivalent yield"—use the formula:

$$\frac{\text{annualized appreciation}}{\text{purchase price}} \times \frac{365}{\text{days to maturity}} = \text{bond equivalent yield}$$

■ **EXAMPLE**

For a 1-year $10,000 bill selling at $9,200 the current return is found by dividing the appreciation (from $9,200 to $10,000) by the purchase price. So we have:

$$\frac{\$800}{\$9,200} = 8.70\%.$$

Yields and quotes Although they can only be redeemed at maturity, T-bills are marketable until that time. Alone among government securities, they are quoted on the basis of yield. This is called the "discount yield." It is calculated as follows:

$$\text{Discount yield} = \frac{(\text{par} - \text{purchase price}) \times 360}{\text{days to maturity}}$$

So, with the example above we have:

$$\text{Discount yield} = \frac{(100 - 94.00) \times 360}{182} = 11.87\%$$

(It is possible to determine the price from the discount yield by inverting this formula):

$$\text{Purchase price} = 100 - \frac{(11.87 \times 182)}{360} = 94.00$$

As noted, the price is almost always quoted in terms of the yield. Changes in price are quoted in terms of "basis points," or $1/100$ of 1% (.01%) of the yield. Thus a typical quote might be:

"March 4, bid 4.30%, asked 4.20%"

This describes the maturity as March 4, and says that someone is offering to buy this bill at $95.70 (the bid) and offering to sell this bill at $95.80 (the asked price).

Treasury notes

These are interest-bearing with payments made semi-annually. Issued in bearer form until mid-1983, they are now available either in registered form without coupons or on a book-entry basis, in which case the purchaser receives a receipt but no certificate.

Treasury notes are redeemable at maturity; they are not callable. Payment at maturity can be in cash, or they can be refunded at that point, *i.e.,* investors are given the option of buying a new security with a new maturity.

Maturities range from 2 to 10 years; denominations range from $1,000 to $1,000,000. They are most appealing to large investors such as banks and major corporations seeking highly liquid assets.

Like T-bills, T-notes are sold at auction, but the notes are offered at a fixed interest rate so the auction involves bids that are equal to, above (at a premium to), or below (at a discount from), par. They are quoted in $\frac{1}{32}$s of a percentage point, written as if it were a decimal. For example:

"Maturing 11/10/90—Bid: 99.16; Ask: 99.24"

means bid at $99\frac{16}{32}$ or $99\frac{1}{2}$ or $995; ask at $99\frac{24}{32}$ or $99\frac{3}{4}$ or $997.50. (Note the convention of .16 for $\frac{16}{32}$.)

Treasury bonds

These are interest-bearing with semi-annual payments and come in bearer, registered, and book-entry form. They are no longer issued in bearer form.

Maturities generally range from 10 to 30 years although only a 30-year bond is now issued. Some have optional call dates, usually 5 years before the stated maturity. These are listed, for example, as "Due 6/30 1992/97" where the first date shown is the call date, the second the maturity date.

If the Treasury decides to issue a call, it must give four months' notice. For obvious reasons, no call is issued when bonds are selling at a discount.

Treasury bond denominations range from $1,000 to $1,000,000; the most usual instrument is a $10,000 bond. They are sold at auction. Like T-notes, they are quoted with variations of $\frac{1}{32}$ of a percentage point and with the same notation, *e.g.,* 104.03 means 104 and $\frac{3}{32}$ percent of par.

("Flower bonds" is the term used to describe certain T-bond issues customarily used to pay estate taxes. They carry a low [less than 4.5%] coupon rate so they can be purchased at a discount. Their special distinction is that they are accepted at face value in settlement of estate taxes. Although flower bonds have not been issued since 1971, and their value has been substantially diminished by changes in the internal revenue code, some are still in circulation with maturities extending up to 1998.)

Under the doctrine of reciprocal immunity, federal obligations are exempt from state and local taxes just as municipal obligations are exempt from federal taxes.

Zero-coupon securities ("Zeroes")

Zeroes are fixed-income securities on which no interest payments are made. Rather, they are sold at a discount and redeemed at par; the difference generates the yield. Conversely, a given yield determines the discount. Since zeroes make no interim interest payments, changes in the yield produce dramatic changes in price.

In 1982, a new type of security was created when interest payments on U.S. Treasury Bonds were separated from the principal. The "stripped" bonds were placed in irrevocable trusts at a custodian bank, and securities representing shares in the trusts were marketed. These became very popular, and different brokerage firms issued their own versions of them.

These are not government securities, but instruments issued by brokerage houses. Nevertheless, the inherent safety of the underlying collateral makes them a very safe investment. In 1984, the U.S. Treasury began to participate in this market by offering its own version of zero-coupon securities called STRIPS (Separate Trading of Registered Interest and Principal of Securities). They are also known as Treasury Receipts.

NON-NEGOTIABLE U.S. GOVERNMENT OBLIGATIONS

These are non-transferable instruments. They can only be redeemed by the purchaser, and can neither be marketed nor used as collateral for loans.

Series EE Bonds or Savings Bonds

These issues are sold at a discount and mature at their face value. The difference represents compound interest. Available only in registered form, EE Bonds can have one owner or two co-owners, or an owner and a named beneficiary in case of death. Commercial banks cannot buy them.

There is a legal maximum to purchases by individuals in one year of $15,000, which represents a face value of $30,000 since they are always sold at a 50% discount. The bonds come in denominations from $50 to $10,000.

Maturity on all issues is eight years, but EE Bonds can be redeemed any time after they have been held for six months. To discourage early redemption, the bonds pay on a sliding scale, offering lower returns in earlier years.

Proceeds are treated as ordinary income and may be deferred until redemption for federal tax purposes. They may be further deferred if on redemption they are traded for HH Bonds instead of cash.

Since November, 1982, government regulations have provided that EE Bonds held five years or more pay a varying rate. This is pegged at 85% of the five-year average for Treasury notes over that time, with a guaranteed minimum of 6% if held to maturity.

HH Series Bonds

These are issued at par, with interest paid semi-annually direct to the holder by Treasury check. They are available in registered form only.

These bonds mature in 10 years. If held to maturity they yield 7.5% annually (8.5% for those issued before 11/1/82). As with EE bonds, payoff is less than face value for bonds redeemed before maturity. They must be held for at least six months and are redeemable only on the first of the month. Redemption requires one month's notice in writing.

Denominations available are from $50 to $10,000. Maximum purchase in one year is $20,000 face or maturity value for one individual (commercial banks are excluded) or $40,000 for two co-owners.

HH Bonds may be purchased from Federal Reserve Banks or U.S. Treasury offices. However, since November, 1982, they cannot be purchased for cash, but only by trading EE (or E) Bonds with a minimum face value of $500, held a minimum of 6 months.

Interest on HH Series Bonds is taxable each year. However, as mentioned above, an investor who exchanges EE Bonds for HH Bonds can defer taxes due on the former at their maturity.

OTHER GOVERNMENT AGENCY OBLIGATIONS

With one exception, noted below, these are not direct obligations of the U.S. government, but are generally issued and backed by agencies—some of them privately owned—sponsored by the government. These securities are considered very safe since the issuers usually show considerable strength in both income and assets, and it is generally assumed the government would not allow any of them to default. Yields on these securities tend to be somewhat higher than on direct government obligations but lower than corporate instruments.

There is considerable variety available in terms of both maturities and types of issues, and an active secondary market exists.

Federal Farm Credit Banks

A system of Federal Farm Credit Banks supplies credit to farmers through the Federal Farm Credit Agency, the Federal Intermediate Credit Banks, and the Central Banks for Cooperatives. This system issues securities called Federal Farm Credit Consolidated Systemwide Obligations. They are the joint obligation of the 37 banks in the system.

Bonds are issued in book-entry form only, through a network of banks and brokers. Once issued, they are traded over the counter.

Federal Home Loan Banks

There are 12 of these banks, owned by nearly 5,000 institutions (such as savings and loan associations). The Home Loan Banks provide capital to those institutions up to a limit authorized by the U.S. Treasury. They do so by buying mortgages from those institutions, thereby providing them with new capital to loan. These guaranteed residential mortgages (along with cash, government securities and bank assets) are the collateral for instruments issued by the Home Loan Banks. These include short-term discount notes (30 to 270 days), interest-bearing notes that mature in less than a year, and bonds with 1- to 20-year maturities. Minimum denomination for the notes is $100,000. Bonds are issued in $10,000, $25,000, $100,000 and $1,000,000 denominations. Interest is paid semi-annually.

Federal Home Loan Mortgage Corporation (Freddie Mac)

This corporation buys residential mortgages from federally-insured savings institutions, and issues mortgage-backed bonds, participation certificates, and mortgage certificates.

The bonds have maturities ranging from 12 to 25 years, and are backed by GNMA (see below). Issued in registered form, they are available in denominations of $25,000, $500,000, and $1,000,000.

Participation certificates are backed by pools of mortgages (but not VA or FHA mortgages), with payments passed through monthly (see next section for a fuller explanation). These certificates usually mature more quickly than the mortgages in the pool. Minimum denomination is $100,000.

Guaranteed mortgage certificates pay interest and a portion of the principal semi-annually. They are available only in registered form, with a minimum value of $100,000.

Federal National Mortgage Association (also called FNMA or Fannie Mae)

This is a publicly held corporation, traded on the NYSE. It buys and sells conventional residential mortgages—insured or guaranteed by FHA, VA, and Farmer's Home Administration—from savings institutions, thus freeing their funds so they can grant new mortgages.

FNMA issues debentures in book-entry form that mature in periods ranging from 3 to 25 years. These are generally non-callable. Denominations range from $10,000 to $1,000,000. FNMA also issues short-term discount notes denominated in multiples of $5,000 up to $50,000. These are bearer notes with maturities ranging from 30 to 270 days. FNMA securities are subject to state, federal, and local taxes, and tend to pay rates similar to, but higher than, T-bills.

U.S. GOVERNMENT-OWNED AGENCY OBLIGATIONS

Government National Mortgage Association (GNMA or Ginnie Mae)

Securities are backed by the U.S. government, but proceeds are not tax exempt in any way. GNMA makes mortgages, insured by the VA and FHA, and issues certificates that represent a stated share of a mortgage pool. These are called "pass-through" certificates, because the monthly payments on the underlying mortgages are literally passed through to GNMA certificate holders. Pass-through payments are partly a return of capital (which is not subject to income tax) and partly interest income (which is taxable).

Selling at a minimum denomination of $25,000, the "pass-through" certificates mature like mortgages over a period of 12 to 40 years, but usually more quickly than the underlying mortgages as mortgage-holders tend to prepay. If the particular pool has many high-interest mortgages, prepayment will be more likely to occur, and yields will therefore be lower than anticipated. Note, however, that the interest payments to investors are determined by the coupon rate of the security, not by the interest rate of the underlying mortgages.

OTHER BOND-ISSUING AGENCIES

Inter-American Development Bank

This agency issues securities in varying currencies and in many parts of the world to finance projects in Latin America. Earnings on IADB issues are fully taxable.

World Bank or International Bank for Reconstruction and Development

They issue securities, including capital stock in various forms (and currencies) to make loans to developing countries.

■ **NOTE**

Several smaller agencies also issue debt instruments. Trading in these is relatively light:

Federal Housing Administration

Issues long-term instruments to holders of FHA mortgages. These are fully guaranteed by the U.S. government.

Export-Import Bank

Issues instruments on the authority of the Treasury, fully backed by the government, to facilitate trade between the United States and other countries.

Farmer's Home Administration

Government guaranteed.

Tennessee Valley Authority (TVA)

Not guaranteed, but backed by power sales and issued with Treasury authorization, TVA instruments include short-term discount notes with a minimum denomination of $1,000,000, and relatively small denomination bonds (minimum $1,000) that are sold like corporate utility bonds.

RULES ON DELIVERY OF U.S. GOVERNMENT INSTRUMENTS

Accrued interest

All government securities are traded "and interest" or "with interest" except T-bills, which are sold at a discount. In calculating interest accrued with these securities, unlike corporate securities, one considers the actual number of days in a month and a 365-day year.

■ **EXAMPLE**

A bond sold regular way on August 5 with interest last paid on April 15 would have accrued the following interest:

April	16 days
May	31 days
June	30 days
July	31 days
August	11 days
	119 days

A bond sold for cash on June 10 with a last interest payment on April 15 would accrue the following:

April	16 days
May	31 days
June	9 days
	56 days

Delivery

As with corporate bonds, contracts for delivery can call for a cash, "regular way" or seller's (buyer's) option. *A cash contract requires same day delivery* by 2:30 PM Eastern time. *Regular way transactions with government issues call for delivery the first business day after trade.* (Transactions completed on the second business day are called "skip day.")

Seller's (or buyer's) option contracts call for delivery sometime from the second business day to no more than 60 calendar days after the trade date. Such transactions may be completed ahead of schedule with one day's written notice.

PART THREE   MUNICIPAL BONDS

This section concerns debt obligations (bonds, notes, etc.) issued by states of the United States, by U.S. territories such as Puerto Rico, by U.S. possessions, or by any political subdivision or public agency that is not federal—a city, school district, airport authority, etc.

These instruments, usually called "municipals," are considered safer than any debt instruments but those of the U.S. government. Nevertheless, their safety depends on the source of revenue backing them and therefore this source is an important consideration. City and county issues, for example, are usually backed by real estate taxes, a steady and predictable source of income. State issues are often predicated on sales or other taxes that can fluctuate. In default, investors have the right to sue a municipality, but not the state.

Like all debt obligations, municipals are issued to raise funds—to build or repair public facilities such as roads, waterworks, bridges, etc. To raise money, government agencies must issue debt instruments; they may not issue equity securities.

Default is quite rare and is more likely to affect interest payments than the principal. With most municipals, interest is paid semi-annually, with principal paid at maturity.

For investors, a principal attraction of these issues is that proceeds are exempt from federal tax. (*This status has been upheld by the U.S. Supreme*

Court.) Obviously, this feature is less attractive to investors in low tax brackets, since a tax break is not so important to them. This tax-free status benefits the issuers as well. It allows them to issue instruments at a lower yield, in effect lowering the cost of the issue.

In effect, the tax status is the reverse of the one that obtains for federal obligations, as municipals are subject to state and local taxes. Some issues, however, are exempt from all taxes and are termed "triple exempt." This is true primarily for instruments issued by territories or possessions. Bonds issued by a state and purchased by residents of that state (intrastate) are also usually triple exempt.

TYPES OF MUNICIPALS

Municipal issues include short-term notes, with terms of one month to one year, and bonds described as short term (1 to 6 years), intermediate term (6 to 19 years) and long term (20 years and more). At issue, they are sold at auction, that is, by competitive or negotiated bidding.

General Obligation (G.O.) bonds

These are backed by the full faith and credit (and by the taxing power) of the issuer. In most cases, no particular property or revenues are pledged, but there is a promise to use taxes—usually income, sales or gas taxes in a state issue; usually real estate (*ad valorem*) taxes for those issued by local governments and smaller agencies. G.O. bonds are used to finance projects that do not produce revenue. They are usually issued under competitive bidding.

These can be "unlimited tax G.O. bonds," which are backed by the issuer's unlimited taxing power. If that taxing power is limited by law to a specified maximum, these are called "limited tax G.O. bonds." Such limits can take several forms. For example, voter approval may be required past a certain point, or a state constitution may have statutory ceilings or limits. The "limited" bonds usually offer a somewhat higher yield to compensate for the increased risk.

One other possible limitation on taxing power is the existence of "overlapping" tax jurisdictions, where more than one entity may be able to tax the same set of taxpayers (for example, residents of a city within a county).

Investors need to consider both direct limitations and the possibility of overlapping jurisdictions in evaluating a bond.

Revenue bonds

The most common type of municipal bond is a revenue bond. These are not backed by the issuer's full faith and credit, but are repayable with proceeds from tolls, user fees, rental payments, etc., generated by the facility or facilities built with the proceeds of the bond issue. Since taxes are not involved, revenue bonds are not subject to statutory limits, nor, in general, does their issue dilute the debt standing of the issuer.

Revenue bonds are supposed to be "self-supporting" or "self-liquidating." The issuer can be a state or subdivision, an interstate or intrastate authority and they are usually underwritten using a negotiated price.

If revenues do not meet expectations, interest payments are sometimes deferred. These issues generally deliver a higher yield than G.O. bonds. In many cases, local law requires that an independent agency conduct a feasibility study of the project(s) to be financed. Such a study usually includes a projection of the scheduled flow of funds. It is part of the Official Statement.

Revenue bonds can have serial, term, or balloon maturity provisions, with serial maturity usually in reverse order. Most are callable under provisions detailed in the Official Statement.

"Net revenues," *i.e.*, any proceeds that remain after providing for operation and maintenance of the facility(ies) built with the bond issue, are pledged for paying off the bonds. They are typically disbursed as follows:

1 Current interest and principal of bond due to mature next.

2 Reserve fund for the next two years of principal and interest.

3 Reserve fund for maintenance and replacement of facility(ies).

4 Surplus, for such purposes as expansion or to retire bonds.

Special tax bonds

These instruments are repayable from the proceeds of a special tax. An example would be a gas tax imposed to repay bonds issued to fund highway construction. (Some of these bonds are backed by the full faith and credit of the issuer as well; they are then considered general obligation bonds.)

Three types of taxation are used:

1 Excise taxes—taxes imposed on liquor or gasoline, etc., or license fees.

2 Special assessments—those who benefit directly from the funds expended (for example, those who live on a street being repaired or where a new sewer system is installed) pay a special tax.

3 *Ad valorem*—in some cases, general property taxes are pledged to pay off these bonds.

New Housing Authority bonds (PHA Bonds)

These are issued by a local housing authority and are payable with proceeds from rentals paid to the authority and by an annual contract with the U.S. Public Housing Authority. These bonds are unconditionally guaranteed by the PHA, which is backed by the U.S. government, and are considered very safe.

Because they are backed by two sources of income, these PHA Bonds are called "double-barreled" or "self-supporting." The same term is applied to any bond backed by two sources of revenue. For instance, a Special Tax Bond which is also backed by the full faith and credit of the issuer is double-barreled.

■ **NOTE**

Other, less common types of municipal bonds include:

Moral Obligation bonds

The issuer is not legally bound to repay these bonds.

Industrial Revenue (or Industrial Development) bonds

Issued to acquire funds to build an industrial plant which is then leased to a corporation. These are a primary obligation of the corporation, not the municipality, and are usually backed by a first mortgage on the property.

Pollution Control bonds

Usually backed by a corporation that leases the equipment built with the proceeds of the bond. Lease payments cover the bond payments. (Some of these could also be double-barreled.)

Both Industrial Revenue bonds and Pollution Control bonds are used as incentives to industry since they allow corporations to borrow money at below-market rates.

SHORT-TERM MUNICIPAL NOTES

These are offered while the issuer awaits the proceeds from a bond sale or the like (a process which can take up to one year) so construction on a project can begin. They are often called "anticipation notes," and there are four basic types:

1 Bond Anticipation Notes (BAN)—short-term general obligation securities.

2 Revenue Anticipation Notes (RAN)—short-term revenue bonds, *i.e.*, paid with proceeds other than taxes (these are usually general obligation securities).

3 Tax Anticipation Notes (TAN)—issued in anticipation of future tax receipts (on special taxes); also usually G.O. securities.

4 Project Notes (PN)—short term (3 month to 1 year) new housing authority bonds, ranging in value from $1,000 to $100,000, but customarily in denominations of $25,000 and up. Issued in bearer form, with interest paid at maturity, they are usually triple-exempt. Like PHAs, they are backed by public housing agencies and the full faith and credit of the U.S. government.

TYPES OF MUNICIPAL ISSUES

Registered to principal and interest

The owner's name is registered on the books of the issuing agency; there are no coupons. Interest is paid by check mailed semi-annually. They must be endorsed to be negotiable. Issued in $1,000 or multiples to $100,000.

Registered to principal only

The owner's name is registered as above, but the bond coupon (which shows the rate of return) must be received before interest is paid. Principal is paid to the registered owner at maturity. Also offered in denominations of $1,000 and multiples to $100,000.

Coupon, bearer, unregistered, or owner bonds

These are negotiable instruments; the holder of the bond is the owner. Since July 1, 1983, all tax-exempt issues of over one year must be registered, but many bearer bonds are still outstanding. If the bond is in default, *i.e.* if interest payments have been missed, these bonds can be delivered only if all past due and future coupons are attached.

LEGAL OPINION

Unlike corporate securities, municipals are not subject to the filing provisions of the Securities Acts of 1933 or 1934 (though the fraud provisions apply), nor to the Trust Indenture Act of 1939. For this reason, investors consider it vital to have an opinion by a municipal bond attorney, an independent attorney who specializes in acting as bond counsel to municipalities. This has become more important since passage of the Tax Reform Act of 1986, which distinguishes among classes of municipal bonds, giving some more favorable tax treatment than others. The legal opinion is the basis for these distinctions. This opinion does not provide any estimate of the worth of the issue, but says the attorney thinks it is both exempt from taxes and a binding debt of the issuer. The opinion may be qualified if some aspect of it is questioned.

Customarily, the issuing agency or municipality employs the bond attorney to ensure that its bonds will enjoy tax-free status, that they do not exceed any statutory debt limit, and that the issue is otherwise legally sound. Once these three matters have been decided, the attorney issues an opinion as to the "validity, legality, and tax-exempt status" of the issue. In addition, the legal opinion includes terms of the offering and call provisions and makes note of any limitations on the issuer's taxing power. This opinion must be on the face of the bond. If no attorney has been retained, the bond must be stamped "EX-LEGAL."

INDENTURE

Although an indenture is not required, as it is with corporate bonds, the issuer's obligations are often spelled out on the face of the bond in a series of "covenants," also called a "bond resolution." Almost all revenue bonds have these. Among the most likely covenants are those concerning:

☐ rates—under this heading, the issuer promises to maintain rates sufficient to meet expenses and service the debt

☐ redemption—the call privilege

☐ insurance—a pledge to insure facilities built with proceeds of the bond

☐ maintenance—a pledge to maintain those facilities

☐ non-discrimination in hiring

☐ feasibility—pledging to ensure the project will be self-sustaining

☐ financial reports and auditing—a promise to issue regular financial reports and to retain an outside auditor

□ additional bonds—like corporates, revenue bond issues can be "open" or "closed"

INTEREST AND PRINCIPAL PAYMENT

Municipal bonds show on their face the interest or coupon rate applied to par. For example, an 8% $1,000 bond will pay $80 a year. Interest is usually paid semi-annually on the dates shown on the face. The principal is paid at maturity.

Municipals come in a wide range of maturities, ranging from one month to more than 50 years. They can be issued in term or serial form.

Term bonds

All bonds in the issue mature at the same time, for example 20 years after issue. These are often used when revenues are estimated, and not for short terms because such estimates can be uncertain. Also called "dollar bonds," they are quoted as a percent of par, thus 97¼ = $972.50. Many term bonds are callable.

Serial bonds

As with corporates, these mature over a series of years. Typically, they are used when revenues are stable, for example, with a waterworks, and are scheduled to mature when income peaks. But they can be issued on a "level debt service" basis, with equal payments (for combined principal and interest) over the life of the bond, like a conventional home mortgage. They are usually quoted on a yield-to-maturity basis.

Balloon serials

A serial issue where most bonds mature in one year, usually with fewer bonds coming due in early years. These are also usually callable.

TENDER, CALL AND PUT

Most revenue bonds include a call provision. When this is not the case, but issuers wish to retire the debt early, they can ask for a "tender offer." This is published in a newspaper and invites holders to "tender" their bonds to the issuer at a stated price.

When call provisions do exist, they usually resemble those in corporate issues. They can be at par or at a premium, usually declining over the life of the bond, can be optional or mandatory, and are usually delayed for some time after issue. Most require a published notice 30 days in advance of the call date.

With serial issues, bonds are usually called in inverse order; *i.e.*, bonds with the most remaining life are called first. Calls of term issues customarily proceed by lot. Calls can be partial (this usually occurs when revenues exceed expectations), or total, as in a refunding.

Recently, in an attempt to attract more investors, some municipal bonds have been issued with a "put" provision. While not truly a Put, as it cannot be traded separately, such a provision does allow the investor to "put" the bonds back to the issuer, *i.e.*, to compel the issuer to redeem the bonds. This opportunity is available only at specified times, and usually not for some time after the bonds are issued.

In effect, the put provision gives the investor some protection against changes in rates. If rates rise, and investors have the right to return the bonds, the issuer can either redeem the bonds or offer to adjust the rate on them.

Trade confirmations for bonds with a call provision have to consider this feature in computing the yields that must be declared on all callable bonds.

MUNICIPAL BOND INSURANCE

Insurance on municipal bonds is available to both issuers and to investors. If issuers buy insurance, it has the effect of increasing the bond's rating, and therefore lowering the rate at which it sells.

Investors with portfolios of at least $50,000 in at least three different issues can also purchase insurance, for example, from the Municipal Guarantee Insurance Corporation (MGIC), a division of American Municipal Bond Assurance Corporation (AMBAC), one of several firms which offer such insurance.

QUOTATIONS

Municipals are generally quoted on the basis of yield to maturity, not percentage of par, as most issues are in serial form. (As noted, term bonds, also called dollar bonds or notes, when issued, are quoted on a dollar basis.) Translating yield to maturity into a dollar price is complicated, so traders generally refer to a "basis book," which contains this information.

SAMPLE BASIS BOOK PAGE

COUPON 4% YTM	9 YRS.	10 YRS.	11 YRS.	12 YRS.
3.80	101.51	101.65	101.78	101.91
3.90	100.75	100.82	100.89	100.96
4.00	100.00	100.00	100.00	100.00
4.10	99.25	99.19	99.12	99.05
4.20	98.51	98.38	98.25	98.12

For example, a 4% coupon with a 4.10% YTM which had 11 years to maturity would have a price of 99.12 or $991.20. Naturally, a 4% YTM would yield a price of 100.00 for any maturity.

A quote on municipals is often called the "basis price," and changes are noted in points. Each point (or "tick") represents 10 cents, so a price of 99.13 would be $991.30. Prices below 100 are at a discount to par. Prices above 100 are at a premium to par.

In using the basis book one often needs to find the price for a yield not listed in the book. Assume, for example, we have a 4% coupon with a yield of 3.95 and a maturity of ten years. Obviously, it has a price between 100 (the price for a 4% YTM) and 100.82 (the price for a 3.90 YTM). Since 3.95 is exactly halfway between 4.00 and 3.90, the price for this security would be 100.41, halfway between the corresponding prices.

This process, called "arithmetic interpolation," can be formalized as follows:

To find the price for a YTM not given in the basis book, choose the next highest and next lowest YTMs (with the same coupon and years to maturity) that do appear in the book. Then find a price that is at the same relative distance from those neighboring prices.

■ EXAMPLE

A yield of 3.96 is 60% (or .6) of the way from 3.90 to 4.00. The corresponding price is computed by subtracting 60% of the difference between the yields (.6 × [100.82 − 100]) from the price of the 3.90 YTM. Thus, 100.82 − .492 = 100.328, or $1,003.28 the price for a 3.96 YTM.

YIELDS AND TAXATION

The yield to maturity, or any other yield, is computed as for any bond; however, the special tax status of a municipal bond does create some changes.

Tax treatment of municipal yields

While interest income from municipal bonds is free from federal taxes, any capital gain realized in the purchase and sale of a municipal bond is subject to capital gains tax.

This last must be modified when, as sometimes occurs, municipals are issued at a discount. Then the difference between the discount and par is considered as interest income which accrues over time, and is not subject to federal tax.

■ EXAMPLE

For a 5% coupon 20-year $1,000 bond issued at $800, the $200 appreciation to par would be considered as accruing at the rate the interest is paid—that is, not at $10 per year for 20 years, but at the compound interest rate. If, for example, after some time, $50 of interest had accrued and the bond were sold for $925, then $50 of the $125 increase over the issue price is not considered a capital gain but the other $75 is.

For bonds issued at a premium, however, the premium is amortized on a straight-line basis over the life of the bond. Thus a bond purchased at $1,050 which matures in ten years has its cost basis adjusted downward by $5 per year, so that if it were sold at $1,010 after six years the investor would incur a $10 loss.

$1,050 − (6 × $5) = $1,020 cost basis; $1,020 − $1,010 = $10 loss

If the bond is held to maturity and redeemed at $1,000, the investor experiences neither a loss nor a gain but has benefited from the tax-free interest income for the life of the bond.

Equivalent yield

Though municipal yields are computed in the same way as for taxable instruments, to compare the two, one must compute the equivalent yields, *i.e.,* take into account the marginal tax rate (tax bracket) for this income.

The equivalent municipal rate (to a taxable rate) is found by multiplying the latter by $(1 - \text{marginal rate})$.

■ **EXAMPLE**

A 12% taxable instrument for someone in the 28% bracket is equivalent to an 8.64% municipal rate:

$$12\% \times (1 - .28) = 8.64\%$$

For a person in the 33% bracket the equivalent municipal rate would be 8.04%:

$$12\% \times (1 - .33) = 8.04\%$$

In other words, the higher the tax bracket, the more attractive any specific municipal bond is.

To find the equivalent taxable rate for a given municipal rate, simply reverse the algebra: divide the municipal rate by $(1 - \text{marginal rate})$.

■ **EXAMPLE**

For someone in the 15% tax bracket, an 8% municipal is equivalent to a bond with a taxable yield of

$$8\% \div (1 - .15) = 9.41\%$$

In general, to compare two bonds—one taxable, the other tax-free— an investor should convert both to the taxable equivalent for his or her own tax bracket and determine which has a higher yield. Alternatively, an investor could convert both to the tax-free equivalent rate and again find the higher rate. Both methods always yield the same result.

Yield to maturity

As with corporate issues, YTM is approximated by the formula:

$$\frac{\text{Coupon} + (\text{change in price/years to maturity})}{(\text{purchase price} + \text{maturity price}) / 2} = \text{YTM}$$

Note that the change in price may be negative, for instance, with a bond purchased at a premium, where the premium would be amortized over the remaining life of the bond.

■ **EXAMPLE**

A 6% coupon $1,000 bond maturing in 10 years that sold at $1,200 would have the following YTM:

$$\frac{\$60 + (- \$200/10 \text{ years})}{(\$1,200 + \$1,000)/2} = \frac{(\$60 - \$20)}{\$1,100} = 3.636\%$$

Yield to Call or Put

These yields are similar to the yield to maturity, and can be computed by replacing the years to maturity with the years to call or put. Thus YTC can be found as:

$$\frac{\text{Coupon} + (\text{net change in price/years to call})}{(\text{purchase price} + \text{call price})/2} = \text{YTC}$$

■ **EXAMPLE**

A 6% coupon $1,000 bond callable in 6 years at 130 would have the following YTC:

$$\frac{\$60 + (\$100/6)}{(\$1,200 + \$1,300)/2} = \frac{\$76.66}{\$1,250} + 6.1328\%$$

TRADING IN MUNICIPALS

There is a steady market for municipals—both a primary and a secondary market—because of their reputation for safety, and because they can be used as collateral. Traditionally, banks and insurance companies have held these instruments, but not charitable organizations or pension funds that have no need of tax benefits.

The major figures in the municipal market are dealers who specialize in municipal bonds, large banks, and those large brokerage firms with separate municipal bond departments. Banks are allowed to make a market in general obligation bonds but not in revenue bonds. They can also act as brokers for revenue bonds, but a bank may not act in this capacity for its own trust department when it buys or sells for client trust accounts.

Although some firms act solely as brokers for other dealers, traders in municipals typically act as principals (see Chapter 8). That is, they maintain an inventory of such bonds and sell from that inventory to investors wishing to purchase municipal bonds. If the broker does not hold the bond, he or she will consult the *Blue List* to find such bonds, purchase them, and then resell them to the client.

The usual face value for a municipal obligation is $5,000, though some come in $1,000 or $10,000 denominations. This is intended to make trade and payment more efficient. A "round lot" usually refers to $100,000 in bonds.

When issued, municipals trade like corporates. Most trading is over-the-counter, through brokers, specialist dealers, and major banks. Available issues are shown in the *Blue List*, a daily publication which describes the issues, showing the quantity available and the yield to maturity. The *Blue List* also has a computer service and a news ticker called Munifacts.

Another publication, called the *Daily Bond Buyer*, shows average yields, but not average prices, and publishes a weekly *Index*. It also gives figures on the proportion of offered issues that have been placed. Another publication, *Moody's Manual*, is used mostly for background information.

Trading in municipal securities is subject to the governance of the Municipal Securities Rulemaking Board (MSRB). These rules are discussed in Chapter 16.

Terminology

Some special language is used in municipal bond transactions. For example, dealer Smith calls and requests a firm offer from dealer Brown. Brown responds "7.20 basis firm for two hours with five." Smith understands this to mean:

☐ The bonds are offered at a yield to maturity of 7.20%.

☐ The offer is firm.

☐ The offer is good for two hours—that is, Smith has two hours to decide if she wishes to buy the bonds at the offered yield of 7.20%.

□ If a third broker wants to buy these bonds and makes a firm bid to dealer Brown, Brown must call Smith and give her five minutes to decide. After five minutes, Brown can sell the bonds to the third broker. (This is the meaning of "with five.")

"Workable quote" The price at which a dealer is willing to buy a municipal bond. It is firm at the moment it is given, but the buying dealer cannot be held to that figure if the selling dealer must first consult a client to see if he wishes to sell the bond at that price.

"Concession" In this context, a discount from the quoted yield on an interdealer transaction. For instance, a transaction at "8¼ less ⅜" means that a bond was sold to yield 8¼% minus a concession of ⅜, or $3.75 for each $1,000 bond.

A concession is usually available on bonds quoted by yield. Dealers purchase term bonds, which are offered at a price in dollars, at the quoted price with no discount, *e.g.*, a bond quoted at 102¼ would be bought at $1,022.50.

Accrued interest

The purchaser of a municipal bond must pay the interest which has accrued since the last coupon payment. Recall that interest on municipals is computed on the basis of 12 months, each 30 days long. Accrued interest is computed by counting from the last coupon date up to, but not including, the settlement date. If the transaction is "for cash," which means same-day settlement, interest is computed up to the day before the sale.

■ **EXAMPLE**

A bond with April 15 and October 15 coupon dates is sold on June 12 for settlement on June 19. Accrued interest would total:

April 15–30	16
May	30 [sic]
June	<u>18</u>
	64 days

This accrued interest would be included in the price the buyer paid and would appear on the trade confirmations to both parties.

Bond swaps

If interest rates rise, the market value of a bond portfolio will fall. An investor holding a portfolio of tax-free bonds could take advantage of this situation with a "bond swap." This involves the following steps:

The investor sells the bonds, thereby incurring a capital loss which can be used to offset other income. At the same time, the investor buys a similar portfolio of municipal bonds at a comparable discount, thereby setting up a potential capital gain in the future. The effect is to defer taxes, which can be of advantage in some situations.

A bond swap is especially attractive to banks, which must treat all proceeds from municipal bond investments as ordinary income and therefore not subject to the limitations on capital losses.

To avoid violating the restrictions on "wash sales" in the tax code, the swap should involve bonds from different issuers or, if that is not possible, bonds that differ substantially in coupon and/or maturity.

JUDGING MUNICIPALS

Like corporate issues, most municipal bonds of sizable issue carry quality ratings from an independent firm—Moody's, Standard & Poor's, Fitches, and Dun & Bradstreet all offer such services. These represent a measure of the relative worth of an issue, and are based on an examination of the legality of the issue, the record of the issuer in past offerings, and, most importantly, on the ability to pay.

Beyond the ratings, it is possible to examine individual offerings in a number of ways.

Evaluating general obligation bonds

Here are some questions to ask in judging the strength of a general obligation municipal issue:

☐ What is the issuer's history—has there ever been a default in the past?

☐ How economically healthy is the issuing community? Answering this can involve looking at overall wealth, for example, property values, retail sales, bank holdings, and bank activity. Other indications may come from examining the mix of economic activity: is it diverse, or over-reliant on one firm or one type of activity? Is the community growing?

☐ What is the character of city officials—have there been cases of malfeasance or corruption?

☐ Is the issuer in sound financial shape? For example, what is the current ratio of debt to property values (remember, G.O. bonds are backed by property taxes) or to overall annual revenues? Are any of the issuer's other debt service obligations about to come due?

☐ Is there "overlapping debt"? This term refers to obligations of other government entities which overlap the issuing body—a simple example would involve a city that bears some obligations as part of the surrounding county.

☐ Other related questions involve finding the issuer's direct debt—*i.e.*, debt that is not self-liquidating (for example, a revenue bond), especially in relation to the value of real property.

☐ Does the issuer show a likely ability to pay? Under this broad heading, one could see whether there are any legal limits on taxation, whether an outstanding issue has prior claim on taxes, and how great a percentage of taxes is actually collected.

Evaluating revenue bonds

Many of the questions about the worth of revenue bonds should be answered in the feasibility study. Chief concerns are:

☐ Is the proposed project justifiable on economic grounds?

☐ Will earnings be adequate to meet the debt obligation?

□ Are there existing or proposed facilities that might compete with the facility funded by this issue?

□ Are the covenants and the "flow of funds" arrangements adequate?

Default

Technically, if a bond issued by a state is in default, the investor has no direct legal redress since the sovereign states cannot be sued without their consent. This is not the case for municipalities or subdivisions of a state, which are subject to court action in case of default.

TERMS

Bonds Long-term debt obligations offering fixed interest do not represent ownership.

Corporate bonds Issued to raise long-term capital; issuer obliged to pay interest before any stock dividends

Rights No voting rights, but precedence over shareholders in liquidation

Terms Usually $1,000 denominations, 20- to 30-year maturities, interest paid semi-annually

Forms

Bearer bonds Negotiable, interest paid when coupon submitted, no corporate record of ownership

Registered Corporate books show owner's name; transfer procedure as with stocks

Book-entry Computerized record only; no certificate

Trust indenture Contract required by law for most bonds stipulating rights and obligations of issuer and creditors

Secured

Mortgage bonds Backed by corporation's fixed assets; can be open end (may issue more bonds of this class) or closed end

Collateral trust bonds Backed by negotiable securities

Equipment Trust Certificates (ETCs) Backed by specific piece of equipment; usually issued by transportation companies

Unsecured

Debentures Backed by issuer's good faith and credit (if "subordinated," honored after debentures in liquidation)

Other types

Income (adjustment) bonds Pay principal at maturity, but interest only if declared

Guaranteed bonds Backed by corporation(s) other than issuer

Zero-coupon Pay no interest but sell at discount, redeemed at par on maturity

Convertible Debt instruments (usually debentures) can include right to convert to stock shares, sometimes with rights

Call provisions Corporation can force redemption of bonds

Put provisions Investor can demand redemption of bonds

Serial bonds One offering with maturity over a range of years

Series bonds Issued over several years, maturing in the same year

Sinking fund Separate fund to assure redemption; required in some indentures

Balloon maturity Serial bonds with most maturing in one year

Trading

Prices Quoted as percentage of par and ⅛ths of a percentage point; above par is "at a premium"; below par "at a discount"

Points Bond price changes of $10 (1% of par)

Yields

Nominal yield Rate of return at par

Current yield Rate of return at current market price

Note current yield is in inverse relationship to price

Yield to maturity Return actually received at time of redemption

Accrued Interest Bonds sold after interest payment date; must include interest due calculated:

$$\text{principal} \times \text{rate} \times \text{time} = \text{accrued interest}$$

where time begins the morning of the last interest payment and ends the day before the settlement date; each month is calculated at 30 days

Trade dates

Regular way Settlement on 5th business day

Seller's or buyer's option Settlement delayed, but no more than 60 calendar days

Cash Settled same day when issued

When issued

Bond ratings

Offered by investment services; reflected in yields

U.S. Government Issues
Exempt from state and local taxes

Negotiable Highly liquid, heavily traded

Treasury bills (T-bills) Short term (3-, 6-, 12-month); sold at discount; book-entry; min. $10,000 denomination; sold at auction

Current return (bond equivalent yield):

$$\frac{\text{Annualized Appreciation}}{\text{purchase price}} \times \frac{365}{\text{days to maturity}}$$
$$= \text{bond equivalent yield}$$

Only governments quoted on basis of yield ("discount yield"):

$$\text{Discount yield} = \frac{(\text{par} - \text{purchase price}) \times 360}{\text{days to maturity}}$$

Changes in prices quoted in "basis point" or .01% of yield

Treasury notes Medium term (2- to 10-year) interest-bearing notes; registered or book entry; $1,000-$1,000,000 denominations; sold at auction; offered at fixed interest rate; sold at percentage of par; quoted in ⅓₂nds of a percentage point

Treasury bonds Long-term (10- to 30-year) interest-bearing; come in any form (no longer issued in bearer form); $1,000 - $1,000,000 denominations; sold at auction; can be callable; quoted and sold like T-notes

"Flower bonds" Low-rate T-bonds sold at deep discount; no longer issued

Zero Coupon Securities ("Zeros") No interest paid but sold at discount and redeemed at par

Strips T-bond interest separated from principal placed in trusts; securities representing shares in the trusts are marketed. U.S. Treasury version called STRIPS or treasury receipts

Non-Negotiable government issues Non-transferable; no loan value

Series EE ("savings") Sold at discount; mature at face in eight years; registered form only; $50 to $10,000 denominations

Series HH Issued at par; interest paid semi-annually; registered form only; $50 to $10,000 denominations

Obligations of other government agencies

Federal Farm Credit Banks Issues Federal Farm Credit Consolidated Systemwide Obligations

Federal Home Loan Banks Short-term notes (minimum denomination $100,000) and bonds (1- to 2-year maturities; $10,000 - $1,000,000 denominations)

Federal Home Loan Mortgage Corporation (Freddie Mac) Mortgage-backed bonds (12-25 years), registered, $25,000 to $1,000,000 denominations; participation certificates (min. $100,000); registered mortgage certificates (min. $100,000)

Federal National Mortgage (FNMA; Fannie Mae) Publicly held corporation, issues debentures (3- to 25-year maturity), $10,000 to $1,000,000; short-term discount bearer notes ($5,000 to $50,000), maturing in 30-270 days

Obligations of U.S. Government-owned agencies

Government National Mortgage (GNMA; Ginnie Mae) "Pass-through" certificates, shares of a mortgage pool; min. $25,000; maturities 12-40 years

Delivery of governments

Accrued Interest Calculated in terms of actual calendar days, 365-day year

Delivery Regular way = first business day after trade; seller's (buyer's) option (from 2nd day to 60 calendar days); cash

Municipal bonds

Debt obligations of non-federal governmental entities Exempt from federal tax; short-term notes and bonds of all terms; sold at auction when issued

General Obligation (G.O.) Bonds Backed by issuer's full faith and credit; based on taxing power ("limited" if that power is limited)

Revenue bonds Repaid by fees from users of facility(ies) built with proceeds; may require feasibility study

Special tax bonds Repaid from proceeds of special tax; can be G.O. bonds as well

New Housing Authority (NHA) Bonds Repaid by rent on housing built by authority; guaranteed by federal agency

"Double-barreled bond" Backed by two sources of income

Moral obligation bonds Issuer not legally bound to repay

Industrial revenue bonds Funds used to build a plant leased to corporation; usually mortgage-backed

Municipal Notes Short-term notes issued while awaiting proceeds from bond sale; called "anticipation notes"

Forms of municipals

Registered To principal and interest, or to principal only (with coupon); in multiples of $1,000 to $100,000

Bearer bonds No longer issued, but many outstanding

Legal opinion On bond face; legal, tax-exempt; appears on bond face; if no opinion, bond is "Ex-legal"

Delivery Regular way = first business day after trade

Indenture Not required; covenants on face of bond cover issuer's obligations

Flow of funds How receipts will be applied on some revenue bonds

Payment At stated interest rate; principal paid at maturity

Term bonds All mature at one time; quoted at percent of par

Serial bonds Mature over a series of years; usually quoted on yield-to-maturity

Tender, Call and Put Revenue bonds usually callable; if not issuer can make "tender offer" to retire issue early; some have put provision

Insurance Available to both issuers and to investors

Quotations Usually in terms of yield to maturity, translated into dollar price by basis book; changes in "points" (10 cents)

Taxation Interest income tax-exempt, but gains realized in trading are taxable; if issued at discount or premium, difference from par is tax-exempt

Equivalent yield After-tax yield on municipal compared with corporate yield

corporate yield rate $\times$ (1 − tax rate) = equivalent municipal rate

Yield to maturity

$$\frac{\text{Coupon} + (\text{change in price/years to maturity})}{(\text{purchase price} - \text{maturity price})/2} = ytm$$

Trading in municipals

Over the counter Mostly involving specialist dealers, banks, and brokerage firms; banks cannot make a market in revenue bonds; traders typically maintain inventory

"Workable quote" Price at which dealer is willing to buy municipal bond

"Concession" In this context, the discount from quoted yield on interdealer transaction

Accrued interest Purchaser must pay interest accrued since last coupon payment, computed on basis of 12 30-day months

Evaluation

Ratings Offered, as with corporates

REVIEW QUESTIONS

1. A general obligation bond would be backed by which of the following?

   (A) taxes
   (B) the full faith and credit of the issuer
   (C) general revenues
   (D) obligations on equipment

2. A capital gain could not be registered on:

   (A) T-notes
   (B) T-bills
   (C) T-bonds
   (D) corporate bonds

3. Which of the following would be most unattractive to the purchaser of a corporate bond?

   (A) high interest rate
   (B) convertibility
   (C) callability
   (D) sinking fund requirement

4. Bonds that mature in a sequence of years are called:

   (A) convertible
   (B) serial
   (C) series
   (D) balloon

5. A basis point is what percentage of yield?

   (A) 10%
   (B) 1.00%
   (C) 0.1%
   (D) 0.01%

6. Par value for most corporate bonds is:

   (A) $100
   (B) $1,000
   (C) $10,000
   (D) $100,000

7. A one-year T-bill with a discount yield of 5.00% would sell at approximately:

   (A) 94.50
   (B) 95.00
   (C) 95.25
   (D) 95.75

8. If interest rates fall the price of previously-issued government bonds will generally:

   (A) fall
   (B) rise
   (C) be unaffected
   (D) vary

Questions 9-11 refer to a 7% corporate bond with par at $1,000 due to mature in 10 years which is bought at $700.

9. The nominal yield on this bond is:

   (A) 6.5%
   (B) 7.0%
   (C) 10%
   (D) 14.28%

10. The current yield is:

   (A) 6.5%
   (B) 7.0%
   (C) 10%
   (D) 14.28%

11. The yield to maturity is approximately:

   (A) 6.5%
   (B) 7.0%
   (C) 11.8%
   (D) 14.28%

12. An issue of bonds that mature at different times with a smaller amount maturing early and most late is:

   (A) term
   (B) serial
   (C) series
   (D) balloon

13. Debentures are backed by:

   (A) the benchmark for revenues
   (B) equipment
   (C) real estate
   (D) general credit

14. A $10,000 government bond priced at $104.04 would sell

   (A) $10,400.04
   (B) $10,404.00
   (C) $10,412.50
   (D) $10,440.00

15. The interest on corporates is computed on the basis of:

   (A) actual days of the month and a 360-day year
   (B) actual days of the month and a 365-day year
   (C) 30-day months and a 360-day year
   (D) 30-day months and a 365-day year

16. The interest on government bonds is computed on the basis of:

   (A) actual days of the month and a 360-day year
   (B) actual days of the month and a 365-day year
   (C) 30-day months and a 360-day year
   (D) 30-day months and a 365-day year

17. A purchase of $10,000 worth of T-bonds for cash on May 18 would settle on:

   (A) May 18
   (B) May 19
   (C) May 24
   (D) May 25

18. Which of the following is "triple exempt"?

   (A) U.S. Bonds
   (B) U.S. Treasury bills
   (C) GNMAs
   (D) Puerto Rico bonds

19. A corporate bond quoted at $98.25 would normally cost:

   (A) $98.25
   (B) $980 and $^{25}/_{32}$ dollars
   (C) $982.50
   (D) $9,825.00

20. Bonds callable at 104 are currently selling at 105½. If the bonds were called, an investor who owned $30,000 face of these bonds would receive:

   (A) $30,000
   (B) $31,200
   (C) $34,000
   (D) $35,500

21. The yield to maturity is the yield an investor would earn if the security is held to maturity. It is arrived at by:

   (A) taking account of difference between purchase price and par
   (B) considering the difference between coupon and current yield
   (C) considering the difference between nominal and current yield
   (D) averaging the discount and the premium on the bond

22. Which S & P rating is highest?

   (A) Aaa
   (B) AAA
   (C) A+
   (D) Al

23. The *Blue List* quotes:

   (A) corporate bonds
   (B) US. Government Agency obligations
   (C) municipal bonds
   (D) Treasury bills

24. A bond with a conversion rate of 20:1 selling at par would be convertible into:

   (A) 20 shares of common at $20
   (B) 50 shares of common at $20
   (C) 20 shares of common at $50
   (D) 50 shares of common at $50

25. The *Bond Buyer Index* measures on a weekly basis an average of:

   (A) 20-year Treasury Bond yields
   (B) 20-year Treasury Bond prices
   (C) 20-year municipal bond yields
   (D) 20-year municipal bond prices

26. The maximum amount (face value) of Series EE that an individual can purchase in any year is:

   (A) $7,500
   (B) $15,000
   (C) $22,500
   (D) $30,000

27. A municipal bond is purchased on November 22. It is a March 15 - September 15

bond. How many days of accrued interest will the purchaser of the bond have to pay?

(A) 66 days
(B) 68 days
(C) 72 days
(D) 73 days

28. In evaluating a Water and Sewer Revenue Bond, which of the following would be taken into account?

I. size of the customer base
II. rate covenants
III. the issuing authority's past performance
IV. the state in which the municipality is located

(A) I only
(B) I and II
(C) I, II, and III
(D) III and IV

29. A feasibility study is required for:

(A) revenue bonds
(B) general obligation bonds
(C) school bonds
(D) special assessment bonds

30. The lowest rating for bonds which are considered investment grade is:

(A) A+ or Al
(B) A or A
(C) BBB or Baa
(D) BB or Ba

31. Municipal bonds which are in bearer form and in default are traded:

(A) flat and stripped of coupons
(B) with accrued interest from the time of default
(C) flat with all unpaid coupons attached
(D) with accrued interest and a default penalty

32. Over a period of years, T-bill investments will have which of the following characteristics?

I. stable interest rates
II. varying interest rates

III. stable principal
IV. varying principal

(A) I and III
(B) I and IV
(C) II and III
(D) II and IV

33. An investor owns 10 corporate bonds with face value of $1,000 callable at a 5% premium. If the bonds are held to maturity the investor will receive:

(A) $10,000
(B) $10,050
(C) $100,000
(D) $100,500

34. A corporation which does not show a profit will still pay interest to holders of all of the following EXCEPT:

(A) convertible bonds
(B) callable bonds
(C) debentures
(D) adjustment bonds

35. An investor buys $20,000 face value corporate bonds at a price of 92 in the secondary market. If he sells them three years later at 96 he will realize:

(A) a capital gain of $400
(B) a capital gain of $800
(C) interest income of $400
(D) interest income of $800 with 60% long term

36. Which of the following is true of U.S. T-bonds?

(A) they are issued at a discount
(B) interest is not subject to federal income tax
(C) maturity at issue is at least 10 years
(D) the price will not fluctuate much over time

37. A bond selling at a premium with a coupon of 5% if held to maturity would have a yield:

(A) lower than 5%
(B) at 5%
(C) higher than 5%
(D) cannot be determined

38. None of the following is guaranteed by the U.S. government EXCEPT:

(A) revenue bonds

(B) Fannie Mae bonds

(C) GNMA certificates

(D) tax anticipation notes (TANs)

39. If a legal opinion on a municipal bond was "qualified," it would mean:

(A) the municipality is able to issue the bond

(B) the bond counsel is in a position to offer an opinion

(C) there are some conditions on the legal opinion

(D) there is a debt ceiling on the issue

40. The information on municipal issues scheduled to be offered would be found in

(A) *Blue List*

(B) 30-day visible supply

(C) *Bond Buyer's Guide*

(D) pink sheets

ANSWERS TO REVIEW QUESTIONS

1. (B) A general obligation bond is backed by all of the resources of the issuer, hence full faith and credit.

2. (B) The difference between the purchase and sale prices of a T-bill is always considered as interest.

3. (C) This is unattractive because it potentially reduces the time period over which the investor will receive the agreed upon return.

4. (B) By definition. Not to be confused with series, which are bonds issued over a series of years all maturing in the same year.

5. (D) By definition. It can also be .01% of the yield.

6. (B) This is typical for corporates, not for governments.

7. (B) Discount yield of 5% means price is $100 − 5 = $95.00.

8. (B) Since they were issued before rates fell, they pay a higher rate and therefore are more valuable than current issues. Hence the higher price.

9. (B) A 7% bond means the nominal yield is 7%.

10. (C) The current yield is $70 (interest) ÷ $700 (price) = 10%.

11. (C) Since it will mature in ten years and pay $1,000, we approximate the yield to maturity by amortizing the $300 over this period. Hence we say that the gain is $70 + $30 = $100 per year and this divided by the average of the purchase and redemption prices $700 and $1,000 yields $100 ÷ $850 = 11.8%.

12. (D) The word balloon refers to the large later payment.

13. (D) Debentures are not backed by any specific assets.

14. (C) The .04 is ⁴⁄₃₂ and since each whole point is $100, ⁴⁄₃₂ is $12.50. 104⁴⁄₃₂ is $10,412.50.

15. (C) This is different from government bonds which are computed on actual days and a 365-day year.

16. (B) By definition.

17. (A) Cash settlement for U.S. securities is same day.

18. (D) In fact, all of the others are subject to federal tax.

19. (C) The usual par value for corporates is $1,000.

20. (B) The investor receives $104 for every $100 of bonds. If possible the investor would have sold these bonds and received $105.50 for every $100 worth of bonds.

21. (A) The formula is

$$YTM = \frac{\text{Annual interest + prorated difference between purchase price \& par}}{(\text{purchase price + par})/2}$$

22. (B) Moody's highest rating is Aaa.

23. (C) *The Blue List* shows quantity available and the yield to maturity.

24. (C) The 20:1 means 20 shares of common to 1 bond. If selling at par we have 20 × $50 = $1,000.

25. (C) The *Index* measures on a weekly basis an average of 20-year municipal bond yields.

26. (D) These are sold at 50% discount to mature at face so an investor can put $15,000 into these bonds each year.

27. (D) Accrued interest would be 16 days in September, 30 days in October, and 28 days (up to, but not including, delivery day) in November = 74 days.

28. (C) The state would have no direct obligation here.

29. (A) Since the payments depend on these revenues rather than any taxing ability, a feasibility study is required.

30. (C) Ratings below this are considered speculative.

31. (C) Since they are in default there is no accrued interest and they are traded flat. Naturally those coupons which have not been paid yet should be attached.

32. (C) The interest rates of T-bills vary with time but since they are short term instruments the principal is not subject to great variation.

33. (A) If they are held to maturity the call option has not been exercised and there is no reason for paying a premium.

34. (D) Income or adjustment bonds include a promise to repay the principal at maturity but interest is contingent on the company's earnings and must be declared by the board of directors.

35. (B) The purchase price of 92 means he paid $18,400 for $20,000 of face value bonds. The sale is at $19,200.

36. (C) T-bills have maturities up to 1 year and T-Notes have maturities up to 10 years.

37. (A) If held to maturity the investor receives face value and hence loses the amount of the premium. This reduces the yield.

38. (C) All of the others are issued by agencies or other entities and are not directly guaranteed by the U.S. government.

39. (C) If the opinion is "qualified," there are some conditions on it.

40. (B) This is a daily compilation of the total dollar value of municipal securities scheduled to come out within the next 30 days.

CHAPTER THREE

Money market instruments

Money market instruments are very secure debt obligations which have maturities of less than one year. This category includes all short-term U.S. government and U.S. government agency obligations, discussed in Chapter 2: Treasury bills; Treasury and agency-issued notes; and bonds maturing in less than one year. It also includes Federal Funds and non-governmental debt obligations like certificates of deposit, bankers' acceptances, and commercial paper, which are described in this chapter. These highly liquid instruments come in a number of forms.

FEDERAL FUNDS

The Federal Reserve System requires each bank to hold a specified proportion of its funds in reserve. To meet these requirements, banks at times borrow from other banks which have a surplus, or from the Fed itself. These are usually unsecured "overnight" borrowings, in amounts of $1 million and up. Interest, usually one day, is calculated on the basis of a 360-day year.

The interest rate, called the "federal funds rate," is extremely volatile, changing from day to day depending on the demand for money. The Federal Reserve will change this rate when it wishes to tighten or ease credit.

REPURCHASE AGREEMENTS

Repurchase agreements, or "repos," occur when a security is sold with an agreement to buy it back, often the next day, at a higher price. Both the time and price of this repurchase are fixed and these together determine the interest charge in the transaction.

These agreements are typically used by dealers in government securities. Dealers often require large amounts of cash in order to hold the large inventories of government securities which they need to conduct business. For this reason, they will, at times, sell some portion of their holdings to the Federal Reserve Bank or to a cash rich corporate lender under an arrangement which includes a pledge to repurchase (repossess, or "repo") those securities, at the selling price plus interest, in the future. (Dealers also raise cash using government issues as collateral for demand loans; see page 65.)

Funds can be borrowed under these agreements overnight, for some days, or even longer. The Federal Reserve Bank participates directly in these arrangements in part because dealers play a vital role in maintaining an active market in government securities, especially when new issues are placed.

When securities are sold to a lender under a repurchase agreement, dealers can realize a profit if the market price of the instrument rises more than the interest paid. Similarly, if the price of these securities declines they can suffer a loss.

The minimum denomination of repurchase agreements is $1,000,000. Interest, paid at repurchase, is calculated in terms of actual days on the basis of a 360-day year.

This procedure works in the opposite direction with a reverse repo: a dealer buys securities and agrees to sell them back at a specified later date. The dealer is effectively lending money, using very secure collateral.

Repos of either type have no secondary market since they represent contracts between a specified buyer and seller.

BANKER'S ACCEPTANCES

Used in international trade, a banker's acceptance can be thought of as a post-dated certified check. These are basically commercial bank drafts, ordering the bank to pay a specified amount to the holder on a specified date (usually 90 days from date of issue). The term "acceptance" comes into play when the bank accepts responsibility—gives its promise—to repay.

Once the bank does guarantee payment at maturity, a banker's acceptance becomes a money market instrument and is traded between banks and in security markets, usually at a discount, with the discount tied to the time until maturity. (They are also discounted if presented for payment before they mature.) Holders of acceptances receive full payment from the bank at maturity. One way to understand the use of banker's acceptances is through an example:

Suppose a Baltimore wholesaler wishes to import mangoes from Malaysia. The wholesaler does not want to pay cash, and the Malaysian Mango Monopoly will not extend credit. The wholesaler then gets a "letter of credit" from his bank and presents it to the Malaysians. The Malaysians ship the mangoes and present the shipping documents and letter of credit to a Malaysian bank. This bank, in turn, draws a draft on a U.S. bank; when the U.S. bank gets and "accepts" this draft, it becomes a banker's acceptance.

Note that this does not involve financing, which is separate. The bank is only guaranteeing payment at maturity. The discount at which it is sold determines the interest rate.

Maturities can range from 1 to 270 days, though 90 days is usual.

COMMERCIAL PAPER

This term covers unsecured promissory notes, in bearer form, for a fixed amount at a fixed date. They are only issued by the most credit-worthy corporations. Issuance is at a discount and redemption at face value. Such notes have become a substitute for bank borrowing for those corporations which can issue them. Purchasers are mostly corporations, commercial banks, insurance companies, and mutual funds.

Commercial paper is sometimes sold directly to investors ("direct paper") and sometimes to dealers ("dealer paper"). Dealers can act as agents, selling to investors and collecting a commission, although dealers sometimes buy the paper directly and then resell it to investors. Maturities are up to 270 days. Denominations start at $100,000. Interest (in this case, the difference between the discounted price and payment at maturity) is calculated on the basis of a 360-day year.

NEGOTIABLE CERTIFICATES OF DEPOSIT

These are tradeable certificates issued by commercial banks in exchange for time deposits. They are quoted on the basis of yield. They usually mature in one year, but can be for shorter periods if the depositor agrees.

Interest is paid at maturity calculated in terms of actual days on the basis of a 360-day year.

BROKER'S LOANS (CALL LOANS)

These are loans made by commercial banks to brokers to finance security purchases made by the broker's customers (margin purchases). The effect of this practice is that funds borrowed from brokers by individuals actually come from banks. As collateral, the broker pledges securities purchased in a "street name."

Broker's loans can be in the form of time notes or demand notes. Time notes pay a fixed interest rate and have varying maturities, usually up to six months. In contrast, interest on demand notes, or "call loans," varies daily. Basically, the call loan is payable on demand the day after it is made; if no demand is made, the note is renewed for another day at that day's interest rate. Such loans can last up to 90 days.

Note that brokers who make a market often use U.S. government bonds and bills as collateral for demand loans needed to pay for their inventories, and that interest on these loans governs the interest charges on margin accounts. Like the "prime rate" the broker's loan rate is fixed by each bank individually; however, competitive conditions force rates to be comparable. Figure 3.1 shows credit ratings for commercial paper.

Figure 3.1　Credit Ratings for Commercial Paper

EXPLANATION	MOODY'S	STANDARD & POOR'S
Highest degree of safety	P-1 (a)	A-1 +
Very strong degree of safety	P-1 (a)	A-1
Strong degree of safety	P-2	A-2
Satisfactory degree of safety	P-3	A-3

NOTE: Moody's assigns a single credit rating to securities in the top two categories.

TERMS

Money Market Instruments Short-term debt obligations, usually very secure, including T-bills, notes, and bonds

Federal funds Overnight borrowings, $1,000,000 and up, by banks from Federal Reserve; rate changes daily

Repurchase agreements (repos) Security sold with agreement to repurchase, usually at fixed time and price. Minimum of $1,000,000

Banker's Acceptances Commercial bank drafts agreeing to payment on a specified date; used in international trade

Commercial paper Unsecured promissory notes of $100,000 and up; issued at discount; can be sold to dealers or investors

Negotiable Certificates of Deposit

Broker's Loans (Call Loans) Notes covering commercial bank loans to brokers to finance margin purchases

REVIEW QUESTIONS

1. All of the following are money market instruments EXCEPT:

   (A) CDs
   (B) Banker's Acceptances
   (C) ADRs
   (D) Fed Funds

2. If the yield on a T-bill is increased by .10, it has increased by:

   (A) 20 basis points
   (B) 0.1 basis points
   (C) 10 basis points
   (D) 100 basis points

3. The instrument with the least active secondary market is the one for

   (A) T-bills
   (B) negotiable CDs
   (C) commercial paper
   (D) banker's acceptances

4. Which of the following is used to finance foreign trade?

   (A) ADRs
   (B) Fed Funds
   (C) Banker's Acceptances
   (D) CDs

5. Federal funds are generated if:

   (A) the Federal Reserve does repos
   (B) a federal bank sells securities
   (C) a bank has excess reserves to lend
   (D) a non-federal bank buys T-bills

6. Which of the following is the most volatile?

   (A) federal funds rate
   (B) prime rate
   (C) T-bill rate
   (D) broker loan rate

7. Auctions for 3- and 6-month T-bills take place:

   (A) daily
   (B) weekly
   (C) bi-weekly
   (D) monthly

8. The maximum maturity on commercial paper is ordinarily:

   (A) 90 days
   (B) 180 days
   (C) 270 days
   (D) 1 year

9. If the rate on Treasury bills dropped this would mean:

   (A) the Fed had tightened
   (B) the cost of bills had risen
   (C) the cost of bills had dropped
   (D) interest rates had risen

10. The money market instrument which most closely resembles a time deposit is:

    (A) negotiable CD
    (B) banker's acceptance
    (C) T-bill
    (D) federal funds

ANSWERS TO REVIEW QUESTIONS

1. (C) American Depository Receipts are certificates that represent ownership of stock in foreign companies.

2. (C) 100 basis points represents 1 point of yield, *e.g.*, from 6.00 to 7.00.

3. (C) Commercial paper is for the most part not bought and sold.

4. (C) Banker's acceptances are time drafts usually used for collections of payments on foreign trade.

5. (C) These are the funds that the Federal Reserve requires a bank to set aside. When too much has been set aside fed funds are created.

6. (A) This changes rapidly, often several times within a single day.

7. (B) The 12-month bills are auctioned monthly.

8. (C) This allows them to be issued without going through registration as securities.

9. (B) If the rate went from 6.50 to 6.00 the price would go from 93.50 to 94.00.

10. (A) In fact, it is a time deposit with the additional proviso that it is negotiable.

CHAPTER FOUR

Investment companies— mutual funds

This chapter describes a class of securities very different from those discussed in the first three chapters. These are not individual securities, but securities issued by companies whose primary purpose is to invest their capital in the securities of other entities. Not unreasonably, these companies are called investment companies. The most important type of investment company is the mutual fund, and most of this chapter will be devoted to that subject.

Investment companies acquire funds by selling shares to shareholders, and they invest those funds in a portfolio of securities. Owning shares in an investment company means owning some part of this portfolio. The company income is the stream of dividends and interest payments that it receives from its portfolio of stocks and bonds. Similarly, the value of the company, as reflected in the worth of its shares, rises and falls with the rise and fall of the portfolio of securities.

There are some advantages to such an investment. It enables an investor to diversify holdings even with a small investment, it helps to reduce record-keeping (one need only keep the records pertaining to the investment company), and it provides the benefits of having one's investment decisions made by professional investment managers. Naturally, these benefits have a price: this is reflected in fees charged by the company, and sales commissions charged for buying shares.

There are three kinds of investment companies: unit investment trusts (UITs), face-amount certificate companies, and management companies (the most common form of which is known as mutual funds). We begin by discussing the first two kinds.

Unit Investment Trusts

Unit Investment Trusts invest in an identified portfolio of securities. Units (shares) of the trust represent ownership of some percentage of this portfolio. There are two types of UITs, fixed and non-fixed.

Fixed UITs typically buy a portfolio of bonds, collect the interest and repayments on those bonds, and cease to exist when the last bond matures. In other words, they last for the life of the bonds. The original portfolio is never changed and thus there are no expenses related to trading.

Non-fixed UITs also invest in an identified portfolio, but this consists of shares in a professionally managed pool of funds. Investors contract to buy shares in the UIT over time, and, as these funds flow in, the trust buys more shares in the pool.

The important distinction here is that while the non-fixed UIT portfolio consists solely of shares in the pool, the pool itself is professionally managed and the holdings in the pool (called the portfolio) vary over time.

Face-Amount Certificate companies

Face-amount certificate companies issue securities which require the company to pay the holder the "face amount" at some specified date. They are generally guaranteed as to principal and interest and are backed by identified securities such as corporate bonds, preferred stock, or U.S. government-backed securities. These certificates can be purchased either with a single payment or through some installment plan.

FORMS OF MANAGEMENT COMPANIES

There are two general formats for management companies: closed-end and open-end (or mutual funds).

Closed-end companies

These authorize and issue stock at their inception, after which no more shares are sold. The company does not redeem its shares; they are, however, traded on the open market. This form of investment company was much more popular before 1940.

Value of shares The shares of the company represent ownership of its assets. These assets, minus the liabilities, constitute the *net asset value*; when divided by the number of shares outstanding this becomes *net asset value per share*, NAV.

Pricing of shares There is obviously a relationship between the NAV and the cost of these shares on the open market. However, since the company does not redeem these shares there is no direct exchange between asset value and the price of shares. As a result the price of shares in a closed-end company is not the same as the NAV. They are traded on exchanges as well as over the counter.

In fact, shares tend to sell at a discount to NAV, although not always. The relationship between share price and NAV is dictated partly by

PUBLICLY TRADED FUNDS

Thursday, December 24, 1987
Unaudited net asset values of publicly traded investment shares, formerly listed as Closed End Funds, as of Friday Also shown is the closing listed market price of each fund's shares, with the percentage difference between the net asset value and the stock price.

DIVERSIFIED COMMON STOCK FUNDS

	N.A. Value	Stk Price	% Diff.
AdmExp(b)	16.25	14⅝	− 10.0
Baker	48.88	35¼	− 27.9
Blue Ch Vol	6.81	5¾	− 15.5
Clemente-Gl(b)	7.55	5⅝	− 25.5
Eafy-Guard(b)	8.41	7⅜	− 6.4
Gemil Cap	14.34	11⅛	− 22.4
Gemil Inc	9.88	11⅞	+ 20.2
GenAin	17.05	14¾	− 13.5
GlobalGr Cap	7.81	8¾	+ 7.2
Global Gr Inc	9.32	8½	− 8.7
GSD Trust	9.19	9½	+ 3.4
Lehman	13.55	11⅛	− 17.9
Libty A-Star	8.03	6⅜	− 20.6
NiagSh	14.70	11⅞	− 19.2
NchAp GrEq	7.53	5⅞	− 22.0
QuestFValCap(a)	9.06	6¾	− 25.2
QuestFVolInc(a)	11.69	8⅝	− 26.2
Royce Value(g)	8.04	6⅞	− 14.5
Schafer Valu	8.24	6⅜	− 16.6
Source	35.63	34	− 4.6
Tri-Cont	24.35	21¼	− 12.7
Worldwd Vol	16.75	12⅛	− 27.5
Zweig Fn	9.85	8⅞	− 9.9

BOND FUND

	N.A. Value	Stk Price	% Diff.
ACM Gov.	n.a.	n.a.	n.a.
CIM High	9.30	9⅛	− 1.9
Hi Yld Inc	9.21	9⅛	+ 4.5
Muni Ins	9.49	10⅛	+ 8.0

SPECIALIZED & CONVERTIBLE FUNDS

	N.A. Value	Stk Price	% Diff.
AmCap	25.33	24	− 5.2
ASA(bXc)	n.a.	n.a.	n.a.
Asia Pac	6.79	4⅞	− 28.2
Bancat	21.42	20⅞	− 2.5
BGR Prec Mtls(b)(e)	15.29	11½	− 26.4
Casile	21.24	21⅛	− 0.5
CenFd Canada	6.64	6	− 9.6
CentS	10.54	8⅜	− 20.5
Claremt(f)	48.11	44¼	− 8.0
Couns Tndm C	6.28	4¼	− 32.3
Cypress Fd	9.04	6¾	− 25.3
DufPh Util	7.61	7⅜	− 3.5
Ellswth Cv	7.76	6⅞	− 11.4
EmgMed	n.a.	n.a.	n.a.
Engex	10.24	7⅜	− 27.9
Fln New C	16.69	13⅜	− 19.9
1st Australia	9.14	7⅛	− 22.0
Fst Fn Fd	7.41	5⅞	− 20.7
France Fd	10.99	8½	− 22.7
Gabelli E	9.86	8	− 18.9
Germany	7.35	6⅝	− 9.9
H&Q Heath	n.a.	n.a.	n.a.
Helvetia Fd	12.14	9¼	− 23.8
Hopper Sal	17.11	8½	− 50.3
Italy Fd(b)	10.31	6⅞	− 33.3
Korea Fd	34.36	51⅞	+ 50.9
Malays Fd(a)	7.57	6⅝	− 12.5
CNV Hldg Cap	8.55	4⅛	− 51.7
CNV Hldg Inc.	9.35	10½	+ 12.5
Mexico(b)	4.48	3⅜	− 24.7
MG SmCap	7.42	5¾	− 22.0
Pete&Res(b)	24.74	21⅞	− 11.6
PilReg	8.18	6¼	− 23.6
Prg Inc	8.56	8⅛	− 5.3
Reg FinlShs	6.94	5⅜	− 22.6
Scandinavia(b)	8.36	6⅞	− 17.8
ScudderN Asia	10.62	7⅛	− 32.9
Taiwan Fd(b)	25.04	33½	− 33.8
TCW CvlSec(a)(b)	7.72	6½	− 15.8
Tmpl Emrg M(b)	7.51	6¾	− 23.4
UTD Kgdm Fd(a)	10.76	10⅞	− 23.3
Z-Seven(d)	15.13	16	+ 5.8

(a) Ex-Dividend.
(b) As of Wednesday's close.
(c) Translated at Commercial Rand exchange rate.
(d) N.A.V. reflects $1.16 a share for taxes.
(e) In Canadian dollars.
(f) On Dec. 31, 1987 the N.A.V. will be reduced approximately $1.50 a share for Federal income tax capital gain.
(g) 21 cents ex-dividend, one cent capital gains.
n.a. - Not available.

Figure 4.1   Publicly Traded Funds

tax considerations and partly by past performance of the investment company.

Offerings of shares Although closed-end funds issue shares only at their inception, they can raise additional funds by issuing preferred stock or bonds.

The original offering of a fixed number of shares is made through a prospectus, similar to the one described in discussing common stocks. (See Chapter 6.) After this initial offering, there is no longer any need for this prospectus. This, and the fact that they do not redeem their shares (remember these are bought and sold, through a broker and for a commission, on the open market for whatever price they can bring), distinguishes closed-end from open-end companies (see chart, page 80).

Open-end investment companies (mutual funds)

These companies do redeem their shares. By law, they may only issue *common stock.* Since they do this continually, they must always have an appropriately revised prospectus on offer. The prospectus must describe the investment objectives of the mutual fund as well as the strategy that it plans to use to meet those objectives. By now, there are many kinds of mutual funds with varied objectives.

EARNINGS

Dividends

From time to time, mutual funds declare and pay dividends on net income. These represent:

- □ all the fund's dividend earnings on stocks plus
- □ interest income from debt obligations less
- □ operating fees and costs (management fees, commissions paid to brokers for buying or selling stocks, custodial fees, legal and accounting fees, and the costs of producing prospectuses and reports, and, in some cases, advertising expenses)

Rules for dividends

1 There is no fixed term for dividends; some funds declare dividends daily.

2 By law, to avoid taxation the investment company must pay as dividend at least 90% of the net earnings from dividends (see page 79).

Gains

Any net gains realized by the fund from the sale of securities can also be distributed to investors in proportion to shares held. Short-term gains are often distributed along with dividend income. Long-term distributions usually take place once a year and are paid separately from dividends.

Tax treatment of earnings

The dividends that an investor receives from a mutual fund are exactly like those received from any other company and are treated as such for tax purposes.

Capital gains dividends are treated as long-term capital gains for the investor, regardless of how long the investor has held the shares.

Under the Tax Reform Act of 1986, there is no "holding period" that distinguishes short-term from long-term capital gains, though that distinction and the distinction between gains and ordinary income are retained in case differential tax treatment is restored in the future.

FEATURES OF MUTUAL FUNDS

Advantages to investors

Individual investors find mutual funds attractive because they offer:

- □ the services of full-time professional managers
- □ safekeeping of securities
- □ the chance to invest in terms of dollar amounts, as funds offer both full and fractional shares

□ the ability to reduce the amount invested without reducing diversity

□ shares which can be used as collateral

Some funds also offer automatic reinvestment and/or the right to convert to other funds in a "family of funds."

Types of mutual funds

Mutual funds diversify their holdings in a variety of ways among different companies, or among different industries, or by mixing various instruments. Their objectives are often described broadly as "growth," "income," or "safety" funds. An investor should choose the fund which best meets his or her investment objectives.

Diversified common stock Mostly common stocks. If the objective is income then the portfolio contains stocks that pay high dividends. If the objective is growth, the fund will concentrate on companies reinvesting their profits for research or expansion. A fund which bought highly volatile growth stocks would be called an aggressive growth fund.

Specialized funds Common stock in one industry (for example, oil), or a group of related industries (such as energy companies), or in one geographical area in the U.S. or overseas. Such funds will subdivide again into growth, income, or safety.

Balanced funds Usually a varying mix of bonds, common and preferred stocks. These tend to be more conservatively managed than common stock funds, and less subject to fluctuation. Their objective is often to preserve capital while producing a moderate income.

Bond and preferred stock funds These offer safety, and, customarily, a fixed income.

Municipal bond funds Usually only investment grade municipal issues (BBB or above).

Money market funds Invest in liquid, short-term debt securities; hence they are often called liquid asset or cash funds. Money market funds usually calculate and reinvest interest on outstanding shares daily, and credit it to shareholders periodically. They also often provide limited "check writing" privileges as a convenient method for redeeming shares.

U.S. Government securities These are government instruments, keeping principal well protected.

Hedge funds engage in aggressive trading practices, including short selling, and usually can hold any type of security.

Dual-purpose funds issue two classes of shares: dividend and capital gains. The former receive all income distributions but no gains, the latter all gains but no income. Investors choose one class and receive that class' stream of funds.

MANAGEMENT COMPANY STRUCTURE

All these funds, of whatever type, have certain common structural features. The entity is the fund. The fund has some stated objectives and sets policies about sales and redemption. The fund chooses an underwriter for its securities and appoints a custodian bank, which performs some clerical functions and holds the actual portfolio of securities. It also chooses a board of directors which makes policy decisions and generally is responsible for meeting the fund's objectives and carrying out its policies. The board in turn chooses a fund manager or management company.

The management company

Basically, the management company functions as investment advisor, and is charged with meeting the fund's goals as spelled out in the prospectus, maintaining an appropriate mix of investments, deciding when to buy or sell or hold, monitoring the tax status of fund holdings, and conducting business efficiently.

Usually, the management company has complete administrative powers: it pays salaries of fund officers and employees and other costs of running the corporation. In return, the fund pays a fee, typically, between 0.5% and 1% of average net assets; in some cases, the percentage declines as assets rise.

Management fees *cannot* be based on increases in value of the fund's portfolio (realized or unrealized). All management fees must be stated clearly in the prospectus.

CALCULATING MUTUAL FUND YIELDS

Under SEC regulations, the only mutual fund yields that may be discussed are those arising from income, dividends, and interest. Within these restrictions, yield may be calculated in any way that is not misleading. For instance, current yield could be calculated with or without including the past year's capital gains in the denominator.

As including capital gains would make yield lower, investors must be alert to the different methods of calculating yields in comparing different funds.

$$\text{current yield} = \frac{\text{annual dividends paid over the past year}}{\text{today's price} + \text{any capital gains paid}}$$

and

$$\text{historic yield} = \frac{\text{average annual dividends}}{\text{average annual price}}$$

PRICING OF SHARES

"Bid" and "ask" prices

Mutual fund prices are quoted as "bid" and "ask." The bid is the price at which the fund will redeem its shares. It is the same as the NAV

MUTUAL FUNDS

	N.A.V.	Buy	Chg.		N.A.V.	Buy	Chg.		N.A.V.	Buy	Chg.
MuniB	8.02	8.44	−.03	FixBd	7.30	NL	−.02	Bond r	11.98	NL	...
Value	14.20	14.95	+.09	Fredm	16.36	NL	+.16	Calif	11.16	11.63	−.04
Citibank IRA:				GloBd	10.62	NL	−.02	Gwth r	15.45	NL	+.16
Balan f	1.75	NL	−.03	GNMA	10.79	NL	−.01	Optin r	9.65	NL	+.08
Equity f	1.95	NL	−.05	Gvt Sec	10.16	NL	...	GvtSc r	...	...	...
Incom f	1.60	NL	...	GroInc	16.12	16.45	+.10	Basic r	13.84	NL	+.08
Sh Trm f	1.34	NL	...	GroCo	17.05	17.58	+.12	Natl	12.09	12.59	−.03
Claremont Fds:				HiInco	9.96	NL	−.01	NY Mu	11.41	11.89	−.04
GovBd	10.93	NL	...	Hi Yld	13.32	NL	...	PrcM r	18.51	NL	−.14
Stock	12.37	NL	+.02	InsMu	11.39	NL	...	SpEq r	15.84	NL	+.22
Combd	13.62	NL	+.07	Lt Mun	9.73	NL	...	IRI Stck	9.24	9.68	+.02
Clipper	44.54	NL	+.09	Magel	59.86	61.71	+48				

Figure 4.2 Quotation of Mutual Funds
Reprinted with permission from the NY Times April 1,1987

(a redemption fee may reduce the amount actually received). The ask or "offer" is the price that an investor must pay to purchase the shares.
Figure 4-2 shows quotations of mutual funds.

"Load" and "No-load"

Mutual funds can be divided into two broad classes: "load" and "no-load." The latter do not have any sales charges and therefore have identical bid and ask prices. This can be seen in Figure 4.2 where some funds have "NL" in the offer column. For those funds where the offer price differs from the bid, the difference is the load or sales charge which is being levied.

Determing NAV

The net asset value per share must be determined at the close of each business day, on the basis of closing prices. The actual price paid by a buyer is the NAV for the day of sale, that is, the price listed on the day after the order is received. However, when shares are sold, the seller receives the *next calculated NAV after the order was received.*

CALCULATING SALES CHARGES AND REDEMPTION FEES

Sales charges are regulated by the Investment Company Act of 1940 and Investment Company Amendment Act of 1975. Those Acts limit the maximum sales charge to 8.5% of the offering price and further hold that this charge can be imposed only if certain benefits are provided to the public. These benefits include discounts for lump-sum purchases, the chance to reinvest dividends, and "rights of accumulation"; *i.e.,* the right to include previous purchases in determining whether or not an investor qualifies for a sales charge discount. If these are not provided, the maximum sales charge is correspondingly reduced.

Sales charges

Sales charges are imposed only when mutual fund shares are sold to an investor. The charge is based on the *asking price*, not NAV.

■ **EXAMPLE**

If the bid price (or NAV) is $15.00 and the ask is $16.00, the sales charge (or load) is $1.00 and the rate is $1.00 ÷ $16.00 = 6.25%.

This can be deceptive if one is provided with a quote of "NAV = $14.49, sales charge 8%." The actual sales charge is 8% of the ask price which is computed as follows: Ask price × (100% − 8%) = $14.49, or $14.49 ÷ 92% = $15.75. Thus the sales charge is $15.75 − $14.49 = $1.26, and not 8% of $14.49 which would be $1.16.

Mutual fund shares cannot be sold for less than the public offering price, and that price cannot include a sales charge of more than 9% (see page 81).

Redemption fees

When a redemption fee is imposed, it is usually 1% or less and is based on NAV.

■ **EXAMPLE**
Bid $20; Ask $21. Redemption fee ¾%. An investor selling 1,000 shares would be charged $20,000 × .0075 = $150 and would therefore receive $20,000 − $150 = $19,850.

Sales charges and redemption fees must be shown in the prospectus.

BREAKPOINTS

Many funds offer reduced sales charges on large purchases, for example, at $10,000, $25,000, etc. These are called "breakpoints."

The Investment Company Act of 1940 allows reductions to any person who buys at the specified levels either at one time ("lump sum") or over a period of time, through "rights of accumulation" or by signing a "letter of intent."

Note that the Act limits the definition of "person" to:

☐ an individual

☐ an individual, spouse, and children under 21 purchasing for one or all of their number

☐ a trustee or fiduciary purchasing for a single estate or account

Groups such as "investment clubs" are specifically excluded.

Rights of accumulation

Investors are entitled to reduced sales charges when their purchases accumulate to the breakpoints.

For instance, a fund cuts its sales charge from 8% to 6% for purchases of $10,000 to $25,000. A buyer who puts $1,000 a month into the fund with rights of accumulation will pay 8% per month for the first 10 months, then 6% from the 11th month through the 25th month. Shares added to an account through reinvestment are included in the total.

Letter of intent

An investor announces the intention to make purchases at breakpoint levels over a period of *13 months*. Such letters can be *backdated as much as 90 days* to include an earlier purchase.

This is not a contract, as the investor is not bound to fulfill the plan. It is, however, binding on the fund: if the sales charge rises, rates stated in the letter hold; if they fall, the investor gets the lower rate. If purchases do not reach breakpoint volume, the higher sales charge is imposed. The fund can hold some of the shares purchased under the letter in escrow and redeem them to pay those added charges.

Note that such a plan, unlike rights of accumulation, allows lower sales charges on all shares purchased.

■ EXAMPLE

On April 1, a customer signs a letter of intent backdated to the beginning of the year agreeing to purchase a total of $10,000 worth of ABC Fund within the next ten months. If he had already purchased $2,000 during that year and purchased $800 more in each of the following ten months, then he would pay the reduced sales commission on the entire $10,000 purchase (assuming $10,000 is a breakpoint).

DOLLAR COST AVERAGING

This plan involves investing a specific sum at regular intervals. As share prices fluctuate, the number of shares purchased will vary.

The attraction of this approach is that, so long as the share price does go up and down, the buyer will be paying less per share than the average price computed by buying the same number of shares in each purchase period, as he or she purchases more shares when the price is low.

■ EXAMPLE

If the prices of a mutual fund in four successive quarters were $20, $15, $12, $25, respectively, then the average price for these periods would be $72 ÷ 4 = $18. An investor who used a dollar cost averaging program of $300 for each period would accumulate 15, 20, 25, 12—or 72 shares for which he would have paid $1,200 for an average cost of $16.67 ($1,200 ÷ 72 = $16.67) in contrast to the average of $18 if equal numbers of shares were purchased each period.

Such a method requires patience and persistence, and cannot offer protection against loss if shares continue to fall, or if the investor must sell when the share price is below his average cost.

This approach is also called "cost averaging," "dollar averaging," etc., but mutual fund sales literature must use the word "cost" in describing these plans.

REDEEMING SHARES

The mutual fund must honor a request to redeem shares. The request can be executed in any of several ways:

If shares are held by a custodian or transfer agent (usually a commercial bank), the investor must write to the mutual fund, in care of the transfer agent. The letter must include the investor's account number and a signed stock power with the signature guaranteed (usually by an NASD member or a national bank).

If the investor holds the share certificates, he or she writes the mutual fund directly or informs the dealer (some funds redeem shares only through a dealer), presenting the certificate or a stock power with a guaranteed signature.

With no-load funds, all transactions are often made through the mails, including redemptions.

The redemption price is the next NAV per share computed after the fund (or transfer agent) receives a properly executed order. Under the Investment Company Act of 1940, the net amount due (less redemption fees, if any) must be remitted to the investor within 7 days.

The 7-day requirement can be avoided only if NYSE trading is restricted or halted for some extraordinary reason, if the SEC has allowed the fund to stop redeeming shares to protect shareholders, or if some emergency makes it impractical to find the NAV or to dispose of shares.

RULES GOVERNING OPEN-END INVESTMENT COMPANIES

Registration requirements

All open-end investment companies must be registered under the Investment Company Act of 1940. Under the Act such firms:

- must have a net worth of at least $100,000 before making a public offering of their shares
- can issue only common stock, not preferred stock or bonds
- can borrow from banks

Rights of shareholders

Like common stock shareholders, holders of mutual fund shares have the right to vote on directors and on matters which could affect their holdings. Proposed changes in the fund's objectives or investment practices, in the way NAV is calculated, in management or other fees, or in redemption privileges, all require a vote of more than 50% of all outstanding shares. Shareholders must be sent proxy forms that describe the fund's contract with its investment advisors and the connections between those advisors and fund officers.

Shareholders also have the right to receive a complete financial statement *semi-annually*.

Custodian

The Investment Company Act of 1940 states that open-end investment companies must employ a custodian. This is usually an institution like a trust company or a national bank. The custodian is charged with safeguarding the company's physical assets, disburses funds needed to purchase securities, and receives funds realized from the sale of securities.

In some instances, the custodian also acts as transfer agent and registrar, and issues new shares, cancels redeemed shares, distributes dividends and capital gains to investors, and performs clerical tasks—preparing reports, handling proxies, and keeping the books.

The custodian cannot take any part in share selling or offer any protection against depreciation of the company's assets.

OWNERSHIP

Mutual fund shares can be owned in any of several ways:

□ in a joint tenancy with rights of survivorship; if one owner dies, the shares go to the other owner

□ under tenancy in common, where each owner holds a specified proportion of the shares; should one die, that person's heirs receive that portion

□ held in trust for a minor under the Uniform Gifts to Minors Act, which may have tax advantages for some investors

□ in trust accounts

To decide on form of ownership, the investor should consult an attorney. Registered representatives cannot recommend any form, as that is construed as practicing law.

TAXATION

Taxation of mutual fund companies

Under the Internal Revenue Code (Section M), a mutual fund does not have to pay tax on income from equities it holds or on any capital gains realized from sale of those equities *provided* (a) those gains are distributed to shareholders and (b) the fund meets the definition of a "regulated investment company." The theory is that these companies are simply a "pipeline" or "conduit" between corporations and investors.

A company is considered regulated under the Code if it is a domestic corporation registered (as a management company or a unit investment trust; see pages 82-83) with the SEC for the tax year. Further:

□ *at least 90% of the firm's gross income must be from dividends, interest, and capital gains*

□ *at least 97% of the firm's net investment income and at least 90% of its capital gains net income in each calendar year must be distributed to shareholders as taxable dividends.* Any amounts held in excess of the required distribution are subject to a non-deductible 4% excise tax

□ *less than 30% of the firm's income can be derived from the sale of securities held less than 3 months*

Shareholders must report dividend earnings and capital gains to the IRS even if they are reinvested. The former are taxed as regular income. Capital gains distributions are also treated as income, though they are taxed at a maximum of 28%.

Individual investors can deduct as a business expense the management fees they pay as mutual fund shareholders, but only if all their business expenses exceed 2% of gross income. Mutual funds will show management expenses as a separate component of income on annual 1099 statements.

If a shareholder liquidates holdings, capital gain or loss is treated like gain or loss from any capital asset for tax purposes. Losses on mutual fund shares held less than six months cannot be claimed if the shareholder received tax-exempt dividends on those shares (*i.e.,* from municipal bond funds).

CLOSED- AND OPEN-END INVESTMENT COMPANIES

The most convenient way to discuss closed-end investment companies is to compare them with open-end.

OPEN	CLOSED
Always sells with a prospectus.	Can sell without prospectus after initial issue.
Can issue only common stock—no bonds or preferred stock.	Can issue bonds or preferred stock to raise additional funds and to buy more securities.
Shares continuously offered—as new investors come in, the company adds to its portfolio.	Fixed capitalization. Fixed number of shares outstanding; no continuing offer of shares.
Sells and redeems (sometimes through intermediaries) its own shares; no exchange market is involved. Redeems share at NAV—never less. May borrow from bank up to ⅓ of its assets. Value computed daily.	Issuer does not redeem shares. Traded on exchange or over-the-counter after initial public offering. Price determined by supply and demand; could be below NAV.
Investors may pay a sales charge.	Investors pay market price plus commission or normal brokerage fees.
Can charge redemption fee.	No redemption fee.

INVESTOR ACCOUNTS

Types of accounts

Typically, mutual funds offer investors several types of accounts:

Regular or open account Involves no periodic purchase; all investments are purely voluntary.

Periodic payment plan An investor agrees to invest a minimum amount, say $100, at certain intervals, at least four times a year.

Voluntary accumulation plan The investor decides when and how much to invest, but may reach breakpoints under rights of accumulation.

Contractual plan

In this form of periodic payment plan, the investor agrees to invest a specified amount over a specified time by making payments at regular intervals, for example, $48,000 over 20 years by buying $200 in shares each month.

The prospectus for a contractual plan must describe both the plan itself and the fund. These plans are actually a form of unit investment trust, with each share representing an undivided interest in the underlying mutual fund.

In a contractual plan, a custodian holds both money and securities for investors and issues "plan certificates" as evidence of the investor's holdings. In addition, the custodian acts as registrar and transfer agent, and must be notified if the investor wishes to assign or transfer shares.

Many plans offer "plan completion insurance," which completes the plan by making payments to reach face value if the investor dies before the end of the designated period. This is like decreasing term life insurance, and has no cash value. The policy names the plan custodian as beneficiary, but proceeds are considered part of the deceased's estate for tax purposes.

■ **EXAMPLE**

If a customer contracts to buy $200 per month for ten years and dies after five years, the insurance will pay the custodian $200 per month for the remaining five years.

Sales charges on contractual plans

While the sales charge on mutual funds cannot exceed 8.5%, the sales charge on any contractual plan can reach 9% of the amount invested. On long-term acquisition plans, the Investment Company Amendments Act of 1975 allows accelerated collection of sales charges under one of two plans: "front-end load" or "spread load." The prospectus must say which is in use.

With either method, the plan custodian is required to send investors a statement of total charges within 60 days after the plan certificate is issued, and inform the investor of the *right to withdraw within 45 days* from the date the notice is mailed. An investor who leaves the plan within that time receives the current value of the shares, plus all sales charges, custodial fees, and insurance payments.

Front-end load Up to 50% of the sales charges may be deducted, in equal amounts, from the first 12 monthly payments. Remaining sales charges are deducted proportionately over the life of the plan. If the plan is liquidated *within 18 months* of the date the certificate is issued, the investor receives a refund of sales charges paid in excess of 15% of the total invested in addition to the current value of all shares.

■ **EXAMPLE**

An investor agrees to a 10-year $100-per-month front-end load plan with a 6% cumulative sales charge. If he chooses to terminate the plan after 40 days, during which time he has accumulated 30 shares, he would receive 30 × NAV less any redemption fee. If he did not terminate until after his 15th payment the sales charge would be computed as follows:

Total sales charge = 6% × $1,200 per year × 10 years = $720
Front-end load = 50% × $720 = $360
Balance of sales charge = $360/9 years = $40 per year, or $3.33 per month
Total sales charge for 15 months = $360 + (3 × $3.33) = $370
Allowable sales charge = 15% of $1,500 = $225
Sales charges refunded = $370 − $225 = $145

After the 18th month, an investor can receive only the existing share value.

Spread-load plan Up to 64% of the investment over the first four years can be deducted for sales charges, but no more than 20% in any one year. The allowed 64% may be divided to average 16% a year. With a spread-load plan investors have only the 45-day grace period in which to withdraw, after which time they receive only the value of their shares.

■ **EXAMPLE**

If the investor of the previous example had chosen a spread-load plan with a 16% average per year, his sales charges would have been computed as follows:

Total sales charges = $720 as above
Spread-load for 4 years = 64% × $720 = $460.80
Sales charge for 15 months = 15/48 × $460.80 = $144

Note that the entire $144 would have been deducted from his investment.

With both plans, fund sponsors are required to have reserves to allow them to refund sales charges if necessary.

WITHDRAWAL PLANS

Many mutual funds provide plans for systematic withdrawal of funds, *i.e.*, for periodic payment to the investor. These usually require a minimum investment of $10,000.

Plans can be for a fixed dollar amount (*e.g.*, $100 per month), or a fixed percentage (*e.g.*, 6% a year), or a fixed number of shares (*e.g.*, 15 shares a month); or they can call for liquidation over a fixed time (*e.g.*, all shares over 10 years). Shareholders must approve such a plan in writing, usually to the custodian, authorizing the custodian to redeem shares to meet planned withdrawals if dividend payments will not suffice, or to reinvest dividends in additional shares if they exceed the withdrawal amount.

If shares must be sold to meet the planned withdrawals, the investor's principal could be eroded. Once begun, such a process could accelerate, especially in a falling market, and wipe out the principal entirely.

THE INVESTMENT COMPANY ACT OF 1940

This act is intended to insure investors are fully informed and fairly treated. It defines three specific categories of investment companies:

Face amount certificate company

These issue installment-type certificates. The holder makes regular, periodic payments to the issuer who promises to pay the face value at maturity, or a surrender value if redeemed in advance.

Unit investment trust

These issue redeemable securities, each representing an undivided interest in a unit of a specified security, which can be a mutual fund portfolio. Most contractual plans are in fact unit investment trusts. Other examples are investment companies which pay *no management fee,* have a low sales charge, and hold a *fixed portfolio of municipal or corporate instruments.* Some of these are closed-end companies.

Management company

Under the Act, any investment company other than those defined above is considered a management company. They can be open- or closed-end, and must manage a diversified portfolio of securities according to specific stated objectives.

These are divided into non-diversified and diversified companies. To be considered diversified, a firm must:

□ have at least 75% of its total asset value in cash and securities but

□ no more than 5% of assets may be invested in any one issuer's security, and

□ cannot own more than 10% of the voting stock of any corporation.

The Act also requires that any investment company operating interstate must register with the SEC, and that the company's objectives, practices, and policies must be announced in detail in regular statements to shareholders.

Requirements of ICA 1940

Many of the requirements of the act have been mentioned in this chapter, but a summary should be helpful:

1 Sponsor(s) must invest at least $100,000 of their own funds before offering securities to the public.

2 Open-end companies may issue only common stock. Closed-end companies may issue bonds (but only to ⅓ the value of company assets) and preferred stock (but only to ½ the value of assets). They can issue only one class of bonds or preferred stock.

3 Face Amount Certificate companies must have a minimum capitalization of $250,000. They cannot issue preferred stock.

4 At least 40% of the company's directors must be "outsiders," that is, neither an officer or employee of the company or of its investment advisor.

5 A majority of the directors must be independent of the fund underwriter, and a majority may not be persons who are officers or directors of the fund's investment bank.

6 Directors must be elected by holders of outstanding shares.

Other elements of the Act include:

□ cannot borrow more than ⅓ of assets

□ must compute NAV once each business day

□ cannot buy on margin or sell short without SEC permission ("hedge" funds routinely get such permission)

□ must have a written contract with the management company approved by the board of directors or a majority of shareholders; fees paid the management company must be based on a percentage of assets and must be set forth in the prospectus

□ must use custodian banks

□ shareholders must approve any change in the fund's objectives

□ redemption of shares must be made within seven business days

ICA says sales literature, broadly defined (the rule includes not just advertising but also, for example, financial statements), cannot be untrue or misleading. Most of the specific prohibitions have been discussed in this chapter in one connection or another: such literature cannot state or imply any assured return, discuss returns without advising of risk, etc.

Open-end investment companies, like other issuers of securities, must be registered with the SEC under the Securities Act of 1933 (see Chapter 15), and issue a prospectus.

Because they continually issue new shares, all mutual fund offerings must be accompanied by a prospectus. This must include all the essential information in the registration statement (see page 313), and, as noted above, must: describe the type of investment company, its objectives and policies; explain how the offering price is computed; include information about breakpoints, rights of accumulation, etc, and set out rights of transfer (if there is a "family" of funds), redemption procedures, etc. The fund must also *issue a financial statement semi-annually.*

NASD RULES ON MUTUAL FUNDS

The SEC imposed stringent rules on the sale of mutual fund shares in a 1950 Statement of Policy extending the Securities Act of 1935. That Statement is now incorporated into the NASD Rules of Fair Practice. Among the most important of these rules is a limit of 8½% on sales charges instead of the 9% allowed under ICA 1940. Note, however, that 9% is still valid for contractual plans. The following are also worth noting:

Prohibitions on RR activity

Representatives *cannot*:

□ combine profits and dividends. If a fund has paid $1.25 from capital gains and $.50 from income, these cannot be combined as "earnings" or "return," or the like

□ "sell" dividends. This is the practice of urging an investor to buy shares in a fund in time to profit from a just-declared dividend. Net assets decline after a dividend is paid, so this is already figured into the price

□ make unfair comparisons—such as with a fixed investment or a non-managed investment, like the Dow Jones average—without pointing out the differences

□ promise future earnings on the basis of past earnings

- fail to mention that risk is involved (although they can say risk may be reduced in a particular plan)
- say that custodian banks safeguard the investment
- say that mutual funds provide capital for new companies
- make loans for mutual fund purchases (no margin sales)
- make any claims about the ability of fund managers, particularly guaranteeing against loss or guaranteeing a return

Requirements for RRs

Representatives *must*:

- say the redemption value of shares may be higher or lower than the purchase price
- file all mutual fund sales literature (including a statement of sales charges) with NASD 10 days *after* it is used
- send a prospectus before, or with, sales literature. This is true whether or not a sale is made. Simply intending to make a sale requires a prospectus. The only exception is when a customer asks for general information on mutual funds.
- sell to customers at the next calculated price; not at an earlier price, nor waiting longer, though specific limit orders are allowed
- inform a customer wishing to switch funds, in writing, that he or she will pay a new service charge, as trading in mutual fund shares is prohibited

Other rules

- performance charts must cover at least 10 years, or the life of the fund, and must show the maximum sales charge, capital gains as reinvested, and dividends as taken in cash
- there can be no "special deals" between a fund sponsor and NASD member to favor one fund. Specifically, underwriters or their associates or affiliates cannot offer, and registered representatives or their affiliates cannot accept, anything of "material value," *e.g.*, gifts or advertising of over $50 per person per year (exceptions are an occasional dinner or tickets to a reception or the like that is part of a genuine business meeting)
- dealers must pay the underwriter (or custodian) for shares within 10 days or underwriter must notify NASD
- a registered representative may earn continuing commissions on contractual plans after leaving his or her firm if prior agreement exists
- a NASD underwriter cannot sell open-end investment company shares to a NASD member for less than NAV
- dealers may buy open-end investment company shares from an underwriter only to cover a customer's order or for personal investment

TERMS

Investment companies Invest in securities of other entities; acquire funds by selling shares

Advantages to investors Can diversify holdings, simplify record-keeping, have decisions made by professional managers

Kinds of investment companies

Unit Investment Trusts Invest in an identified portfolio; if "fixed," hold bonds and cease to exist when bonds mature; if "non-fixed," hold portfolio of shares in professionally managed pool; holdings vary over time

Face-Amount Certificate Companies Issue securities which pay "face-amount" at some specified date

Closed-end investment companies Issue stock at inception and not after, do not redeem shares, shares represent ownership of company's assets, trade on open market

NAV Assets divided by the number of shares outstanding

Open-end investment companies (mutual funds) Redeem their own shares, may only issue common stock, shares always accompanied by a current prospectus

Dividends Can be declared and paid on net income for any term

Types of funds Growth or income, stock, bond, municipals, etc.

Structural features Fund has stated objectives and policies, chooses underwriter, custodian bank, directors; directors choose fund manager

Management company Functions as investment advisor, usually has complete administrative powers, earns fee based on net assets—not on increases in value of fund portfolio

Yields Under SEC rules, only mutual fund yields arising from income, dividends, and interest may be discussed

$$\text{current yield} = \frac{\text{annual dividends paid over past year}}{\text{today's price} + \text{any capital gains paid}}$$

and

$$\text{historic yield} = \frac{\text{average annual dividends}}{\text{average annual price}}$$

Bid Price at which fund will redeem shares, same as NAV

Ask or offer Price to investor

No-load No sales charges; bid and ask prices are identical

Load Sales charge; shows as difference between offer and bid

NAV Determined by price at the close of each business day

Price to buyer NAV for day of sale

Seller Receives next calculated NAV after order was received

Sales charges Imposed when shares are sold; based on asking price, not NAV; cannot exceed 8.5% except 9% on contractual plans

Redemption fees Usually 1% or less, based on NAV

Breakpoints Specified quantities at which sales charges may be reduced; only to an individual, family, or trustee, not a group; can be one-time purchase or over a period through:

Rights of accumulation Sales charges reduced when purchases accumulate to breakpoints or

Letter of intent To purchase given amount, can stretch over 13 months, can be backdated 90 days, not binding on investor, binding on fund

Redeeming shares Fund must honor request to redeem shares and remit amount due within 7 days, except in extraordinary circumstances

To register under ICA 1940 A fund must have minimum net worth of $100,000 before public offering made, can issue only common stock, can borrow from banks, directors must be "outsiders"

Shareholder rights Voting

Custodian Fund must employ custodian (usually financial institution) which can also act as transfer agent and registrar; perform clerical tasks; cannot sell shares or offer any protection against depreciation of the company's assets

Forms of ownership Joint tenancy with rights of survivorship, tenancy in common, in trust for a minor under UGMA, in trust accounts

Taxation of fund To avoid tax, fund must pay out at least 90% of net dividends' earnings as dividends and meet requirements of regulated investment company

Taxation of investors Dividend earnings and capital gains are considered income even if reinvested, management fees can be a business expense

See chart comparing closed-end and open-end investment companies on page 80.

Types of accounts

Regular or open account No periodic purchase

Voluntary accumulation plan

Periodic payment plan Can be a contractual plan:

Contractual plan Agreement to invest specified amount over specified time, unit investment trusts, custodian holds money and securities, issues plan certificates, acts as registrar and transfer agent

Sales charges Accelerated collection allowed, "front-end load" or "spread load" plans; limited right to withdraw

Withdrawal plans Can be for fixed dollar amount, percentage, number of shares, time; shareholder must approve in writing

Categories of investment companies

Face Amount Certificate Company Issue installment-type certificates, holder makes regular payments, issuer promises to pay face value at maturity

Unit Investment Trust Issue redeemable securities, each represents an undivided interest in a unit of a specified security

Management Company Any other investment company

NASD Rules of Fair Practice

Limit sales charges, restrict RR

RR cannot combine profits and dividends into "earnings" or "return," sell dividends, make unfair comparisons, fail to mention risk, sell mutual fund shares on margin, guarantee against loss

RR must say shares may be above or below purchase price at redemption, file all fund sales literature with NASD 10 days after it is used, send a prospectus before or with sales literature, sell to customers at next calculated price

Other Rules See Chapter 16.

REVIEW QUESTIONS

1. When an investor sells her shares back to a mutual fund the amount she receives is the:

   (A) NAV
   (B) offer
   (C) bid less commissions
   (D) asked price

2. The primary difference between open-end and closed-end funds is:

   (A) their capitalization
   (B) their investment objectives
   (C) diversification
   (D) their tax status

3. Capital gains distributions from investment companies are taxed:

   (A) as ordinary income
   (B) as long-term capital gains
   (C) only if not reinvested
   (D) when the shares are sold

4. Shareholders must receive financial statements from investment companies:

   (A) monthly
   (B) quarterly
   (C) semi-annually
   (D) annually

5. An investor in a contractual plan has completion insurance. In case of his death the proceeds would go to the:

   (A) investment company
   (B) estate
   (C) beneficiary of the estate
   (D) custodian

6. This completion insurance would pay:

   (A) 100% of the contracted amount of the plan
   (B) 50% of the contracted amount of the plan
   (C) 50% of the unpaid amount in the plan
   (D) 100% of the unpaid amount in the plan

7. In a spread-load plan, the maximum that can be deducted from contributions in any of the first four years is:

   (A) 9%
   (B) 16%
   (C) 20%
   (D) 50%

8. In a front-end load plan the maximum sales charge that can be deducted from contributions in the first year is:

   (A) 9%
   (B) 16%
   (C) 20%
   (D) 50%

9. If one purchases an open-end fund on Tuesday the price paid is:

   (A) Monday's closing NAV
   (B) Tuesday's NAV
   (C) the next NAV after the order is entered
   (D) the average of Monday and Tuesday closing NAV

10. If the shares of a mutual fund can be purchased at Net Asset Value (NAV) it is a:

    (A) no-load fund
    (B) dual purpose fund
    (C) closed end fund
    (D) low cost fund

11. All of the following are purchased at or above NAV EXCEPT:

    (A) open-end funds
    (B) closed-end funds
    (C) no-load funds
    (D) funds which issue only common stock

12. An investor pays a 7.5% selling charge on the purchase of 1,000 shares of a mutual fund offered at $15. If he must pay a .5% redemption fee and the fund has not changed in value at redemption, he will receive approximately:

    (A) $13,730
    (B) $13,800
    (C) $14,925
    (D) $15,000

13. The NAV of a mutual fund is $14.80. If the maximum sales commission is 7½%, what price is it offered at?

(A) $14.80
(B) $15.86
(C) $16.00
(D) $16.20

14. How long after the plan custodian mails notice of charges does the customer have to cancel a front-end load and still receive a full refund?

(A) within 30 days
(B) within 45 days
(C) within 60 days
(D) within 90 days

15. To qualify as a regulated investment company a mutual fund must pay out as dividends at least:

(A) 75% of investment income
(B) 80% of investment income
(C) 90% of investment income
(D) 97% of investment income

16. An investment company has had an average price of $15.00 over the past year. If the year-end price is $14.50, and it had a $.75 income distribution and a $.70 capital gains distribution for the year, its (historical) yield can be described as:

(A) 4%
(B) 4.66%
(C) 5%
(D) 9.66%

17. The "conduit theory" for a regulated investment company says that:

(A) the flow of revenues should be unimpeded by redemptions
(B) investment income flows to the investor after taxes
(C) the investor and the fund are taxed as a single entity
(D) the investment income is taxable to the investor only

18. The responsibility for safeguarding the securities of a mutual fund belongs to the:

(A) fund manager
(B) investor
(C) NASD
(D) custodian bank

19. The "breakpoint" for a mutual fund is the:

(A) point where sales break even
(B) minimum investment at which one gets a volume discount
(C) minimum number of shares for a volume discount
(D) point at which one gets a break on a letter of intent

20. An investor interested in capital appreciation would most likely buy which of the following?

(A) an income fund
(B) a growth fund
(C) a closed-end fund
(D) a specialized fund

21. With respect to a letter of intent all of the following hold EXCEPT:

(A) it is good for 13 months
(B) it may be backdated for 90 days
(C) shares purchased under it can be held in escrow
(D) the investor may not redeem shares while the letter is in effect

ANSWERS TO REVIEW QUESTIONS

1. (C) The bid is the same as the NAV.

2. (A) Closed-end funds issue shares once when they are formed and never redeem shares. Open-end funds are continually issuing and redeeming shares.

3. (B) Current tax law no longer makes this distinction but the category may reappear in the future.

4. (C) They also receive monthly statements about trading in their own accounts.

5. (D) The custodian also receives payments from the investor and holds securities for him.

6. (D) Hence the name completion.

7. (C) Up to 64% of the first four years investment may be deducted but no more than 20% in any one year.

8. (D) This may be deducted from each monthly payment.

9. (B) If one *sold* then one would receive the next NAV after the order was entered.

10. (A) The bid is always at NAV. If the offer is, too, it is a no-load fund.

11. (B) Closed-end funds are not redeemed by the fund and hence their price is not directly related to NAV. They often sell at a discount and sometimes at a premium.

12. (B) $15 \times (1 - .075) =$ Bid $= \$13,875$. If a 0.5% redemption fee is charged the investor receives approximately $13.80 which if multiplied by 1,000 shares gives $13,800.

13. (C) $\$14.80 \div (1 - .075) = \$16.00$.

14. (B) The notice of changes must be sent within 60 days after the plan certificate is issued.

15. (D) It must also distribute at least 90% of its capital gains income.

16. (C) $\$.75 \div \$15.00 = 5\%$. Only investment income may be used to describe yield.

17. (D) The investment company merely acts as a conduit for the flow of income to the investor.

18. (D) In addition, the custodian collects and disburses funds from the purchase and sale of securities for the fund.

19. (B) The breakpoint is a fixed dollar value rather than a fixed number of shares. The latter would commit the investor to an indeterminate dollar sum.

20. (B) These funds invest in companies that pay little if any dividends, instead using the money to invest in company growth.

21. (D) The letter of intent would no longer be in effect if the shares were redeemed.

CHAPTER FIVE

Tax-advantaged investments, annuities and retirement plans

PART ONE   TAX-ADVANTAGED INVESTMENTS

This chapter begins with a discussion of certain specialized investment plans known as "tax shelters." In general, these were originally devised for individuals in high tax brackets—those paying 50% or more. As designed, tax shelters allowed investors to defer taxes, or to incur certain losses that they could write off against other income, while still enjoying both current and potential net income. A good example would be a real estate investment in which year-by-year depreciation produced a loss on paper that could be charged off against income from other sources. Investments which have no economic function other than tax avoidance are labelled abusive and are illegal.

TAX SHELTERS TODAY

The Tax Reform Act of 1986 essentially decrees that losses from tax shelters can no longer be used to shelter other income, such as wages, interest or dividend income, or profits on securities trading. There are some specific exceptions: losses from tax shelters can be used to offset income from the same or other tax-sheltered investments; certain types of real estate still offer tax advantages.

Note that the new law affects only so-called "passive losses." Individuals actively involved in running a business can still have expenses which exceed their income. Real estate developers are specifically excluded, but an investor actively managing rental property still receives some limited special treatment: landlords with an adjusted gross income of less than $100,000 can take up to $25,000 in tax losses. This allowance declines as income rises, disappearing completely at an income of $150,000.

Despite these new restrictions, some analysts think there is still a role for tax shelter programs, except that they will now be structured for profitability, to offset losses in shelters set up under the old law.

DIRECT PARTICIPATION PROGRAMS

As the name implies, direct participation programs (DPP) allow investors to participate directly in the benefits of the investment. That participation involves both economic gain or loss and tax consequences.

One type of DPP is a "subchapter S" corporation. This gives investors the benefits of a corporate shield (that is, they do not have personal responsibility for corporate debt) while allowing all profits and expenses to flow directly to investors as income (or loss). Investors pay taxes on this income but the corporation does not, so the program avoids double taxation.

The most important type of DPP is a limited partnership, and the remainder of this section will be devoted to those programs.

Qualifications for limited partnership

To qualify for the tax treatment afforded a limited partnership it must differ from a corporation in at least two of these six fundamental characteristics:

- □ being a profit-directed business
- □ providing limited liability
- □ being an association of individuals
- □ having central management
- □ having perpetual life
- □ being freely transferable

The last two ways are most commonly used to differentiate limited partnerships from corporations: to provide that the partnership has a limited life and to place some restriction on the ability to transfer ownership.

■ NOTE

The investor interested in a partnership is well advised to seek a tax opinion from an independent attorney as to whether the proposed partnership meets IRS requirements; if not, it will be taxed as a corporation.

Types of partners

A limited partnership has two kinds of partners: a general partner, who has unlimited liability with respect to the obligations of the partnership and is usually active in management; and one or more limited partners, who provide most of the capital, share any profits or losses, and who are not actively involved in management. These investor-partners have limited liability, *i.e.*, their potential loss is limited to the amount of their investment.

Formation of limited partnership

To form a limited partnership, a certificate must be filed in the state of origin, generally (except in Louisiana) under the Uniform Limited Partnership Act, which governs the interrelationships of the partners among themselves, and the partnership's relationships to creditors. A sponsor (or syndicator), who is often the general partner, organizes and registers the partnership with state and federal authorities. This person may also serve as the partnership manager, who is charged with choosing investments and for overall management.

The certificate includes the following information:

- the name of the partnership, the names of each of the general and limited partners and the business purpose for which it was formed
- the degree of participation of each partner as to both contribution and the allocation of profits and expenses
- the methods of changing membership, if any, including new partners, the transfer of partnership rights, and provision for dissolution in case of the death of the general partner
- the life span of the partnership

In addition to the Certificate of Limited Partnership, there is an Agreement of Limited Partnership that describes the rights and responsibilities of both the limited and general partners. This contract between the partners is not a public document. The agreement can be modified with the written consent of the partners. This consent is often called "partnership democracy."

EVALUATING A LIMITED PARTNERSHIP

Under NASD rules, the managing underwriter of a DPP must exercise due diligence. In addition, a registered representative should evaluate the suitability of such an investment for any client. Nevertheless, it behooves each investor to take particular care to examine the proposed program in light of his or her own needs and resources. Especially under the new law, this means assessing the soundness of the projected activity(ies) in terms of both its stated objectives and its general economic validity.

In addition, prospective investors should investigate the sponsor's earlier offerings in the same area to get some indication of ability and knowledge. Another important consideration is whether the type of investment proposed fits the investor's ability and/or willingness to deal with risks (*e.g.*, oil and gas limited partnerships often bring no return, but pay off handsomely when they do succeed; real estate programs fail far less often but pay far lower returns).

Potential conflicts of interest should also be a focus. Is the sponsor or the general partner involved with other programs which might conflict with the one proposed? One common example involves "adjacent leases," where the sponsor is raising funds to drill on a plot adjacent to one where a producing well has already been located under the same sponsor.

Other warning signs of potential conflict would include plans which do not strictly control the use of funds (for example, allowing them to be mixed with other offerings), and those that do not limit the sponsor's use of funds or compensation for sponsor's services.

In short, potential investors should be assured that the sponsor is committed to giving the limited partners a fair chance to protect their investment. If the program involves purchasing real property, investors should ascertain the basis on which it is appraised and should see whether the expected gain in value is reasonable. If the plan involves oil and gas production, the geological analysis is crucial.

Of particular concern in evaluating returns in these programs is the fact that they are often stretched over a long period of time. Thus straightforward evaluations that do not take into account the time value of money can be misleading. For example, a dollar received in eight years would be worth $.50 if interest rates were at 9% throughout that period.

In addition to looking at potential returns, of course, it is necessary to examine the risks of the venture. Two general risks are inherent in all such offerings: a limited partner can lose the entire amount invested and there is no guaranteed return.

Other risks include the fact that these investments are relatively illiquid; these agreements also usually make it difficult to transfer interests (see page 92). Investors should also be confident that the IRS will approve the deductions taken by the partnership, that the level of leverage is not too great, and that cost projections are sufficiently realistic. Especially with the new restrictions on tax losses, it is necessary to look at projected returns from the project in light of one's own tax situation.

Finally, most programs have a considerable front-end load: expenses for organizing the partnership, fees involved in acquiring property, sales and other expenses, are all deducted from invested funds. An inordinately high front-end load reduces the amount actually invested, which means that returns on the net investment must be significantly higher.

METHODS OF FUNDING A LIMITED PARTNERSHIP

□ Letter of credit—partners sign a letter that guarantees obligations of the partnership

□ Installment payments—also called "staged payments;" partners make their contributions in designated amounts over a specified time

□ Subscription amounts—these include both all initial investments and installments

□ Capital contributions—cash or property

□ Assessments—in such schemes, the general partner can assess the limited partners an additional amount

□ Loans to the partnership—tax shelters may borrow money. These are called "recourse loans," as the lender has recourse in the sense that the limited partner is personally liable for payment of the loan. As we shall see, real estate tax shelters (and only real estate shelters) can incur nonrecourse loans, under which the lender has no such claim.

TYPES OF OFFERINGS

Managed offerings

Direct participation programs, usually limited partnerships, can be sold by underwriters in "managed offerings." The procedures resemble those with mutual funds (see Chapter 6): the issue can be purchased on a firm commitment basis or sold ("best efforts") on commission; underwriter's compensation may not exceed 10% of the total amount of the offering.

Non-managed offerings

The issuer can sell directly through registered representatives at various firms or through a "wholesaler" who hires representatives to work on commission. In any case, the 10% limit obtains for total compensation for selling the issue. Registered representatives are required to notify their firms in writing if they are selling a non-managed account.

THE SUBSCRIPTION AGREEMENT

Investors in a direct participation offering are considered "subscribers"; they enter into a subscription agreement with the general partner or sponsor. In this, limited partners accept the terms of the agreement and attest to their ability to satisfy net worth and income requirements, and to their ability to analyze the investment. No sales are completed until the general partner accepts the subscribers as limited partners.

It is the registered representative's responsibility to make reasonable inquiry about those parts of the agreement that attest to the participant's reading of the prospectus, understanding of the risks involved, income, net worth and suitability, state of residence, tax identification number, nature of ownership, and powers of attorney, if any.

As the general partner can refuse to admit an investor who does not meet certain requirements—for example, in terms of net worth, ability to absorb the potential loss, etc.—he or she must also assess the information shown in the individual's subscription agreement.

Before investing, the individual should consider the amount of liability and risk, tax effects, the difficulty in getting out of the program, and that there is little governmental protection or regulation compared to other investment plans.

The most popular types of programs are real estate, oil and gas, and equipment leasing. Programs involving cattle, movies, and other industries have been cut back substantially by the new tax laws.

REAL ESTATE PROGRAMS

In a real estate program, investors usually have a completely passive role. A partnership manager selects and arranges to buy or lease properties, a property manager is in charge of daily operations. Both are appointed by the general partner.

The basic incentives in such programs are fourfold. They are: income, capital appreciation, diversification, and the opportunity to participate in an investment that requires substantial expertise and provides some tax relief. Tax relief comes because the investor is able to deduct expenses, mortgage interest, and depreciation. With depreciation, it is possible to create income losses while investors still enjoy cash flow. While this benefit has been curtailed somewhat by the 1986 Tax Reform Act, it remains a significant factor in real estate investment.

Real estate programs have an additonal advantage. In most limited partnerships, the maximum deduction available is the amount involved or "at risk," including loans for which the limited partners are personally liable ("recourse loans"). But the law allows real estate investors to write off nonrecourse loans as well. With these loans, the lender may foreclose, but cannot hold limited partners liable for any balances due. This increase in allowable write-offs means that investors in real estate programs may enjoy greater potential tax benefits.

This advantage does not come without costs, however. Holding greater debt means that a larger percentage of revenues must be used for debt service. If rental income does not cover this debt service, partners may have to make additional contributions or face foreclosure.

A second concern is that any cash distributions in such a plan are treated as return of capital. At some point, when depreciation and other expenses wane, income rises. The limited partners' cash contribution may then be smaller than the taxable income attributable to that partner. This creates "phantom" income, which is taxable. Typically, a partnership will arrange to sell or refinance the property before this "crossover point" is reached.

There are several different types of real estate programs:

New construction

These programs are primarily vehicles for capital gains as opposed to income. The risks of such programs are all those inherent in building something: cost overruns, delays, inability to sell the finished product. They do however have the potential for enormous capital gains.

Government-aided housing

These programs were significantly changed by the 1986 tax bill, but do still provide some opportunities for tax relief and for very modest income and capital gains. The same is true for programs that focus on the rehabilitation of historic structures.

Existing properties

Investment in existing property is designed for those willing to give up some capital appreciation for cash distributions and a diminution of risk. Most real estate syndicates try to purchase existing properties, improve them, and sell at a profit. Because this happens so often, it is possible to predict cash flows with some certainty, and to receive accurate valuations from independent appraisers. However, it is still essential to be sure that the sponsor's projections are realistic. Two areas to look at are lease restrictions (which may severely limit needed changes) and tenant stability (tenants' leases should not be so loose that continued income is endangered nor so tight or long-lasting that they threaten returns once improvements are made).

Land

Undeveloped or "raw" land offers the potential for appreciation if there is change in land use, or even when it remains unused but there is population growth nearby. These ventures usually involve experienced, professional developers.

As there is no income until the land is used, investors must be able to deal with a long-term cash outflow and consistent repeated costs, including taxes and interest. At times, the general partner may assess investors for additional funds to avoid foreclosure. These investments also face certain external risks, for example, development plans are often vigorously opposed by local agencies or environmental groups. Finally, there is no depreciation on land, making such investments less attractive to those who need a tax shelter.

Condominium securities

A condominium may be a security under certain conditions, specifically if there is evidence of investment intent or if management is by a third party. If a condominium is classified as a rental pool, *i.e.*, is operated as a management company like a hotel, then all of the condominiums in the pool are securities. The benefits of such a program are primarily the potential for capital gains and significant tax advantages. A key element to be considered in calculating potential tax advantages is that the owner may not personally use the property for more than two weeks, or 10% of the rental days, without running the risk of losing the privileged tax status with respect to depreciation, fees and expenses, and interest. The tax benefits of a condominium include the possibility of deducting real estate taxes for the unit itself and for the unit's proportional share of taxes on common grounds. Interest payments are also deductible.

A limited partnership can buy a property and then lease it back to the seller. This is called a "sale-leaseback." Its primary advantages are the tax benefits of depreciation and the ability to deduct interest expense. Typically, a sale-leaseback involves a long-term lease in which the seller-tenant agrees to pay maintenance costs, property taxes, and insurance premiums along with the rent. These are called "triple net leases" because they are net of those three charges. The principal risk arises when the lessee cannot make the payments, as the partnership must then find a suitable replacement tenant.

REITs

Another type of real estate investment is called a Real Estate Investment Trust or REIT.

Purpose of REITs These trusts invest in income property or mortgage loans, and pay dividends from interest income or realized gains, or both. For investors, Real Estate Investment Trusts offer the possibility of buying shares in a mix of real estate holdings. For the real estate industry, REITs offer a chance to attract capital investment from individuals who are not customarily involved in direct real estate investment.

REIT shares are sold on stock exchanges and over the counter. Market price tends to reflect current yield because they are required to distribute 95% of their earnings from interest or rents or both. The Tax Reform Act of 1986 allows the REIT to act much more like a real estate operator in that it substantially liberalizes the amount that the trust can hold in reserve for both ongoing and future investment in the property, *e.g.*, maintenance and improvements.

The REIT Act Under the REIT Act of 1960, qualified REITs are offered special tax treatment: only the retained earnings are subject to federal income tax.

Qualifications for REITs

To deserve the special tax treatment, a REIT must meet a number of requirements in addition to distributing at least 95% of its earnings:

Organization The trust must be legally unincorporated. This could mean shareholders face some liability, but as the trust indenture states they are not responsible for debts of the trust, there is no real risk, practically speaking.

Holdings At least 90% of REIT holdings must be in real estate investments. The trust cannot, under the law, hold property primarily for sale.

Trust indenture A trust indenture must be established. Shareholders elect the trustees, who are responsible for managing the trust; most often they contract with an adviser (usually a bank or insurance company or other financial institution with real estate expertise) to handle daily operations, and to investigate and recommend investments.

Ownership REITs must issue certificates of beneficial ownership as evidence of shareholding, and these shares must be transferable. REITs operate like closed-end investment companies (see page 70): they market a fixed number of shares, and do not redeem them on request. Those who wish to liquidate their holdings must do so in the market, so shares may sell for more or less than their net asset value. The trust must have at least 100 beneficial owners; no five (or fewer) can own more than 50% of the stock.

Assets At least 75% of the trust's total assets must be in real property at the end of every quarter. Real property is defined as mortgages, shares of other REITs, cash or government securities.

Income At least 75% of gross income must be from activities related to real estate, for example, rents, interest on mortgage-secured property, gains from property sales, etc. Another 15% must come from such sources or from the sale of securities, including other REITs. Only 10% may come from such items as clients' fees or other business income.

OIL AND GAS PROGRAMS

The law provides certain specific incentives to make exploration for, and production of, gas and oil more attractive. These include:

The chance to deduct "intangible drilling costs" Basically, these are the expenses involved in getting the oil or gas, as distinguished from capital expenses for equipment which would last a year or more. Thus, costs for labor and gear used to prepare a site, testing, and the like would all be considered intangible drilling costs.

A "depletion allowance" This is a form of depreciation that reflects the using up of estimated reserves. This is computed in one of two ways: the percentage depletion method, in which a flat percentage of gross income is deductible each year; or the cost depletion method, in which the adjusted cost of the property is assumed to be reduced by the percentage of the recoverable oil which is actually sold in that year. The next year, the cost is adjusted by subtracting the previous year's depletion to get a new adjusted cost basis. For example, if the property costs $1,000,000 and includes an estimated 100,000 barrels (or $10 a barrel), and 20,000 barrels are sold in one year, then $200,000 can be deducted and the following year the cost basis is $800,000.

"Sharing Arrangements"

On oil and gas programs, the costs and revenues involved can be allocated in one of four ways:

Overriding royalty interest The sponsor takes a share of revenues but does not contribute to costs. As this tends to encourage drilling wells without concern for their overall profitability, it is generally not considered an ideal choice for investors.

Reversionary (or subordinate) working interest Again, the sponsor does not contribute to the cost, but also does not share in any revenues until investors have recovered their investment.

Functional allocation Investors contribute all deductible costs, the sponsor all non-deductible costs. The sponsor contributes capital only for the development of productive wells.

Disproportionate sharing arrangement The sponsor does share in the program's cost, but disproportionately. Typically, the sponsor would pay 25% of the costs and be entitled to 50% of the revenues.

Types of oil and gas programs

Oil and gas programs are conventionally divided into two types, "drilling programs" and "income programs." The first of these drills wells in hopes of finding new sources of oil and gas and the second type buys productive wells.

Drilling programs are further subdivided into exploratory and development programs:

1 Exploratory ("wildcatting") involves drilling wells in an unproven area. The risk of no return (a dry hole) is high, but potential return is also high. The principal benefits of such a program are tax advantages and the opportunity for high return.

2 Development programs involve drilling in or near proven fields. Less risky than an exploratory program, but also with less potential for really spectacular return, as these are generally costlier to lease, and also often on land which other drillers have chosen not to try. These also provide tax benefits and the opportunity for income partially sheltered by the depletion allowance.

Income programs Acquiring producing properties. The purchase price is based on a geologist's estimate of the reserves discounted to present value and allowing for risk factors. The benefit here is in sheltering income since with no drilling they offer little in the way of tax relief.

Combinations of the above Often designed to combine these types of programs in ways that provide some or all of their potential benefits.

EQUIPMENT LEASING PROGRAMS

The purchase and subsequent leasing of major capital cost equipment is another type of DPP. The principal tax benefit reflects the depreciation of the equipment. Using accelerated depreciation provides the investor with substantial early write-offs.

If the lease arrangement provides rentals which cover the entire price of the equipment (a "full-payout lease"), the investment is less risky. However, because of depreciation, such a situation is likely to generate phantom income.

To avoid this, the partnership can sell the equipment before the crossover point is reached. This may generate a capital gain because of the recapture of depreciation expenses.

Operating lease arrangements are short-term. They present the investor with an additional risk as the equipment will probably not be as valuable or as rentable when the original lease expires.

TAXATION AND ACCOUNTING PRACTICES

An accounting method called Accelerated Cost Recovery System (ACRS) applies to both new and used assets and does not consider salvage value in computing depreciation.

For tax purposes, expenses such as organization and syndication costs are capitalized and must be amortized over the life of the partnership. All depreciation and depletion deductions are recaptured when the asset is sold for a gain.

The partnership basis (*i.e.*, the cost of the property) is adjusted upward to reflect income, capital gain, new contributions, and new debt for which the partner is personally liable; it is adjusted downward to reflect distributions, losses, depreciation, and partial sales.

The alternative minimum tax affects many items of tax preference resulting from DPPs.

DISSOLVING A LIMITED PARTNERSHIP

There are several situations in which a limited partnership might be dissolved before the date specified in the partnership agreement. These include:

- retirement, insanity or death of general partner
- the sale of all partnership assets
- a vote by a majority of the ownership to dissolve

In any case, the certificate of limited partnership should be cancelled; otherwise, partners can lose their limited liability protection.

On dissolution, creditors have first call on the assets of the partnership; the general partner is liable for any remaining debt. After creditors are satisfied, assets go to reimburse limited partners and then general partners, but the agreement can modify this.

PART TWO   ANNUITIES

Some types of investment instruments are expressly designed for individuals who want future income, particularly at retirement. These include annuities and other plans discussed in Part Three of this chapter.

An annuity is a contract between an insurance company and an individual investor. The insurance company agrees to pay a stipulated amount to the investor (the "annuitant"), for life or for some specified period, in return for a single payment or a series of payments; benefits may begin immediately or at some later date. The major types are fixed and variable annuities.

FIXED ANNUITY

With a fixed annuity, the insurance company guarantees to pay a fixed dollar amount at each specified period for the term of the contract, typically the life of the annuitant.

This means that the insurer assumes the "mortality risk," the possibility that the annuitant will survive beyond the actuarially expected life span. The insurer also assumes the investment risk, since it guarantees the rate of return on invested principal. Even if the insurer's investment return is lower than this guaranteed rate, the insurance company still must pay the guaranteed rate. Indeed, in many contracts the annuitant receives additional payouts for those periods where the insurer's return is higher than anticipated.

The annuitants, on their part, assume the risk that inflation will lower the real value of the payout.

VARIABLE ANNUITY

The variable annuity attempts to deal with this inflation risk. It is designed to keep pace with inflation. However, neither the amount of payout nor the interest rate is guaranteed. Payments vary according to the market value of the portfolio used to fund the annuity. In other words, the annuitant assumes the investment risk.

In 1959, the U.S. Supreme Court ruled that because the investment risk was borne by the purchaser, these contracts were subject to regulation as securities. Therefore, they must be registered with the S.E.C. and under the Investment Company Act of 1940 as open-end investment companies.

Because no fixed payment is involved, the variable annuity is valued in units, not in dollars (see below).

Note the resemblance to mutual funds—both involve participation in a portfolio of securities, and both are subject to federal regulation. But mutual fund participation is measured in shares, not in units, and while holders of mutual funds may seek income or growth in a long-term investment, the primary objective of variable annuity is retirement income. The most important difference, however, is that earnings on a variable annuity are tax deferred while mutual funds are taxed on distributions and gains each year.

Separate account

The insurance company puts moneys paid to it for variable annuities into a "separate" or "segregated" account. This serves the dual purposes of shielding the insurer's other assets (*e.g.*, from life insurance or fixed rate annuities), and allowing the insurer to invest in securities that may not be appropriate for the insurer's regular business. Funds are usually invested in a portfolio including common stocks, and often in the shares of mutual funds to avoid the costs of managing a portfolio.

Over time, this account grows as dividends and interest are paid in, and changes with gains and losses from the sale of securities. It also fluctuates daily, reflecting market ups and downs in the securities portfolio.

A professional investment advisor manages the fund under the supervision of a board of managers. As with mutual funds, firms that offer variable annuities are prohibited from making any statement implying that their management skills or investment policies guarantee against loss.

Regulations affecting variable annuities

Variable annuities are subject to regulation at two levels: first, all insurance companies must comply with the rules set by the state insurance commission in their state; second, at the federal level, three laws apply:

1 The separate account is considered an investment company, so all accounts which represent a pooling of variable annuity funds must be registered under the Investment Company Act of 1940.

2 A variable annuity contract is a security and subject to registration under the Securities Act of 1933.

3 Any firm selling variable annuities is considered a broker/dealer and must register under the Securities and Exchange Act of 1934.

Value of variable annuity contract

The value of a variable annuity is expressed in "units" of two kinds: "accumulation" units while the annuitant is paying in, and "annuity" units during distribution.

Accumulation units These are an accounting measure of the contract owner's proportionate interest in the separate account during the accumulation period. The units vary in value daily as the investment portfolio varies in value. Thus on any given day, one accumulation unit equals the value of the separate account portfolio divided by the number of accumulation units outstanding.

This is just like net asset value per share with mutual funds. The value of a contract at any point in time is thus the value of a single accumulation unit times the number of units. If a contract currently has 2,000 units and each unit has a value of $7.50, then the value of the contract is $15,000.

The contract usually specifies the date at which accumulation ends and payout begins. At that point the annuitant will receive a lump sum payment or (by "annuitizing" the accumulation) regular monthly payments for some fixed period, or for the length of his life, depending on the contractual agreement entered into earlier.

Annuity unit This is the accounting measure used to determine how much the annuitant will receive during the payout period if a monthly payment plan was chosen. It is the value of an accumulation unit at the time that the payout period begins.

The *first* month amount is fixed by the contract as follows:

When payout begins (usually at retirement), the value of the contract is determined by multiplying the number of units accumulated by the value of one accumulation unit at that point.

The first monthly payment is then calculated on the basis of the insurance company's annuity tables. These are actuarial tables showing monthly payment-per-$1000 of value. They take into account the annuitant's age, the payout option chosen, any charges, and the "assumed interest rate" of the portfolio. So the monthly payment-per-$1000 times the value of the individual account determines the first payment.

This first payment is then divided by the current value of an accumulation unit to determine the total number of annuity units required to make that first payment. The number of annuity units remains fixed. Every month the annuitant receives the dollar amount of that fixed number of units times the *current* value of a unit.

■ **EXAMPLE**

If at retirement an annuitant had 20,000 accumulation units and each had a value of $6, the value of the contract would be $120,000. Suppose that for this annuitant actuarial tables show a monthly payment per $1000 of $8.50; so the first month's payment was

$$120 \times \$8.50 = \$1,020.$$

Then $1,020 ÷ $6 = 170 units would have to be sold in order to make this payment. From then on, the contract-holder would get 170 units' worth of payment for each succeeding month. If for some later month units were worth $7 (rather than the $6 value at the time of retirement), that month's check would be for $170 \times \$7 = \$1,190$.

The annuitant hopes that these payments would increase at least at the same rate as inflation; however, that is not at all certain: the annuitant assumes the investment risk.

Two final notes:

If the annuitant dies before the units are exhausted there is often provision for the unspent units to be transferred to the estate or to some beneficiary.

If the annuitant outlives the time required to use up all of the units, he or she still continues to receive the annuity. Thus the insurer is still accepting the insurance risk.

ANNUITY PURCHASE OPTIONS

As noted above, an annuity can be purchased in one payment or in installments and payout can begin at once or at a set future date. The possible combinations are:

Single payment immediate annuity

The value of the account is simply that of the initial lump-sum purchase, less any sales and administration charges, so payout is determined immediately and begins "one full payment period" after purchase. Any capital gains or investment income is reinvested in the separate account.

Single payment deferred annuity

Again, there is a lump-sum purchase, but payout only begins after an agreed waiting period (usually a set number of years) or at some occurrence (e.g., retirement or death). Until payout begins, income and gains accumulate tax deferred.

Periodic (or installment) payment deferred annuity

The annuitant makes a series of payments, usually at regular intervals. During this accumulation period, any net income and gains are added to the value of the account. Once payout begins, this continues as "reinvestment."

ANNUITY PAYOUT OPTIONS

The possible forms of payout (or "resettlement") are:

Life annuity

Provides monthly (or other periodic) payment for life of annuitant, however long. This option offers the highest regular payments. The insurance company's obligation ends at death.

Life annuity, joint and survivor

Payments go to both the annuitant and a second person. If one should die, benefits go to the survivor. The insurance company's obligation ends with the death of both.

Life annuity, period certain

Payments continue for a specified period (usually 10, 15 or 20 years). If the annuitant dies, payment goes to the beneficiary.

Life annuity, unit refund

Regular payments are made during the annuitant's life. At death, a named beneficiary receives a lump-sum payment for the remaining value of the account.

Installment for designated period (also called limited installment, fixed period)

Payments to the annuitant continue only for a specified period.

Installment for designated amount

Payments continue until the account is exhausted.

Investment income

Pays only from income, leaving the principal untouched.

Note that many of these payout options are available with either fixed or variable annuities or a "combined annuity," with a fixed portion paying a stated dollar amount, the variable in units.

OTHER FEATURES

Contract terms

The insurance company usually guarantees payment as long the annuitant lives (payment for this risk is built into the annuity tables). In addition, the company guarantees it will not reduce payments because its expenses go up.

If the annuitant should die before payout begins, a "death benefit" provision states that the value of the account goes to the beneficiary. If the investor stops paying for any other reason, a "non-forfeiture" provision ensures that he or she retains the accumulated units purchased and can redeem them at current value. Finally, some contracts include loan privileges, allowing the annuitant to borrow on units in the account.

Sales charges (and management and administrative fees)

When such charges are imposed on variable annuities, this must be noted in the prospectus. These are usually a fixed percentage of payment. As with mutual funds they can be reduced at breakpoints or with rights of accumulation.

Some plans deduct most sales charges in the first year ("front-end load"). These have rights like those with mutual funds (full refund of sales charges if withdrawn in 45 days; if the front-end load is 50%, the purchaser can withdraw in up to 18 months with a refund of any charges over 15% of all payments).

TAXATION OF ANNUITIES

Tax treatment of annuities requires a number of distinctions. All interest, dividends, and capital gains accumulate on a tax-free (actually tax-deferred) basis; however, once payout begins, some part of the money received is taxable. The distinction here is between contributions made on a before-tax basis and those made after-tax.

Thus, that portion of the payout that represents the original contribution is considered a recovery of money paid in (this is determined by IRS-approved actuarial formulas for the cost basis) and is not taxed. The remainder—any gains in the separate accounts—is taxed as ordinary income; of course, this rate is usually somewhat lower for those over 65.

PART THREE   RETIREMENT PLANS

Many individuals are covered by retirement plans. Some of these are employer-sponsored; others are individual plans. This section provides an overview of the various types of plans.

A key element here is the concept of "tax-qualified" plans. This refers to whether contributions to the plan are deductible from income—either the income of an individual taxpayer or of a corporation sponsoring the plan.

With a tax-qualified plan, funds that go into the retirement account are deducted from income at that time, although they are taxed (according to rules outlined below) when they are distributed; such plans must meet certain rigorous requirements. In non-qualified plans, funds deposited cannot be deducted from income; at distribution, this original contribution is not taxed again, though any accumulated investment income is.

EMPLOYER PENSION PLANS

Approximately half of all employees in the country are covered by employer plans. The employee is liable for taxes on the money in these plans only when he begins to receive it at retirement. Employer contributions are a deductible expense if the plan is "qualified." To be considered qualified, a pension plan must meet certain standards set by IRS and by ERISA, the Employment Retirement Income Security Act. These standards deal with vesting rights, eligibility, and fairness.

Vesting To be "vested" in some property is to have the right of ultimate ownership to that property. Under the 1986 Tax Reform Act, employer-sponsored plans must vest eligible employees in one of two ways: either they are fully (100%) vested after five years or 20% vested after three years, and 20% in each succeeding year to become fully (100%) vested after seven years.

Eligibility Eligibility requirements vary, but must include the following minimum standards. For employees aged twenty-one or older, eligibility cannot be delayed for more than one year. Regardless of the vesting schedule (even if the employee is fully vested at once), participation may not be delayed for more than two years and must be within three years. (Employees include all who work more than 1,000 hours during the year).

Fairness The act requires that coverage be available to employees other than those who are highly paid. One criterion is that at least 70% of all non-highly compensated employees are covered.

Benefit plans

Benefit plans are labeled as either "defined contribution" or "defined benefit." In a defined contribution plan, a specified amount is contributed each year. The funds accumulate, including any interest earned, and are available for distribution at retirement very much like an annuity.

In a defined benefit plan, the benefit to the employee is defined as some percentage (often between 1% and 2% for each year of service) of the employee's average salary during his last five years of employment. For example, a 2% formula for an employee with 30 years of service would define a benefit of 60% of the average of salary earned between the years 26 through 30.

Contribution deadlines

For qualified plans, corporate contributions must be made by the date the corporate tax return is filed.

INDIVIDUAL RETIREMENT PLANS

Aside from employer pension plans there are a wide range of individual plans which offer some tax advantages. These include Individual Retirement Accounts (IRAs), Keogh (HR-10) Plans, Simplified Employee Pension Plans (SEPs), and Section 401(k) Plans.

Individual Retirement Accounts (IRAs)

Any individual may open and maintain an IRA. The 1986 Tax Reform Act limits the deductibility of contributions to these accounts, but they still offer individual investors the chance to shelter funds for retirement.

Contribution limits Individuals who are not active participants in an employer-sponsored retirement plan may contribute up to 100% of income or $2,000, whichever is less, into an IRA and deduct that from income before figuring taxes. For a couple with only one wage earner the limit is $2,250; with two wage earners, the maximum is $2,000 each.

For those who are active participants in an employer-sponsored plan, the deduction is phased out when income reaches $25,000 for individuals and $40,000 for couples. For those earning more, an IRA contribution is no longer tax-deductible; however, any interest earnings or other gains in the account are tax-deferred until withdrawals begin.

Any contribution above the limits described is considered an excess contribution and is subject to a 6% excise tax. An IRA may be established up to the date that the return is due (April 15, for those on a calendar year).

Distributions Once established, IRAs are treated much like the plans described above: taxes are deferred on any gain to the account, funds distributed before age 59½ are subject to a 10% penalty and income tax, distribution of funds must begin by age 70½ and meet minimum distribution requirements or a 5% penalty must be paid for "insufficient distribution."

An additional feature concerns an individual who receives a lump-sum distribution from a qualified employer plan, for example on leaving a job. The distribution may be "rolled over" by placing it in an IRA. The $2000 limit does not apply, but the money must be be rolled over within 60 days. All or part of the sum can be so handled. If only part is rolled over, the balance is taxed as normal income.

At payout, IRA distributions are taxed as regular income. Lump sum distributions are subject to the same treatment as with annuities.

If the investor withdraws (or borrows) funds, or redeems the annuity during the accumulation period, any increase in value over the cost is taxed as income. If current value is lower than the cost, the difference is deducted from income. Any such early withdrawals may be subject to tax penalties.

During the payout period, part of the payment is considered return of cost, and is not taxable. This is based on an IRS formula, where total cost is divided by a "life expectancy multiple" to get the yearly amount of nontaxable income. The balance is treated as ordinary income.

Keogh plans (H.R.10) for the self-employed

Keogh (pronounced "Key-oh") plans offer tax advantages on retirement-oriented investments for self-employed individuals and their employees. These funds can be invested in any investment approved by the IRS. These include annuities, mutual funds, trust or savings accounts, most securities, non-term life insurance, and mortgages.

One feature of Keogh plans is that all eligible employees must be covered at the same rate. Physicians who set up Keogh plans and contribute the maximum 25% of net compensation must contribute that proportion of their nurses' salary as well.

Contribution deadlines A Keogh must be established by the end of the tax year. However, additional contributions—up to the limits allowed—can be made up to the time the tax return is due—April 15 of the following year.

Self-employed individuals include those who are employed by others but have separate earned income from consulting, royalties, or from work as an independent contractor.

Contribution Limits Contributions are limited to 25% of net compensation with a maximum of $30,000 for a defined contribution plan. Eligibilities, vesting and fairness requirements for all employees of self-employed individuals are the same as those for employee pension plans.

Simplified Employee Pension Plans (SEPs)

A Simplified Employee Pension plan allows a small employer to set up a pension plan with individual retirement accounts for each covered employee. It greatly reduces the paperwork and is in other ways simpler than an employer benefit plan.

Under these plans, the employer may, but is not compelled to, make contributions to the individual accounts each year. In addition, the employee may elect to have his or her salary reduced by up to 25%, which is then deposited in the account. The maximum for this elective contribution by an employee is $7,000 annually. The total contribution, including amounts from the employer and those elected by the employee, is limited to 15% of compensation but no more than $30,000.

Vesting in an SEP is immediate. Eligibility requirements are like those for employer pension plans.

401(k) plans

A final pension option is the tax-deferred retirement plan known as 401(k). These resemble employer pension plans but are less restrictive. Contributions to such plans are treated like additions to a defined contribution plan. Elective employee contributions to such a plan are again limited to the smaller of 25% of compensation or $7,000 and employer contributions are allowed up to 15% of compensation with a $30,000 maximum.

Note the total contribution by an employee to all SEP and 401(k) plans is limited to 25% of compensation with a maximum of $7,000.

To qualify as a tax-deferred plan, a 401(k) may not discriminate in favor of highly-compensated employees. That is, the actual deferral percentage for highly-compensated employees cannot exceed that of lower-paid employees by too large an amount. Vesting is immediate.

TERMS

Tax shelters

Specialized investment plans, allow investors to defer taxes, or incur paper losses. Under the Tax Reform Act of 1986, such losses cannot be used to shelter income except from tax shelters; certain types of real estate still offer tax advantages.

Direct Participation Programs (DPP) allow investors to participate directly in gain or loss and tax consequences

Limited Partnership (LP) most important type of DPP

Qualifications for LP must differ fundamentally from corporation; *e.g.*, have limited life, restrict transferability

General partner unlimited liability, usually active in management

Limited partner(s) provide most of capital, share profits or losses, not active in management, limited liability

Sponsor (syndicator) organizes and registers partnership with authorities

Formation certificate must be filed in state of origin; gives details of partnership, partners

Agreement describes rights and responsibilities of limited and general partners

Evaluating limited partnership assess economic soundness, examine sponsor's earlier offerings, especially potential conflicts of interest, real basis of investment, gauge potential risks (lack of liquidity, etc.)

Recourse loans due the partnership limited partner personally liable to partnership

Managed offerings like mutual funds

Non-managed offerings sold directly through a wholesaler or RR

Subscription agreement between investors and general partner or sponsor; investors attest they can satisfy all requirements
RR must assure that participants understand the program
No sales until general partner accepts subscribers as limited partners

Real estate programs

Investors usually completely passive

Basic incentives income, capital appreciation, diversification, and tax relief

Non-recourse loans no claim on limited partner's assets

Tax relief expenses, mortgage interest, and depreciation allow income losses and cash flow

Types of programs New construction; government-aided housing; existing properties; land; condominium securities; REITS

Oil and gas programs

Chance to deduct intangible drilling costs and depletion allowance

Overriding royalty interest sponsor shares revenues but not costs

Reversionary (subordinate) working interest sponsor does not share cost, shares revenues only when investment recovered

Functional allocation investors contribute all deductible costs; sponsor all non-deductible costs

Drilling programs exploratory (in unproven area) or development (drilling in or near proven fields)

Income programs acquiring producing properties

Combination programs

Equipment Leasing Programs purchase and subsequent lease of major capital cost equipment

Annuities

Annuity contract between insurance company and investor ("annuitant"); company agrees to pay stipulated amount for specified period for one or several payments; benefits may be immediate or deferred

Fixed annuity company guarantees to pay fixed dollar amount at specified intervals; assumes mortality risk and investment risk, annuitants assume inflation risk

Variable annuity no guarantee of payout amount or interest rate, annuitant assumes investment risk

Contracts must be registered as open-end investment companies

Taxation earnings tax deferred

Separate account moneys paid for variable annuities must be segregated

Investment advisor manages funds under board of managers

Guaranteeing against loss prohibited

Accumulation units expresses value of variable annuity while annuitant paying in, measure of proportionate interest in separate account

Value of contract value = accumulation unit × number of units

Annuity unit measure of how much annuitant will receive during payout period, based on value of accumulation unit when payout begins and actuarial tables

Purchase/payout combinations Single Payment Immediate Annuity; Single Payment Deferred Annuity, Periodic (Installment) Payment Deferred Annuity

Possible forms of payout Life Annuity; Life Annuity, Joint and Survivor; Life Annuity, Period Certain; Life Annuity, Unit Refund; Installment for Designated Period (Limited Installment, Fixed Period); Installment for Designated Amount; Investment Income

Charges and fees usually fixed percentage of payment, can be reduced at breakpoints or with rights of accumulation; front end load like mutual funds

Tax treatment contributions accumulate income tax free, treatment of payouts depends on whether contributions made after-tax or before-tax

Retirement plans

Employer-sponsored plans to be tax-qualified, must meet standards of vesting, eligibility, fairness

Individual plans include:

IRA any individual may open except active participants in an employer-sponsored plan

Keogh plans up to 25% of all earned income from self-employment

Simplified Employee Pension (SEP) Plans

401(k) Plans

Review Questions

1. If a Direct Participation Program does not have a legitimate economic purpose it is called:

    (A) a tax shelter
    (B) a direct shelter
    (C) a deduction shelter
    (D) an abusive shelter

2. Due diligence must be exercised on a real estate limited partnership by the:

    (A) registered representative
    (B) managing underwriter
    (C) investor
    (D) SEC

3. The Ozark Oil Drilling Partnership requires the limited partners to pay labor costs and the general partner to pay for producing well equipment. This type of arrangement is called:

    (A) functional allocation
    (B) overriding royalty interest
    (C) reversionary working interest
    (D) disproportionate sharing

4. All of the following are risks of a direct participation program EXCEPT:

    (A) there is no guaranteed return
    (B) the program may not get favorable tax treatment
    (C) the investment may be illiquid
    (D) potential loss could be larger than contracted for

5. A limited partnership is most likely to differ from a corporation in which of the following ways?

    I.   limited liability
    II. centralized management
    III. difficulty of transferring ownership
    IV. continuous life

    (A) I and II
    (B) II and III
    (C) III and IV
    (D) I and IV

6. An investor in a buy-leaseback arrangement would expect all of the following EXCEPT:

    (A) risk of default
    (B) freeing up of capital
    (C) depreciation deductions
    (D) regular cash distributions

7. The Keogh Act would allow each of the following to set up a self-retirement fund EXCEPT:

    (A) a lawyer in private practice
    (B) a municipal employee with an income from selling paintings
    (C) a broker with the funds from a Christmas bonus
    (D) a salaried plumber from free-lance plumbing income

8. One may rollover the proceeds from an IRA (for the benefit of the same person) tax-free as long as the transfer occurs within:

    (A) 30 days
    (B) 60 days
    (C) 90 days
    (D) 6 months

9. Eligibility for an employee in a Keogh Plan takes place:

    (A) at once
    (B) after one year
    (C) after three years
    (D) after five years

10. An individual can receive distributions from an IRA without penalty at the age of:

    (A) 59
    (B) 59½
    (C) 60
    (D) 60½

11. He must begin distributions by age:

    (A) 62
    (B) 65
    (C) 70
    (D) 70½

12. All of the following are permissible investments for an IRA EXCEPT:

    (A) options
    (B) variable annuities
    (C) corporate bonds
    (D) CDs

13. The maximum allowable annual contribution to a Keogh Plan is:

    (A) $2,000
    (B) $7,500
    (C) $15,000
    (D) $30,000

14. The value of an accumulation unit in a variable annuity is directly dependent on:

    (A) the prime rate
    (B) the Dow Jones Industrials Average
    (C) the NAV in the separate account
    (D) a broad-based securities index

15. If an investor purchases insurance completion with a variable annuity, who receives the benefit if the investor dies?

    (A) the fund's custodian
    (B) the estate's executor
    (C) the fund's trustee
    (D) the estate of the deceased

16. The potential advantages of a tax shelter investment are:

    I. long-term capital gains
    II. generation of current losses which can offset income
    III. generation of current income

        (A) I and II
        (B) I and III
        (C) II and III
        (D) I, II, and III

17. All of the following are true of variable annuities EXCEPT:

    (A) there is a guaranteed minimum return
    (B) the portfolio may include convertible bonds
    (C) the portfolio may include mutual funds
    (D) the payout may begin 10 years after contributions end

18. To qualify, a Keogh Plan must cover the following employees EXCEPT:

    (A) there are no exceptions
    (B) full time employees of at least 1 year
    (C) employees who work more than 1,000 hours for one year
    (D) employees who work less than 1,000 hours for two years

19. A basic feature of oil and gas drilling programs is:

    (A) depletion allowance
    (B) current income
    (C) investment tax credit
    (D) safety of investment

20. All of the following are true about REITs EXCEPT:

    (A) they invest in long-term mortgages
    (B) they pass 95% of net earning to investors
    (C) they make short-term loans
    (D) there are at least 100 beneficial owners

ANSWERS TO REVIEW QUESTIONS

1. (D) In order to qualify for the favorable tax treatment it must have a legitimate economic purpose.

2. (B) The underwriting firm is responsible for due diligence.

3. (A) The sponsor contributes for the development of productive wells.

4. (D) The point of such a program is that liability is limited.

5. (C) These are the two ways in which limited partnerships differ from corporations.

6. (B) The seller-lessee would have capital freed up, not the buyer-lessor.

7. (C) All of the other sources of income are from self-employment. This one is from income at his regular job.

8. (B) This rollover can only occur once in any year. It is not limited to $2,000 but rather can be all of any existing IRA.

9. (B) Vesting occurs after five years of eligibility or in increments of 20% from year 3 to year 7.

10. (B) Death or disability also allow penalty-free distributions.

11. (D) At that time the moneys are subject to income tax.

12. (A) While options are generally not a permissible investment a mutual fund which wrote covered options to enhance return would be permissible

13. (D) The maximum is the smaller of $30,000 and 25% of income.

14. (C) A variable annuity must have a separate account. This is different from a fixed annuity whose assets may be commingled with those of the insurer.

15. (A) The custodian is responsible for seeing that the premiums in the plan are paid.

16. (D) All of these are potential advantages of such a program.

17. (A) A variable annuity does not guarantee any fixed return but does offer the possibility that the return will be sufficient to offset the effects of inflation.

18. (D) All those employed for at least 1 year, except those who work less than 1,000 hours per year, must be covered.

19. (A) None of the others are basic features of a drilling program.

20. (C) They are required to invest in real property or government securities.

CHAPTER SIX

New issues

W hen a corporation wants to raise money for long-term needs, it usually issues securities. (Bank borrowing is generally reserved for short-term use and relatively small amounts.) This chapter describes the mechanisms and rules involved in issuing new securities.

THE INVESTMENT BANKER

Corporations can sell their own securities to investors, but customarily work with an investment banker. This relationship is a long-term one, since the services provided require that the investment banker have an intimate knowledge of the corporation.

These investment banking firms act as middlemen between a corporation seeking capital and individuals or institutions seeking to invest. Working with responsible corporate officers, the investment banker decides on the amount of money to be raised, the type of securities to offer, and how and when to offer them.

Most often, the investment banker underwrites the issue, that is, buys securities from the issuer and resells them to the public. These transactions require considerable capital, and margins (the difference between the cost of buying securities and the price at which they are resold) are relatively low, so investment banking is considered a risky and highly technical business. Especially because of the risk, regulations prevent commercial banks from entering into the investment banking business (see Chapter 15).

TYPES OF OFFERINGS

Offerings of securities can be divided into two basic types:

Primary offerings

Here the investment banker distributes previously unissued securities. (The first time a firm offers shares publicly is called the "initial public offering.") *Proceeds from primary offerings go directly to the issuer and they cannot be bought on margin.*

Secondary offerings

Here the investment banker distributes securities held by individual owners (for example, a large block of stock belonging to a corporate official). Treasury stock (see page 10) can fall into this category. *Proceeds from these transactions go directly to the seller. Margin purchases are sometimes permitted.*

At times, an issue of stock will include both a primary and secondary offering. This is called a "split offering" or "combined distribution."

PRIVATE PLACEMENTS

A completely separate category of new issue is one that can go directly to one or several major individual or institutional investors. This is called a "private placement." Under this procedure, the security is never made available to the general public. (See page 315.)

The advantage of a private placement is that it is not regulated as stringently as a public offering and is therefore much less costly for the corporation. It does not have to be registered with the SEC, on the assumption that the private investors are sophisticated and do not need the protection that the general public does. Investors supply an investment letter attesting to this.

In addition, it affords the issuing company a great deal more privacy about its finances than a public offering. Most private placements are for bonds, and the purchaser of a privately placed issue is drawn by the fact that these pay a slightly higher rate than comparable public offerings.

NEGOTIATED OFFERING

Most new issues of corporate securities involve a "negotiated offering." (Some involve competitive bidding, but since this is more common with municipal issues, it is discussed later in this chapter). In the process of negotiation the investment banker will investigate the issuer's financial condition, relations with employees, plans for future growth, etc., and the general condition of the industry in which it is engaged, as well as examining the saleability of the securities to be offered.

Once both sides are satisfied, the issuer and the investment banker enter into a contract under which the investment banker agrees to buy the issue at a specified price. (The securities are subsequently sold to the public at a higher price; see below.)

THE UNDERWRITING AGREEMENT

This contract is called the underwriting agreement. It must be filed with the SEC as part of the registration statement (see Chapter 15), and is usually not finally signed until just before the new issue goes on sale to the public.

The agreement includes the following elements:

- □ name and amount of securities being offered
- □ the issuer's pledge that the issue will meet SEC requirements
- □ the issuer's agreement to sell a stated amount of securities
- □ the investment banker's agreement to buy a stated amount of securities
- □ *the price at which securities will be offered to the investment banker*
- □ *the price at which securities will be offered to the public (the public offering price or POP)*
- □ *dealer concession*
- □ provisions concerning payment—how, where and when the issuer will be paid for the securities
- □ conditions required for the underwriter to meet its commitment (for example, independent review of the issue's legality and of the issuer's financial statements)
- □ responsibility for meeting both federal and state registration requirements and for preparing and distributing the prospectus and registration
- □ *indemnifying each side from liability for anything not its fault*
- □ *terminating with "market out" clause (see below)*
- □ provisions dealing with the possibility of default by the underwriter
- □ postponement in case of some catastrophic event

TYPES OF UNDERWRITER COMMITMENTS

As principal

Usually, the investment banker buys outright the full amount of the new offering and guarantees the proceeds to the issuer—that is, the underwriter assumes financial liability for any unsold shares, and acts as a principal in the transaction. This is called "firm commitment" underwriting.

"Standby" The issuer tries to sell its securities directly to investors (for example, to existing shareholders as part of a rights offering) and the investment banker "stands by" to assist in selling any remaining shares.

"Mini-max" The investment banker makes a "firm commitment" to sell a certain portion of the issue and agrees to make a "best effort" with the balance. The agreement is not cancelled if the minimum is met, even though the maximum is not sold.

■ **EXAMPLE**   In a "1 million, 1.5 million mini-max" agreement, the underwriter commits to purchasing 1 million shares and to make a "best effort" to sell the remaining .5 million shares without actually buying these shares.

As agent

The investment banker or underwriter can also act as an agent in one of several ways:

"Best Efforts" The underwriter agrees to make its "best effort" to sell as much of the issue as it can, but assumes no actual financial liability. This entails less risk, and is most common with relatively small issues or where the issuer does not feel particularly pressed for funds.

"All or none" (AON) The investment banker again makes a best effort, but must work within a time limit (usually some days or weeks). If the entire issue is not sold in that time, the agreement (and the offering itself) is cancelled. With such an approach, no sales to investors are final until and unless all shares are sold.

Market-out clause

All types of underwriter commitments may, and usually do, include a "market-out clause." This allows the agreement to be cancelled in case of a dramatically unfavorable turn of events, for example, a strong downturn in the market, a sudden change in the issuer's financial position, some adverse government ruling, or some drastic change in the economy as a whole.

FORMATION OF UNDERWRITERS' SYNDICATE

If the new issue is too large for one investment banker to handle, the underwriter will usually turn to other investment bankers and form a syndicate to sell the issue. Typically, the issuer would select a senior manager and perhaps several junior managers. This management group would then choose other investment bankers to join them in an underwriting syndicate. Members of the syndicate sign an "agreement among underwriters" that details arrangements between the several members, and between members and the managing underwriter. It generally includes provisions on:

☐ terms of the offering

☐ proportion of each underwriter's participation

☐ the length of the association (30 days is usual)

☐ appointment of the managing underwriter to represent the syndicate and a listing of its responsibilities

☐ the fee for management

☐ member's obligations for expenses

☐ the method of handling the liability for unsold issues

☐ the time and method of delivering the securities and paying for them

An important feature of most such agreements (sometimes called purchase group agreements) is a clause penalizing members who sell shares to customers interested in a speedy profit. The "penalty syndicate clause" says that if a member's customer sells to the managing underwriter in the after-market at the stabilizing price (see page 121), then that syndicate member earns no commission on the transaction and is subject to other penalties.

TYPES OF UNDERWRITERS' AGREEMENTS

These Agreements can be:

Divided account (or Limited Liability or Western Account)

This arrangement is the one usually employed with corporate issues. Syndicate members are "severally, but not jointly" liable, *i.e.*, each member is liable only for his agreed-upon participation. For example, a firm with 5% participation in a $20 million issue is responsible for only $1 million of the shares, and bears no responsibility for other unsold shares, nor would it share in any profit from those other shares.

Undivided account (Eastern Account)

Here each member is "severally and jointly liable"—responsible both for its own and for other members' participation. This approach is normally used only with municipal issues. If a member takes 5% participation in a $20 million issue, it is liable to sell $1 million, but even if that commitment is met—even exceeded—each member is still responsible if other members fail to sell their allotted shares. Thus if $2 million remained unsold, the member would be responsible for 5% of that $2 million.

In all cases, the syndicate dissolves when the transaction is complete.

The managing underwriter has several duties, including forming the syndicate, that are discussed in the following sections. For their part, members of the underwriting syndicate agree to offer the securities at the established price. They can be released from this pledge if the issue proves particularly difficult to sell, but only with the authorization of the managing underwriter.

THE SELLING GROUP

If the managing underwriter decides that the underwriting syndicate will not be able to sell the entire new issue without assistance, it will put together a "selling group" composed of NASD member firms for help in marketing the issue. Securities held by the syndicate and sold directly, not through the selling group, are called "retained shares" or the "retention."

Members of the selling group do not actually buy the securities, that is, they take no financial responsibility, are not underwriters. But each one commits to sell a certain amount, either as allotted by the syndicate or as subscribed to. This is often called a "firm subscription." Members of the group sign an agreement with the syndicate manager that generally echoes the underwriters' own agreement. These firms receive a "selling concession," which is part of the underwriter's spread (see page 123).

PREPARATION OF NEW ISSUES

Registration

All new issues of securities must be registered with the SEC. (Some smaller, intrastate, and government instruments are exempt; see Chapter 15). The investment banker usually assists in preparing the registration statement, which is supposed to provide "full disclosure" about the issue to potential investors.

Cooling-off period

Once this statement is filed, a "20-day cooling-off period" begins to allow the SEC to review the statement. In actual practice this period can be—and most often is—extended in 20-day increments, but 20 days is the minimum time that must elapse before the "effective date," *i.e.,* the date on which securities may be sold to investors.

During this period, both issuer and underwriter take a number of steps, including:

"Preliminary prospectus" May be issued. This is designed to provide potential investors with information sufficient for them to judge the worth of the offering. Though they cannot yet purchase securities, they can make "indications of interest."

This preliminary prospectus is also called a "red herring" because it includes these words, stamped or printed in red: "this is not an offer to sell and any solicitation of sale is unlawful." It contains much of the information in the SEC registration statement and in the final prospectus, with some important omissions: *it does not show the public offering price, the underwriter's spread, the date securities will be available or the total amount of the sale.* In most cases the underwriter distributes the preliminary prospectus. It may indicate an expected price range, *e.g.,* "$20–$25 per share."

"Blue-skying" During the cooling-off period, the managing underwriter registers the issue in each state where securities are to be offered for sale, under the laws of that state. This is called "blue-skying" the issue. Additionally, registered representatives who sell in any state must register in that state.

"Due Diligence Meeting"

At or near the end of the cooling-off period, the managing underwriter calls a "due diligence meeting." This involves not only the underwriters, but also responsible officers of the issuing corporation and, usually, accountants and attorneys acting on behalf of both parties.

At the meeting, participants review the registration statement and the final prospectus to make sure that all is in correct order before the public sale begins.

An underwriter wishing to withdraw can do so at this meeting without incurring any liability. Formal terms of the contract between issuer and underwriter are usually negotiated. The underwriter establishes the final public offering price, the spread, and the sales concession. By that time, responses to the preliminary prospectus should have provided a good idea of how the public will receive the offering.

SALE OF NEW ISSUES

Although actual sales to the public can start at any time beginning with the effective date on the registration statement, they usually begin on the day following.

Once sales open, syndicate and selling group members contact those who have given indications of interest and ask for firm orders.

All purchasers must receive a final prospectus. The final prospectus must remain available for 40 days following offering date of a primary or secondary distribution, and for 90 days following an initial public offering.

"Tombstone Announcements"

When sales to the public begin, the underwriter may place a "tombstone" announcement in the press. This is specifically an announcement, not an advertisement designed to sell the issue. It includes the name of the issuing company, the type of securities being offered, the amount of the issue, and the price of each unit. Names of underwriter(s) are included, with the managing underwriter(s)'s displayed above that of the other underwriters.

Opening and closing the books

When sales begin ("opening of the books"), the managing underwriter receives subscriptions from members of the selling group and from outside dealers. If enough subscriptions are received the managing underwriter may "close the books."

"Closing the books" is at the discretion of the managing underwriter, and can take place almost immediately. Such quick closings are often accompanied by an announcement that the issue is "oversubscribed." This does not necessarily mean that all the securities have been sold, but only that dealers—who may still have to sell the securities—have subscribed for the entire issue.

In general, a certain amount of oversubscription is anticipated. Along with providing for clerical errors the underwriter must anticipate some last-minute cancellations.

"Stabilizing the Issue"

If public interest in the issue proves lower than expected, the underwriter may be required to engage in "stabilizing the issue." This requirement, if it exists, is usually described in the prospectus.

Stabilizing is an effort to keep the issue from losing value too quickly. For a time after the sale date until the price stabilizes on its own, the underwriter may need to stand ready to buy the securities back at or below the public offering price.

Obviously, stabilizing never requires purchases when the price is at a premium to the offering price. Stabilizing is the only type of price manipulation allowed by the SEC. This readiness to buy provides a partial floor for the market value at or close to the offering price.

An agreement among underwriters may state that subscribers can sell securities back to the managing underwriter if the price falls, but at a penalty.

This announcement is not an offer to sell or a solicitation of an offer to buy any of these securities. The offering is made only by the Prospectus, copies of which may be obtained in any State in which this announcement is circulated only from underwriters qualified to act as dealers in securities in such State.

NEW ISSUE   May 26, 1988

2,666,400 Shares

CAROLCO PICTURES INC.

Common Stock

_____

Price $9.375 Per Share

_____

PaineWebber Incorporated

Bear, Stearns & Co. Inc.

Furman Selz Mager Dietz & Birney
Incorporated

Alex. Brown & Sons Incorporated	The First Boston Corporation	Donaldson, Lufkin & Jenrette Securities Corporation
Drexel Burnham Lambert Incorporated	A. G. Edwards & Sons, Inc.	Goldman, Sachs & Co.
Lazard Frères & Co.	Montgomery Securities	Morgan Stanley & Co. Incorporated
Prudential–Bache Capital Funding		Shearson Lehman Hutton Inc.
Smith Barney, Harris Upham & Co. Incorporated		Crowell, Weedon & Co.

Advest, Inc. Bateman Eichler, Hill Richards William Blair & Company Blunt Ellis & Loewi
Incorporated   Incorporated

Cowen & Co.   First Albany Corporation   Ladenburg, Thalmann & Co. Inc.

Neuberger & Berman Oppenheimer & Co., Inc. Stifel, Nicolaus & Company Sutro & Co.
Incorporated   Incorporated

Thomson McKinnon Securities Inc.   Wheat, First Securities, Inc.

Arnhold and S. Bleichroeder, Inc.   First Manhattan Co.   Gruntal & Co., Incorporated

Josephthal & Co.   Mabon, Nugent & Co.   Newhard, Cook & Co.
Incorporated   Incorporated
Rowland, Simon & Co.   Wedbush Securities, Inc.

Figure 6.1 Tombstone

"Hot Issues"

Some issues of stock are labelled "hot issues" because there is a larger public demand for them than the existing supply. Such an issue is likely to sell at a premium immediately in the secondary or after market. (Trading in the new issue after the effective date by broker-dealers is called trading in the "after-market.")

Typically, some purchasers of these shares are eager to take a profit and therefore offer to resell immediately. For this reason, the underwriter will often "overallot" or "oversell" the issue, that is, allot or sell more securities than actually exist (usually up to 10%), and buy up the shares offered for resale to make up for this oversold condition.

Any losses incurred because such purchases were made at a premium are pro-rated among syndicate members in the manner specified in the agreement among underwriters.

In many cases, the issuer grants the underwriter the option to buy additional securities at the public offering price less the spread, and these can be used to cover the oversold position. Any new stock issued for this purpose must be registered with the SEC in an amendment to the registration statement.

Profits, if any, from distributing these additional shares are pro-rated among syndicate members.

NASD rules governing the handling of hot issues (see page 332) are designed to ensure that broker-dealers make a genuine effort to distribute a new issue at the public offering price, and forbid members from withholding a portion of the allotted securities for their own use. In general, these rules say that all potential customers must be treated equally and that no individual or group gets favored treatment.

COMPENSATION

Usually, the issuer pays all expenses connected with getting securities to the underwriter—preparing and distributing the registration and both preliminary and final prospectus, and blue-skying the issue. The underwriter is responsible for its own legal expenses, for any advertising costs, and for the costs of stabilizing the issue and distributing securities to syndicate members.

The spread

The difference between the public offering price ("POP") and the actual amount paid to the issuer is called the underwriter's "spread" or gross spread. This discount for the managing underwriter will vary according to the type of securities. Spreads are generally higher on common stocks than on preferred, higher on preferred than on bonds, and usually increase with smaller issues, more speculative issues or issues that are expected to be difficult to sell.

Management fee

In exchange for his extra responsibilities the manager of the syndicate usually receives some part of the spread on every share sold. This is called the management fee.

Underwriter's concession ("takedown")

Shares distributed by the rest of the syndicate earn the spread minus the management fee. The difference between this price and the POP is called the "underwriter's concession" or the underwriter's takedown.

Selling concession

Members of the selling group then can earn the "selling concession," a portion of the underwriter's concession.

Reallowance

Finally, for shares ultimately disposed of by non-members of the selling group, including syndicate members who require more shares than they are allotted by the syndicate managers, there is a reallowance that is typically less than half of the selling concession.

■ **EXAMPLE**

If the public offering price for a stock was $20. and the spread was $.75, then the managing underwriter would earn $.75 on each share that he sold. If the management fee was $.05 the syndicate members would earn an underwriter's concession or takedown of $.70 on shares that they distributed (and the manager would earn $.05). Members of the selling group would earn the selling concession, say $.40, leaving $.35 for the syndicate member which, of course, includes the $.05 management fee. Finally, a reallowance of $.20 might be earned by a non-member of the selling group who distributed shares. The selling group member then earns $.20 on these shares and the syndicate member the remaining $.30, never forgetting the additional $.05 management fee.

Discount to:	Manager	Underwriter's Concession	Selling Concession	Reallowance
	$.75	$.70	$.40	$.20
Price to:	Manager	Underwriter	Selling Group Member	Non-member
	$19.25	$19.30	$19.60	$19.80

NEW ISSUES OF MUNICIPALS

Though there are many similarities, the process of offering new municipal securities usually differs from new corporate offerings in important ways. Perhaps most significant is the fact that competitive bidding by underwriters—rarely required with corporate issues—is the rule. Indeed, it is required by law in most states for general obligation municipal bonds.

Where there is competitive bidding, prior contact with underwriters is strictly forbidden. Competition occurs in the sense that syndicates bid for this issue and for the right to resell it to the public. To begin with, the issuer publishes an official Notice of Sale which describes details of the proposed new offering. The underwriters submit sealed bids, and the bid that provides the lowest net interest cost (NIC) to the issuer wins the competition. Sometimes bids are stated in terms of True Interest Cost (TIC), which also takes into account the time value of money. However, it is the NIC which determines the winning bid.

Some firms act as financial advisors to municipalities. If such firms wish to participate in an underwriting, they must alert the issuer in writing of their intention, providing details on the amount of remuneration they expect to receive from the underwriting. This is particularly applicable in smaller municipalities where government officials may be part-time and may also practice law or work in financial businesses.

There are several sources of information on these matters. The most commonly used are:

The Blue List

This publication covers only the secondary market, showing yields to maturity on dealer-held inventories of municipal bonds. It provides a listing of the current supply of such bonds being offered by dealers. It contains no background information, not even bond ratings. An additional service of the *Blue List* is called *Munifacts*. This is a wire service which provides constantly updated information about prices and new issues.

Daily Bond Buyer

This publication indicates new issue market conditions, as it shows the "placement ratio," that is, what proportion of new issues placed on sale have actually been sold. It also includes the *Bond Buyer Index* which lists 20 bonds of 20-year terms and shows the average yield to maturity each month, thus indicating current interest rates in the market.

Additional indices are a G.O. index of eleven 20-year AA-rated bonds and a revenue bond index that consists of 25 three-year revenue bonds of different types—transportation, housing, etc. Lastly, it has the *Visible Bond Supply*, a listing of municipals scheduled to be sold in the coming 30 days. This is significant because if too many issues are entering the market, this will tend to lower the price of a new issue, and vice versa.

MUNICIPALS: BIDDING AND SELLING PROCEDURES

If a municipality or agency decides to issue securities in a situation requiring a competitive bid, it must publish an Official Notice of Sale in the financial press (usually the *Daily Bond Buyer*). This Notice must contain complete information about the proposed issue itself, and about bidding procedures. It includes:

- the date, time and place of sale
- a description of the issue (the purpose, type, and amount of securities; maturities and amounts maturing in each period)
- manner of bidding (oral or sealed written bid)
- class of bond (general obligation or revenue issue)
- agency or official authorizing the sale
- limits on interest rates (if there is a statutory ceiling)
- dates on which interest will be paid
- denomination of securities and form (book-entry, registered, etc.)
- minimum acceptable bid
- "good faith deposit" required with a sealed bid
- name of the bond attorney
- place and method of settlement
- right to reject any and all bids
- person authorizing the sale

Naturally, the Official Notice of Sale does not specify the underwriter nor the rating of the proposed issue. One difference between municipal underwriting and corporate underwriting is that municipal syndicates can take indications of interest from prospective investors even before they are awarded the issue. Investors can enter pre-sale orders knowing that the order will not be filled if the syndicate does not win the bidding.

The winning syndicate tries to sell the issue out as quickly as possible. Sometimes, the issue is completely sold out in pre-sale orders; if not, there is an "order period" during which the issue is sold. If an issue is over-subscribed, MSRB specifies a strict order for allocations of these bonds. This is:

1 Pre-sale orders.

2 Group net orders. These have the highest priority during the order period. An investor wishing highest priority stipulates as much. These orders are credited to the entire syndicate no matter which member brings them in.

3 Net designated orders. These are orders brought in by syndicate members in which an investor specifies who is to receive credit for the sale. For example, an order for 1,000 bonds might specify that 500 be credited to member A, 300 to member B, and 200 to member C.

4 Member at takedown (or member takedown orders). These are orders for bonds entered by a member and credited to that member only.

As an illustration of the compensation to underwriters consider the following example:

■ **EXAMPLE**

A $1,000 face value bond is bought by a syndicate for $975, giving a spread of $25. Suppose the manager's fee is $4 (that is, the manager collects $4 for each bond sold), and the syndicate fee is $6 (*i.e.*, $6 goes into a syndicate account for each bond sold). This syndicate account is then divided among the members. A syndicate member with a 5% participation would get 5% of the syndicate account value.

For all pre-sale orders (item 1 above), the $15 remaining after the manager's and syndicate's fees are deducted (the "takedown") also goes into the syndicate account. Similarly, for group net orders (item 2) the remaining $15 is deposited to the syndicate account.

For net designated orders, however, the takedown is distributed to the members in proportion to their participation as specified by the investor. In the illustration above, member A gets $15 on 500 bonds, B on 300, and C on 200 bonds.

Members at takedown (item 4 above) receive the takedown for the entire order.

Finally if these orders do not sell out the issue, and a member of the selling group (but not a syndicate member) gets an order, he or she can buy the bond with a concession—a portion of the takedown—and the remainder is added to the syndicate account. In this example, if the selling group member receives $7, then $8 goes into the syndicate account.

Before the underwriter will buy the issue, he customarily ensures that the legal opinion (see Chapter 2) is on the face of the bond or attached to it. If this is missing, the bond is not in "good delivery form." Such bonds can be traded (as "ex legal"), though usually only at a discount.

Since municipals always trade "with interest," newly-issued securities always include the "dated date," *i.e.*, the day on which interest begins to accrue. New issues are usually traded "when issued."

This announcement is not an offer to sell or a solicitation of an offer to buy any of these securities.
The offering is made only by the Prospectus.

NEW ISSUE   September 30, 1986

2,148,315 Shares

M. A. Hanna Company

$2.125 Convertible Exchangeable Preferred Stock

The shares of $2.125 Convertible Exchangeable Preferred Stock, with a liquidation preference of $25 per share, of the Company are convertible at the option of the holder at any time, unless previously redeemed, into shares of the Common Stock of the Company at a conversion price of $24.875 per share, subject to adjustment under certain conditions.

The Preferred Stock also is exchangeable in whole at the option of the Company on any dividend payment date beginning December 30, 1989, for the 8.50% Convertible Subordinated Debentures Due December 30, 2016 of the Company at the rate of $25 principal amount of Debentures for each share of Preferred Stock. The Debentures, if issued, will be convertible at the option of the holder at any time, unless previously redeemed, into shares of Common Stock at a price equivalent to the conversion price applicable to the Preferred Stock for which the Debentures were exchanged.

Price $25 Per Share

plus accrued dividends, if any, from date of issuance.

Copies of the Prospectus may be obtained in any State in which
this announcement is circulated only from such of the Underwriters as are qualified to act as dealers in securities in such State.

PaineWebber Incorporated		The First Boston Corporation
Bear, Stearns & Co. Inc.	Alex. Brown & Sons Incorporated	Dillon, Read & Co. Inc.
Donaldson, Lufkin & Jenrette Securities Corporation	Drexel Burnham Lambert Incorporated	A. G. Edwards & Sons, Inc.
Goldman, Sachs & Co.	Hambrecht & Quist Incorporated	E. F. Hutton & Company Inc.
Kidder, Peabody & Co. Incorporated	Lazard Frères & Co.	Merrill Lynch Capital Markets
Montgomery Securities	Morgan Stanley & Co. Incorporated	Prudential–Bache Securities
L. F. Rothschild, Unterberg, Towbin, Inc.	Salomon Brothers Inc	Shearson Lehman Brothers Inc.
Smith Barney, Harris Upham & Co. Incorporated	Wertheim & Co., Inc.	Dean Witter Reynolds Inc.

Figure 6.2   Tombstone

TERMS

Investment bankers Middlemen between corporation seeking capital and investors; cannot be commercial bank

Underwriter Buys securities from issuer and resells to public

Primary Offerings Previously unissued securities, proceeds directly to issuer; cannot be bought on margin

Secondary Offerings Securities held by individual owners, proceeds directly to seller; margin purchases permitted

Split offering or combined distribution Both primary and secondary offering in one issue

Private placement Securities not available to public, SEC registration not required

Underwriting agreement Contract between issuer and investment banker, must be filed with the SEC

Firm commitment Underwriter/investment banker buys full offering and guarantees proceeds to issuer; *i.e.*, acts as a principal

Best efforts Underwriter assumes no financial liability, acts as agent

All or None Best effort within a time limit, cancelled if entire issue not sold in that time

Standby Issuer tries to sell directly to investors, investment banker stands by to assist in selling any remaining shares

Mini-max Firm commitment to sell portion of issue, best effort with the balance

Market-out clause Agreement can be cancelled in case of a dramatically unfavorable turn of events

Managing underwriter(s) Underwriter(s) who form a syndicate

Agreement among underwriters Details arrangements between members

Divided (Western) Account Each member liable only for agreed-upon participation

Undivided (Eastern) Account Each member responsible both for its own and other members' participation

Selling group Put together by managing underwriter to help market issue, takes no financial responsibility

Retained shares ("retention") Securities held by syndicate and sold directly, not through the selling group

Firm subscription Selling group members commitment to sell a certain amount

Selling concession Amount received by selling group

Registration New issues generally must be registered with SEC, statement provides full disclosure

Cooling-off period 20-day period after statement filed to allow SEC review, can be extended

Effective date Date when securities may be sold to investors

Preliminary prospectus May be issued during cooling-off period

Blue-skying Registering issue in each state where securities are to be sold

Due diligence meeting Underwriters, corporate officers review registration statement and final prospectus, establish final public offering price, spread and sales concession

Final prospectus Must go to all purchasers

Tombstone announcement May be placed when sales begin, provides basic information, not an advertisement

Opening the books Sales begin

Closing the books At discretion of managing underwriter

Stabilizing the issue Underwriter may buy securities back at or below public offering price to keep the issue from losing value too quickly

Hot issues Where public demand exceeds existing supply

Overallotment In hot issue, underwriter can allot or sell more securities than actually exist, and buy up shares offered for resale; any profits or losses incurred are pro-rated among syndicate members

Spread Difference between public offering price and amount paid issuer

Management fee Portion of spread given syndicate manager

Underwriter's concession or takedown Spread minus the management fee

Selling concession Selling group member's portion of underwriter's concession

Reallowance Amount allotted for shares sold by non-members of selling group or by syndicate members who require more shares than allotted

Municipal Securities Underwriting usually by competitive bidding, issuing agency must examine market

Blue List Covers secondary market, showing yields to maturity, lists dealer-held inventories, publishes *Munifacts* wire service

Daily Bond Buyer Shows proportion of new issues actually sold

Bond Buyer Index Shows average yield to maturity on selected bonds

Visible Bond Supply List of municipals to be sold in next 30 days

Official Notice of Sale Must contain complete information about proposed issue and bidding procedures

Precedence for filling muni orders
□ pre-sale orders
□ group net orders
□ net designated orders
□ members at takedown

Good delivery form Bond with legal opinion, otherwise bonds can only be traded "ex legal"

Dated date Day on which interest begins to accrue

Blue Sky Laws State laws dealing with registration of representatives and securities

REVIEW QUESTIONS

1. The preliminary prospectus would contain all of the following EXCEPT:

   (A) a description of the uses to which the funds will be put
   (B) the names of the officers of the company
   (C) the offering price
   (D) a disclaimer of SEC approval

2. In an underwriting syndicate arrange the following in order from largest to smallest:

   I.   underwriting spread
   II. reallowance
   III. selling concession

       (A) II, III, and I
       (B) III, II, and I
       (C) I, II, and III
       (D) I, III, and II

3. If the manager says that the retention is 80% for an underwriter who has 100,000 shares, the shares available to that underwriter for his own customers is:

   (A) 20,000
   (B) 80,000
   (C) 100,000
   (D) 100,000 plus 80% of the remainder

4. Which of the following occurs during the cooling-off period?

   (A) stabilization
   (B) reallowance
   (C) due diligence meetings
   (D) setting of the final price

5. The selling price of a new issue is affected by all of the following EXCEPT:

   (A) anticipated earnings
   (B) the underwriter's feel for the market
   (C) the selling group
   (D) anticipated dividends for the first year

6. An underwriter in an Eastern account has a 15% participation. The underwriting is for $10 million and he has sold $1.5 million.

If $1 million remains unsold what is his liability?

   (A) nothing
   (B) $100,000
   (C) $150,000
   (D) $1 million

7. A broker who is a member of the selling group would get which of the following discounts?

   (A) spread
   (B) concession
   (C) takedown
   (D) reallowance

8. Which of the following is not allowed to the manager of an underwriting?

   (A) Increasing the number of shares offered
   (B) Increasing the offering price
   (C) Stabilizing after distribution begins
   (D) Setting aside some percentage of each member's share, for institutional buying

9. If an investment banker may return to the issuer all securities not sold, we have a:

   (A) best effort offering
   (B) contingency offering
   (C) firm commitment
   (D) limited offering

10. Another name for a tombstone is:

    (A) preliminary prospectus
    (B) final prospectus
    (C) request for bids
    (D) announcement of a new offering

11. An investment banker is likely to participate in which of the following?

    I.   Arranging a 6-month loan
    II. Arranging a 15-year bond issue
    III. Participating in a third market distribution
    IV. Arranging a new issue of securities

        (A) I and III
        (B) II and IV
        (C) II, III, and IV
        (D) All of the above

Questions 12–15 are based on the following information: A Western syndicate agrees to purchase 10 million shares from a corporation for a total of $89 million. These are to be offered to the public at $10 per share.

12. If the manager is to receive $.10 per share then the underwriter's concession is:

(A) $1.00 per share
(B) $1.10 per share
(C) $1.20 per share
(D) subject to further negotiation

13. If an underwriter with a 10% share has sold 900,000 shares and if the entire syndicate has sold 8 million shares this underwriter is responsible for an additional:

(A) 100,000 shares
(B) 200,000 shares
(C) 1,000,000 shares
(D) 2,000,000 shares

14. If the selling group concession is $.40, then a member of the selling group would receive:

(A) $.40 per share
(B) $.60 per share
(C) $.70 per share
(D) none of the above

15. Which of the following would be an example of stabilizing?

(A) A pre-sale bid of $11
(B) A pre-sale bid of $9
(C) A post-distribution bid of $11
(D) A post-distribution bid of $9

16. If an underwriter agreed to an All or None offering he would:

(A) take all of the unsold issue for his account
(B) take none of the unsold issue for his account
(C) sell all of the issue to an institution
(D) sell all of the issue or return it all to the issuer

17. Which of the following new issue debt instruments is most likely to be purchased through competitive bidding?

(A) corporate debentures
(B) corporate adjustment bonds
(C) municipal general obligation bonds
(D) municipal water and sewer bonds

18. A "best effort" underwriting can be characterized as one where the underwriter is a(n)

(A) broker
(B) dealer
(C) principal
(D) owner

19. A firm is to make its first public offering. The firm is located in New York and does some business in New Jersey and Connecticut and therefore the broker will offer the shares in those two states as well. Which of the following hold?

I. registration takes place in New York only
II. blue-sky laws of all three states must be satisfied
III. tombstones must be published in all three states
IV. registered reps must be licensed in any state in which they sell the issue

(A) I and III
(B) II and III
(C) II and IV
(D) II, III, and IV

20. The solicitation of an investment letter from a prospective purchaser is normally associated with:

(A) secondary distributions
(B) private placements
(C) no-load funds
(D) Rule 144 distributions

21. A new stock offering suggests that between 2 million and 2.5 million shares will be sold depending on the market. This is called a:

(A) conditional underwriting
(B) best effort
(C) all-or-none underwriting
(D) mini-max offering

22. A "due diligence" meeting is called for a new issue in order to:

    (A) establish the reallowance and the selling concession
    (B) set the final price of the offering
    (C) allow the underwriter to meet with the issuing firm
    (D) all of the above

Questions 23–25 are based on the following information: An initial offering of Consolidated Amalgamated Incorporated is to be underwritten by a syndicate. Of the 10 million shares being offered, 2.5 million are allocated to the selling group. The public offering price is $18 per share, of which CAI is to get $17. Assume the management fee is set at $.15 and the selling concession is $.60.

23. How large is the spread?

    (A) $.40
    (B) $.60
    (C) $.85
    (D) $1.00

24. What does the managing underwriter get for his services?

    (A) $ 400,000
    (B) $ 850,000
    (C) $1,000,000
    (D) $1,500,000

25. How much will a syndicate member realize on each share that he sells to a member of the selling group?

    (A) $.25
    (B) $.40
    (C) $.60
    (D) $.85

ANSWERS TO REVIEW QUESTIONS

1. (C) The price is not set until just before distribution begins.

2. (D) The underwriting spread is the largest. From this the selling concession would be offered to the selling group who might in turn offer a reallowance to others.

3. (A) The retention is those shares that are retained by the syndicate for group sales.

4. (C) All of the others occur later.

5. (C) The selling group does not take part in the price setting.

6. (C) In an Eastern account each underwriter is jointly and severally responsible. Therefore, this underwriter is responsible for 15% of the unsold shares.

7. (B) The concession goes to members of the selling group.

8. (B) The price may never be changed after the offer price has been made; however, a lower bid may be made to help stabilize the issue.

9. (A) The underwriter makes his "best effort" and the issuer accepts whatever he gets.

10. (D) The tombstone is merely an announcement.

11. (B) (I) would be done by a bank and (III) involves listed stocks, not new issues.

12. (A) The total spread is the difference between the offering price, $10 and what the issuer receives, $8.90 less the $.10 manager's fee leaves $1.00.

13. (A) In a Western syndicate each underwriter is responsible for his share, in this case 10% of 10 million is 1 million shares.

14. (A) This is the definition of the selling concession.

15. (D) Stabilizing takes place only after distribution and at a price no higher than the offering price.

16. (D) The definition of "All or None."

17. (C) In most cases this is a legal requirement.

18. (A) The underwriter does not actually buy the issue but rather takes a commission for any shares sold.

19. (C) The issue must be registered in any state where it is offered. The tombstone is not required anywhere.

20. (B) The letter asserts that the investor is sophisticated and aware of the risks.

21. (D) The lower bound is a firm commitment, the rest is on a best efforts basis.

22. (C) The meeting allows a review of the registration statement and the final prospectus.

23. (D) The difference between the price and what the issuer gets.

24. (D) $.15 × 10 million shares.

25. (A) After the $.15 management fee and the $.60 selling concession, there is $.25 left.

CHAPTER SEVEN

Over-the-counter market (OTC)

THE FOUR MARKETS

Traders distinguish four types of transactions:

□ trading of listed securities on an exchange

□ trading of unlisted securities over-the-counter (These are called the "secondary market" or "after market" to distinguish them from new issue transactions, which are known as the "primary market.")

□ "third market" refers to trading of listed securities in OTC markets. This occurs, for example, with some listed securities that can be traded only by members of the listing exchange, but can be sold over-the-counter to a non-member broker/dealer. Third market transactions are also popular with institutional traders who do not want to place a large block of stock on an exchange at one time as such an action might depress the price of the security.

□ "fourth market"—direct trades between institutions, for example, mutual funds or insurance companies, without using any middleman or broker. Some of these transactions take place through "Instinet."

OVER-THE-COUNTER TRADING

The term "over-the-counter" or OTC is used to describe securities trading that does not take place on an exchange. There is no single centralized marketplace for this trading. Rather, individual firms are willing to make a market (have an inventory from which they are willing to buy and sell to others) in some securities. Different firms make a market in different securities, although a single firm may make a market in several securities.

The types of securities that are traded over-the-counter include all securities not listed on an exchange, of course, but any security can be traded over-the-counter. There are significant differences between trading on an exchange (discussed in Chapter 8) and OTC trading.

Differences between OTC and exchange markets

The exchanges are auction markets, with transactions made on the exchange floors, subject to the rules of the exchanges and with prices determined by bidding. In the OTC market, price is reached through negotiation: someone who wishes to buy will make a bid; someone who wishes to sell will ask or offer a certain price. The difference between bid and asked price is called "the spread."

OTC transactions are governed by NASD rules. On the exchanges, there are "listing requirements" which a security must meet in order to be eligible for exchange trading. In contrast, in the OTC market there are no such requirements. These exchange requirements set certain minimums for capitalization, number of shares outstanding, and breadth of ownership. Thus most unlisted securities tend to be smaller and newer than—though not necessarily inferior to—those traded on an exchange.

Types of issues traded OTC

In addition to unlisted securities, traders generally prefer the OTC market for closely-held issues, for high-value shares, and for instruments that tend to be traded in large blocks.

The following securities—listed and unlisted—are commonly traded over-the-counter: shares of bank and trust companies and insurance companies, U.S. government securities, municipal bonds, open-end investment company (mutual fund) shares, new issues, corporate bonds, foreign securities, and ADRs. Overall, more issues of all types are traded over-the-counter than on the exchanges, although overall trading volume is greater on the exchanges.

THE MARKET-MAKER

Some over-the-counter dealers "make a market" in certain securities. In some respects, the market-maker is like a stock specialist (see page 153) but he acts as a dealer, not a broker.

In general, the market-maker owns (has a position in) a particular security and sells to or buys from customers—individual investors, or other broker/dealers. Earnings come from a markup or markdown rather than from a commission. The market-maker regularly publishes bid and offer quotes and stands ready to buy or sell securities at the quoted price.

BROKER OR DEALER

It is important to distinguish between an agent acting as broker and one acting as dealer:

A dealer sells securities to (or buys securities from) a customer from (or for) his own inventory. This is acting as a principal. The dealer earns money on the difference between the price he is willing to pay and the price he will sell at. This is called the *markup*.

A broker acts as an agent, bringing a buyer and seller together, or buying for a customer from a market-maker and charging a fee, or commission, for this service. In OTC transactions, the price the customer pays, including the markup, is called the "net price."

One may not act as broker and dealer in one transaction—i.e., one cannot earn both a markup and a commission.

However, "dual agency" is possible. The broker can act as agent for both buyer and seller *and can earn commissions on both transactions*. This must, however, be disclosed when confirming the transaction.

CONFIRMATION

When a trade is completed, the broker/dealer must send the customer a written notice of confirmation. For trades between dealers, this confirmation must be sent by the end of the first business day after the trade date. For trades involving retail customers, confirmation must be sent by the date on which the transaction is completed (the settlement date).

The notice of confirmation must say whether the broker/dealer acted as a broker or a dealer. If as a broker, the confirmation must include the name of the other party to the transaction (or an offer to provide the name) and the amount of commission earned. If the firm acted as dealer, selling from its inventory, it need not disclose the amount of markup; however, if it buys the securities for immediate resale to the customer in what is known as a "riskless" trade, it must disclose the amount of markup.

TYPES OF QUOTES

In the OTC market, quotes can be "subject" or "firm."

"Subject Quotes"

The quoted price is subject to confirmation. The quoting broker/dealer may or may not buy or sell at this price. Here are samples of subject quotes:

"It is quoted 15 - 15½" (where 15 is bid, 15½ offered).

"It is 15 - 15½ subject."

A variation is the "work out" quote. This indicates a possible buying or selling price if the broker/dealer is given time to execute the order. Such a quote might occur when a broker/dealer has so many buy and sell orders for a particular security that he must "work out" his position before filling an order. The quote "15 - 17 work out" means that any trade will be executed in that range.

"Firm Quote"

This is the actual buying or selling price for a security (sometimes called "actual quote"). Examples would be:

"It is 15 - 15½."

"The market is 15 - 15½."

A dealer giving a firm quote must be ready and able to buy or sell at the quoted price in a quantity equal to at least one usual trading unit—usually 100 shares of stock or five bonds.

"Bid or Offer Wanted"

When a broker/dealer wants to trade in a security, but is receiving no orders, he may make a "bid wanted" ("BW") quote. This shows no price, but requests bids from potential buyers. Conversely, an "offer wanted" ("OW") comes from a broker/dealer seeking possible sellers of a particular security. These are usually found in the "sheets" described on page 139.

TYPES OF ORDERS

Because the OTC is a negotiated market, there are basically two types of orders allowed, Market Orders and Limit Orders.
The various kinds of Stop Orders are not allowed.
In a Market Order the customer asserts that he is willing to pay (or receive) the best currently available price. In a Limit Order he says that he will pay no more than (accept no less than) some specified amount, his limit. Either order may be for one day only or may remain open until it is filled or cancelled.

■ **EXAMPLE**

A client puts in an order to buy 100 ACI "at the market." If your firm makes a market in ACI and it is currently 20 - 21, you would sell them to the client at 21. If you did not make a market in that stock, you would call a market-maker and buy from him. If you bought at 21 you would sell it to the client at 21 and would charge a commission of perhaps $.80 per share bringing the cost to $2,100 plus $80 in commission.

WHOLESALE AND RETAIL TRADING

A trade between brokers is a wholesale transaction. A trade between a firm and a client is called a retail transaction. A market-maker or a broker/dealer who trades only with other dealers or with large institutions is called a wholesale trader. Dealers who sell to the public (often after buying from wholesalers) are said to operate in the retail market. In general, the spread between the bid and offer price is greater in the retail market.

THE NASDAQ SYSTEM

The channel for negotiating many over-the-counter prices is the NASD Automated Quotation Service, or NASDAQ. This electronic system links broker/dealers, market-makers, and others through a network of computer terminals. It gives quotes by registered market-makers on authorized securities, as well as some indications of trading volume. Note that NASDAQ is not an up-to-the-minute record of trades. It shows the volume of trading for each security at day's end, not trades or volume as they occur.

There are three levels of NASDAQ quotes. Level 1 is essentially for retail trade. It provides the highest bid and lowest offer (the inside price) currently available. Level 2 shows all market-makers and their current bids and offers. Finally, Level 3 is used by market-makers. It allows them to enter changes in their current quotations. Thus, an order room would see the quotes and the firms making them on its Level 2 but only a Level 3 system would enable one to make changes in a current quote. *All of these quotes are firm quotes.*

Requirements for NASDAQ listing

To be included in the NASDAQ system, securities must be registered under the Securities Act of 1934 or the Investment Company Act of 1940, have at least 100,000 publicly-held shares and at least 300 shareholders. In addition, to be listed:

- they must have a minimum bid price of $5
- the issuer must have capital and surplus of at least $1 million and assets of at least $2 million
- there must be at least two market-makers for domestic issues, three for foreign issues

To qualify for participation in NASDAQ, a market-maker:

- must remain open for business from 8:30 a.m. to 4:30 p.m. Eastern time
- must maintain a net capital position of at least $2,500 for each security in which he makes a market ($500 for securities priced at $5 or less)
- must execute a trade for at least the normal trading unit (100 shares of stock or 5 bonds) at the price shown on the screen when the order is received; in other words, the NASDAQ quote is a "firm quote"
- must provide bid and ask quotations
- must report volume for his securities daily and monthly

OTHER SOURCES OF OTC INFORMATION

The National Market System, NMS Introduced in 1982, the National Market System marked a significant improvement in providing information about the market. NMS provides up-to-the-minute reports of actual transactions and total volume, as well as the quote information available on

NASDAQ. Over 3/4 of the securities in NASDAQ are eligible for the NMS. The SEC encourages the inclusion of eligible issues and the Federal Reserve allows stocks in the NMS to be bought on margin.

Small Order Execution System A further improvement instituted in 1984, the Small Order Execution System (SOES) allows trades in NMS and NAS-DAQ stocks to be executed automatically at the inside price. Up to 1,000 shares for NMS stocks and up to 500 shares of NASDAQ stocks can be traded without contacting other brokers. Market and limit orders can be filled this way.

Computer-Aided Execution System The Computer-Aided Execution System (CAES) allows automatic execution of both listed securities and NMS stocks. There is some overlap with SOES, but CAES accepts listed (but not all NASDAQ) stocks and does not limit the size of the trade while SOES accepts NASDAQ (but not listed) stocks and limits the size of the trade.

The National OTC-NASDAQ list or "national list" Published daily in the *Wall Street Journal* and other financial pages, it includes issues with the highest trading volume (in dollar terms). Figures shown in these listings are the last dealer-to-dealer quotes for that day, not the public price (*i.e.*, they do not include commissions, markups or markdowns). These are "subject" quotes.

Additional list 950 additional issues that don't qualify for the national list.

Local lists Several separate lists are published in specific areas and include items of interest in those localities. These can include both NASDAQ and non-NASDAQ securities.

Pink sheets Published every business day, these sheets show the names and telephone numbers of market-makers and the subject quote of each market-maker. If there is no quote from a market-maker it will show a blank and will have OW (BW) if the market-maker is looking for offers (bids). These are inter-dealer "subject" quotes and do not include commissions or markups. NASDAQ stocks have their symbols listed and marginable stocks have an M preceding their listing.

Yellow sheets These sheets cover OTC trading in unlisted corporate bonds and their market-makers.

NASD MARKUP POLICY

NASD Rules of Fair Practice make reference to "fair" and "reasonable" prices and commissions. This has led to the "5% markup policy" for markups and markdowns in OTC trading. The basis for this markup is always the current offer to other dealers. Specifically, it is *not* the price which this dealer actually paid for the shares originally. That price is irrelevant. This is a guideline, not a firm rule; a greater (or lesser) percentage may be reasonable under certain conditions. Under the Rules, the following factors may be considered in deciding on the fairness of a markup (or commission):

Type of security For example, the markup percentage is usually higher on common stock than on a bond, higher on a more speculative than on a less speculative issue.

Market activity Markups should be lower on an actively-traded security. Unusual effort required to obtain an inactive security may justify a higher markup.

Price In general, the percentage markup goes down as the price of the security goes up as handling costs involved in trading low-priced issues are proportionately higher.

Dollar value of transaction Handling expenses may be greater, in percentage terms, with a small transaction.

Disclosure Telling a customer that the markup is high (and explaining why) does not itself justify unfair charges, though such a practice would be considered if a dealer were to be accused of imposing an excessive markup.

Patterns While each transaction must be fair, the pattern of a broker's markups overall will be considered.

Services offered Some broker/dealers provide more, or more elaborate, services for their clients, and such costs may be considered, to some degree, in deciding on the fairness of the markup. Note that "excessive expenses" cannot be used to justify unreasonable markups.

The 5% guidelines apply on the following types of OTC transactions:

"Riskless" or "simultaneous" transactions This is where a dealer has an order for a security and buys the same security to fill that order.

Sales from dealer's inventory The markup is calculated on the basis of the current market price. Profit (or loss) experienced because the dealer's inventory has appreciated (or depreciated) is not considered.

   The same rules apply when making purchases of securities from customers—the markdown (amount deducted from the price dealers bid in interdealer transactions) must be reasonable. Also, when acting as an agent in a transaction, the broker/dealer must charge a fair commission.

"Proceeds transactions" If a client sells securities to a dealer, and uses the proceeds of that sale to purchase other securities from the same dealer, this must be viewed as one transaction—*i.e.*, any profit or commission on the first part of the transaction must be considered in deciding on the fairness of the markup charged on the second part.

■ **NOTE**

The 5% is a guideline and some of the factors mentioned above may justify some modification. Also note that in calculating markup or markdown, one begins with the current offering (or bid) price of the security among dealers, not the dealer's original cost.

   This guideline does not apply to exempt securities. These include issues sold with a prospectus or at a specific public offering price, in other words to new issues (or registered secondary issues) or to open-end investment company shares.

OTC MUNICIPAL BOND TRADING

As all municipal bonds are traded OTC, it will be helpful to review some of the material covered in Chapter 2.

The primary source for information on municipal bond trading is the *Blue List*, the daily publication that lists the securities each dealer has available for sale. It describes the bonds, the quantity available, and the price (usually expressed in terms of yield to maturity). In addition, the *Blue List* offers a computer service showing current yield, which is displayed on a terminal.

The *Daily Bond Buyer*, a newspaper for the bond market, includes articles and statistics about bonds. It also provides indices of average yields for different categories of bonds and has a wire service with up-to-the-minute information about bonds, syndicates and winning bids.

Transactions between dealers are done on a concession basis. That is, they are sold at some given yield less a discount to the purchasing broker. For example, in a sale of 20 bonds at "8¼ less ⅜" the bonds are priced to yield 8¼% and the buyer received a concession of $75 (20 × $3.75).

TERMS

Types of transactions:

Trading of listed securities on an exchange

Trading of unlisted securities over-the-counter (OTC) "secondary market"

Third market Trading of listed securities OTC

Fourth market Direct trades between institutions

OTC trading Can involve any security, price reached through negotiation, transactions governed by NASD

Spread Difference between bid and asked price

Market-maker Like exchange specialist but acts as dealer, must maintain certain holdings, honor NASDAQ quotes, etc.

Dealer Acts as principal, sells or buys securities, earns a markup or markdown

Broker Acts as agent, earns commission

One party may not act as broker and dealer in one transaction

Subject quotes Price subject to confirmation

Work out quote Possible price given time

Firm quote Actual price to buy or sell at least one usual trading unit

Bid or offer wanted Request for bids or offers from potential buyers or sellers

Market order Customer will pay (or receive) best available price

Limit order Customer will pay no more than (accept no less than) specified amount

Stop orders Not allowed OTC

Time limits Orders may be for one day only, or good until filled or cancelled

NASDAQ NASD Automated Quotation Service, electronic link, gives firm quotes, volume only at day's end

National Market System, NMS Gives last-sale prices and current volumes for some NASDAQ securities

Small Order Execution System (SOES) For trades in NMS and NASDAQ stocks

Computer Aided Execution System (CAES) For executing orders for both listed securities and NMS stocks

The National OTC-NASDAQ List ("National List") Published daily in financial pages

Pink sheets Show market-makers and subject quotes from each

Yellow sheets Cover OTC trading in unlisted corporate bonds

Markup policy NASD Rules of Fair Practice call for "fair" and "reasonable" prices and commissions

5% markup policy Maximum for markups and markdowns, guideline, not a rule, does not apply to new issues or mutual fund shares, based on current offer

REVIEW QUESTIONS

1. In an agency transaction, an over-the-counter dealer would consider all of the following in determining the commission EXCEPT:

   (A) dollar value of the transaction
   (B) actual costs of execution
   (C) liquidity of the market for that security
   (D) original price to the dealer for the security

2. Which of the following are traded over-the-counter?

   I.   municipal bonds
   II. treasury bonds
   III. corporate bonds
   IV. common stocks

      (A) I and II
      (B) I and III
      (C) I, II, and III
      (D) I, II, III, and IV

3. Firm A acting for Firm B makes securities transactions not for Firm A's account. Firm A is said to be acting as a:

   (A) principal
   (B) broker
   (C) dealer
   (D) middleman

4. In an over-the-counter transaction, the "spread" refers to the:

   (A) mark-up from cost
   (B) difference between the current bid and asked
   (C) difference between purchase and sale prices
   (D) allowable charge on the transaction

5. All of the following are true of the over-the-counter market EXCEPT:

   (A) it is a negotiated market
   (B) it is a secondary market
   (C) it is an auction market
   (D) it handles large secondary distributions

6. On the NASDAQ System all of the following would be shown EXCEPT:

   (A) market-makers' change of quotes
   (B) transactions as they occur
   (C) report on daily volume
   (D) quoting requirements

7. An investor sells $50,000 of ACI and uses all of the proceeds to buy stock in CAI. A single firm acts as a dealer in both transactions. Which of the following is true?

   I.   each mark-up is determined separately
   II. a "fair" mark-up must take both transactions together
   III. this is illegal
   IV. this is a "proceeds transaction"

      (A) I only
      (B) I and IV
      (C) II and IV
      (D) III only

8. On the NASDAQ, Level III provides which of the following?

   (A) firm quotes
   (B) level quotes
   (C) subject quotes
   (D) negotiated quotes

9. A purchaser of stock from a market-maker in that stock can expect to pay:

   (A) no markup
   (B) a markup and a commission
   (C) a markup
   (D) a commission

10. Exchange-listed securities which are traded over-the-counter are involved in the:

   (A) first market
   (B) second market
   (C) third market
   (D) fourth market

11. If a dealer were said to have a position in a security he would:

   (A) own the security
   (B) have issued a position paper on this security
   (C) be recommending it
   (D) be in a position to acquire a large block of it

12. A market-maker has purchased stock for his account at prices ranging from $3 to $10, with an average of $8. If the stock is currently selling at 4 bid, 4¼ asked, NASD Rules of Fair Practice require him to base his offer on:

   (A) $3
   (B) $8
   (C) $10
   (D) the current market price

13. For over-the-counter securities, the inside market is:

   (A) the highest bid available coupled with the lowest offer
   (B) the bid and offer of any market-maker
   (C) the lowest bid available coupled with the highest offer
   (D) the narrowest bid and offer from some market-maker

14. Which of the following would be considered a firm quote?

   I. "We can do ACI at 20 - 20⅜"
   II. "ACI is 20 - 20⅜"
   III. The market in ACI is 20 - 20⅜"
   IV. "ACI is quoted around 20 - 20⅜"

   (A) I only
   (B) I and II only
   (C) III and IV
   (D) I, II, and III

15. In the over-the-counter market, stock prices are determined by:

   (A) negotiation between buyers and sellers
   (B) bidding among buyers
   (C) bidding among sellers
   (D) the 5% mark-up rule

16. A quote of "8.0 for one hour and five" means:

   (A) a firm offer of 8.50
   (B) a firm offer good for 1 hour and 5 minutes
   (C) a firm offer good for 1 hour
   (D) a firm offer of $8.05

17. The SOES:

   I. handles only National Market System shares
   II. is an automated trading system
   III. handles trades of no more than 1,500 shares
   IV. is part of the Computer-Assisted Execution System (CAES)

   (A) I and II
   (B) II and IV
   (C) I, II, and III
   (D) II and III

18. Which of the following is governed by the NASD 5% policy?

   (A) exchange distributions
   (B) underwriting spreads on new issues
   (C) simultaneous or riskless transactions
   (D) secondary distributions

19. Level I of the NASDAQ has:

   (A) the most recent transaction for every security
   (B) the highest bid and the lowest offer for every security
   (C) average bid and offers for each security
   (D) none of the above

20. A pension fund buys 10,000 shares of ACI from some other fund. We would call this a trade on the:

   (A) second market
   (B) third market
   (C) fourth market
   (D) over-the-counter market

ANSWERS TO REVIEW QUESTIONS

1. (D) As an agent he charges a commission. The first three are relevant to this commission.

2. (D) All four are traded OTC although some stocks and bonds are also traded on exchanges.

3. (B) Choices A and C are incorrect and D is not common usage.

4. (B) This spread is the quote that a customer would get.

5. (C) The exchanges are auction markets.

6. (B) There are no transactions reported on NASDAQ.

7. (C) It is not "fair" to charge for two transactions.

8. (A) These are always firm quotes, however, they can be changed at will.

9. (C) A commission would be charged by a broker and it is illegal to charge both.

10. (A) None of the other choices describe having a position.

11. (A) None of the other choices describe having a position.

12. (D) The 5% rule applies to the current price.

13. (A) The quote which has the "inside track."

14. (D) Only IV is not a firm quote.

15. (A) It is a negotiated market.

16. (C) An offer good for 1 hour with a five minute warning that someone else wants to accept.

17. (D) It is an automated system which handles up to 1,000 shares of NMS and 500 shares of NASDAQ securities.

18. (C) None of the others come under the 5% rule.

19. (B) This is called the inside price.

20. (C) The fourth market represents trades between investors.

CHAPTER EIGHT

Exchange markets

An exchange market is a place where buyers and sellers come together to trade securities. The best-known and largest exchange is the NYSE, which handles well over half of all transactions. The AMEX, the Boston Stock Exchange, the Pacific Stock Exchange, the Midwest Stock Exchange, the Philadelphia Stock Exchange, and other exchanges have rules and procedures not unlike those of the NYSE. Therefore, our description of the NYSE will serve as a model for the others.

The NYSE is a large room dotted with booths known as "trading posts," staffed by "specialists," each of whom handles certain securities. All transactions in listed securities take place on the floor of that room.

The exchange is not itself involved in the market, though it acts to enforce certain rules to ensure fairness. A board of directors (the NYSE is a corporation) sets policy, decides which stocks are eligible for listing and who will be a member of the exchange, and approves specialists.

MEMBERSHIP

Membership is limited to 1,366 "seats" and is *open only to individuals*. Corporations or partnerships may not hold seats. Seats are sold by bid to any qualified person. The price varies according to demand and has ranged from under $50,000 to over $1,000,000. Brokerage firms can operate on the floor if a member of the firm (usually a partner or director) holds a seat; these are called member firms. Only a member of the exchange, or a person who has leased a seat from a member, can transact business on the floor. The board of directors (10 from the public, 10 exchange members and a full-time chairman who can vote only to break a tie) is chosen by a nominating committee of exchange members not on the board.

Categories of membership

Commission house brokers Act for themselves or for non-members; execute customers' orders for their firms and charge a commission for their services.

Floor brokers or "Two Dollar Brokers" Execute orders for other brokers when the latter are too busy to execute orders themselves. They usually charge a fee for each transaction (once $2, hence the name).

Registered trader or competitive trader Usually execute orders for their own account; if they do agree to act for others, they must give those orders strict priority.

Specialist or market-maker This role is discussed in detail below. The specialist is always at his post, the booth where the security he specializes in is traded. A broker will come to that booth to trade that security. The specialist will not handle every transaction in the stocks in which he specializes (most trades are handled directly between members) but he is responsible for all odd-lot trading (see page 156).

Bond members Deal exclusively in bonds.

Allied members Are allowed on the exchange floor, but not to trade. They include general partners, directors, and executives of member firms.

NYSE listing requirements

Only certain securities are traded on the NYSE, namely those listed there.
   To be eligible for listing on the NYSE, stocks must meet minimum requirements as to market value, number of shares outstanding, number of shareholders, and corporate earnings. These requirements are periodically changed.
   Directors also consider whether there is national interest in the firm (a corporation with strength concentrated in one region might be held to higher standards) and the general condition and future prospects of the corporation. The listing agreement requires that the firm solicit proxies and provide timely disclosure of information important to investors.

Delisting

The NYSE generally disapproves of delisting a corporation which remains eligible. However, a firm that wishes to be delisted can do so if:

□ holders of ⅔ of the outstanding common stock vote to delist *and*

□ holders of no more than 10% of outstanding shares object *and*

□ a majority of the corporation's directors agree

A corporation can be involuntarily delisted if it fails to issue proxies or issues non-voting common stock.

OPERATION OF THE EXCHANGE

Trading on the exchange involves a "double auction." In the usual auction, one seller hears bids from many potential buyers. This, however, is a two-way affair: buyers shout bids while sellers shout offers. In all cases, the highest bid and lowest offer prevail. Although prices are quoted per share, the basic trading unit is 100 shares (a round lot).

Thus, a broker who bids "29½" is willing to buy 100 shares at $29.50 each. One who offers "29¾" is willing to sell 100 shares at $29.75. A quote includes the current highest bid and lowest offer (*e.g.,* "29½ bid, 29¾ offered" or just "29½, 29¾"). The difference between bid and offer is called the spread.

A quote may also include the quantity being bid or offered ("quote and size"). For example, "29½, 29¾, 200 either way" would mean 200 shares are bid at 29½, 200 offered at 29¾. The same price quote followed by "100 by 300" or "1 by 3" would mean 100 bid, 300 offered. When no size is mentioned, all trades are for one round lot.

Auction rules

The minimum bid from a buyer must be ⅛ point higher than the last bid, from a seller ⅛ point lower. A bidder cannot enter a lower bid in an attempt to confuse other bidders. All bids must be audible; no secret deals are allowed.

Once all offers or bids are removed by a trade or trades, a new auction begins. Since so many transactions in a particular security take place at one trading post, exchange rules determine the order in which bids (and offers) must be considered.

Priority Since the highest price or best offer succeeds, the first to make a bid or offer at a given price is given priority. Only one individual can have priority, even if he is no longer at the trading post.

Precedence If more than one broker makes the high bid at the same time, the largest order prevails. For example, Broker A enters the highest bid of 25 for 400 shares of PDS. Simultaneously Broker B also bids 25 but for 700 shares. Broker C, who is offering 700 shares, must sell to B, as he can fill the order.

Parity If two or more members offer the same price at the same time for the same quantity (*i.e.,* no one has priority or precedence) they must match (usually by tossing a coin) to see who gets the order. In other words, once the priority order is filled, others who have offered the best price are equal. If one can fill all orders, he wins the bid; if more than one can fill all orders, the first to bid wins. If no one is first, they match.

TYPES OF ORDERS

Investors can enter different kinds of orders which limit transactions in terms of price, time or broker's discretion.

Market order

An order to move at the "best available price," *i.e.*, to buy or sell at the lowest offer or highest bid when the order is received. The customer knows the order will be executed, but not at what price.

Limit order

An order to buy or sell only at a specified price "or better," *i.e.*, a minimum selling price or a maximum buying price. If the limit is not reached, the order is not executed.

As a limit order is always entered above the current selling price (or below the current buying price), the broker will seldom be able to fill the order on the floor. So he usually leaves the order with a specialist to execute if and when the limit is reached.

The specialist enters such orders in his book (see page 154) in the order received. The most recent will not be executed until all those entered earlier are filled. A limit order can be partially filled, *e.g.*, on an order to sell 500 shares of ABC at $30 only 200 shares might be sold.

For a customer, the advantage of a limit order is that he knows what price he will receive (or pay) for a security. The disadvantage is that there is no assurance a transaction will take place: the limit may not be reached. Even if it is reached other orders may have priority.

Stop order

This also sets a specified price, but automatically becomes a market order when that price is reached. Thus, if the stop price is reached, execution is guaranteed—but not the price, as the transaction is executed at the next available price.

For example, consider an order to buy 200 XYZ at 80 on a stop. If successive transactions were 79, 79½, 80, the order would become a market order and the specialist would take the next offer whether it was at 80 or above (or below).

Both buy and sell stop orders can be entered. They are usually executed by a specialist since the stop price is not (usually) at the market price and a broker would be reluctant to wait at the booth until the order could be filled. Stop orders are used in two ways: to protect profits or limit losses, and (by technical traders) to trigger orders at support levels (see Chapter 12).

■ **EXAMPLE**

An investor is willing to risk $500 on the 100 shares of XYZ which he purchased at $55. By placing a sell stop order in at $50 he is assured that even if he is not following the stock carefully his loss will be limited to about $500 because if the price falls to $50 his sell stop becomes a market order and is automatically executed.

This same order could be used to protect a profit. If the customer in the previous example had actually bought XYZ at $25 and it was now trading at $55, he might still put in a sell stop at $50 guaranteeing himself most of his current profit. In a similar fashion an investor could use a buy stop if he currently were short (see Chapter 11).

Stop-limit orders

A stop order that automatically becomes a limit order (not a market order) once the stop limit is reached. For example, "Sell 100ABC at 50 stop 49½ limit." Though this avoids the risk of a stop order (not being filled at 50), there is the possibility that the market may move in the wrong direction once the stop price is reached, and the order might not be executed.

Time qualifications on orders

Day Order—good only until the close of trade that day, and cancelled if not executed by then. Orders are assumed to be day orders unless otherwise marked.

Good-till-Cancelled (GTC) or Open Order—valid until it is executed (or cancelled). Such orders are automatically cancelled twice a year: at the end of April and the end of October, to clear the specialist's book. They can then be immediately renewed and retain their priority order position.

Shorter term orders, good for a week or good for a month, are handled by the broker, who places a GTC order with the specialist, then cancels it. *It is the broker's responsibility to cancel such an order and a customer would not be liable for an order executed after his cancellation date.*

Not Held Order or Market Not Held

This is a market order with the additional proviso that the floor broker is given some leeway in filling it. If he feels that it should not be filled immediately he may wait to get a better price. The broker is, however, "not held" responsible if the order is not filled within a particular time or at a particular price. This type of order is often used with a large order where the broker may prefer to sell a little at a time.

Time qualifications on orders

At the opening An order to buy or sell at the opening price. If it is not executed then, it is to be cancelled.

At the close To be executed at the close of trading with no guarantee that it will be done at the closing price.

Other qualifications on orders

Fill or Kill This must be completed entirely immediately in one trade or the order is cancelled.

Immediate or Cancel Like Fill or Kill, but can be partially filled, the remainder is then cancelled.

All or None An order (for bonds only) that must be filled in its entirety or not at all. Unlike Fill or Kill it does not require immediate execution. The order can be either a market or a limit order.

Do Not Reduce (DNR) and Do Not Increase (DNI) The price named should not be adjusted for ex-dates or for stock splits.

Automated Order Execution Systems

Each exchange has an automated system to help speed the execution of relatively small orders. The NYSE has DOT (Designated Order Turn-around System) and Super DOT. Others, modeled on DOT, include PACE (Philadelphia Exchange Automated Communication and Execution System); MAX (Midwest Automated Exchange), and AUTO PER and AUTO AMOS for equity and options transactions on the AMEX.

With DOT, an order form completed by a registered representative is sent from the firm's wire room directly to the DOT system. The system looks for an order to sell that matches the order to buy; if the system does not already contain such an order, the buy order is directed to a specialist, bypassing the floor broker.

Orders can be both market and limit orders. The volume on the auto-mated systems continues to grow.

BLOCK TRADES

Because a large buy or sell order for a particular security can distort the market, the NYSE has developed special procedures for dealing with what are called block trades. With respect to these procedures, there is no fixed definition of a "block." The amount varies according to the typical volume of trading in a security, which can change from time to time.

The NYSE does record the number of trades involving 10,000 or more shares and calls them block trades but these are not the only trades for which the special procedures can be invoked. If a broker decides the market cannot absorb a particular large trade in some security, he can get permission from the exchange to use one of the special methods described below.

Block trade procedures may require notification of the SEC and some-times registration of the stock. In particular, notification is required if:

- the stock is not registered
- the stock was acquired through stock options
- the owner is an officer (or insider) of the firm
- the owner has more than 10% of the shares outstanding

The four basic methods are: special offer or bid, exchange distribution or acquisition, specialist block purchase or sale, and secondary distribution.

Special offer, special bid

This involves the sale (or purchase) of a large block. Special offer is an announcement on the tape, offering a block with no commission to the buyer. Trading is executed on the floor and reported on the tape. Price shown is net to buyer plus a commission which is offered as an inducement to brokers. If the offering is oversold, each bidder receives a proportionate share (*e.g.*, if 90,000 are offered, and bids for 100,000 shares are received, each bidder gets 90% of his bid).

Conversely, in a special bid, a firm will announce its intention to buy a large block at a price (and the commission it will pay) on the tape. Unless otherwise announced, the offer (or bid) must remain open for at least 15 minutes.

■ EXAMPLE

XYZ Pension Fund wants to sell 100,000 shares of Amalgamated Consolidated (ACI), currently at 23. After negotiations, your firm agrees to purchase the block at 21½ in a private transaction. With exchange permission, you then print notice of a special offer on the tape:

Myfirm Special Offer ACI 100,000s.23 less 1.

This means your firm is willing to pay $1 for every share ordered. As orders are received, they are crossed ("crossing" occurs when a member holds buy and sell orders within the current market for an equal number of shares of the same stock) on the floor and appear on the tape in the usual manner until the order is complete.

While this procedure is supposed to protect the seller from having his block drive the price down, news of the offer will sometimes affect the market. In such cases, the special offer can be withdrawn.

Special bid procedures are just the opposite of those outlined above. In either case the tape announces "deal is done" once the offer or bid is completed.

Exchange distribution (exchange acquisition)

The broker representing a client with a large sell (buy) order finds buyers (sellers) privately. When he has assembled enough orders to complete the transaction and with the approval of the exchange, he crosses the block on the floor of the exchange.

Notice of the sale appears on the tape once the transaction is completed but not before with the symbol DIST. All brokerage costs are paid by the seller (buyer), allowing the broker to attract buyers (sellers) with a lower (higher) net price.

■ EXAMPLE

Your client wants to sell 45,000 shares of ACI, now on the market at 25. After negotiation, your firm buys the stock for 24½ in a private transaction. Your sales people then offer these shares at 25 net, *i.e.*, the customer pays no commission. When they have sold 45,000 shares, those orders are accumulated into one block and brought onto the exchange floor with the sell order from your firm's account, and the two blocks are crossed. The transaction must take place during market hours and involve only member firms.

Specialist block purchase or sale

This is basically a private sale, where the broker feels that activity in a particular security is so thin that selling (buying) a block would cause a sharp drop (rise), yet the quantity involved does not justify a special bid or offer, or exchange distribution or acquisition.

A specialist block transaction may also be necessary when speedy execution is important. In a purchase, a broker will ask the specialist if he is interested in the block. As the specialist can expect to have to hold the securities in inventory for a time, he usually offers a price below the market.

The transaction, which must be approved by a floor governor of the exchange, is completed privately off the floor and never appears on the tape. *It also does not appear on the specialist's book.* A specialist block sale involves the same procedure on the sell side.

Secondary distribution

For an extremely large block of shares, the methods outlined above may not be practicable and the seller will turn to a secondary distribution. Some of these must be treated as new issues and require SEC registration, a cooling-off period, a prospectus, etc. (see Chapter 6). Others also resemble a new offering in that an underwriting syndicate is formed which buys the shares, then sells them to the public, but they are handled, with special permission, on the exchange.

A secondary distribution is announced on the tape, usually near the market close. The message will show the name of the head of the syndicate, the code for the stock, number of shares available, the price and the commission offered.

The stock is offered at a net price, *i.e.*, with no commission. After the announcement, trading in these securities takes place off the floor. *Although the other types of special block sales can involve only exchange members, non-members can participate in a secondary distribution because the number of securities involved is usually very large.*

THE SPECIALIST

To work properly, an exchange market must continuously offer the opportunity to buy and sell in an orderly fashion. Much of a specialist's work is directed to ensuring that such a market exists: he is ready to trade when no one else will and he acts to stabilize the market in the issues in which he is a specialist. Often several specialists will combine in partnerships or joint accounts. Specialists are selected by the exchange board of directors.

Exchange rules say the specialist is required to meet at least once a year with the officers of the corporation(s) whose securities he specializes in. However, neither the specialist nor his associates (including clerks) may serve as officers or directors of those corporation(s). They are also not permitted to participate in proxy contests in firms whose stock they are specialists in.

On the floor of the exchange, about 25% of the members are specialists. They act as both agents and dealers. As an agent, a specialist is in effect a broker's broker, filling orders for floor brokers. For this, he earns commissions from the floor broker's firm. As a dealer, the specialist buys or sells for his own account. When trading for his own account he *must* buy only on a downtick and sell only on an uptick. In short, he trades against the market to help stabilize it.

He plays a further stabilizing role by stepping in to buy or sell when no one else will. Specialists typically form specialist units as partnerships or joint accounts. They are required to meet minimum capital requirements as well as minimum requirements on maintaining positions in stocks for which they are specialists.

Trading rules for specialists

A specialist's trading practices are subject to specific restrictions. The specialist cannot accept orders from:

- officers, directors, or principal shareholders of a corporation in whose shares he is a specialist
- profit-sharing funds or pension funds
- a bank, trust company, insurance company, or investment company

In addition, the specialist:

- may not make a transaction for his own account that causes a stop order to be executed. Thus if the last transaction is at 47½ and he has a buy stop at 48, he may not offer stock at 48 himself. *In general, the specialist stops stock when he is acting as an agent. As a dealer he may not stop stock. Thus he may never stop stock for his own account.*
- may not buy or sell for his own account while holding a market order not yet executed. (Though he may buy while holding a sell order and vice versa.)
- may not buy (or sell) at a limit order before a customer recorded in his book
- may not, acting for his own account, trigger a limit order on his book
- may not act as both broker and dealer in the same transaction

One final, and important, restriction on a specialist is that he may not "cross" orders without first offering the stock higher than his bid (*e.g.*, if a specialist has an order to buy 300 shares at 32 from one broker, and an order to sell the same quantity at the same price from another broker, he must ask 32⅛ or more (or bid 31⅞ or less) in an attempt to get a better price before making a cross).

The specialist's book

To keep his transactions as an agent firmly separated from his transactions as a dealer, the specialist enters other broker's orders in his book. These are kept according to price, and within each price in the sequence in which they were received. This book is closed to all but exchange or SEC officials.

The specialist accepts only limit and stop orders (no market or not held orders) on either a day or GTC basis. A day order re-entered as a GTC order is treated as a newly-entered order and is placed last in line.

Each page is headed by the symbol for the stock and usually covers only one point beginning with the point and ending at 7/8. See Figure 8.1.

A specialist will always quote the highest bid and lowest offer currently in his book, *i.e.*, the price at which a market order to buy or sell can be immediately executed. Thus with ACI, as shown in Figure 8.1, the quote would be "20¼ - 20½," meaning he will execute a buy order at 20¼ or a sell order at 20½.

The specialist may quote prices more favorable than those in his book. For example, floor brokers or other specialists trading in one of "his" stocks may make a higher bid (say 20⅜ in our example), so the current quote becomes "20⅜ - 20½."

SPECIALIST'S BOOK

BUY	ACI	SELL
	20	
2 ML	⅛	
1 DW		
3 BACHE		
1 DW (STOP)	¼	
2 SCHWAB		
	⅜	
	½	3ML
		1 SCHWAB
	⅝	2 DW
		I DREX
		2ML
	¾	
	⅞	

Figure 8.1   Page from Specialist's Book

While he may not show his book, the specialist will, on request, announce the number of shares at the current quotation level *but not above or below these levels*. Thus, "300 by 400" or "3 by 4" indicates the 300 buy and 400 sell orders in ACI.

It is not always possible for the specialist to execute limit orders, even though the limit price is reached. He may be holding earlier orders ("stock ahead"). In the illustration, the 300 to buy for Bache would not be filled even if 300 were sold, since Merrill would get 200 and DW 100 before that order could be filled; or he may lose a match.

Stopping stock

If—and only if—a broker asks, the specialist can agree to "stop" an order. This means he guarantees to execute a market order at the current price, while allowing the broker a (usually short) time to shop for a better price. The specialist must honor his guarantee, that is, must buy or sell at the stop price, even if he has failed to act on time. Under NYSE rules, a specialist:

□ cannot stop stock for his own account, for another specialist in the same stock, or for another exchange member. *Stopping is for public orders only.*

□ cannot stop stock unless the currently quoted spread is greater than the minimum (in other words, ¼ point or more)

□ cannot reduce the size of an offer on his book once a stop is granted

□ cannot guarantee the stop once another trade has been executed at the stop price (except to correct an error)

Again using Figure 8.1, the specialist could buy for his own account at $20\frac{3}{8}$ since any lower purchase would trigger the stop. In the same way he could sell from his own account at $20\frac{3}{8}$.

"Arranging the opening"

Before trading begins for the day, the specialist will review orders received since the previous close (often from foreign clients), and attempt to match them so the day's trading will begin in an orderly fashion.

If the volume of buy orders considerably exceeds the volume of sell orders (or vice versa), the price may move swiftly up (or down) at the opening. To prevent this, the specialist will often supply (buy) stock from (for) his own account. If this is not possible, and the security will open significantly up or down ($2 on stocks at $20 or more, $1 on stocks less than $20) from its previous closing price, he must get exchange approval to open at the new price and the symbol OPD (opening delayed) appears on the tape.

If supply and demand are grossly unequal, the specialist may not begin trading until late in the day or not at all. In the most extreme situation, the specialist may ask the exchange governors to halt trading in the security.

Ex-sales and the specialist

Once a stock goes ex-dividend or ex-rights, it often drops in price. Thus the specialist reduces the price in his book on certain orders entered below the current market. These are:

Open Buy Limit Orders   Open Sell Stop Orders

(Remember the initials OBLOSS.) These are orders where the buyer (or seller) is interested in the "value" of the security.

Orders entered above the current market are not changed:

Open Sell Limit   Open Buy Stop

DNR (do not reduce) orders are also not changed. Since dividends may not exactly equal a trading unit, the specialist rounds to the next lowest $\frac{1}{8}$, *e.g.*, a dividend of 55 cents would mean a reduction down $\frac{5}{8}$.

■ **EXAMPLE**

If Consolidated Amalgamated Inc. (CAI) selling at $30\frac{1}{4}$ goes ex-dividend of $.70, the specialist (rounding up to $\frac{3}{4}$) would reduce a limit order to buy at 29 to the new price of $28\frac{1}{4}$ and a sell stop order at $29\frac{5}{8}$ would be lowered to $28\frac{7}{8}$. A buy stop at 34 and a limit sale at 32 would be unaffected. Similarly, any order marked DNR would be unchanged.

ODD-LOT TRADING

Orders to buy or sell less than a round lot (usually 100 shares) are also handled by the specialist. In these transactions, he acts as a principal. Only round-lot transactions appear on the tape. A specialist may buy several odd lots adding up to a round lot. If he then trades those shares, the transaction will appear on the tape.

Share price in an odd-lot purchase is based on the round-lot price, so an odd-lot order cannot be executed until a round-lot sale of that security has been recorded. This is called the "effective sale price." Most specialists charge a "differential fee" for handling odd-lots, usually ⅛ point (12.5 cents) per share, buy or sell.

"Part round lot" is the term for an odd-lot order entered as part of a round lot, for example, 150 shares. The odd-lot portion is executed at the round-lot price.

"Bunched orders" If several customers (or one broker acting for several accounts) enter odd-lot buy or sell orders, they can be bunched into a round lot with customer approval. Dividing round lots into odd lots is not allowed.

Types of odd-lot orders

Odd-lot orders can be market, limit or stop orders. A market order is executed at the next round-lot buy or sell price, plus the differential. Short sales in odd lots are subject to the plus-tick and zero-plus-tick rules based on the next round-lot sale.

■ **EXAMPLE**

A market order to buy 70 shares of CAI would be executed after the next round-lot transaction. If this occurred at 25½ (the effective price), the order would be filled at 25⅝ (the execution price). At the same time, a market order to sell 30 shares would be executed at 25⅜.

Limit orders are handled similarly to those for round-lots, but must consider the differential. A buy limit order, for instance, is based on the first round-lot sale *below* the odd-lot limit by at least ⅛ point. Thus, a buy limit order for 70 shares at 28 would not be executed until the stock reached 27⅞. Similarly, a sell limit of 50 shares at 28 would not be executed until the price reached 28⅛. In both cases the customer would then be assured of getting at least the price that he set.

Stop orders Odd-lot stop orders are also handled as with round lots, and are allowed on both the NYSE and the American Exchange. Thus an odd-lot stop is triggered by the first round-lot sale at or above the stop price on a buy order (at or below on a sell order), and is executed on the next round-lot sale, whatever the price. The differential is not considered.

■ **EXAMPLE**

With the market at 31 for ACI, an order to buy 40 shares at 31½ on a stop is received. Subsequent round-lot trades occur at 31⅜, 31½ and 31¾. The client's order would be triggered by the 31½ and become a market order. The *next* sale at 31¾ would be the effective price and the customer would pay 31⅞. A sell stop would work in the opposite direction.

BOND TRADING

Most corporations which list their stocks on the exchange also list their bonds. However, trading on the exchange is relatively light as most bonds are traded in over-the-counter markets. Bond brokers typically act as broker's brokers for a "give-up commission" since the volume and trading does not warrant individual firms maintaining their own operation. The exchange bond room includes the "free" or "active" crowd, and the "cabinet" crowd.

Types of trading

Active trading involves verbal bids and offers on an "all or none" basis for lots of at least 50 bonds (the usual trading block). A typical transaction would be "Bid 104 for 50 ACI; Offer 50 ACI at 104½. Take them." Notice the *bid* begins with price, then volume, and finally name, whereas the *offer* has volume, then name, then price. This is the standard procedure for trades in the active crowd. Only GTC and day orders are handled; market, limit and stop orders may be used.

"Cabinet" trading literally involves filing bids and offers in a cabinet. Orders can be day orders or good for a week or month or GTC. Stop orders are not accepted.

A broker wishing to buy who finds a filed offer card at an acceptable price takes it to the ring and makes a verbal bid at that price. If no better offer is available, the filed offer consummates the trade. An offer on file can be cancelled only by physically removing the offer card.

Pricing

Bond trading has the same auction rules as do stocks. New bids must be better than existing bids (by at least ⅛) to get priority, and lower bids are not allowed. Similarly, offers must be lower to get priority.

The "nine-bond rule"

To encourage trading on the exchange, especially by small traders, the NYSE has promulgated a "nine bond rule." This holds that any order for nine bonds or less must be shown on the floor before being traded over-the-counter. If there is no sale in a reasonable time (l hour) the broker may go outside the exchange. This rule does not apply to:

□ federal, state or municipal securities

□ bonds with a call or redemption date within 12 months

□ bonds for which the customer orders no trading on the floor

□ lots of 10 or more

Bond quotations

In bond quotes, the letter "M" is used to indicate $1,000. Thus an order for 4M is an order for four bonds with a face value of $1,000 each.

READING THE TAPE

News of stock transactions is carried on the "consolidated tape," which shows information about volume and price seconds after a transaction occurs. The selling broker sends this information. The tape has two channels, or "networks."

Network "A" covers trades in all stocks, warrants, rights, etc. listed on the NYSE, whether executed on the NYSE or on regional exchanges and in the third and fourth markets. The "B" Network shows AMEX trades and transactions on regional exchanges for stocks that meet the listing requirements of the NYSE or AMEX.

Tape symbols

The "ticker symbol" (abbreviation) for a particular stock appears on the top line; the number of shares sold and the price are shown immediately below. If the trade involves 100 shares, only the price appears.

Trades in multiples of 100 are shown with a single digit followed by an "s." Thus 3s is 300 shares, 7s is 700 and so on. The "s" is always placed between the volume and the price: "6s33" means 600 shares at $33. If the transaction being reported involves more than 10,000 shares the entire amount appears on the tape: 11,000s35 means 11,000 shares traded at $35.

If more than one transaction is being reported, a period is used to separate them. Thus 24.7s23½ means 100 shares at 24, 700 shares at 23½. A series of trades at the same price is reported in a string: 3s 5s 2s25 indicates separate trades, in sequence, of 300, 500, and 200 shares at 25.

Reporting of errors

When they occur, errors are corrected on the tape. (Note that a quote to a customer based on a tape error does not hold; the customer must pay the correct price.)

Late reports Although all trades are supposed to appear on the tape as soon as possible, a trade will sometimes appear out of order. These late trades carry the symbol "SLD." Thus: SLD T/ 2s.90 means that 200 shares of Telephone were traded at $90 sometime earlier. It is not possible to tell how much earlier.

Abbreviated quotes When volume is particularly heavy, the quotation may be "abbreviated" by removing the first digit of the price. Thus for a stock where the last trade was 33, the tape might show 4s3½, indicating 400 shares at 33½, etc. The full figure would reappear if the shares went up or down through the next ten-point level, *i.e.* to 40 or 20.

Inactive or rarely-traded stocks If listed on the NYSE, normally trade in round lots of 10 shares. There is no trading booth for inactive stocks, rather orders are filed in a cabinet, as with inactive bonds. When traded the number of shares sold appears on the tape with the symbol §. Thus 4 §35 means 40 shares traded at 35. This is not an odd-lot trade.

Preferred stocks The symbol Pr identifies preferred stocks. Thus T Pr/75 indicates 100 shares of Telephone preferred traded at $75 per share.

When-issued shares If new shares of an already-traded stock are being issued because of a stock split, these are shown on the tape as W/I, for "when issued." For example, if PDS stock is trading at 70 and the corporation offers a two-for-one stock split, the when-issued stock will trade at 35.

A sale of 700 new shares after the split would show on the tape as PDS 7s35 W/I.

Rights Trades in rights are signified with the symbol RTS. These values (rights customarily trade for less than $1) are expressed in fractions: those below 50 cents trade in 32nds; those at 50 cents to $1 trade in 16ths.

Thus XYZ.RTS /900s 12/16 means 900 shares of XYZ rights traded at 12/16.

Bankruptcy Companies in bankruptcy that continue to trade are identified with the letter Q. So PDS Q/ 5s.3 means the bankrupt PDS company traded 500 shares at $3.

Other tape messages From time to time, the tape will carry messages not strictly related to a particular transaction, for example, to report "TRADING HALTED" or "OPENING DELAYED" (or the code OPD) for a particular security.

Finally, as noted above, certain block trades (special offers and special bids, exchange distributions and exchange acquisitions) appear on the tape with the codes SP OFF, SP BID, DIST and ACQ.

TERMS

NYSE Membership 1,366 seats

Types of members

Commission House Brokers Act for themselves or for non-members

Floor brokers Execute orders for other brokers, usually for a fee

Registered trader Usually acts for own account, if acting for others, must give their orders priority

Specialist or market-maker

Bond members

Allied members

Exchange Practices

Listing requirements To be listed, stock must meet certain financial and other tests

Trading on exchange Double auction, highest bid and lowest offer prevail

Basic trading unit 100 shares (a round lot)

Spread Difference between bid and offer

Quote and size Includes quantity being bid or offered

Auction Rules Minimum bid difference $\frac{1}{8}$ point

Order in which bids (and offers) must be considered

Priority First to make a bid or offer at given price

Precedence If more than one broker enters high bid at same time, largest order prevails

Parity If no one has priority or precedence, they must match for the order

Types of Orders

Market Order Order to move at "best available price"

Limit Order Order to act only at a specified price "or better"

Stop order Sets a specified price, automatically becomes a market order when that price is reached

Stop-limit orders Stop order that automatically becomes limit order once stop limit is reached

Day order Good only until close of trade that day

Good-till-cancelled (GTC) or Open Order Valid until executed (or cancelled)

Shorter term orders Broker places GTC order, takes responsibility for cancelling

Not held order (or market not held) Market order which broker can wait to execute

Fill or Kill Completed entirely in one trade or cancelled

Immediate or Cancel Like Fill or Kill, but can be partially filled

All or None Order for bonds that must be filled entirely or not at all

At the Opening (or At the Close) To be executed as near as possible to opening (or closing) price

Do Not Reduce (DNR) and Do Not Increase (DNI) Named price not adjusted for ex-dates or splits

Automated Order Execution Systems DOT (NYSE), PACE (Philadelphia), MAX (Midwest), AUTO PER, AUTO AMOS (AMEX)

Block trades special procedures

Special offer, special bid Announced on tape, trade on floor reported on tape

Exchange Distribution (Exchange Acquisition) Broker finds buyers (sellers) privately, stock crossed on floor, notice of sale appears on tape

Specialist block purchase or sale Private sale off floor, never appears on tape

Secondary distribution For extremely large blocks, announced on tape, trade off floor

Specialist

Works to ensure an orderly market, acts as both agent and dealer, as dealer must trade against the market in accord with strict trading rules

Specialist's book For other broker's orders; only limit and stop orders, day or GTC; always quotes highest bid and lowest offer in book

Stopping stock Specialist can agree to stop an order, guaranteeing execution at current price, while broker seeks better price; stopping for public orders only

Arranging the opening Specialist attempts to match orders received since the previous close so day's trading will begin in orderly fashion; must get exchange approval to open at price significantly up or down; in extreme situation, may ask to halt trading in the security

Ex-sales When a stock goes ex-dividend or ex-rights, specialist must reduce price in book on Open Buy Limit orders, Open Sell Stop orders (OBLOSS)

Odd-lot share price Based on recorded round-lot price

Part round lot Odd-lot order entered as part of a round lot

Bunched orders Several customers' odd-lot orders can be bunched into a round lot with customer approval

Odd-lot order Can be market, limit, or stop orders based on applicable round-lot sale

Bonds

Active trading Verbal bids and offers, "all or none" basis, minimum lot 50 bonds; only GTC and day orders; market, limit, and stop orders allowed

Cabinet trading Bids and offers filed; day, week, month, GTC orders allowed; no stop orders

Nine-bond rule Generally, any order for nine bonds or less must be shown on the floor before being traded over-the-counter

Pricing Bond auction rules like stocks

Bond Quotations "M" indicates $1,000 value

REVIEW QUESTIONS

1. An investor enters an order valid for six weeks. Who bears responsibility for cancelling the order at the end of the six week period?

   (A) the investor
   (B) the registered representative
   (C) the specialist
   (D) the member firm

2. An investor enters an order to buy 100 ACI at 55, GTC. ACI is currently selling at 60 and goes ex-dividend $1 before the order is filled. The specialist's book will contain an open order to:

   (A) buy 100 at 60
   (B) buy 100 at 59
   (C) buy 100 at 58⅞
   (D) buy 100 at 54

3. The quote "40 to 40½ 300 either way" on the NYSE signifies:

   (A) the broker will sell 300 shares at 40 or better
   (B) quote and size
   (C) the broker will buy 300 shares at 40½ or better
   (D) all of the above

4. All of the following are acceptable on the AMEX EXCEPT:

   (A) stop-limit orders
   (B) round-lot limit orders
   (C) odd-lot orders
   (D) all are acceptable

5. A group of brokerage firms organize to sell a large block of stock off the floor. This is called a(n):

   (A) secondary distribution
   (B) special offer
   (C) exchange distribution
   (D) special bid

6. An order to be filled immediately is most likely to be:

   (A) a market order
   (B) a stop order
   (C) a fill or kill order
   (D) a limit order

7. All of the following are reported on the Consolidated Tape EXCEPT:

   (A) options trades
   (B) preferred stock trades
   (C) exchange distributions
   (D) third market trades

8. All of the following would be accepted by a specialist EXCEPT:

   (A) GTC orders
   (B) day orders
   (C) not held orders
   (D) limit orders

9. What does the symbol OPD on the NYSE tape mean?

   (A) the daily opening
   (B) opening delayed
   (C) delete the trade in OP
   (D) none of the above

10. The number of members of the NYSE is:

    (A) 500
    (B) 1,066
    (C) 1,366
    (D) 2,001

11. A buy order which converts to a market order after a transaction at or above a specified price is called a:

    (A) market order
    (B) buy stop
    (C) buy limit
    (D) buy stop-limit

12. None of the following can take place on the NYSE floor without prior announcement EXCEPT:

    (A) special bid
    (B) exchange distribution
    (C) secondary distribution
    (D) special offer

13. The following symbols appeared on the tape: ACI 25s 45. One would read this as saying:

(A) 2500 shares of ACI were sold at 45
(B) 250 shares of ACI were sold at 45
(C) 2500 shares of ACI were sold short at 45
(D) 25 shares of ACI were sold at 45

14. A specialist can stop stock for himself if:

(A) he gets approval from an exchange officer
(B) he gets approval from an exchange governor
(C) he chooses to
(D) under no circumstances

15. A stock closes today at 45½. The stock will trade ex-dividend tomorrow morning. The most recent dividend was $1.40. If the stock were to open unchanged it would open at:

(A) 44
(B) 44⅛
(C) 44¼
(D) 45

16. An order for corporate bonds is marked "3M92." What is the dollar amount which the customer proposed for these bonds?

(A) $276
(B) $2,760
(C) $3,000
(D) $30,000

17. The "nine-bond" rule on the NYSE requires that orders for listed bonds be presented for execution on the floor of the exchange EXCEPT when:

(A) the order is for less than ten bonds
(B) the bonds are revenue bonds
(C) the bonds are debentures
(D) the bonds have been called

18. A sell stop could be used in any of the following situations EXCEPT:

(A) to safeguard a profit on a long position
(B) to limit a loss on a long position
(C) to limit a loss on a short position
(D) to establish a new position

19. An investor sells 100 shares of CAI at 45. That afternoon his broker informs him that the sale was at 44¾. The investor:

(A) can demand a sale at 45
(B) must accept the sale at 44¾
(C) can cancel the order
(D) has grounds for a grievance

20. A broker receives an order to buy 1,000 ACI at 40 "fill or kill." The following trades appear on the tape: ACI 5s403s416s40. How many shares will the customer get?

(A) 500 shares
(B) 600 shares
(C) 1,000 shares
(D) no shares

21. Which of the following can own a seat on the NYSE?

I. Mr. Smith
II. Smith & Jones Partners
III. Smith & Jones Inc.
IV. Jones and Jones Brokers

(A) I only
(B) I and II only
(C) I, II, and III
(D) I, II, III, and IV

22. The DOT system:

(A) is an automated order system
(B) is an AMEX system
(C) is used by floor brokers
(D) never goes through the specialist

23. If ACI is currently selling at 45 and an investor enters an order to buy 200 shares at 48 stop and will not pay more than 49, what kind of order has he entered?

(A) a buy stop order
(B) a market "not held" order
(C) a buy limit order
(D) a buy stop limit order

24. Two of the functions of this individual are to maintain an orderly market and to act as a broker for other brokers. He is a(n):

(A) principal
(B) floor trader
(C) specialist
(D) odd-lot broker

25. To be listed on the NYSE, a firm is required to have all of the following EXCEPT:

   (A) pre-tax earnings of $2.5 million in the previous year
   (B) at least 2,000 round-lot owners
   (C) one million shares outstanding
   (D) net worth of $5 million

26. An investor buys 300 shares of CAI at $90. After a 3 for 1 split and no other changes, he will own:

   (A) 300 shares at $30
   (B) 900 shares at $30
   (C) 300 shares at $90
   (D) 900 shares at $90

Questions 27–28 are based on the following stretch of ticker:

CAI. SLD 45 ACI Pr 45s 102 ACI 2s 55

27. The CAI trade shows

   (A) 100 shares of CAI were sold
   (B) 100 shares of CAI were sold short
   (C) 100 shares of CAI were sold and reported out of sequence
   (D) 100 shares of CAI were part of a secondary distribution

28. The first trade in ACI preferred shows:

   (A) 45 shares of ACI preferred sold at 102
   (B) 450 shares of ACI preferred sold at 102
   (C) 4500 shares of ACI preferred sold at 102
   (D) 450 shares of ACI preferred sold short at 102

Questions 29–30 are based on the following excerpt from a specialist's book:

Amalgamated Consolidated Incorporated

BUY		SELL
200 Bache	55	
100 Reynolds	$\frac{1}{8}$	
100 Shearson	$\frac{1}{4}$	
	$\frac{3}{8}$	
	$\frac{1}{2}$	200 Merrill
	$\frac{5}{8}$	100 Kidder
	$\frac{3}{4}$	300 Schwab
	$\frac{7}{8}$	

29. What is the size of the quote?

   (A) 400 by 600
   (B) 200 by 100
   (C) 200 by 300
   (D) 100 by 200

30. For his own account, the specialist may bid as low as:

   (A) 55
   (B) 55¼
   (C) 55⅜
   (D) 55½

ANSWERS TO REVIEW QUESTIONS

1. (B) The registered rep would cancel any order longer than a day order.

2. (B) Remember open buy limit and open sell stop (OBLOSS) orders are reduced.

3. (C) This quote gives both the "bid and asked" and the size on each side.

4. (D) Only stop limit orders for round lots are permitted on the AMEX.

5. (A) All of the others take place on the floor of the exchange.

6. (A) Choices B and D are not immediate and C may not be filled.

7. (A) The others are all carried for listed stocks.

8. (C) These can be accepted by a broker who would use his discretion as to when it is filled.

9. (B) By definition.

10. (C) This number is fixed and membership is limited to individuals.

11. (B) If there is also a maximum price which may be paid it is a buy stop limit.

12. (B) Choices A and D require prior announcement and C is done off the floor.

13. (A) The symbol "s" following a number means that number of round lots.

14. (D) He may only stop stock for public orders.

15. (B) The adjusted price of 44.10 would be rounded to the next highest eighth.

16. (B) This means three $1,000 bonds selling at $920 each.

17. (D) The rule does not apply to bonds callable within one year.

18. (C) The order is executed as the price is falling and could decrease a loss, never limit it.

19. (B) He must accept it unless his was a limit order.

20. (D) Since he couldn't fill the order in one transaction, it is killed.

21. (A) Seats may only be purchased by individuals.

22. (A) The DOT system is an automated system which bypasses floor brokers. If it cannot match orders, it sends them through the specialists.

23. (D) There is a triggering stop and a limit on the price.

24. (C) These are the main functions of the specialist who must also keep a book on orders to be filled.

25. (D) This is not required but it is necessary that the market value of outstanding shares be at least 16 million dollars.

26. (B) With no other changes the value must remain the same and hence if the number of shares tripled, the value of each share must be cut into a third of its original value.

27. (C) The symbol SLD means trade reported out of sequence.

28. (C) The Pr means preferred and the s is the number of round lots.

29. (D) The size is the amount of the highest bid and the lowest offer.

30. (C) For his account he must bid higher than any of the bids of his customers.

CHAPTER NINE

Options

An option is the right to buy something at a specified price and within a given time; the buyer pays for this *right*. For example, a film producer takes an option on a book, or a real estate agent takes an option on a house. These payments don't provide title to the book or the house but rather give the holder the option to acquire title. With securities, options involve the right to buy (call) or sell (put) securities (usually 100 shares of a stock) at a set price and until a specified future date.

The holder, or buyer, of the contract pays the writer (or seller) a fee, called a "premium." The holder need not exercise the right to buy or sell, but has the "option" to do so. If the holder does "call," the writer must sell the called securities at the specified price. If the holder "puts," the writer must buy the securities at the specified price.

Trading in options

Options contracts are negotiable. They are traded both over-the-counter and through exchanges; the latter are called "listed options." OTC trading in options, as with other securities, takes place in a negotiated, rather than an auction, market. But trading is not continuous, as there is no active secondary market. This is particularly crucial since options have a limited life.

In the OTC market, one can have an option in any security for which someone is willing to write an option. These differ from listed options in important ways: there is no need to meet any regulatory requirement, no mechanism for getting continuous price information, and no limit on the number or amount of options an individual may hold; in addition, settlements are on the same day, expirations are not uniform, and exercise prices are not standardized. For all of these reasons, the OTC market is very small and the remainder of this chapter concerns only listed options.

167

The Options Clearing Corporation

In 1973, the need for a really liquid market, standardized terms, and a centralized marketplace led to the establishment of the Options Clearing Corporation. Working with several national exchanges, the OCC sets option terms, provides forms for traders, ensures a continuous market for securities (just as the NYSE provides for common stocks listed there), and supplies daily quotations to the financial press. The OCC acts as principal in every options transaction for listed options contracts. It is owned by the five exchanges where options are currently traded. These are the American, Pacific, Philadelphia and New York Stock Exchanges and the Chicago Board Options Exchange.

As principal it issues all listed options, guarantees the contracts, and is the legal entity on the other side of every transaction. In effect, the OCC makes it possible for buyers and sellers to act independently.

FORMS OF OPTIONS

Options contracts are traded in two forms: the contract to buy is classified as a "call option"; the contract to sell as a "put option."

Call options

The holder of the call has the right to buy *at a specified price* (to call) securities from the person who writes the contract. The writer in turn has the obligation to sell if the holder calls. The right and obligation have a finite lifetime, after which they simultaneously expire.

Thus, the call-holder has the *right* to call from the writer; the call-writer has the *obligation* to sell if the option is called (or exercised.) The call-buyer pays a fee (the premium) for this right.

Put options

With a put, the holder has a right to sell (to put) securities to the writer at a specified price. The writer is obliged to buy if the holder exercises his option. The put-holder has the *right* to sell to the writer; the writer has the *obligation* to buy if the option is exercised. As with the call option, the right and obligation have a finite lifetime.

■ NOTE

The holder or buyer of the contract is said to be "long" the option. The terms "long a call" or "long a put" are sometimes used to describe this position. Conversely, the writer or seller is "short" the option. Here the terms "short a call" or "short a put" are used.

TERMINOLOGY

The following terms are used in describing options trading.

Exercise price or strike price

This is the price fixed in the options contract at which the option can be exercised; *i.e.,* the price at which the call-holder can buy or the put-holder can sell. With listed options, choices for this price are set by the OCC, usually in $5 intervals for stocks under $100 and at $10 intervals for stocks trading at over $100. On the over-the-counter market, the exercise price is usually set at the current market value per share of the underlying stock.

Expiration date

The month in which the contract expires is the expiration date. These are set by the OCC for all listed options.

In that month, all listed options expire on the Saturday following the third Friday of the month at 11:59 P.M. Eastern Time.

OTC options usually are for terms of 90 days or 6 months plus 10 days, but can be for as little as 35 days or last up to 1 year 10 days.

Type

The two basic types of options are calls and puts.

Class

All options of one type for a given stock are a "class" of option. For example, all IBM calls or all IBM puts are termed a class, whatever the price or expiration date.

Series

Series are options that are identical in class, expiration date, and execution price; *e.g.* all IBM Aug 60 Puts.

Premium

A premium is the fee charged by the writer whether or not the option is exercised. It varies with the price of the underlying stock and other factors. (See page 171.)

■ **EXAMPLE**

With these definitions in mind, we can read the following quote:
"3 PSM Nov 60 C at 2"

3—the number of contracts for 100 shares of the underlying stock,
PSM—abbreviated name of the underlying security,
Nov—expiration month,
60—execution price or strike price,
C—type of option (call or put),
2—premium (these trade in fractions as small as $\frac{1}{16}$, though most examples here use whole numbers).

Thus, 3 PSM Nov 60 C at 2 describes an option giving the buyer the right to buy 300 shares (3 × 100) of PSM for $60 per share until some time in November for a premium of $600 ($2 per share × 3 × 100 shares). Note that the standard contract is for 100 shares of stock.

BASIC OPTIONS POSSIBILITIES

Every options contract involves one of two present actions (buying or writing) *and* one of two potential actions (calling or putting). Let us look first at the four basic possibilities (for simplicity, we will generally ignore premiums in this section).

Call-holder (or buyer)

The call-holder has the option to buy at a particular price. He hopes the market price of the underlying stock will rise. If it does, he will exercise his option to buy the stock at the strike price, and then profit by reselling it at the higher market price.

■ **EXAMPLE**

Mrs. A buys a PSM Nov 70 Call when the market price of the underlying stock is 70. PSM rises on the market to 76. She calls 100 shares at 70, sells them in the market at 76, and makes a profit of $600 minus whatever premium she paid. If the stock falls below 70, Mrs. A simply lets the option expire, since to exercise would mean buying at 70 a stock which she can buy in the market for less than 70.

Call-writer (or seller)

The call-writer sells the option to buy. He hopes the price of the underlying stock will not go up. If it doesn't, the call-holder will let the option expire, and the writer will profit by the amount of the premium collected at the time the option was written. If the security's market price rises, however, the option will be exercised, and the call-writer must provide the stock at the agreed price taking whatever loss this involves.

■ **EXAMPLE**

If Mr. B. wrote the option that Mrs. A (in the example above) exercised at 70 when the stock went to 76, he must buy at 76 (or provide from his portfolio) and sell at 70. Mr. B will lose $600, again minus the premium which he collected originally.

Put-holder

The put-holder purchases the right to sell at a specified price. He hopes the market price of the underlying stock will fall. He will then exercise his option to sell to the writer at the (now higher) strike price, buy in the market at a lower price, and realize a profit on the difference.

■ **EXAMPLE**

Mrs. A. buys PSM Nov 70 Put when the market price of PSM is $70. The price drops to $63. She can exercise the option, sell at $70 a share securities which she can buy at $63, and realize a gain of $7 a share or $700 for the contract (less the premium). If the market value of the stock rises, she will let the option expire, since exercising it would create a loss.

Put-writer

The put-writer has sold the right to sell; *i.e.*, he has assumed the obligation to buy from the put-holder at the exercise price. Thus, the put-writer hopes the market value of the underlying stock will not fall. Then the put-holder will not exercise the option and the writer will profit by the amount of the premium.

■ **EXAMPLE**

Mr. B writes PSM Nov 70 Put when the market price of PSM is $70. The stock drops to 63. He must now buy from Mrs. A at $70 per share PSM which has a value of only $63 in the market, a loss of $7 per share, or $700 minus the previously collected premium.

■ NOTE

In general, if an option is exercised, the holder's gain from exercising is offset by the writer's loss. If the writer already owns the stock or, in the case of a Put, is short the stock, the loss is an opportunity loss, *i.e.*, loss of the opportunity to sell at the (better) market price since the writer must sell (or buy back the short) at the exercise price.

In summary, the put-holder has the right to sell at a specified price and hopes the market price falls; the put-writer must buy if the option is exercised, and hopes the price doesn't fall.

PREMIUMS

While bidding determines the actual price of an option, it is customary to distinguish two components of the value of an option.

Intrinsic value

This is the value reflected in a call option with an exercise price below the current price of the underlying stock or a put option with an exercise above the current value of its underlying stock. It is the amount of money the owner of the option can make by exercising the option at the moment and immediately reversing that transaction in the stock market. For this reason, such an option is called "in the money."

For example, a call option with a strike price of $40 on a stock selling at $50 has an intrinsic value of $10, since one could exercise the option getting the stock for $40 and then selling it at once for $50. Options with a strike price below market price are called "out of the money," and those whose strike prices exactly equal market prices are called "at the money."

For put options, in and out of the money are reversed. A put with a strike price of $40 on a stock selling at $50 is out of the money, and one with a strike price above market price (*e.g.*, market price at $30) is "in the money." *However, even out of the money options are worth something.*

Time value

In general, we ascribe all value not explicitly intrinsic to time value. For in the money options this value is the difference between premium price and intrinsic value. For out of the money options, all value is time value. The actual length of time until expiration of the option plays a role, and the premium tends to go up if the time to expiration is longer, *i.e.*, there is greater time value to the option.

Here are several examples, all of which involve buying PSM Nov. 40 Calls.

- □ if the premium is $4, but PSM itself is trading at $38 a share, or $2 out of the money, the buyer is not paying for any intrinsic value, but rather hopes for PSM stock to rise over time.

- □ if the premium is $6 when PSM is selling for $44, it reflects a time value of $2 above the intrinsic value.

With a put, obviously, the situation is reversed. For example, a PSM Nov 70 Put is in the money by $4 if PSM sells at $66. In this case, $4 of the premium would represent the intrinsic value.

Volatility

To understand premium pricing one additional element must be included, namely the volatility of the underlying stock price. If this is high, if the stock price fluctuates greatly, then the value of an option is increased since the likelihood that the option will have substantial intrinsic value is increased. Conversely, if the stock price tends to be stable, the option will have less time value.

Notice that while the time value increased with volatility, only the intrinsic value could be cashed in by exercising the option. Of course, since options are traded as instruments in their own right, one can buy an option and resell it later at a higher price.

COVERED VS. UNCOVERED OPTIONS

Writing options can be extremely risky. If a call option is exercised, the call-writer must pay the difference between the market price and the strike price; the greater this difference, the greater the loss. In principle, there is no limit to the writer's risk since there is no limit to the price the underlying security might reach before the option expires. The put-writer must pay the difference between the market price and the strike price. This limits the risk to the price of the underlying security, since that could go to $0.

Limiting risks on call-writing

These risks can be moderated. If a call-writer owns the underlying security which has been called, then he merely needs to deliver it. His risk has now been converted to an opportunity loss (since he no longer owns this security and cannot himself benefit from its rise). Of course by owning the security, he also assumes the risk that this underlying security might fall in price.

A writer who owns the underlying security is referred to as a "covered writer." Those with no such protection are termed "uncovered" or "naked" option writers. Variations of covering include owning a security convertible to the underlying stock, or owning an escrow or depository receipt, *i.e.*, legal evidence that the writer has the stock on deposit. (This is often used by large institutions.)

A call-writer can also limit risk by holding an unexpired long call on the same stock at the same or some other strike price. If the call he wrote is exercised, he can, where necessary, exercise his own long call to obtain the stock needed to fill his obligation.

■ **EXAMPLE**

A writer of a 50 ACI Call who owns a 60 ACI Call has his risk limited to the $10 between 50 and 60. If the price rises above $60 he exercises his call and delivers the shares to the 50 call holder. The writer's loss is limited to $10 per share (minus the premium he collected but plus the premium he paid for the 60 call).

Limiting risks on put-writing

A Put-writer can limit risk by selling the underlying security short or by owning a put on the same security. If he is short the security, he of course assumes the risk that the security will rise in price.

■ **EXAMPLE**

A writer of a 50 ACI Put who owns a 35 ACI Put risks a maximum of $15 since he can sell ACI at 35 and must buy at 50. Of course if he owns a higher put, say an ACI 60, then he has no risk; if exercising the 50 put makes sense, then so does exercising the 60 put and he will make $10 per share.

■ **NOTE**

In this case the premium he paid for his 60 put is probably higher than that which he received for writing his 50 put.

BREAK-EVEN POINTS

The break-even point is that point at which an investor who trades in options literally "breaks even" in regard to some transaction or combination thereof. We will analyze such points *before the imposition of transaction costs.*

Buyers

For buyers of options the break-even point is readily determined. The buyer of a call will break even when the underlying security is priced at the strike price plus the premium. The buyer of a 40 call with a premium of 5 breaks even when the stock goes to 45. By exercising there, he would buy at 40 and sell at 45, thereby recapturing the premium of 5 which he paid originally.

Conversely, the buyer of a put will break even when the stock price equals the strike price minus the premium. The buyer of a 40 put at a premium of 5 needs to have the stock price at 35 in order to break even.

Writers

For writers the issue is somewhat more complex. For a covered call-writer, the break-even point is the original cost to the writer of the underlying security *minus* the premium. For example, if ACI was originally purchased at 35 and a call was written at 35 with a premium of 7, the writer is said to break even when the stock reaches 28. The loss of 7 per share on the stock is exactly made up by the 7 premium collected when the option was written.

It is worth noting that if a stock goes up in price, there is no break-even point—the writer is always ahead. This is true because the break-even is now based on two combined transactions.

Similarly, for a put-writer who is short the stock, the break-even is the short sale price *plus* the premium. If ACI was shorted at 35 and subsequently a 35 put is written for a premium of 4, the writer breaks even at 39. Here again two transactions are combined.

For an uncovered call-writer the break-even is the strike price *plus* the premium. If one writes an uncovered call on ACI with a 35 strike price and collects a 4½ premium, the break-even occurs when ACI reaches 39½.

Conversely, an uncovered put-writer breaks even at the strike price *minus* the premium. A 35 put with a premium of 6 causes the writer to break even at 29.

STRATEGIES: HEDGES, STRADDLES, COMBINATIONS, SPREADS

Aside from the basic strategies of buying and writing puts and calls there are other more complex strategies. In this section the more common of these investments will be outlined.

Hedges

Hedges are strategies similar to insurance policies. Just as with insurance one pays a premium and is then protected against catastrophic loss. There are two basic hedges: long call/short stock and long put/long stock.

Long call/short stock Buying a call on a stock and selling the same stock short. This procedure, "hedging a short sale," provides insurance to a short seller who otherwise faces unlimited risk. It guarantees the right to buy at a price that puts a ceiling over any loss from the short sale.

■ **EXAMPLE**

Sell 100 shares PSM short at 50 and buy 1 PSM Nov 50 Call at 5. If PSM went to 100, the short seller would lose $5,000. With the call, however, the loss is only the premium, or $500, since the investor has the right to buy the stock at 50 for the term of the option. If the stock falls, the short seller will not realize a profit unless and until the drop exceeds the amount of the premium, which in the above example, is below 45.

The maximum loss for the call buyer would be the $500, and his theoretical maximum gain—if the stock went to $0—would be $5,000 − $500 = $4,500. A naked writer of the call would have no limit on his potential maximum loss and would have a maximum possible gain of $500 if the call was not exercised.

Long put/long stock This means buying a put and buying shares of the same stock. It limits risk if the market price of the stock falls.

■ **EXAMPLE**

Buy 100 PSM at 50 and buy 1 PSM 50 put at 5. The put guarantees being able to sell the stock at 50. Thus the loss cannot exceed $500, *i.e.*, the premium or cost of placing the put. Again, no profit will be realized until the stock rises enough to cover the premium; which means the break-even point is the cost of the stock plus the premium, or 55 in the above example.

Again, the maximum loss for the put buyer is the $500 premium, but his theoretical maximum gain is now unlimited.

■ **NOTE**

Writing covered options is a partial hedge. It insures against some limited amount of loss. For instance, writing a covered call on ACI at 70 for a premium of 6 provides the writer with protection against a fall in the price of ACI up to 64. The writer is thus partially protected, but should ACI fall below 64 he again assumes the risk.

Straddles

A straddle is the simultaneous buying (or writing) of a put and a call on the same stock with the same expiration date and strike price.

Long straddle (buy a straddle) This means buying a put and a call of the same expiration date and execution price for one security. The buyer expects movement in the stock but is unsure whether it will rise or fall.

■ **EXAMPLE**   Buy 1 PSM Nov 70 Call at 7 and buy 1 PSM Nov 70 Put at 5. Assume the underlying stock goes to 74, the call is exercised, and the put expires. The holder of the straddle has paid $1200 in premiums ($700 for the call, $500 for the put), and earned $400 from the exercised call (buy at 70, sell at 74)—a net loss of $800. Here the break-even point is reached when the underlying stock rises or falls in the market enough to cover both premiums—in this example, up to 82 or down to 58.

The maximum loss for the purchaser is now $1,200, equaling the maximum possible gain for the writer. This occurs only if both options expire unexercised.

■ **NOTE**   In the above example, if the call were exercised at 74 before the put expired, and subsequently the stock fell to 62, that would also represent a break-even.

Short straddle (write or sell a straddle) Writing a put and a call on the same security, with the same expiration date and execution price. Here, the writer hopes for relatively little movement in the market price of the underlying security. He gets two premiums. This, like call-writing or put-writing, is often used to improve the return on capital.

■ **EXAMPLE**   Sell 1 PSM Nov 70 Call at 5; sell 1 PSM Nov 70 Put at 3. If by expiration date PSM goes to 73, the call is exercised and the put is allowed to expire. The writer has received $800 in premiums and this gain is offset by a loss of $300. The writer's break-even points would be 78 or 62, *i.e.,* he would make money if the stock remained within that range and would lose outside of it.

Combinations

Combinations are variations on a straddle. They involve the purchase (or sale) of a put and a call on the same security with different expirations, different strike prices, or both. Two examples follow.

□ buy 1 ACI May 60 Call and buy 1 ACI Aug 60 Put
□ sell 1 ACI May 60 Call and sell 1 ACI May 50 Put

Like the long straddle, the first example would be employed when considerable movement was expected, especially if one thought it might first go up and then down. The second combination might be used if the writer believed the price would fluctuate between 50 and 60. In that case neither option would ever be in the money.

Spreads

Buying and selling a call or buying and selling a put on the same security, *i.e.,* on options of the same type and class, with either different expiration dates or different strike prices or both, is called "putting on a spread" or "spreading." Such a procedure involving self-cancelling positions—any gain on one side would be offset, dollar for dollar, by a loss on the other—may seem odd. However these positions are not exactly opposite. Here the term "spread" refers to the difference between the premium paid and the premium received on the two positions (*e.g.,* long call/short call), and determines the gain or loss.

If the only difference is the strike price, this is called a "vertical spread" or "price spread." If they differ in expiration date only, it is called a "horizontal spread" or "time spread." Spreads which differ in both time and price are called "diagonal spreads." (These terms reflect the way options are listed in the newspaper: successive strike prices are shown one above the other, successive expirations along one line.)

Let us examine the two situations:

Debit spread (also called a bull price spread or "buying the spread") If the premium paid for the long call is greater than the premium received for the short call, the transaction is called a "debit spread." The position is more profitable if the market price of the underlying stock goes up and widens the spread.

■ **EXAMPLE**

With PSM at 76, buy 1 PSM Nov 70 C at 7, and sell 1 PSM Nov 80 C at 1; net debit, $600. With this spread, the maximum loss would come if the market price drops below 70—both calls expire "out" and the $600 net premium cost is lost.

Alternately, maximum gain occurs if the price rises above 80. The written call would be exercised and the spreader would have to deliver at 80. He, in turn, exercises the held call at 70, for a gain of $1000 less premium of $600 or a total of $400.

■ **NOTE**

The difference between the long and short call—10 points here—is the maximum possible gain, whatever the market price. Of course, some lesser gain is possible if the underlying stock reaches a point between 70 and 80. The break-even here is obviously at 76.

Credit spread (also bear price spread or "selling the spread") If the premium paid on the long call is less than the premium received on the short call, a "credit spread" occurs. There is greater profit if the market price falls and the spread narrows.

■ **EXAMPLE**

Buy 1 PSM 80 C at 1, sell 1 PSM 70 C at 7; net credit $600, assuming market price is 76. This situation is the reverse of the bull spread. Maximum gain is realized if the price falls below $70, leaving both calls "out of the money" so that both options expire and the spread earns $600 net (premiums). Maximum loss occurs if the underlying stock climbs above 80. Both calls are then in the money, will be exercised, and the holder of the spread must deliver shares purchased at 80 for 70. The loss is $1,000 less the $600 gain on premiums, or a net loss of $400. Here again the break-even is at 76.

OBJECTIVES OF OPTIONS TRADERS

It is possible to identify four separate but related objectives for options purchasers:

1 To speculate in a security while limiting risk. For example, a $10 ACI 100 call would return a profit of $2,000 on a $1,000 investment if ACI goes to 130, or 200%. Purchasing ACI outright would require a $10,000 investment and bring a return of 30%.

2 To diversify a portfolio. An investor with $5,000 who believed the market was due to rise could buy calls *on five different* stocks (assuming a $10 premium on each) but could only buy 100 shares of *one* $50 stock.

3 To hedge a position. An investor owning 100 shares of ACI could protect that investment against catastrophic loss by buying a put on ACI. If ACI drops sharply, the investor's loss is limited to the premium on the put option, and he can still profit from any rise in ACI (minus the cost of the put).

4 To delay a decision. A relatively small investment in a call allows an investor to take advantage of a rise in the price of the security while not committing a large amount of capital. This is an important advantage in cases where the capital might not be available until some later date. By buying a call, the investor defers the decision without giving up all the potential gain.

MARGINS

Though margins are covered in detail in Chapter 11, some margin requirements pertain specifically to options. Only writers of uncovered options must meet margin requirements.* Buyers, under OCC rules, must settle on the next business day. The buyer of a put or call must pay the full amount of the premium, even if that individual has an active margin account for stocks, *i.e.*, long options have no loan value and the broker cannot loan against them even if they appreciate.

Applied to a margin purchase, "covered" means the brokerage firm is not at risk, while covered writer, on the other hand, refers to protecting the investor.

On calls

A call-writer is considered covered for margin purchases if he holds:

□ a long position in the underlying stock, or

□ a security convertible to the same stock, or

□ has an escrow or depository receipt showing the stock is held in a bank and will be delivered if the call option is exercised, or

□ holds a long call option on the same stock with the same or later expiration date and the same or lower strike price.

In any such case there is no margin requirement on the writer of a call.

* The margin requirements are changed from time to time by the various exchanges.

On puts

A put-writer is covered if he

- □ is short the underlying stock, or
- □ holds a long put option with same expiration date or longer, or
- □ holds a long put option with same strike price or greater. Technically being short stock and writing a put is not a covered put position, but for margin purposes it is covered since there is no additional margin requirement.

Deposits

Uncovered writers are required to have a minimum on deposit, in most cases $2,000, before any transactions are undertaken. After that the requirements are governed by maintenance margin, and further deposits are not required except to meet those margins. For options traded through OCC, the minimum margin on one transaction is $250 per contract.

Margin for writers of naked equity options

The current requirement is that 20% of the value of the underlying stock plus the premium collected from the buyer be on deposit as margin. This total is decreased by the "out of the moneyness" of the option, and there is a minimum requirement of the premium plus 10% of the value of the underlying stock.

For uncovered puts, the requirement is similar, namely 20% of the market price plus the premium and minus any out of the moneyness, again with a minimum of 10% of market value. Further, this requirement is "marked to market" at the end of each day. That is, every day at the close, the new premiums and market prices are used to determine the necessary amount.

■ **EXAMPLE 1**

If ACI is selling at 52 and the investor writes 3 ACI Nov 50 calls at 3, the required deposit would be:

$$3(20\% \times \$5,200 + \$300) = 3(\$1,040 + \$300) = \$4,020$$

■ **EXAMPLE 2**

If ACI is selling at $58 and the investor writes 5 ACI Nov 60 calls at 1, the required deposit is:

$$5(20\% \times \$5,800 + \$100 - \$200 \text{ [out of money]}) = \$5,300$$

■ **EXAMPLE 3**

If CAI is selling at 24 and the investor writes a CAI Nov 30 call at 1/2, the required deposit would be:

$$20\% \times \$2,400 + \$50 - \$600 = -\$70$$

Since this is less than the 10% minimum, the required deposit becomes:

$$\$50 + 10\% \times \$2,400 = \$290$$

Spread margins

Covered spreads Although there is no margin requirement for covered spreads, the difference between the premium collected on the written option and that required for the purchased option would have to be deposited.

Call spread A call spread is covered when the long option has a strike not higher than, and an expiration not earlier than, the short option. For example:

- □ buy 1 ACI Jun 55 Call at 7
- □ sell 1 ACI Jun 60 Call at 3

If the 60 Call is exercised, then the 55 can be as well. There is no margin requirement, but the $400 difference in premiums must be deposited.

Put spread If the long option has a strike price no lower, and an expiration not earlier than the short option, then the put spread is covered. For example:

- □ buy 1 ACI Sep 60 Put at 6
- □ sell 1 ACI Jun 60 Put at 3

Here, a later date is chosen for the long put rather than a higher price. In any case, if the short put is exercised, the long put can be as well. Again, there is no margin requirement, and the $300 between premiums must be deposited.

OPTION TRANSACTION PROCEDURES

Issuing a contract

The option contract is issued by the OCC as a "new offering" of a security. Therefore, under the Securities Act of 1933, all potential purchasers must receive a prospectus and any solicitation of a customer to buy (or write) an option must be accompanied by a prospectus. Whenever a prospectus is updated, existing customers must get a copy of the new prospectus with or before the confirmation of their next trade. In options, the prospectus is often called the "Option Disclosure Document" or "Option Disclosure Statement."

Ordering options

To order listed options, the following steps occur. After the customer enters an order for a buy or sell option contract through a brokerage firm, the order is executed on the floor of a member exchange. After the trade is completed, it is then submitted to the OCC which "clears" the transaction and issues the option contract to the buyer or seller.

Exercising an option

When a customer exercises an option, he notifies his broker; the brokerage firm notifies the OCC directly; and then the OCC assigns the contract to one of the firms representing writers on a random basis. That firm in turn must assign the contract among its clients equitably. This can also involve random selection, or "first in first out," but must be fair—for example, not to the customer who has the largest position. In short, the OCC holds the option contract obligation, and acts as intermediary between buyer and seller.

Required forms

Because option trading is risky and specialized, the OCC will not issue a contract until certain documentation is completed. No customer can participate in options transactions unless and until all four of these forms are completed.

Option information form This form concerns the customer's financial standing, background, and interests. It must be signed by both the customer and the registered representative who is recommending the customer for this type of trading, and approved by the firm's branch manager (who must be a Registered Option Principal if the branch has four or more registered representatives involved in options transactions). This approval must be confirmed in writing within 15 days by a Compliance Registered Options Principal (CROP). In addition, the CROP must also approve any promotional or educational material. Said materials must also be submitted to the Options Exchanges at least 10 days before they are used.

Standard option agreement This explains the firm's procedures for dealing with the account, any transactions, notices of execution, delinquencies, etc. It must be signed by the customer within 15 days after the account is opened.

Prospectus (Options Disclosure Document) At or before the time that options trading begins, the client must be provided with the risk disclosure statement "Characteristics and Risks of Standardized Options," published by the OCC.

A New Account Form (See Chapter 10)

Options clearing agreement Finally, within 15 days after the account is approved, the customer must sign an agreement with the OCC itself. This "Options Clearing Agreement" specifies OCC regulations pertaining to the customer.

Trading in listed options is carried out without certificates. Rather, confirmations of transactions and regular statements are sent by the broker.

"Opening" and "closing" transactions

Options orders must show if the customer is "opening" or "closing" a position, and if that position is long (buyer or holder) or short (seller or writer). There are only the following four possibilities:

Opening buy—Long, *i.e.,* establishing a long call or put position as holder.

Closing sell—Long, *i.e.,* liquidating a long call or put position.

Opening sell—Short, *i.e.,* establishing a short call or put position as writer.

Closing buy—Short, *i.e.,* liquidating a short call or put position.

These designations allow options trading exchanges to provide a daily accounting of "open interest" which is an important indicator of liquidity in particular options contracts. This figure, published in the financial press, shows the number of contracts still open in a given series.

OPTIONS PRICING

When a listed option of a particular series expires, the options exchange will introduce a new series based on the current market price of the underlying stock. The offered puts and calls usually "bracket" this price. For example, if PSM is selling at $68 when the January contracts expire, the exchanges will offer October PSM 65 and October PSM 70.

In general, strike (exercise) prices are offered at $2.50 intervals for equities below $25/share, at $5 intervals for stocks up to $200, and at $10 intervals for those above $200.

OCC RULES AND REGULATIONS

Expirations

All options contracts expire at 10:59 P.M. Central Time (since much options trading takes place in Chicago, times are often given in both Central and Eastern zones), 11:59 P.M. Eastern Time, on the Saturday following the third Friday of the expiration month.

Although options contracts expire on a Saturday, trading in a particular option must cease at 3 P.M. Central (4 P.M. Eastern) time the business day preceding the expiration date. In addition, even though trading in the option has been halted, an option can be exercised until 5:30 P.M. Eastern time on the business day preceding the expiration date. An option can be exercised, but not sold, even if trading in the option and the underlying stock have been suspended.

Each listed option has a cycle of four expiration months, *e.g.,* Jan, Apr, Jul, and Oct; or Mar, Jun, Sep, and Dec. At any given time, only the next three of these expirations are available. For instance, if Feb, May, and Aug are available, then Nov does not become available until Feb expires.

Adjustments in contracts

Cash dividends With exchange traded options, there is no adjustment in price when a cash dividend is issued for the underlying stock. With over the counter options, the option price is reduced by the amount of the dividend. The dividend belongs to the stockholder, hence the ex-dividend date represents the dividing line for options contracts. Thus the holder of a call must exercise before that date to get the dividend, and the holder of a put may not exercise until the ex-dividend date in order to keep the dividend.

Stock dividends For a stock dividend, the number of shares is increased and the exercise price is decreased to reflect the dividend, beginning on the ex-dividend date. These changes are made to the nearest whole share and the nearest ⅛ of a point. This keeps the dollar amount needed to exercise close to the amount before the dividend.

■ **EXAMPLE**

If ACI declares a 5% stock dividend, then a May ACI 50 Call would become a May ACI 47⅝ of 105 shares ($5,000 ÷ 105 = $47.6190). The premium is now multiplied by 105 after the split.

Stock splits For whole number splits (*e.g.*, 2 for 1), the number of contracts is increased and the price reduced.

■ **EXAMPLE**

1 PSM Nov 90 Put after a 3 for 1 stock split becomes 3 PSM Nov 30 Puts.

In a fractional split (*e.g.*, 5 for 4), the number of shares per contract is increased, and the price reduced.

■ **EXAMPLE**

1 PSM Nov 90 Put becomes one PSM Nov 60 Put for 150 shares after a 3 for 2 stock split.

Exercise notice

The option agreement sets forth the customer's responsibility to deliver stock if exercised on a call or to deliver money (to buy stock) if exercised on a put. An American-style option can be exercised as soon as ownership is confirmed. There are a few European-style options that permit exercise only in the time just before expiration. Once exercised, the stock must be delivered, and settlement made, in five business days. For the writer, this will be four business days after assignment.

POSITION LIMITS

Because a large investor could conceivably use leverage to control the market, the OCC limits the number of contracts an individual investor can hold at any one time. "Individual" includes investors acting in joint accounts or partnerships, investment advisors, and those representing many accounts.

An individual investor cannot exceed the position limit on the "same side" of the market, *i.e.*, such that they would benefit from moves in the same direction. The easy way to think of this is in terms of "bullish" and "bearish" holdings. In other words, a long call and a short put are both bullish; short calls and long puts are bearish.

Position limits are currently set on three levels by the OCC.*

1 8,000 contracts on a side for options where the underlying stock meets one of the two following criteria:

* Position limits may also change from time to time.

□ 120,000,000 shares outstanding and a trading volume of at least 30,000,000 shares during the most recent six-month trading period.

□ trading volume of at least 40,000,000 shares during the most recent six-month trading period, independent of shares outstanding.

2 5,500 contracts on a side for options where the underlying stock meets one of the two following criteria:

□ 40,000,000 shares outstanding and a trading volume of at least 15,000,000 shares during the most recent six-month trading period,

□ trading volume of at least 20,000,000 shares during the most recent six-month trading period, independent of shares outstanding.

3 3,000 contracts on a side for all other listed options.

□ These same limits apply to the number of contracts that an investor may exercise in any consecutive five-business-day period.

EXCHANGES

The OCC is owned by five exchanges on which options are traded. They are:

New York Stock Exchange—NYSE
Chicago Board Option Exchange—CBOE
American Stock Exchange—ASE
Philadelphia Stock Exchange—PBX
Pacific Stock Exchange—PSE

Options are bought and sold on these exchanges in an auction market similar to the stock markets. Commission charges, set by brokers and the exchange, are based on premiums. Limit and market orders are permitted.

All exchanges but the CBOE use a specialist system similar to that described in Chapter 8, with firms acting as both brokers and dealers on the floor. On the CBOE, there are no specialists. Instead, a "board broker" maintains a book like the specialist's book, but acts only as agent.

The OCC guarantees puts and calls listed on its exchanges, and supervises the listing of options. An option to be listed must meet the following rigorous requirements as to value, volume traded, and financial health of the issuing firm.

1 The underlying stock must have a value of at least $10 per share.

2 At least 8 million shares of the underlying stock must be publicly held, with at least 10,000 different shareholders.

3 At least 1.2 million shares must have traded each year in the two preceding years.

4 The firm issuing the underlying stock must have had a net after-tax income of at least $1 million in three of the last four fiscal years, including the most recent fiscal year.

5 The issuing firm must be current in its dividend and sinking fund obligations to preferred shareholders and in its debt payments.

TAX ON OPTIONS

A chapter of this book is devoted to taxes. This section will describe some options trading tax consequences. An investor who closes out an option position always realizes a capital gain or loss. For tax purposes, gain or loss is defined by the way the option position is ended, *i.e.*, expired, exercised, traded or sold.

Expired options

When an option expires, it is treated as worthless for tax purposes. It is therefore a capital loss to the owner. The writer of such an expired option always has a short-term capital gain.

Traded options

The liquidation of an options position by sale generates a capital gain, or loss, of net proceeds less acquisition cost. Thus an investor who bought a contract with a premium of $300 and resold it at $600 realizes a $300 capital gain. The gain is found in similar fashion with the repurchase of a written option.

Exercising

Taxes are calculated only when the security is sold, and call premiums are included in the basis or cost of acquisition.

Buy a call A customer buys PSM Nov 60 Call at 3 on June 4, and exercises the option August 12. The cost of acquiring the stock is $63 per share. If the stock is sold for $64 per share, the gain is $100. The holding period begins on the day the option is exercised, in this case August 12. Note that for tax purposes, the cost basis for the stock acquired by exercising now includes the cost of the option.

Write a call A customer writes PSM Nov 60 Call at 3 on June 4 and is exercised on August 12. Net proceeds would be $6,300. Acquisition cost must be the price actually paid for the stocks. If this is an uncovered option, then the current market price is used. For the writer, the holding period ends when the call is exercised.

Write a put A customer writes a PSM Nov 60 Put at 3 on Sep 4 which is exercised. He must buy at $60, but acquisition cost is $57.

Buy a put An investor buys a PSM Nov 60 Put at 4 on Aug 6 and exercises Sep 7. His proceeds are $5,600. If he had owned stock long term the put does not affect its status; however, for stock owned short term the holding period is eliminated and cannot begin again until the put is disposed of.

Spreads

For spread transactions each option is taxed separately.

SUITABILITY

Options are inherently risky. A registered representative must exercise special care in determining the suitability of this type of investment for each client. This includes recognizing that a situation in which covered options are suitable is not automatically a situation in which the riskier uncovered options are suitable and that in general no more than 15% or 20% of a client's assets should be involved with options. In addition, a client must be advised of the generally higher fees and commissions charged in options trading. The RR (Registered Representative) should also alert clients to the possible tax consequences of options trading on existing stock positions.

STOCK INDEX OPTIONS

Stock indexes are weighted averages of groups of stocks. Recently, options based on these indexes have been introduced. Although trading in these options resembles other options trading, there are some significant differences.

Trading in index options is a way to diversify over a range of equities without having large amounts of capital and without the problems and paperwork of trading many separate stocks. In this way, stock indexes resemble mutual funds. They differ in that there are no management fees associated with index trading and no professional management of the portfolio; one simply chooses an index, *e.g.*, S & P 100, and trades it.

Some indexes are quite broad, like the Value Line Index of 1,500 stocks or the S & P 500. Others are much narrower or more specific, such as indexes comprised exclusively of stocks in a single industry, *e.g.*, computer technology.

Indexes are computed in several ways. The most straightforward method is to sum the prices of all included stocks and divide that total by the number of different equities, without considering the size of each component. Another method is to multiply each stock by the number of shares outstanding before finding a total and then averaging. Finally, some indexes are computed by averaging the percentage change over a stated period in each component stock.

In all cases, the value at some given date is considered a base value of the index. This base may be modified periodically to reflect changes in the capitalization of a component stock, or even by adding or dropping a stock. Finally, the value of an index changes each day with changes in the prices of the component stocks.

Reasons for buying index options

Recall that investment risk is often separated into several components, including "company risk," which is the risk that a particular company will not perform as expected. Diversification can overcome this risk. Similarly, the indexes provide opportunities for moderating "industry risk" (the risk associated with a particular industry) and "market risk" (the risk that the entire equities market will not perform as expected).

Investors use index futures and index options just as they do stock options. An investor who feels that computer stocks are going to appreciate, but is unsure which stock will do best, might buy a call on an index of computer stocks.

Options also provide a method for hedging stock portfolios. For example, an investor who holds stocks with large capitalizations could augment the return on such a portfolio by writing options on MMI (Major Market Index), an index of blue chip stocks. The premiums collected would augment the return on this portfolio.

Characteristics of index options

Contract size The value of an options contract is, with some exceptions, $100 times the value of the index. Thus, if the S & P 100 is at 275.40, the value of one options contract for that index is $27,540. In this way, the 100 multiplier is like the 100 shares of stock in a stock option.

Settlement The major difference between index and stock options is that all settlements in index options are cash transactions. They take place the next business day. There is no opportunity to call an index in the sense of actually buying the securities. Rather, when an index option is exercised, the short (writer) pays the long (holder) the difference between the strike price and the index value times the multiplier (usually 100) at the time of exercise. This difference affects margins in that there are no covered options. The basis for payment is the closing price on the day of the transaction rather than the price at the time of the transaction.

Exercise and expiration Exercise prices for these options are in dollars. They are set at five-point intervals, or as necessary. Expiration and exercise times are exactly like those for stock options: all contracts expire at 10:59 CT (11:59 ET) on the Saturday following the third Friday of the expiration month. Trading ends at 3 p.m. CT (4 p.m. ET) on the business day preceding the expiration date, but an option can be exercised until 4:30 CT (5:30 ET) on that day.

Other features All options are issued by the OCC.

Most of these options are "American-style," *i.e.,* they can be exercised at any time before the expiration date. A small number, however, are European-style options, which may only be exercised during a specified period, usually the last day before expiration. For such options the idea of intrinsic value (outside the exercise period) is less clear since one can take advantage of this value only by selling the option itself. In principle, even an option well in the money might be priced at less than its in the moneyness since one cannot actually capture this money by exercising the option.

Margin requirements*

For long positions, 100% of the premium must be deposited. As mentioned earlier, there are no covered short positions. In calculating margins, "narrow-based" are distinguished from "broad-based" index options. The former are indexes of a specific industry and entail greater risk.

The margin requirement for a broad-based index is 15% of the value of the index plus the premium and minus the out of the moneyness.

* These too are subject to change.

The minimum requirement is 10% of the value of the index plus the premium. In either case—exactly as with stock options—the premium which has been collected would be subtracted from the margin requirement to determine the cash requirement, and a minimum $2,000 initial deposit would be required.

■ **EXAMPLE 1**

With the S & P 100 at 272.50, a 275 Call with a premium of 7 would have a margin requirement of

$$\$700 + (15\% \times \$27,250) - \$250 = \$4,537.50$$

■ **EXAMPLE 2**

With the MMI at 440, a 400 Put with a premium of 1/16 would require

$$\$6.25 + (15\% \times \$43,000) - \$4,000 = \$2,456.25$$

which is obviously below the minimum, so the requirement becomes

$$\$6.25 + (10\% \times \$43,000) = \$4,306.25$$

For narrow-based indexes, the requirement is 20% of the value plus the premium and minus the out of the moneyness, with a minimum of 10% of value plus the premium.

■ **EXAMPLE 3**

With the Gold and Silver Index at 95.00, a 100 Put with a premium of 6.50 means that the requirement is

$$\$650 + (20\% \times \$9,500) = \$2,550$$

Position limits

As with stock options, concern about an individual's ability to influence the market has caused the SEC to establish position and exercise limits of 25,000 on the same side of the market for index options.

INTEREST RATE OPTIONS

At times, options on interest rates—including a long-term interest rate index, T-note, and T-bond options—have been offered through the OCC and traded on major exchanges. The primary use of these options is to speculate on the direction of interest rates or to hedge portfolios of fixed income securities.

For instance, if rates are expected to rise (and hence prices to fall), puts might be bought. If these expectations are realized, one could exercise and reap the reward; if not, one's loss would be limited to the cost of the puts. On the other hand, the manager of a portfolio of fixed-income securities could write call options, increasing the yield on the portfolio and protecting against some modest rate rise as well. Of course, he has the risk that if the rates fall, his portfolio would be called away.

While these options are not currently available, they may be offered again in the future. A brief discussion of the three most popular interest rate options follows. Note that the details of trade practice are offered here only to give a sense of the strategies involved; actual rules regarding contract size, expiration, and pricing may vary.

T-bill options

The contract size is $1,000,000 of 13-week T-bills. The expiration cycle is Mar., Jun., Sep. and Dec., with the three nearest active at all times, *e.g.*, when March expires December begins trading. The exercise of a T-bill option is settled by delivery of $1,000,000 of 13-week T-bills on Thursday (the usual day of issue) of the following week.

Exercise and strike prices are based on the discount yield for 1-year bills. Thus, if the current discount is 6.20 the current price is given as $100 - 6.20 = 93.80$. As noted earlier, each .01 is called a basis point; 1.00 is 100 basis points. The 6.20 annualized discount is adjusted to a 91-day maturity to compute the actual discount and the resulting principal or exercise price as follows:

$$6.20 \times 91/360 = .015672$$

$$.015672 \times \$1,000,000 = \$15,672$$

the actual discount which results in a principal of

$$\$1,000,000 - \$15,672 = \$984,328$$

Notice that the inverse relationship between rates and prices still obtains. This method of converting discount yield to a price does the inversion automatically. Thus, if yield goes from 6.20 to 6.40 the price declines from 93.80 to 93.60. Strike prices usually are set at 20 basis point intervals bracketing current market price; occasionally they are set at 50 basis point intervals.

While each point represents $1/100$ of 1% or $100 on a $1,000,000 1-year bill, these are 13-week bills (or $1/4$ of a year), so each basis point is worth $25 (or $1/4$ of $100). Thus a 20 point move from 93.80 to 94.00 is an increase of $500.

Premiums are quoted in terms of 100 basis points to the unit. Thus, a premium of 1.24 would cost $3,100 ($25 × 124).

T-note options

Contract size is $100,000 face value of the appropriate notes. Prices are quoted as a percentage of par and $1/32$ of a percent. Quotation style is similar to notes: 102.08 means 102 and $8/32$% of par. Since 1% of par is $1,000, each $1/32$ is worth $31.25, so that 102.08 equals $102,250.

Strike prices are set at two-point intervals bracketing current market price. Premiums are quoted like prices: a premium of 2.10 would mean $2,312.50. Settlement of an exercise notice is in two business days.

T-bonds

The size of this contract is also $100,000 worth of the listed bond. Quotations and premiums are the same as for notes. Strike prices are at two-point intervals. Thus, if the bonds were trading at 98.12 when the option came into existence, its cost would be $98,375 and strike prices would be set at 98 and 100.

Margin requirements

Margin requirements for all debt instrument options have the following qualities in common*:

1 All longs are required to deposit the entire premium.

2 Shorts can be covered or uncovered. They are considered covered if:

□ for calls, the appropriate underlying security is on deposit in the account, or an escrow receipt for the same,

□ for puts, a bank guarantee letter,

□ for calls (puts) being long a similar option with a not higher (lower) and a not earlier expiration date.

Objectives of Interest Rate Options Traders

As noted above, investors in these options have two general objectives: to speculate on the direction of future interest rates and to hedge existing portfolios. The former is not unlike the situation with any options trader: longs want increased leverage and limited risk; shorts hope to collect the premium. Hedging strategies are more complex, however. Here are some typical potential uses of interest rate options:

■ EXAMPLE 1

A portfolio manager has some T-bonds at 90. He believes that rates will rise soon, but is unwilling (for tax or other reasons) to sell his bonds. He buys "at the money" puts, and if bond prices decline (*i.e.*, if rates rise), the decline in the value of his portfolio is offset by the rise in the value of the options. If bond prices rise, then the cost of the options is at least partly offset by the increase in the value of the portfolio. The maximum loss of this strategy is limited to the cost of the options.

■ EXAMPLE 2

A portfolio manager wishes to increase the yield on her T-notes. She can do this by writing call options and adding the premium to the interest collected on the notes. Of course, if rates decline and her notes are called away, she may no longer be able to provide that yield.

■ EXAMPLE 3

A corporate treasurer must commit funds for a project some time before corporate bonds are issued to actually finance the project. Fearing a rise in rates, he buys puts on treasury securities of similar maturity to his bonds. These are not identical instruments, but can act as a partial interest rate hedge since corporate and treasury rates are likely to go in the same direction, and he will be able to offset some of the additional cost of his bonds by selling his puts at a higher price.

FOREIGN CURRENCY OPTIONS

Trading in foreign currencies occurs on an enormous scale. Such trading consists of exchanging one currency for another at a specified exchange rate. Most transactions occur in the following currencies:

* Again, these are subject to change.

- □ U.S. dollars (US$)
- □ Canadian dollars (CD)
- □ Deutsche marks (DM)
- □ Swiss francs (SF)
- □ French francs (FF)
- □ British pounds (BP)
- □ Japanese yen (JY)

There are now three basic marketplaces for these transactions; only one is directly involved with options sales.

Interbank

The Interbank market, as its name implies, involves currency trading among commercial banks. It operates 24 hours, conducts business by telephone and Telex, has no central marketplace, is self-regulated, and is dominated by banks and multinational corporations.

Because trading is continuous, there is no "last trade" information, but rates are extremely uniform due to ease of arbitrage. Quotations are available world-wide via Reuters and other quote systems in one of two formats:

European terms Units of a foreign currency per U.S. dollar (*e.g.*, 2DM = $1) or

U.S. terms Units of U.S. dollars in that currency (*e.g.*, $0.5 = 1 DM).

As our interest is confined to trades between U.S. dollars and all other currencies, we do not consider trades involving only non-U.S. currencies.

The outcome of a currency transaction is to credit an account with some number of units of one currency and debit it the appropriate number of units of the other currency. Two types of transactions can occur on the Interbank market, "spot" and "forward" transactions. Spot transactions settle in two business days, except in Canada where they settle in one day. Forward transactions settle in more than two days, with the usual transactions for one month, three months, six months, and one year.

The International Monetary Market (IMM)

The International Monetary Market in Chicago began trading currency futures contracts in 1972. Unlike Interbank transactions, these contracts are for a fixed size, and for fixed delivery (on the third Wednesday in Mar., Jun., Sep., and Dec. only). It is an exchange market, unlike the Interbank where trades are between individual institutions.

A futures contract is an agreement to buy (or sell) a specified number of units of currency, at a future date stipulated in the contract. An initial margin (technically "good faith money") is required, the account is marked to market every day, and deficiencies from a maintenance margin must be made good immediately. The IMM is monitored by the Commodity Futures Trading Commission, CFTC.

Currency options markets

In 1982, a third market for trading currencies was opened when the Philadelphia Stock Exchange (PHLX) began trading currency options in the six foreign currencies listed above. Trades are all in terms of U.S. dollars and are quoted in U.S. terms. Since then, options on the Australian dollar and the ECU (European Currency Unit) have been added. (At this writing, the ECU is not actively traded.)

Expirations There are six expirations: Mar., Jun., Sep., Dec., and two others chosen so that there are always one-, two-, and three-month options available. Currently, only the three nearby expirations are traded.

Trading rules As with all other listed options, the OCC issues options contracts and the same trading rules prevail: trading stops at 2:30 p.m. ET. Options must be exercised by 5:30 on the Friday preceding the third Wednesday in the expiration month and expire at 11:59 p.m. on the day after trading ends.

Specifications The following table gives specifications on options contracts for the Philadelphia exchange.

The options contract expresses in U.S. terms the exercise price per unit of the foreign currency. As the table shows, the BP, SF, CD, AD, and DM are quoted in cents ($.01), the FF in $\frac{1}{10}$ cents ($.001), and the JY in $\frac{1}{100}$ cents ($.0001). Strike prices were originally at 5-cent intervals for the BP, 1-cent for the SF, DM and CD, $\frac{1}{2}$ cent for the FF and $\frac{1}{100}$ cent for the JY. These are modified as necessary.

CURRENCY OPTIONS SPECIFICATIONS
PHILADELPHIA STOCK EXCHANGE

Currency	Number $ of Units	Usual Strike Price Intervals	Minimum Price Change	Value of a $.01 Price Change
Australian Dollars	50,000	$.01	1/100 of a cent	$500
British Pounds	31,250	$.025	1/100 of a cent	$312.50
Canadian Dollars	50,000	$.005	1/100 of a cent	$500
Deutsche Marks	62,500	$.01	1/100 of a cent	$625
European Currency Unit	62,500	$.01	1/100 of a cent	$625
French Francs	250,000	$.005	1/1,000 of a cent	$250
Japanese Yen	6,250,000	$.01	1/10,000 of a cent	$625

Figure 9.1

■ **EXAMPLE 1**

The contract size for the DM is 62,500. Therefore buying,

1 DM Jun 48 Call at $\frac{3}{4}$

would be the right to buy 62,500 Deutsche marks at $.48 per mark any time between now and expiration. For this right the premium is $\frac{3}{4}$ cent per mark or $.0075 × 62,500 = $468.75. The total value of the contract is 62,500 X $.48 = $30,000.

■ **EXAMPLE 2**

The contract size for the JY on the PHLX is 6,250,000. Therefore buying,

> 1 JY Sep Put 65 at 1

would be the right to sell 6,250,000 Japanese yen at $.0065 per yen. The total value is 6,250,000 × $.0065 = $40,625. The premium would be found by moving the decimal four places, 6,250,000 × .0001 = $625.

■ **EXAMPLE 3**

The PHLX BP contract is for 12,500. A premium of 6 for a BP option would represent a total premium of 12,500 × $.06 = $750.

Premium quotes

Since the units of the currencies involved have very different values in U.S. dollars, premium quotes are also in different units. They conform to the quotes of the currencies as listed above.

Minimum changes are also listed in the table, along with the dollar value of these changes. Thus, the minimum premium change in the FF is .05 and since the FF is in units of $\frac{1}{10}$ cent ($\frac{1}{1000}$ of a dollar) the decimal is moved 3 places to the left and we have

> 125,000 × $.00005 = $6.25

as the minimum change in the total price of a FF option.

Margin requirements

As with all other options there is no margin requirement for long option positions. Rather, the total purchase price must be deposited.

Covered For writers of options, again we distinguish covered and uncovered positions. Here it is useful to bear in mind that the underlying security is money in the form of some currency. Thus, a call-writer must have the foreign currency and a put-writer must have U.S. dollars.

There are two basic forms. The first is an option guarantee letter from an approved bank. The letter states that the bank has on deposit, and will deliver from the investor's account, the appropriate number of units of the named currency (or the requisite number of units from the reciprocal currency). Thus, a call-writer must have foreign currency to be delivered against dollars and a put-writer must have dollars for delivery against the foreign currency.

The second is an irrevocable letter of credit from the bank to the broker. This letter states that it will deliver on demand the requisite number of units of the currency.

Uncovered For uncovered positions (short), the structure of the margin requirement is similar to that for equity options. It is the premium, plus 4% of the current value of the contract, minus the out of the moneyness. There is a minimum margin of the premium plus ¾ of 1% of the contract value.

■ **EXAMPLE 1**

If the spot (current) price of the DM is .48 then

> 1 DM Sep 49 Call at .24

on the Philadelphia Exchange has a margin requirement of $150 (premium) + .04 × $30,000 − $625 (out of the money) = $725. (The minimum would have been $375.)

■ **EXAMPLE 2**

With the same spot price

    1 DM Sep 49 Put at 1.2

on the PHLX would have a margin requirement of $750 (premium) + .04 × $30,000 (spot value) = $1,950.

Spread margins Here again the logic of margins duplicates that of stock options. Call (put) spreads are covered when the long strike price is not higher (not lower) than the short strike price. Covered spreads have no margin requirement but the difference in premiums must be deposited.
    For uncovered spreads the margin is the lesser of:
    (1) the margin on the short position,
    (2) the dollar value of the difference in the strike prices.

■ **EXAMPLE**

With the JY spot at 65.40
    Sell 1 Dec JY 65 Call at 1.00
    Buy 1 Dec JY 66 Call at .60
    (1) $625 (premium) + .04 × 6,250,000 × .006540 = $2,260
    (2) 6,250,000 × ($.0066 − $.0065) = $625
    The lesser of these is $625 from (2).

Straddle margins Long straddles require that the premiums be on deposit. Short straddles require the larger of the two short margins.

■ **EXAMPLE**

On the PHLX with the CD spot at .7450
    Sell 1 Sep CD 75 Call at 0.5
    Sell 1 Sep CD 75 Put at 1.0
    Call Margin: $250 (premium) + .04 × 50,000 × $.7450 − $250 (out of money) = $1,490.
    Put Margin: $500 (premium) + .04 × 50,000 × $.7450 = $1,990.
    In general the (more) in the money option will have the higher margin. In this case it is the put margin of $1,990.

Position and exercise limits

With the usual definition of being on the same side, *i.e.,* long call and short put or long put and short call, the position limit is 100,000 contracts on the PHLX. Furthermore, these limits also govern the number of contracts which may be exercised over any five-consecutive-business-day period.

Option strategies

Individuals, or firms, engaged in foreign trade must continually consider the risks associated with the shifting relationships between the U.S. dollar and other currencies. For example, a firm doing business in Germany does so in DM and must make any purchases in that currency; similarly, any profits from such business would be in marks, and must be converted to dollars before being reverted to the U.S.

Options allow one to hedge the risk in such a future conversion. For instance, if one felt the dollar was going to appreciate relative to the DM one might buy DM puts insuring (at the cost of the put premium) that one could later sell those DM at the strike price rather than at the "anticipated" lower price.

For speculators, the situation is analogous to that in stock options. By thinking of the foreign currency as a security with a current price and an anticipated future price, all of the same strategies apply. For example, if one felt exchange rates were going to remain stable, one might sell (write) puts or calls or straddles. On the other hand, if the opposite were true one would buy such instruments.

TERMS

Option Right to buy at specified price within given time; buyer pays for this right

Call option Right to buy (call)

Put option Right to sell

Holder Buyer of contract

Writer Seller of contract. If holder calls, writer must sell at specified price, if holder puts, writer must buy at specified price

Premium Fee holder pays writer

Securities option Usually 100 shares of stock

Options trading OTC and through exchanges; no active secondary market

Options Clearing Corporation Sets terms, provides forms, makes continuous market, supplies daily quotations; acts as principal in every transaction for listed options

Exchanges trading options American, Pacific, Philadelphia, and New York Stock Exchanges, and the Chicago Board Options Exchange

Call options

Call-holder Has right to call (buy) from writer

Call-writer Has obligation to sell if option called

Put options

Put holder Has right to sell securities to writer

Put writer Has obligation to buy if holder exercises his option

Terminology

Long an option Holder of contract

Short an option Writer of contract

Exercise or strike price Price fixed in contract at which option can be exercised

Expiration month, listed options Set by OCC in three quarterly cycles; expire Saturday following third Friday, 11:59 P.M. ET

Expiration OTC options Varying terms

Types Calls and puts

Class All options of one type for a given stock

Series Options identical in class, expiration date, and execution price

Premium Fee charged by writer

Call-holder (buyer) Has right to buy at particular price; profits if market price of underlying stock rises

Call-writer (seller) Sells option to buy; takes loss if market price of underlying stock rises

Note Call-writer's loss generally equals call-holder's gain and vice-versa

Put-holder Purchases right to sell at specified price; profits if market price of underlying stock falls

Put-writer Sells right to sell; must buy if option exercised; takes a loss if market value of underlying stock falls

Intrinsic value Value reflected if call (put) option exercise price is below (above) the current price of the underlying stock

In the money call Option with strike price above market price

Out of the money call Option with strike price below market price

At the money option Strike price exactly equals market price

Out of the money put Option with strike price above market price

In the money put Strike price below the market price

Time value All value not explicitly intrinsic; increases with volatility

Covered options

Covered call-writer Owns underlying security, or holds unexpired long call on same stock

Covered put-writer Sells underlying security short or holds unexpired put on the security

Break-even points

Call-buyers break-even When underlying security price = strike price + premium

Put-buyer break-even When underlying security price = strike price − premium

Covered call-writer Break-even = original cost of underlying security − premium

Put-writer short the underlying stock Break-even = strike price + premium

Uncovered call writer Break-even = strike price + premium

Uncovered put writer Break-even = strike price − premium

Hedges

Long call/short stock Buy call and sell short same security

Long put/long stock Buying a put and buying shares of same stock

Straddles

Long straddle (buy a straddle) Buy a put and a call of same expiration date and execution price for one security

Short straddle (write or sell a straddle) Write a put and a call of same security, expiration date, and execution price

Combinations

Purchase (or sale) of a put and a call on the same security but with different expirations or different strike prices or both

Spreads

Buying and selling a call or a put on one security with either different expiration dates or different strike prices or both; spread = difference between premium paid and premium received on the two positions

Debit spread (buying the spread) If premium paid is greater than premium received

Credit spread (selling the spread) If premium paid is lower than premium received

Margin requirements

Apply only to writers of uncovered options

Covered call-writer No margin requirement if long underlying stock, holds long call on same stock with same or later expiration date and same or lower strike price

Covered put-writer Short underlying stock or holds long put option with same or later expiration date, same or greater strike price

Deposit requirements Uncovered writers must have minimum deposit before any transactions

Margin for naked equity options 20% of value of underlying stock plus premium minus the out of the moneyness; minimum: premium plus 10% of the value of the underlying stock

Marked to market Day's premiums and market prices are used to determine the necessary amount

Covered spreads No margin requirement; customer must deposit difference between premium collected and the premium required

Call spread Covered when long option has not higher strike and not earlier expiration than the short option

Put spread Covered if long option has strike price no lower and expiration not earlier than short option

Transaction procedures

Issuing a contract OCC contract is new offering under Securities Act of 1933; must provide prospectus (Option Disclosure Document)

Ordering procedure Customer orders through brokerage firm, order executed on exchange floor, OCC clears transaction and issues the option contract

Exercise procedure Customer exercises option; brokerage firm notifies OCC; OCC assigns contract to firm representing writers; firm assigns contract equitably

OCC holds option contract obligation, and acts as intermediary between buyer and seller

Required forms

Option information form Signed by both customer and RR and approved by branch manager

Standard option agreement

Prospectus (Options Disclosure Document)

New account form

Options clearing agreement between customer and OCC

Opening and closing transactions

Opening buy—Long, establishing long call or put position

Closing sell—Long, liquidating long call or put position

Opening sell—Short, establishing short call or put position

Closing buy—Short, liquidating short call or put position

Open interest Number of shares still open long and short in a given series

Price Strike (exercise) prices usually bracket current market price of underlying stock when introduced; then at $2.50 intervals for equities below $25/share, $5 intervals for those up to $200, and $10 above $200

Trading Must cease at 3 P.M. CT on business day preceding expiration date; can be exercised until 5:30 P.M. ET that day

Expirations Each listed option has four expiration months; at any given time, only the next three are available

Adjustments in contracts

Cash dividends Exchange-traded options, no adjustment in price when dividend issued; over-the-counter options, option price reduced by amount of dividend

Stock dividends Number of shares increased and exercise price decreased to reflect dividend on ex-dividend date

Stock splits Number of shares or contracts and price adjusted

Position limits (imposed on same side of option = long call and short put; short call and long put)

Tax

Expired options Capital loss to holder, short-term capital gain to writer

Traded options Sale of options position generates capital gain (or loss) of net proceeds less acquisition cost

Exercising Taxes calculated only when security is sold, call premiums included in cost of acquisition

Spreads Each option taxed separately

Stock index options

Contract size Usually $100 times the value of the index

Settlement Cash transactions, writer pays holder difference between strike price and the index value

Covered options Do not exist

Expiration and exercise times Exactly like stock options

American-style options Can be exercised any time before expiration date

European-style options May only be exercised during some specific period, no intrinsic value except during this period

Interest Rate Options Including long-term index, T-note, and T-bond options, sometimes offered

REVIEW QUESTIONS

1. What percentage of the premium on a listed option must be deposited?

   (A) 25%
   (B) 50%
   (C) 60%
   (D) 100%

2. What would the owner of 1 ACI 45 Call have after a 3-for-2 stock split?

   (A) 1 ACI 45 Call
   (B) 1 ACI 45 Call for 150 shares
   (C) 1 ACI 30 Call
   (D) I ACI 30 Call for 150 shares

3. A writer of a CAI Dec 50 Call would be considered covered by OCC rules if he owned (was long):

   (A) 1 CAI Dec 60 Call
   (B) 1 CAI Sep 50 Call
   (C) 1 CAI Mar 40 Call
   (D) 1 CAI Dec 50 Put

Questions 4-5 are based on the following information: An investor buys 2 ACI Mar 45 Calls for a premium of 4 each. The current market price of ACI is 47. Answer all questions without regard to commissions.

4. What is the most that an investor could lose on this trade?

   (A) $200
   (B) $400
   (C) $600
   (D) $800

5. What is the break-even point?

   (A) $45
   (B) $47
   (C) $49
   (D) $51

6. All listed options are issued and guaranteed by the:

   (A) SEC
   (B) option writer
   (C) exchange on which they are traded
   (D) Options Clearing Corporation

7. All listed options expire at:

   (A) 2:30 Central Time on the third Friday of expiration month
   (B) 3:30 Central Time on the third Friday of expiration month
   (C) 4:30 Central Time on the third Friday of expiration month
   (D) 10:59 Central Time on the Saturday after the third Friday

8. Being long a straddle means:

   (A) short a call and long a put
   (B) short a call and short a put
   (C) long a call and long a put
   (D) long a call and short a put

9. Which of the following is true for listed options?

   (A) cash dividends raise the strike price
   (B) cash dividends reduce the strike price
   (C) stock dividends raise the number of shares
   (D) stock dividends raise the strike price

10. When a brokerage firm is notified that an investor wishes to exercise an option, it notifies the:

    (A) writer
    (B) OCC
    (C) AMEX or CBOE
    (D) exerciser

11. An uncovered put writer will suffer a loss if:

    (A) the option expires unexercised
    (B) the price of the stock rises
    (C) the price of the stock drops by less than the premium
    (D) the price of the stock drops by more than the premium

12. An investor buys 200 shares of ACI at $50. At the same time he writes 1 ACI Dec 55 Call at 2. If the option expires without be-

CHAPTER NINE 199 OPTIONS

ing exercised, what profit (or loss) will the investor realize on the stock?

(A) $-400
(B) $200
(C) $600
(D) cannot be determined

13. An investor bought 100 shares of CAI at 38 and at the same time wrote 1 CAI Feb 35 Call at 5. At what price will he break even?

(A) $30
(B) $33
(C) $35
(D) $38

Questions 14–15 are based on the following information: An investor buys 1 ACI Dec 45 Call at 1½ and simultaneously sells 1 ACI Dec 40 Call at 5½. Assume ACI is selling at 43 at that time.

14. These option transactions would be called:

(A) a long straddle
(B) a short straddle
(C) a bull spread
(D) a bear spread

15. If the options are held to expiration, the investor will have a maximum profit if ACI:

(A) closes above 45
(B) closes at or below 45
(C) closes above 40
(D) closes at or below 40

16. Which of the following are on the same side?

I.   long calls, long puts
II. long calls, short puts
III. short calls, long puts
IV. short calls, short puts

(A) I and III
(B) I and IV
(C) II and III
(D) II and IV

17. The largest limit on the number of listed stock options of the same class held by any individual or group acting in concert is:

(A) 2,000
(B) 4,000
(C) 6,000
(D) 8,000

18. Which of the following would be considered the same class of options?

(A) 1 ACI Dec 50 Call and 1 ACI Dec 50 Put
(B) 1 ACI Dec 45 Call and 1 CAI Sep 40 Call
(C) 1 CAI Sep 40 Call and 1 CAI Mar 60 Call
(D) 1 CAI Sep 45 Call and 1 CAI Mar 45 Put

19. The price an investor pays for buying an option is called:

(A) strike price
(B) exercise price
(C) premium
(D) listed cost

Questions 20–22 are based on the following information: In May of 1987, an investor bought 100 shares of Amalgamated Consolidated Incorporated (ACI) at $53 per share. In July, 1987, he then bought 1 ACI Dec 50 Put at ½.

20. If the put expires without being exercised, what are the tax consequences for the investor regarding the premium?

(A) a $50 capital loss
(B) a $50 income loss
(C) an addition of $50 to his cost of the ACI stock
(D) cannot be determined until the stock is sold

21. If the investor sells the stock for $50 in August, what are the tax consequences of that transaction?

(A) he realizes a $300 capital loss
(B) he realizes a $350 capital loss
(C) he realizes a $300 capital gain
(D) there are no consequences until the option expires

22. If the option is exercised and no other transactions take place, what is the investor's net stock position?

(A) long 0 shares
(B) long 100 shares of ACI
(C) long 200 shares of ACI
(D) short 100 shares of ACI

23. The most speculative of the following options transactions is probably:

(A) sell a call and buy the stock
(B) sell a call and short the stock
(C) buy a call and short the stock
(D) buy a call

Questions 24 and 25 assume that the margin requirement includes 20% of the value of the underlying stock.

24. What is the margin requirement for writing an uncovered CAI Sep 30 Put at 4 if CAI is selling at 28?

(A) $400
(B) $560
(C) $960
(D) $2,000

25. What is the margin requirement for writing an uncovered CAI Jun 40 Call at 2 if CAI is selling at 37?

(A) $200
(B) $300
(C) $640
(D) $940

26. The premium on an option not in the money is said to be

(A) the strike price
(B) its intrinsic value
(C) its time value
(D) its out of the moneyness

27. An investor owns 1 ACI Aug 45 Call. A cash dividend is declared with an ex-dividend date of July 10. The investor is entitled to that dividend:

(A) never
(B) always
(C) if he exercises before July 10
(D) if he exercises after July 10

28. A premium of 1.20 on a T-bill option would require payment of:

(A) $1,200
(B) $3,000
(C) $12,000
(D) $30,000

Questions 29 and 30 assume an investor buys 2 at the money ACI Dec 70 Calls and 2 ACI Dec 70 Puts for a total premium of $2,000.

29. The investor can do no better than break even if:

I.   ACI goes to 80
II. ACI goes to 76 and subsequently falls to 66
III. ACI goes to 50
IV. ACI goes to 60 and then rises to 70

(A) I only
(B) I and III only
(C) I, II, and III
(D) I, II, and IV

30. The maximum possible results from this position are:

(A) $1,000 loss and $7,000 gain
(B) $2,000 loss and $14,000 gain
(C) $2,000 loss and unlimited gain
(D) cannot be determined

ANSWERS TO REVIEW QUESTIONS

1. (D) The full premium price must be deposited when purchasing options.

2. (D) The number of shares is increased and the strike is decreased equivalently. The same is true when stock dividends are declared.

3. (C) The covering call option must have a not higher strike and a not earlier expiration.

4. (D) If they expire unexercised, the investor loses the premium 2 × $400.

5. (C) To break even the investor must recapture the premium. He does this by exercising at 49.

6. (D) The OCC takes the other side on all listed options contracts.

7. (D) Since most options trade in the midwest, expiration time is often quoted in Central Time.

8. (C) A straddle is being long (or short) a put and a call of the same strike and expiration.

9. (C) There is no adjustment for cash dividends. Stock dividends increase the number of shares.

10. (B) When an investor wishes to exercise, he notifies his broker who in turn notifies the OCC (or does so through a clearing member of the exchange).

11. (D) The writer collects a premium. If the exercise price is lower than the strike minus the premium, the writer loses.

12. (D) All that we know is that he collected the premium.

13. (B) By collecting a $500 premium the investor is protected until the price drops below $33, the break-even point.

14. (D) A bear spread is profitable if the price of the stock drops.

15. (D) The maximum profit occurs if neither option is exercised. This occurs at or below 40.

16. (C) Holding II, you would like the stock price to rise; with III you would like it to fall.

17. (D) This limit holds for stock with 120 million shares outstanding and 30 million in trading volume over six months.

18. (C) A class is all options of a type (call or put) in the same stock.

19. (C) Choices (A) and (B), the strike or exercise price, are prices at which the investor can buy the stock, not the option.

20. (A) The asset became worthless.

21. (A) The option has no tax consequence unless sold, exercised or it expires.

22. (A) When the investor exercises a put he sells the 100 shares which had been bought.

23. (B) Choice D risks the premium, A is a covered option, and C loses if the stock goes up. B loses more since he is short a call.

24. (D) The margin is 20% of $2,800 + $400 premium or $960.

25. (C) 20% × $3,700 + $200 − $300 out of the money or $640.

26. (C) The intrinsic value is the amount it is in money.

27. (C) If he exercises before July 10 he then owns the stock and is the owner of record when the dividend is declared.

28. (B) The premium is quoted on the basis of $25 for a basis point. Hence 1.20 or 120 points × $25 = $3,000.

29. (D) If ACI goes to 50, he can do better than break even by exercising the put and collecting $4,000. In all other cases, he can break even.

30. (C) The maximum possible loss is the $2,000 of premium. The maximum gain is unlimited since the stock price can rise without limit.

CHAPTER TEN

Client accounts

T his chapter outlines procedures and rules for opening and maintaining customer brokerage accounts. All customer accounts with a brokerage firm are either cash accounts or margin accounts.

The cash account customer who purchases securities pays the full amount required. A margin account customer pays for his purchases by borrowing some portion of its cost from the firm and putting up the difference himself. Margin accounts are discussed fully in Chapter 11, though they are mentioned here when applicable.

OPENING A NEW ACCOUNT

The registered representative is responsible for knowing the relevant facts about the customer. This responsibility is spelled out in NYSE Rule 405, the "Know Your Customer" rule, which is one of the most crucial of the exchange's regulations.

Under this rule, member brokerage firms, their partners, officers, managers, and registered representatives are charged to "use due diligence to learn the essential facts relative to every customer, every order, every cash or margin account accepted or carried" by the firm.

The new account form

For this reason, every firm requires that a new account form be filed for each prospective customer and approved by the firm's management. Essentially, this is written proof that an individual is legally authorized to open an account. The form varies from firm to firm, but all contain at least the following information:

□ name(s)—family name and at least one full name; an initial is not sufficient

□ address and telephone number—usually for both residence and business

□ social security number (or tax identification number)—required by the IRS to identify dividend recipients, and often also required by transfer agents

□ age

□ marital status

□ occupation and employer and type of business; certain employees connected with financial institutions (see below) cannot open an account without special approval

□ bank reference

□ brokerage reference—from any other brokerage accounts

□ citizenship—non-citizens may be subject to certain taxes on dividends

□ cash or margin account

□ relationship—to the registered representative, if any

□ investment objectives

Information about the customer's income and assets may also be sought. If more than one person is authorized to trade in the account, their names and occupations should also be included. This is particularly important when a husband and wife have independent accounts.

Such a form is required for *every* new account. It must be reviewed and approved by an executive officer or general partner of the firm. In some cases, a branch manager can provide interim approval while the form is forwarded to the responsible official.

Other customer forms

Other forms may be required, often as part of a Customer's Agreement. Depending on the type of account, these include:

Hypothecation agreement An agreement that must be signed for a margin account; it gives the broker the right to pledge the customer's securities as collateral to secure a bank loan (see Chapter 11).

Credit agreement An agreement required for margin accounts to spell out the method of calculating and charging interest on balances.

Loan consent agreement An agreement for margin accounts allowing the broker to lend customer securities to other brokerage firms, *e.g.*, for short sales.

Options agreement As outlined in Chapter 9, this agreement is required if options will be traded in either cash or margin accounts.

Power of attorney If someone other than the customer has authority to act in the account, such a power must be obtained for either cash or margin accounts.

TYPES OF CUSTOMER ACCOUNTS

Individual account

This is a cash or margin account in one name, owned by one person.

Joint account

A cash or margin account in the names of two or more individuals either as:

□ "Tenants in common account" (or agreement)—In which interest is divided; should one of the tenants die, that person's portion of the interest becomes the property of his or her estate or

□ "Joint tenants with rights of survivorship"—In which each party's interest is undivided; should one tenant die, the deceased's portion goes to the surviving party(ies), and not to the estate. This agreement is most common between married couples.

In opening a joint account, the registered representative must obtain a joint account agreement in addition to the new account and other forms mentioned above.

Corporate account

This is held in the name of a corporation. The registered representative and the brokerage firm must be sure they are dealing with a person or persons specifically authorized to conduct securities transactions. For this reason, a copy of the corporate resolution authorizing specific persons to trade, passed by the board of directors and signed by the corporation secretary, is required.

This resolution must state that the corporation is legally incorporated and that its charter and by-laws permit stock-trading. Requirements for a corporate margin account are similar. These forms are required in addition to all pertinent documents mentioned above.

Partnership account

Held in the name of a partnership, these require not only new account and other pertinent forms, but a copy of the partnership agreement, which makes the action of each individual partner binding on the other partner(s).

Unincorporated associations

Accounts held in the name of investment clubs, nonprofit organizations (charities, schools, churches, hospitals, etc.) and hedge funds. These require a copy of the group's constitution or other document authorizing securities transactions, and a copy of a resolution naming specific persons to act for the organization, in addition to any other needed forms.

Fiduciary accounts

"Fiduciary" is the term for a person or institution legally authorized to act on behalf of an individual, such as a trustee or guardian, the administrator or executor of an estate, or a receiver in bankruptcy. A fiduciary can open only a cash account; margin accounts are usually not allowed.

With these accounts, in addition to the new accounts form, the brokerage firm must obtain a legal document certifying the individual's authority to transact business. For example:

- ☐ trustees—must present a copy of the trust whether it has been established in a will or is a "living trust," *i.e.,* one set up by a living person.

- ☐ guardians—must present a court certificate showing their appointment as guardian, *i.e.,* as the person designated to handle the affairs of a minor or of someone deemed incompetent.

- ☐ executors and administrators of estates ("executor" is the person designated in a will, an "administrator" is usually appointed by a court when an individual dies without a will)—must present copies of the death certificate and will, a court order recognizing the executor, waivers on inheritance tax, and proof of domicile.

- ☐ receivers in bankruptcy—must present the court order showing they have been appointed receivers.

- ☐ conservator for an incompetent—must present the court order appointing him or her as conservator of someone judged incapable of handling his or her own affairs.

Unless they are specifically granted legal permission to do otherwise, fiduciary accounts must be handled according to the rules on securities investment in their state. These laws are of two types:

"Legal list" Some states provide a list of approved securities and the fiduciary is allowed to buy only items on that list.

"Prudent man rule" Some state statutes do not restrict the fiduciary's investment, except to say that purchases and sales must be "reasonably prudent," *i.e.,* to bring a reasonable income and preservation of capital.

Investment advisors' accounts

Some individuals may be registered with the SEC as investment advisors under the Investment Company Act of 1940. A registered advisor may open an "omnibus account," which shows the advisor as the person who introduced the customer, but lists each account separately.

The advisor must present a power of attorney, a new account form, and a trading authorization for each customer, as well as written instructions indicating where to send duplicate confirmations. (The original goes to the advisor.)

CUSTODIAN ACCOUNTS FOR MINORS

Minors are not legally entitled to own securities, as they cannot execute a contract, *e.g.,* endorse a stock certificate. Thus, a registered representative can prudently maintain an account for a minor only through an adult custodian. Such accounts are regulated in all states by the Uniform Gifts to

Minors Act (UGMA), which includes the following rules for custodian accounts:

1 All gifts to minors must be irrevocable. This means the donor gives up all rights and may not withdraw the gift, nor can the minor return it. Gifts must be "new;" property already owned by the minor cannot be part of a gift.

2 The donor can give cash or securities of any type; there is no limitation on the amount. In most (but not all) states, gifts under the UGMA cannot be established through a will.

3 The donor appoints the custodian who may be the donor or another party. However, when the gift is bearer securities, the custodian must be someone else.

Specifically with regard to brokerage accounts, the law holds:

4 Custodian accounts cannot purchase securities on margin (be margin accounts) or pledge securities for a loan. Securities donated as a gift cannot be purchased on margin.

5 There can only be *one* custodian and *one* minor for each account. Neither joint custodians nor joint tenants are permitted.

6 Securities bought for or sold from the account must be in registered form, in the customer's name, showing the minor as legal owner. For example, "John Doe as custodian for Sally Doe under the Uniform Gifts to Minors Act of the State of Ohio."

Bearer instruments and stocks held in a "street name" cannot be held in the account. This also excludes options, since there is no evidence of ownership. (Bearer securities can be given to a minor if accompanied by a Deed of Gift, but the donor may not designate himself or herself as the custodian of such securities.)

7 Any payment from the account must be in the name of the custodian acting on behalf of the minor and never in the custodian's name alone.

8 The account must show the minor's tax identification number; the minor bears tax liability for the account.

9 The account is completely controlled by the custodian, who may buy or sell securities, and exercise (or not exercise) rights, warrants, or options solely as he or she sees fit. This also means that the custodian cannot enter into an agreement allowing a third party to trade in the account.

10 If the custodian dies or resigns, a new custodian must be appointed by a court (unless the custodian designates a successor).

11 If the minor dies, the account is terminated and the gift becomes part of the minor's estate.

12 Money may be taken from the account for the minor's benefit; for example, for his or her support or education.

13 Proceeds from sales or dividends may be held in the account for a reasonable amount of time; if they are not then reinvested, they must be put in a bank.

14 The custodian must maintain proper records. He or she is entitled to a reasonable sum for services in operating the account and to reimbursement for expenses if he or she is not the donor.

15 Once the minor reaches the age of majority, all securities and cash in the account must be transferred into his or her name.

■ **NOTE**

A guardian has no control over a custodial account (unless of course the guardian is the custodian).

The term "beneficial owner" is often used in discussing custodial accounts. This is the person for whom property is being held, in this case, the minor. No special documents, beyond the New Account Form, are required to open a custodial account under the UGMA.

RESTRICTIONS ON NEW ACCOUNTS

Restricted persons

Under NYSE Rule 407, a registered representative cannot open an account for certain persons without special written approval. These include:

NYSE employees These employees must have written permission from their employers to open a cash or margin account. This applies to employees and members of AMEX and other exchanges, and to spouses of employees of the above.

Registered representatives and other employees, including partners, of brokerage firms, and their spouses Must have written permission from their employer (or another partner if a partner is involved) to open a cash or margin account. After each trade, duplicate copies of each confirmation must be sent to a designated person (partner or officer) in the employing firm.

Individuals employed by a bank, insurance company, trust company or other financial organization Must have written permission from their employers to open a margin account (but not for a cash account). This does not include officers of such companies, who are not considered employees.

Aliens There are some restrictions on persons who are not citizens of the United States.

"Control persons" and those holding restricted securities They are subject to certain conditions on transactions according to the Securities Act of 1933 and SEC rules (see Chapter 15.)

Other restrictions on accounts

Discretionary accounts The holder of an account can give another party (including a registered representative) the right to make decisions about, and transactions in, that account. In such cases, the account-holder must provide written authorization. All orders for such accounts:

□ must be marked discretionary,

□ must be suitable for the account,

□ must be approved on the day they are entered by a partner or officer of the brokerage firm, or by some person in the firm specifically named to provide such approval.

Discretionary accounts can be either "limited power," which excludes the right to take funds from the account, or "full power," which includes the right to take funds. Under these agreements, the broker decides not only when to buy and sell, and at what price, but chooses the securities to be traded. Thus, an order to sell 100 PSM "when the market looks good" would not be considered discretionary.

Both NYSE and NASD rules require that these accounts be reviewed frequently by a member of the firm other than the person exercising discretion. A particular concern is to avoid "churning," or excessive trading in an account simply to generate more commissions without regard to the benefit of the client.

Power of attorney If a customer wants another party to have the authority to trade in the account, a written power must be obtained. In such accounts, the original confirmation of a transaction is sent to the holder of the power of attorney, and a duplicate is sent to the customer.

"Refusal to receive duplicate confirmation" This refusal can be entered by a customer with an account under power of attorney.

Numbered account A customer who wishes to keep his or her identity a secret may have transactions conducted so that only a number appears. Holders of such accounts must provide the brokerage firm with a letter stating the actual ownership of the account.

Second accounts A customer who opens more than one account with a firm should sign a "Two or More Accounts Form."

REQUIREMENTS IN DEALING WITH DECEASED PERSONS' ACCOUNTS

When an account-holder dies, all unexecuted orders must be cancelled, and all records of the account should be marked to show date of death. Any assets in the account should be considered frozen until the necessary documents are presented by a legally authorized person to transfer ownership to the proper beneficiary. The actual documents need vary according to the type of account.

Individual account

□ copy of will; if there is no will, a Surrogate Court Certificate

□ copy of death certificate

□ appointment of executor as stated in the will; if there is no will, court appointment of administrator

□ tax waivers (this document attests to the payment of inheritance taxes; it may be necessary to have one from both the state of domicile and the state of incorporation)

□ certificate of domicile (showing state in which the deceased resided)

Joint tenants with rights of survivorship

□ copy of death certificate

□ tax waivers

Joint tenants in common

All documents listed for an individual account and written instructions on transferring the securities from the executor (or administrator) are required.

Partnership account

If one partner dies, the partnership no longer exists. Surviving partner(s) must then file a new partnership account form and give written instructions on how to dispose of the deceased's share.

Account with power of attorney

If the signer of the power of attorney dies, the power of attorney is terminated.

ORDER PROCEDURES FOR CLIENT ACCOUNTS

The order ticket

Orders from a customer must be presented, in writing, to the firm's wire room or order room. A standardized form (or order ticket) is used. These vary slightly but must include:

□ client's name and account number

□ registered representative's identification number

□ description of securities involved—name (or symbol) and number of shares or bonds (*e.g.*, 100 shares Xerox, or 5M PG&E 7% of 2015)

□ market on which the security is traded (*e.g.*, NYSE or OTC)

□ price limitations—if it is a limit, stop, or market order

□ time limitations—if it is a day or GTC order

□ nature of the order, *i.e.*, buy, sell (long, short); if an option order: buy, write (covered or uncovered), open, close

□ type of account (cash, margin, etc.)

□ special instructions—*e.g.*, on settlement or payment

The customer's name must appear on the ticket; blank tickets are not allowed. If the name is incorrect, or if the wrong customer's name appears, it can be changed only with the permission of an officer of the firm. All errors on order tickets must be reported to an officer immediately.

Client confirmations

With every transaction, a client must receive a written confirmation. This document must include:

- Client's name and account number
- Broker's name
- Trade and settlement dates
- Price bought [or] sold
- Market on which traded
- Commission
- Interest, taxes, registration fees, and/or postage
- Net amount

In addition, for municipal bond trades, confirmation must disclose whether it is a dealer or broker transaction and the bond's dated date.

Reviewing the report of execution

Once a transaction has been executed, a report is sent to the broker who initiated it. This report must be compared to the order ticket; if there is a discrepancy, it must be reported to an officer of the firm at once before any other action is taken. Customers are not bound by errors arising from this discrepancy.

However, an error *in reporting* is not binding on the broker. That is, if the confirmation is inaccurate but the order was filled correctly, the actual trade is binding on the customer. For example, a registered representative receives a confirmation that a particular "at the market" buy order was executed at 35½. Later, he learns the actual price was 36. The customer must accept the price of 36.

Records of customer's transactions

A broker must keep a cross-indexed record of a client's holdings, *i.e.:*

- a "customer book" which gives details of each client's security positions
- a stock record, which breaks down customer's holdings by security

"Back office" order processing

The clerical duties in a brokerage firm are handled in several departments, usually referred to as "the back office." Following the trail of a transaction, they are:

Order department (or wire room, or order room) The order ticket goes first to this department which transmits it to the proper market for execution. When that market confirms the transaction verbally, this confirmation is noted on the ticket. One copy of the order ticket is retained in the Order Department; the others go to:

Purchase and sales (P&S) department This department prepares a confirmation for the customer, computes all of the consequences of the transaction, records them in customer accounts, and handles billings.

Margin department This section is responsible for collecting monies due from both cash and margin accounts. It learns of a trade from the order ticket but does not act until it receives figures from the P&S department. It then handles all activities involving credit, computing when and how much money customers must deposit in cash or margin accounts.

Bookkeeping department Copies of the order ticket also go to this department, which maintains an updated record of all client accounts for the previous six years.

Registered representative Finally, the order ticket is sent back to the registered representative who gives it a last check for errors.

Other back office functions

Cashiering department This department is responsible for receiving and delivering securities and money. All transactions are recorded daily on a "blotter" kept by the cashier. This department also keeps a record, called a "box," of all securities currently in the firm's possession. Upon receipt of instructions from the margin department (called "transfer and ship") the cashier will remove the named securities from the box, send them to the transfer agent, and then deliver them to the customer once his or her name has been registered. Similarly, the cashier will issue payment on instructions from the margin department.

Securities held by a brokerage firm are usually held in a street name, *i.e.,* the firm's name, until transferred.

Dividend department Ensures that dividends and interest payments on securities held by the firm for customers are properly credited to customer accounts.

Proxy department Ensures that proxy statements and information, such as financial reports, go to customers whose securities the firm is holding.

Reorganization department Advises customers of reorganizations involving securities that the firm is holding for them. This department also oversees calls when issued by a corporation, handles conversions at the customer's request, assists in subscriptions for new shares in a rights offering, etc.

Stock record department This department maintains a record of all securities held by the firm by name of security and customer, and number of shares.

Controller's department (or controller) The controller oversees the cashier's department and is responsible for the firm's internal accounts (payroll, etc.), record-keeping, and for filing reports required by regulatory bodies.

TERMS

Cash account Purchaser pays full amount required

Margin account Purchaser borrows portion of cost from firm

NYSE Rule 405 "Know Your Customer" RR responsible for knowing all pertinent facts about any customer

Required forms

New account form For each prospective customer, reviewed and approved by executive officer or general partner

Margin account Hypothecation agreement, credit agreement, loan consent agreement

Others Options agreement, power of attorney, joint account agreement

Types of accounts

Individual account Cash or margin account owned by one person

Joint account Cash or margin account in the names of two or more individuals, as tenants in common or joint tenants with rights of survivorship

Corporate account Held in name of corporation, requires copy of corporate resolution authorizing trade

Partnership account Held in name of partnership, requires copy of partnership agreement

Unincorporated associations Require copy of document authorizing securities transactions, resolution naming specific person(s) to act

Fiduciary accounts Held by person or institution legally authorized to act on behalf of an individual, margin accounts usually not allowed, require legal document authorizing fiduciary to transact business

Legal list State-approved list of securities for fiduciaries

Prudent man rule Statute holding purchases and sales must be "reasonably prudent," for fiduciaries

Investment advisor's accounts Individuals registered with SEC as investment advisors may open omnibus account, must present power of attorney and trading authorization for each customer

Minors' accounts RR can maintain only through adult custodian under Uniform Gifts to Minors Act (UGMA):

Numbered account Customer must provide firm with letter stating actual ownership

Two or more accounts form From customer who opens more than one account with a firm

Death of account-holder All unexecuted orders cancelled, assets frozen until documents presented to transfer ownership to beneficiary

Order procedure

Order ticket In writing to wire room or order room

Order department Transmits order to proper market; when market confirms, sends copies of order ticket to purchase and sales

Purchase and sales (P&S) Prepares confirmation for customer, records transaction in customer accounts, handles billings

Margin department Collects monies due from both cash and margin accounts, computes amount due from customers

Bookkeeping department Maintains updated records of all client accounts

Cashiering department Receives and delivers securities and money

Dividend, proxy, reorganization departments Ensure that securities held for customers are properly credited with dividends, etc.

Stock record department Maintains a record of all securities held by firm

Controller Oversees cashier, handles internal accounts, files reports required by regulatory bodies

REVIEW QUESTIONS

1. On opening a new account the registered representative has a responsibility to determine which of the following?

    I. the customer's investment objectives
    II. the customer's prior trading record
    III. the customer's financial means

        (A) I only
        (B) I and II
        (C) I and III
        (D) I, II, and III

2. A customer enters a GTC order and then goes on vacation. If the customer wants the stock but will not return in time to pay for it by the settlement day, the account executive should:

    (A) pay for it himself and be reimbursed
    (B) request an extenstion
    (C) cancel the order
    (D) transfer the order to a house account

3. The term limited trading authority allows its possessor to:

    (A) enter orders without further authorization
    (B) withdraw cash from the account
    (C) withdraw securities from the account
    (D) none of the above

4. When a client dies the registered rep must:

    I. close the account
    II. cancel all open orders
    III. await the instructions of the executor
    IV. fill or kill all open orders

        (A) I and II
        (B) II and III
        (C) II and IV
        (D) I, II, and III

5. All of the following customer records must be kept by the registered rep EXCEPT:

    (A) each customer's current position
    (B) each customer's purchase and sale for the past three years
    (C) each customer's dividend income for the past three years
    (D) a cross-indexed file of his entire customer holdings

6. Under the Uniform Gift to Minors Act which of the following is true with respect to the custodian and the donee?

    (A) The relationship is automatically terminated at majority
    (B) The custodian is responsible for all taxes
    (C) Payments from the account can be in the custodian's name alone
    (D) The relationship is terminated after majority when the donee instructs the firm to terminate

7. For a discretionary account which of the following is true?

    I. It must be accepted by a principal of the firm
    II. It must have written authorization on file before any trading takes place
    III. The account must be reviewed periodically by an authorized employee of the firm
    IV. All orders must be marked discretionary

        (A) I and II
        (B) I and III
        (C) I, II, and III
        (D) I, II, III, and IV

8. Stock registered in "street" name has as beneficial owner the:

    (A) brokerage firm
    (B) client
    (C) registrar
    (D) transfer agent

9. "Street" name stock has as owner of record the:

    (A) brokerage firm
    (B) client
    (C) registrar
    (D) transfer agent

10. A confirmation will include all of the following EXCEPT:

    (A) trade date
    (B) broker's ID
    (C) limit or stop order
    (D) settlement date

11. Which of the following would require that all confirmations and statements be sent to the investor's employer?

   (A) an account for an employee of the NYSE
   (B) a margin account for an employee of another broker
   (C) a margin account for an employee of a bank
   (D) none of the above

12. On the death of one tenant of an account with joint tenancy with rights of survivorship the:

   (A) account passes to the other tenant
   (B) account passes to the estate of the deceased
   (C) account is automatically closed
   (D) brokerage firm becomes the custodian of the account

13. Under NYSE rules which of the following requires prior permission from the investor's employer?

   I.   a margin account for an employee of a bank
   II. an account for an employee of the exchange
   III. a cash account for an employee of another broker

      (A) I and II
      (B) II and III
      (C) I and III
      (D) I, II, and III

14. All of the following are allowed under the Uniform Gifts to Minors Act EXCEPT:

   (A) gifts of mutual fund shares
   (B) purchases in margin accounts
   (C) gifts of letter stock
   (D) gifts of real estate

15. In processing an order, the information will go through which sequence?

   (A) Order room, P&S, cashier, margin
   (B) Order room, P&S, margin, cashier
   (C) Order room, cashier, margin, P&S
   (D) Order room, margin, cashier, P&S

16. A custodian account may include:

   (A) a custodian and one minor
   (B) a custodian and two minors
   (C) two custodians and one minor
   (D) two custodians and two minors

17. If a registered rep has been told to use his judgment but has no written authorization, he may make choices about:

   (A) which stock to buy or sell
   (B) what price to execute at
   (C) which bond to buy or sell
   (D) how much of a security to buy or sell

The following information is to be used for questions 18–20: An investor wishes to provide his young ward with a gift of cash and securities. Under the Uniform Gifts to Minors Act:

18. If some of the securities are in "bearer" form, they:

   (A) may not be acccepted in the account
   (B) may be accepted in the account if accompanied by a deed of gift
   (C) must be converted to "street name" to be accepted
   (D) may have the donor as custodian

19. The custodian account must have the Social Security (or Tax I.D.) number of the:

   (A) guardian
   (B) custodian
   (C) minor
   (D) minor and the custodian

20. If the custodian dies, the:

   (A) account is frozen until the minor chooses a new custodian
   (B) court appoints a new custodian
   (C) account is liquidated
   (D) account reverts to the donor

ANSWERS TO REVIEW QUESTIONS

1. (C) The client's prior trading record is not required but detailed information on his background is.

2. (B) He may request an extension as long as the privilege is not abused.

3. (A) The authority is limited to trading. No cash or other assets may be transferred from the account.

4. (B) The account is not closed but it is frozen

5. (C) The dividend record is not required. In particular, if the client received dividends directly, the rep would not know about them.

6. (A) The other choices are incorrect since taxes are the owner's responsibility, and the securities must be marked with the minor as legal owner.

7. (D) All are required. Oversight is especially required out of particular concern that the account not be churned to generate commissions.

8. (B) The beneficial owner is the one who benefits from ownership. This is obviously the client.

9. (A) By definition.

10. (C) The trade price is given.

11. (B) All of them would require prior approval to open an account.

12. (A) The most common form for married couples. It allows the survivor to manage the account immediately.

13. (D) As noted above. For choices II and III this applies to both cash and margin accounts. For I, only to margin accounts.

14. (B) Margin accounts are not allowed.

15. (B)

16. (A) Every such account is set up with one custodian and one minor.

17. (B) This is not trading authority. The broker has been given discretion over price and/or time.

18. (B) The securities must show the beneficial owner; hence, if in bearer form they require a Deed of Gift to identify the owner.

19. (C) The tax liability is the minor's. Therefore his tax I.D. is required.

20. (B) A custodian is court-appointed or is designated by the previous custodian.

CHAPTER ELEVEN

Margins and short sales

PART ONE   MARGINS

Margin accounts are accounts in which the customer puts up only a certain percentage of the amount required to purchase securities and a broker/dealer extends credit for the balance. In effect, the broker/dealer becomes a creditor (lends money), the customer a debtor.

For investors, the principal advantage of such an account is "leverage," *i.e.*, the opportunity to buy a given quantity of securities with fewer dollars than required in a cash purchase.

■ **NOTE**   All securities bought on margin are registered in the firm's name (the "street name") because the customer is a debtor. The brokerage firm is then the "nominee," the customer the "beneficial owner."

Terminology

Terms used in margin transactions include:

Margin The margin is the percentage of the sales price the customer must deposit. Under federal regulation, the current margin requirement is 50%. This means that for every dollar of securities purchased on margin, the customer puts up 50¢, the broker/dealer lends 50¢. This Regulation T requirement varies. It has been as low as 40% and as high as 100%.

Hypothecation Hypothecation is the practice of pledging securities as collateral for loans, *e.g.*, when customers leave securities on deposit with a broker as a pledge for purchases.

216

Rehypothecation Rehypothecation is when a broker pledges a customer's pledged securities with a bank (or other source of funds).

Loan value The percentage of the security's market value that the brokerage firm lends the customer is called the loan value. If the margin requirement is 50%, the loan value is 50%; if the requirement is raised to 65%, the loan value is reduced to 35%.

REGULATION OF MARGIN ACCOUNTS

Under the Securities Exchange Act of 1934, the Federal Reserve Board is given the power to set margin requirements and to regulate credit practices in the securities industry. In addition, the NYSE, NASD, and individual brokerage firms set their own margin requirements which tend to be more stringent than those of the FRB.

The three pertinent FRB regulations are:

Regulation U—limits the amount banks can lend to brokers who use any securities as collateral

Regulation G—limits the amount non-bank lenders can lend to brokers who use customer securities as collateral

Regulation T—limits the amount brokers can lend to customers on securities of various types. Reg T does this in part by specifying the proportion and method of payment required for different types of accounts as follows:

Cash account

Customers holding such accounts may buy any type of security, but must pay in full promptly. "Promptly" is defined as no more than seven business days after the trade date. Reg T covers these purchases as a way of limiting the free credit a broker grants a customer. In fact, firms usually require payment in five business days (to conform with "regular way" settlement).

Long account

The customer may buy stocks by putting up the FRB required margin. As above, payment is due in seven days but most firms demand payment in five to meet "regular way" dates.

Frozen accounts

Under Reg T, if a customer does not pay in seven days, the brokerage firm must cancel or liquidate the transaction and "freeze" the account for 90 days. When an account is frozen, no trades can be made in the account unless they are paid in cash in advance.

There are, however, a few exceptions. Margin requirements of $500 or less need not meet the time requirements; purchases of "when-issued" securities are subject to other requirements; and extensions can be allowed "for exceptional circumstances," including illness, postal problems, etc. The broker may request a time extension for payment from a registered stock exchange or from an NASD district office. To insure that this privilege is not abused, no more than five (5) such extensions may be granted in any one-year period.

■ **NOTE**

An account must be frozen if the broker does not receive payment on time or if a customer sells a security before making payment. For example, Mrs. Y enters a buy order for 100 shares of PSM at $50; the stock goes up to $55 two days later and she sells out, taking a profit, without sending a check for the buy. Her account is frozen. A customer must actually send money to the broker/dealer. If the payment is made within seven (7) days, the account is automatically unfrozen.

CHARACTERISTICS OF MARGIN ACCOUNTS

Since they involve extending credit, margin accounts are subject to some special requirements imposed by regulators and brokerage firms.

Opening a margin account

Registered representatives who open margin accounts must have their customers sign a margin agreement form in addition to the usual new accounts form. The margin agreement form states that all transactions are subject to the pertinent laws and rules of all regulatory authorities, exchanges, etc. In addition, by signing, the customer further agrees, among other provisions, that:

☐ all securities may be pledged or repledged in the broker's general loans,

☐ interest will be charged on debt balances in the account,

☐ if equity is inadequate, the brokerage firm may sell the customer's securities with or without notifying the client.

A margin agreement form is usually combined with a consent to lend agreement, authorizing the firm to borrow the customer's securities for its own use or to lend to other brokers. (This usually involves short sales; see Part Two of this chapter.)

Individuals requiring special approval

In general, customers who must receive prior approval for a cash account also require similar approval for a margin account. Such customers include officers or employees (or their spouses) of other exchange members; employees of the NYSE, NASD, and any of their subsidiaries. All such potential customers must have written permission from their employers before a margin account can be opened. In addition, under NYSE rules, any employee of any organization dealing in any form of securities—such as banks, trust, and insurance companies—must have such permission to trade in a margin account. This does not include, however, corporate officers or independent insurance agents.

Approval

The registered representative may not open a margin account without a branch manager's approval. Many firms also require a credit check and/or a cash deposit.

Ineligible accounts

Margin purchases may not be made for accounts held under the Uniform Gifts to Minors Act (UGMA). Fiduciary accounts are also barred, unless there is specific authorization to engage in such trading.

Eligible securities

Under Reg T, only certain securities may be purchased on margin. They are known as "marginable securities" and defined as follows:

□ any "listed" securities, *i.e.*, those traded on a national securities exchange,
□ securities traded over the counter must be on the OTC margin list, which means they meet certain requirements. This list is updated regularly.

Ineligible securities

All OTC stocks not on the list are "nonmarginable" and have no loan value. Therefore, they may not be purchased on margin.

A nonmarketable security, *e.g.*, a U.S. government Series EE Bond, cannot be purchased on margin.

Finally, new issues may not be purchased on margin.

Exempt securities

Certain securities are specifically exempted from Reg T margin requirements. These include debt securities issued by the federal government or its agencies, and by state or municipal governments, or other taxing entities.

Brokerage firms can assign higher loan values to these instruments because they are exempt.

REG T INITIAL MARGIN REQUIREMENT

Under Reg T, a customer who makes a margin purchase must provide an initial amount equal to stated requirements. If Reg T margin is 50%, and the customer wants to buy $20,000 worth of securities, he or she must put up 50% of the total worth, or $10,000; the brokerage firm lends the rest. The amount the customer must put up is termed the "call" or "initial call."

CALCULATIONS INVOLVING MARGIN ACCOUNTS

Long market value

This is the customer's gross cost, including any charges or commissions (charges and commissions are ignored in the examples below for the sake of simplicity), on the trade date; it is used for purposes of calculating the initial margin requirement. After this, securities in the account are valued at their current market price.

Debit balance

Debit balance is the amount lent to the customer by the brokerage firm (the reciprocal of the margin requirement), and for which it charges interest. With an initial purchase of $20,000 and a 50% margin, the debit balance is $10,000. It is useful to bear in mind that the debit balance (often called the debit record) does not change as market value changes.

Equity

The margin customer's net worth in the account is the equity. To calculate equity, the following formula is used.

Market Value − Debit Balance = Equity

In our example:

Market Value	$20,000
Debit Balance	$10,000
Equity	$10,000

In other words, the customer buys $20,000 in securities by meeting the initial $10,000 margin requirement (the equity), and the brokerage firm puts up $10,000 (the debit balance).

This ability to purchase $20,000 worth of securities with only $10,000 in cash indicates the leverage offered in a margin transaction. This is often called "buying power"; a formula for calculating it would be:

Buying Power = Cash Available ÷ Margin %

in this case $10,000 ÷ 50% = $20,000; a $10,000 investment in a margin account has the buying power of $20,000. If the Reg T requirement is 60%, then the buying power of $10,000 is $10,000 ÷ 60% = $16,666.67.

Loan value

As noted above, the loan value, or the reciprocal of the margin requirement, is the amount the broker can lend to the customer. If the Reg T requirement is at 60%, the loan value of $20,000 would be:

$20,000 × (100% − 60%) = $8,000.

FRB Reg U limits the amount of customer securities a broker can pledge to a bank for a margin loan. Under this regulation, a broker cannot pledge securities worth more than 140% of the customer's debit balance. Continuing with the above example, this means 140% of $10,000; or $14,000 of the $20,000 in securities purchased. The bank, in turn, will loan up to 70% of the value of the securities pledged as collateral, or $14,000 × 70%

= \$9,800. This sum is very close to the amount the broker lends the customer.

With Reg T at 60%, the broker could pledge 140% × \$8,000, or \$11,200 worth of securities. Note that 140% is the most that may be pledged, and if a bank requires less than that in collateral, then the lesser amount is pledged. In any case, securities not pledged must be segregated and marked as belonging to the customer.

The rate that banks charge the brokerage firm on such a loan is called the Broker Loan Rate. The Call Rate, the rate that the firm then charges its customer, is typically 1% higher than this.

Buying power of deposited securities

A customer may purchase on margin by depositing fully-paid securities with the broker. The broker then rehypothecates them to a bank for a loan. In other words, the customer purchases securities with the loan. Just how great a quantity of securities must be deposited depends on the margin requirement. The formula is:

fully paid securities deposit = amount of purchase × margin % ÷ (100% − margin %)

Thus, a customer who wishes to purchase \$5,000 in securities by depositing fully-paid securities with a 50% margin requirement must deposit,

\$5,000 × 50% ÷ 50% = \$5,000 (in fully paid securities)

Or:

Market Value	\$10,000	
Debit Balance	\$5,000	(Loan with securities as collateral)
Equity	\$5,000	(Fully-paid securities on deposit)

This meets the 50% initial margin requirement. Note the loan equals the purchase, and the loan itself is collateralized by the deposit of securities.

Again, with a 60% requirement a customer purchasing \$5,000 of securities would deposit

\$5,000 × 60% ÷ 40% = \$7,500

and the account would read:

Market Value	\$12,500
Debit Balance	\$5,000
Equity	\$7,500

Margin Requirements on Transactions Including Options

Recall that option premiums are not marginable; *i.e.*, they must be paid in full. This affects the margin requirements on certain hedge transactions. For instance, suppose an investor buys 100 ACI at 60 on margin and writes 1 ACI Dec 60 Call at 5. The margin requirement at 50% is \$3,000, but the \$500 premium received can be used to meet this call and the customer would only need to deposit an additional \$2,500 to meet this call.

On the other hand, if a customer wished to hedge the purchase of that 100 ACI by buying 1 ACI Dec 60 Put at 4, the total purchase is $6,000 for the stock and $400 for the put, or $6,400. But recalling that the option is not marginable, the amount required for deposit by the customer in this margin account is $3,000 + $400, or $3,400.

Excess equity

If the market value of the securities in a margin account increases, the equity in the account increases correspondingly. Look again at the example we have used after the initial purchase.

Market Value	$20,000
Debit Balance	$10,000
Equity	$10,000

or a margin of 50% ($10,000/20,000).

Now assume the securities go up in value on the market to $30,000.

Market Value	$30,000
Debit Balance	$10,000
Equity	$20,000

The equity goes up exactly as much as the market value. If the customer were to sell out at this point, he or she would realize $30,000 which, after paying off the $10,000 loan, would leave $20,000 (the equity).

This increase in value, then, creates "excess equity."

To find the excess equity, simply subtract equity required for the new, higher market value from actual equity. In the example above, current equity is $20,000, required equity at 50% is $15,000; therefore excess equity is $5,000. The customer can choose to withdraw the excess equity in cash, apply it to a new margin purchase, or leave it in the account.

Withdrawing cash If a customer withdraws the excess equity in cash, *i.e.*, reduces the account by $5,000 to its allowable position, the debit balance increases, because market value − equity = debit balance. In other words, the loan value increases and interest will be charged on the higher amount.

Purchasing stock Assume the customer uses excess equity to purchase additional securities in the same account. The excess now has buying power, and the $5,000 can purchase $10,000 in securities. The account looks like:

	CURRENT POSITION	NEW POSITION
Market Value	$30,000	$40,000
Debit Balance	$10,000	$20,000
Equity	$20,000	$20,000 (50% margin)

The customer can simply let the account stand as is.

RESTRICTED ACCOUNTS

Consider a situation in which the market value of securities in an account declines. If a customer has purchased $10,000 of PSM stock when the margin requirement is 50%, the account looks like this:

Market Value	$10,000
Debit Balance	$5,000
Equity	$5,000

Just as equity rises along with an increase in value, so it falls with a decrease. If the value of the PSM securities a customer has purchased should fall to $7,500, the account would be:

Market Value	$7,500
Debit Balance	$5,000
Equity	$2,500

Note the margin also declines along with market value: here, from 50% to 33%.

Under Reg T, there is no legal limit on how far the account can decline. Even if the stock loses all value, the FRB would neither take nor demand action. (The NYSE, NASD, and individual firms do set limits, however; these are discussed below.) But such accounts do have a different status: whenever the equity in a margin account falls below the initial margin requirement, it becomes a restricted account, and as such it is subject to certain rules governing any sales. (An account can also become restricted because commissions or other charges have been added to the debit balance.) This is called the retention requirement.

To recap, the Federal Reserve imposes both an initial margin requirement (which dictates how much the customer must put up with a purchase) and a retention requirement (which dictates how much a customer must retain if anything is withdrawn from the account). Federal rules on restricted accounts do not require payment from the customer, or bar new trading or withdrawals from the account.

Additional purchases in restricted account

If a customer with a restricted account wants to purchase additional securities, he or she need only comply with the initial margin requirement for those new shares. Look again at the above example and assume the customer buys an additional $5,000 in securities and the margin requirement is 50%. The account looks like this:

Market Value	$7,500 + $5,000 = $12,500
Debit Balance	$5,000 + $2,500 = $ 7,500
Equity	$2,500 + $2,500 = $ 5,000

The account is still restricted because it is still below the 50% margin requirement.

Selling securities from a restricted account

When selling securities from a restricted account, on the other hand, the retention requirement states that only a portion of the proceeds may go to the customer. The balance stays in the account, reducing the credit balance (raising the margin). This could, conceivably, remove the account from restricted status.

Assume $5,000 worth of securities are sold from the following account:

Market Value	$20,000
Debit Balance	$12,500
Equity	$ 7,500

If the proceeds of the sale were left in the account, then:

Market Value	$20,000 − $5,000 sold	= $15,000
Debit Balance	$12,500 − $5,000	= $ 7,500
Equity	$ 7,500	= $ 7,500

returning the margin to 50%. However, if the customer took the allowable portion of the proceeds of the sale in cash, thereby reducing equity by $2,500 (to $5,000) and increasing the debit balance an equivalent $2,500 (to $10,000), the margin actually drops to 33%.

Withdrawing cash from restricted accounts

Cash may be withdrawn from restricted accounts without selling securities. To do so requires deposit of additional margin securities, while the customer receives only the current loan value of those securities. Should a client wish to take $5,000 cash from an account, with the Reg T requirement at 50%, he must deposit $10,000 in marginable securities.

Withdrawing securities from restricted accounts

Customers may withdraw stock from a restricted account, but must replace it with cash or with other securities. In either case, the amount must meet the retention requirement. For example, if Mrs. Y is holding:

Market Value	$15,000
Debit Balance	$10,000
Equity	$5,000

with equity at only 33%, this is a restricted account. If she wishes to take out $5,000 worth of stock and put cash in the account, she would have to deposit $2,500 because 50% of the value of the withdrawn stock must be retained in the account.

If she wanted to withdraw $5,000 worth of PSM and replace it with another stock she is holding, she must deposit securities with a loan value equal to the retention requirement. In the above example, she must deposit the equivalent of $2,500 to take out $5,000 worth of stock due to the retention requirement. However, this $2,500 is calculated in terms of loan value: if Reg T is 50%, she will have to bring in $5,000 worth of the securities for deposit in the account.

■ NOTE

There are two steps to this calculation: figuring the retention requirement and then finding the loan value.

Liquidation of securities to meet Reg T calls

It is possible to meet a Reg T call for a new purchase by liquidating securities in a restricted account, although this is prohibited as a regular practice. It is necessary, then, to remember the retention requirement, *i.e.*, 50% of the value of the sold stock must remain in the account. Therefore, to meet an initial call of $2,000, for example, the customer must liquidate $4,000 in securities.

Simultaneous purchase

There is an exception to requirements generally facing restricted accounts, namely, same-day substitution of equal dollar amounts. A customer who buys, say, $7,000 of one stock and sells $7,000 of another on the same day need not put up additional margin.

Simultaneous transactions of unequal value

When same-day transactions are not exactly even, then Reg T requirements do come into play. If the buy side is greater than the sell side, the customer must meet the margin requirement on the difference, *e.g.*, buy $7,000, and sell $5,000; he or she must put up $1,000 or 50% of $2,000. If the sell side is greater, only 50% of the difference can be withdrawn, *e.g.*, buying $5,000 and selling $7,000, only $1,000 can be received.

INDUSTRY REQUIREMENTS

NYSE and NASD initial requirements

As noted above, the securities industry's self-regulatory agencies impose requirements on margin accounts which are stricter than those under Reg T.

For new accounts, these rules require the customer to put up an equity of $2,000, or 100% of the cost of the securities if the total purchase is less than $2,000. For example, if a customer wished to open an account by purchasing 100 PSM at 70, and the margin requirement is 50%, the call follows the Reg T pattern.

Market Value	$7,000
Debit Balance	$3,500
Equity	$3,500

This satisfies both the initial margin requirement and the $2,000 minimum. But if PSM is at 35, then

Market Value	$3,500
Debit Balance	$1,750
Equity	$1,750

satisfies Reg T, but not the $2,000 minimum. The customer must be called, and the account looks like:

Market Value	$3,500
Debit Balance	$1,500
Equity	$2,000

In effect, a margin of about 58% has been put up.

However, a customer need never put up more than the full purchase amount. If PSM were selling at $17, with the margin requirement at 50%, the account would be:

Market Value	$1,700
Debit Balance	$ 0
Equity	$1,700

When-issued securities are subject to the same minimum rules.

Industry maintenance requirements

As we have seen, Reg T does not set any limit on how far the market value of securities held in a margin account may fall. However, NYSE and NASD rules do impose a minimum maintenance requirement. In a long account, a customer must maintain equity of 25%, or $2,000, whichever is greater. As with the initial requirement, the account is not required to hold more than the full cost of the securities.

Thus, neither the customer nor the broker/dealer can act in any way that brings the account below $2,000. However, if the market value of the securities in the account drops below $2,000, no call is issued as long as the 25% minimum is satisfied.

These are industry-wide minimums. Many brokerage firms demand even higher minimums which are often called a "house requirement."

Differences between Reg T and maintenance calls

If the market value of shares in a long account falls below the 25% minimum, the firm sends the customer a maintenance call. This must be met immediately (most firms allow 48 hours). If it is not, the broker may sell shares from the customer's account.

The customer may meet the call by depositing cash or additional securities in the account, or by liquidating some of the securities held, as described in the calculations below.

Important differences between a maintenance call and a Reg T call include:

□ the maintenance call, once met, brings equity in the account up to the 25% level, not the 50% of the initial call;

□ a Reg T call must be met in seven business days; a maintenance call is due on demand;

□ a Reg T call must be met by the customer. As indicated above, an initial purchase requires an initial margin payment, even if the shares are sold or increase dramatically in value. A maintenance requirement, however, may be met by market action. If the market price of the securities in the account increases sufficiently to put the account above the maintenance requirement, then the call is met.

Calculations: maintenance calls

Consider the case below where stocks decline in value.

	OPENING $	1ST DECLINE	2ND DECLINE
Market Value	$10,000	$7,500	$7,000
Debit Balance	$5,000	$5,000	$5,000
Equity	$5,000	$2,500	$2,000

The margin here has dropped from 50% to 33% (2500 ÷ 7500) after the first decline, and to about 28% after the second. This is still above the NYSE and NASD minimum although it may be below the house requirement.

However, if the securities drop in value below $6,666, a maintenance call would be issued:

Market Value	$6,666
Debit Balance	$5,000
Equity	$1,666

or a margin of 25% (1,666 ÷ 6,666).

The formula for determining the market value at which a NYSE or NASD maintenance call must be issued is

$\frac{4}{3}$ × Debit Balance = Minimum Maintenance Level Market Value.

In the example above, $\frac{4}{3}$ × $5,000 = $6,666 is the balance triggering a maintenance call.

■ **EXAMPLE**

In an account with a market value of $24,000 and equity of $14,400, the maintenance level is found by determining the debit balance and then multiplying the debit balance by $\frac{4}{3}$.

If:

$24,000 − $14,400 = $9600 × $\frac{4}{3}$ = $12,800

then:

Market Value	$12,800
Debit Balance	$ 9,600
Equity	$ 3,200

where equity is 25% of market value.

■ **NOTE**

This calculation is based on the debit balance, which remains constant. Had 25% been taken from the market value, the result would not be correct ($6,000 in the example above).

Another way to express minimum maintenance requirement is

Equity = $\frac{1}{3}$ of Debit Balance.

Since market value = debit balance + equity, $\frac{1}{3}$ of the debit balance requirement yields

Market Value = ⅘ of Debit Balance

which agrees with the first version above.

Meeting maintenance calls

Assume the stock values continue to drop to:

Market Value	$6,000
Debit Balance	$5,000
Equity	$1,000

The market value has now fallen below the minimum maintenance requirement (25% of $6,000 = $1,500) and a maintenance call for $500 would be issued.

Depositing cash to meet maintenance call

There are several ways to meet a maintenance call. The simplest is to deposit cash. Thus, the equity increases and the credit balance decreases. In our example, a deposit of $500 would create:

Market Value	$6,000
Debit Balance	$4,500
Equity	$1,500

Depositing securities to meet maintenance call

A customer may meet a maintenance call by depositing fully-paid securities. The necessary amount is determined by the formula

⁴⁄₃ Maintenance Call = Securities Required.

In this example, ⁴⁄₃ × $500 = $667. The account now reads:

Market Value	$6,667
Debit Balance	$5,000
Equity	$1,667

and the equity is ¼ of the market value as required. The point is that since ¼ of the amount deposited must be used as maintenance for the increase in market value, ¾ of it is available for meeting the maintenance call. Since ¾ × ⁴⁄₃ × maintenance call = maintenance call, the requirement is met.

Liquidating securities to meet maintenance call

Finally, a customer could meet the call by liquidating securities in the account. Although this is not proper as a regular practice for meeting a Reg T call, it is acceptable for a maintenance call. The formula here is

4 × Maintenance Call = Value of Securities to be Liquidated.

In the example above,

Market Value	$6,000
Debit Balance	$5,000
Equity	$1,000

If $2,000 is liquidated (4 × $500 call) the account reads:

Market Value	$4,000
Debit Balance	$3,000
Equity	$1,000

SPECIAL MEMORANDUM ACCOUNT OR SMA

The Special Memorandum Account (SMA) is so called because amounts are kept on the basis of a "memorandum" entry. Funds are not actually moved into the account; an SMA is more like a line of credit than a bank account. A customer who uses the money in an SMA increases the debit balance in the margin account, and therefore pays interest on the amount withdrawn.

An SMA *balance* is created in a margin account when there is excess equity. This means that the client can either purchase new securities or remove cash from the account without violating any of the margin requirements. The account serves to protect the buying power of that excess equity because the amount in an SMA is not affected by a drop in the value of the securities in the account.

The SMA balance can be created by a rise in the value of the securities in a margin account.

Effect of excess equity on SMA balance

Look again at a margin account holding securities which have risen in value:

Market Value	$30,000
Debit Balance	$10,000
Equity	$20,000

The $5,000 excess equity is credited to an SMA. SMA, like excess equity, can be withdrawn in cash (in which case the debit balance is increased), used to buy additional securities under the buying power formula, or simply allowed to stand.

Note what happens in the above example if the securities decline in value:

	ORIGINAL	DECLINE
Market Value	$30,000	$24,000
Debit Balance	$10,000	$10,000
Equity	$15,000	$ 9,000
SMA	$ 5,000	$ 5,000

The result is that equity is reduced (because the debit balance is unchanged but market value has dropped); but the SMA balance remains unaffected and its buying power is preserved.

Adding to SMA

The SMA balance can be generated in a number of ways in addition to a rise in the market value of stock beyond Reg T requirements:

Cash A customer may deposit cash in a margin account which is credited to the SMA if it is not needed to meet a margin call.

Marginable securities When a customer deposits marginable securities into an account, the securities' loan value is transferred into the SMA.

Cash dividends and earned interest If stocks held in the account pay dividends, those dividends may be credited in full to SMA. A customer is entitled to withdraw all dividends and interest from the SMA even if the account is restricted.

Liquidating securities When a customer sells securities in a margin account, 50% of the proceeds are automatically released to an SMA. This reflects the retention requirement.

Reducing SMA

Cash withdrawals from an SMA mean the customer must pay interest on a larger credit balance. These withdrawals are allowed even if the account is restricted. There is, however, one important proviso: SMA withdrawals cannot leave the equity in the account below the maintenance level.

Equity is involved because the debit value is increased, which decreases equity. Assuming an SMA of $14,000, consider the following example,

Market Value	$24,000
Debit	$14,000
Equity	$10,000

Margin is now at 42% (10,000 ÷ 24,000), making the account restricted; the SMA is the result of earlier activity. How much may this customer withdraw before the account reaches the maintenance level? If there is no change in market value, the maximum withdrawal is $4000.

Market Value	$24,000	$24,000
Debit	$14,000 + $4,000 = $18,000	
Equity	$10,000 − $4,000 = $ 6,000	

Withdrawing securities With no SMA, as noted above, the margin account customer must make a cash deposit of 50% of the value of the withdrawn securities. Similarly, with an SMA, the SMA is debited by 50% of the value of the withdrawn securities.

This requirement is imposed because the broker has made outstanding loans using the securities as collateral. By making the customer replace securities with cash, the broker's position is unchanged. The formula here is

SMA ÷ 50%

thus a customer with $4,000 in an SMA could withdraw $8,000 in securities, leaving nothing in the SMA.

Other possibilities include combining SMA and cash. For a customer with $2,000 in an SMA who then wishes to withdraw $7,000 worth of securities, a total of $3,500 is needed.

$7,000 × 50% = $3,500 Total Needed

From this amount, subtract the amount of the SMA,

$3,500 − $2,000 SMA = $1,500 cash must be deposited

A customer with an SMA could also withdraw securities from the account by replacing them with other marginable securities (see below). In this case, one would determine the deposit required, then divide that by the loan value to calculate the amount of securities needed.

For example, a customer wishes to withdraw securities worth $6,000 and replace them with fully paid securities. He has $2,000 in an SMA.

Initial requirement	= $3,000 ($6,000 × 50%)
Less SMA	$2,000
Net required	$1,000

Therefore, the client will have to deposit $2,000 ($1,000 ÷ 50% loan value) in fully-paid securities.

Summary of SMA calculations

Consider the following margin account (with Regulation T at 50%):

Market Value	$60,000	SMA	$10,000
Debit Balance	$20,000		
Equity	$40,000		

At this point the customer can choose one of the following three options:

Withdrawing cash By withdrawing cash from the account, the client, in effect, borrows some (or all) of the cash available in the SMA, thereby increasing the debit balance. If the customer took $5,000 the account would now read:

Market Value	$60,000	SMA	$5,000
Debit Balance	$25,000		
Equity	$35,000		

Buying additional securities The customer could buy up to $20,000 of additional securities without putting up any money. If Reg T were at 60%, then his buying power in the account would be,

Buying power = SMA ÷ 60% = $10,000 ÷ .6 = $16,667.

Inactive account If the account were left alone and the market value dropped precipitously so that the account showed:

Market Value	$35,000	SMA	$10,000
Debit Balance	$20,000		
Equity	$15,000		

the margin would now be 42.86% ($15,000 ÷ $35,000) and the account would be restricted, *i.e.*, between the 25% maintenance and 50% Reg T. At this point, either buying or selling could be considered.

◻ Buying securities—The customer could still buy up to $20,000 in marginable securities using the SMA.

Market Value	$55,000	SMA	0
Debit Balance	$40,000		
Equity	$15,000		

Notice that the margin has now dropped to 27.27% ($15,000 ÷ $55,000) which is very close to the 25% maintenance requirement.

◻ Selling securities—If the customer sold securities the situation would be reversed. Assume instead of buying $20,000 in securities the customer sold $10,000. The client can either take the proceeds, in which case the account would read:

Market Value	$25,000	SMA	$10,000
Debit Balance	$15,000		
Equity	$10,000		

or leave them in the account, in which case the account would read:

Market Value	$25,000	SMA	$15,000
Debit Balance	$10,000		
Equity	$15,000		

With market value at $25,000 the equity in the account cannot go below $6,250, which is 25% of the market value.

PART TWO   SHORT SALES

A short sale is any sale of security which the seller either does not own, or owns but chooses not to deliver. Thus, a short sale is any sale which is consummated by the delivery of a borrowed security by, or for the account of, the seller. To make delivery in such a transaction, the broker borrows the subject stock. Because the customer does not own the stock, he must buy the stock at some future date to meet his sales commitment ("cover the short position") or deliver some stock he owns.

At this time, the Reg T requirement on short sales is 50%. Thus, a customer selling short 100 shares of ACI at 50 would be required to deposit $2,500 into his account. Notice that by selling short the customer is effectively creating additional shares of ACI. The required deposit mitigates the effect of this new wealth in the economy. Additionally, this deposit acts as security for the broker since the customer does not actually have the stock which has been sold.

Customers who sell short expect the value of a security to decline. If the stock appreciates in value, the short-seller loses the difference between the amount he must pay when he eventually buys the shares and the amount he received when he sold them originally. Alternately, if the security declines in value, the strategy is profitable as the customer can buy back for less than the selling price.

■ **EXAMPLE**

An investor sells short 100 shares of ACI at 50. Subsequently the price of ACI falls to 40. The investor buys back the ACI at 40 realizing a profit of $1,000 less transaction costs. Of course, if ACI had risen to 75 instead, and the investor, afraid of even further rises, bought it back at that point, he would realize a loss of $2,500 plus commissions.

■ **NOTE**

Short sales may only be transacted in margin accounts. Legally, any security can be sold short, in practice, however, only "marginable" securities are usually so traded. The reason is that in a short sale the broker must be able to borrow the actual securities. This is difficult or impossible with nonmarginable securities, since they generally are not available for borrowing purposes. Customers sign loan agreements allowing the broker to borrow securities in a margin account, but these would not include nonmarginable securities. Indeed, most firms limit short sales to listed securities and avoid over-the-counter issues.

Note further, that while short sales take place in margin accounts they do not involve borrowing money from the broker creating debit balances; rather credit balances are created by the sum of the market value of the securities sold and the required margin deposit.

In the above example we have:

Credit Balance $5,000 (100 ACI at 50) + $2,500 (margin) = $7,500.

The equity in the account is the credit balance less the market value of the securities. Here, it is simply the $2,500 deposited by the client.

PURPOSE OF SHORT SALES

Speculation

Many of those who sell short are simply speculating. This means the client expects a stock to drop in price, and hopes to make a profit on that drop. Such transactions often include stop and limit orders (see Chapter 8).

Hedging

Another use of short sales is as part of a hedging strategy, *e.g.*, taking a short position in a firm's common stock while holding a long position in a convertible debt instrument issued by the same firm. These strategies are covered in some detail in Chapter 9.

Tax purposes, or sales against the box

Sometimes a customer will sell short securities he owns, or will soon own, "against the box." In these transactions, the seller makes delivery by borrowing stock, not using his own holdings. Later, he may use his stock to repay the lender or buy in the open market to close out the transaction. The usual reason for such sales is to lock in a profit on a security without actually realizing that profit in that tax year.

■ **EXAMPLE**

A customer owns 100 shares of CAI which he bought at 40 and is now selling at 75. If he were to sell, the customer would realize a capital gain of $3,500 and incur the accompanying tax liability. If, instead, he were to sell CAI short against the box at 75, a profit of $35 per share is guaranteed without actually realizing that profit at that time. This is often called "locking in" the profit. At some later date, in another taxable year, he can unwind the transaction by covering his short and selling the security he owned.

Short sales against the box are also used to hedge a long position.

Future delivery

A customer can sell short simply to delay delivery. For example, someone who is traveling and cannot actually endorse the certificates might sell short until he can deliver the requisite instrument.

Market arbitrage

This sophisticated trading technique involves trading the same stocks in different markets. For example, if PSM were trading at a slightly higher price on the Pacific Exchange than in New York, the trader might buy in San Francisco and sell in New York—but sell short because regular-way delivery is not physically possible.

Arbitrage between equivalent securities

It is sometimes profitable to buy a convertible bond and simultaneously sell short the equivalent stock. This usually involves a newly-issued convertible instrument in which the arbitrageur would hold the new issue as a hedge against a short position in the common stock.

RIGHTS OF LENDERS

As defined above, a short sale can be effected only when a broker can borrow stock to deliver to the buyer. The short-seller's broker can supply the securities from its own stock (in other words, lend them to the customer). Or, the broker can borrow from another firm, in which case the borrowing firm must deposit the total market value of the securities in cash with the lender. The lender of the stock can lend the deposited funds and earn interest. For this reason, such loans of stock are usually without charge ("flat"), though a premium can be charged. Sometimes, when interest rates are high, the lender actually pays interest on the money received for the loaned stock, effectively splitting the amount earned on the money.

CLOSING OUT A SHORT SALE

Normally, a short position is closed out when the short-seller "covers" by buying the requisite securities and delivering those shares to the lender who returns the deposited funds.

The following special rules can apply to these transactions.

Mark to the market

If the market value of the borrowed securities rises, the lending broker may demand that the borrower deposit enough additional cash so that the total equals the new, current market value of the borrowed stock. This is called "mark to the market." As a stock loan for a short sale must be 100% secured by cash, the borrower must meet the demand for additional funds immediately. If the market value declines, the lender returns surplus cash.

Dividends from loaned stock

If a dividend is declared on this borrowed stock there are two claimants for it: the investor and the lender. The investor who bought the stock and has the securities will get the dividend from the corporation; however, the lender of the stock also owns shares. Therefore, the short-seller must pay the lender an amount equal to any dividends paid on loaned shares. This amount is usually charged to the short-seller's account. The short-seller must also pay in a timely fashion, *i.e.,* when the dividends are normally paid. The lender does lose the privilege of voting the shares which he has lent.

Return of stock

Under NYSE rules, a loan of securities can be cancelled by either side at any time. The lending firm may return the money and demand the securities, or vice versa. This is usually done through a clearing corporation, but it can simply involve the two firms.

MARGIN REQUIREMENTS FOR SHORT SALES

As noted above, in a short sale the customer's account is credited with proceeds from the sale of the securities. In an example which we will carry forward for further transactions, suppose a client sells short 100 PSM at 100 with Reg T at 50%. The account looks like this:

Credit Balance	$15,000
Market Value	$10,000
Equity	$ 5,000

In this case it is the credit balance which remains constant as the sum of the market value and the equity.

NYSE rules

In addition, NYSE rules require a $2,000 initial deposit on any margin account. However, the alternative ("or 100% of purchase") is not applicable in short accounts; even if the initial transaction is for less than $2,000 a $2,000 deposit is required.

Minimum maintenance (NYSE/NASD)

In short accounts, minimum maintenance is set by the NYSE and NASD at $2,000 or 30% of market value, whichever is greater. For stocks valued at less than $5.00 per share, a margin of $2.50 per share, or 100%, whichever is greater, must be maintained. For stocks valued at $5 or more, the minimum is $5 a share or 30% of the market value, whichever is greater.

REGULATION OF SHORT SALES

The Securities Exchange Act of 1934 gives the Federal Reserve Board power to fix margin requirements on short sales. It also prohibits a firm's directors, officers, and principal shareholders from selling stock short in their own companies. It also sets legal penalties for those who sell short on a national security exchange in violation of SEC rules. Perhaps the most important of these is the "plus-tick rule" adopted in 1937.

The plus-tick rule

This rule is designed to prevent investors from driving down the price of a stock by continuing to sell it short. The rule holds that individuals, whether acting as principal or agent, may not make a short sale on any national security exchange except at a price higher than the last change in price.

The plus tick terminology is straightforward, and includes:

Plus-tick A plus-tick is a movement upward by a minimum price change. It is usually ⅛ point above the previous transaction. For example, in the following series of trades:

(a) 34   (b) 34⅛   (c) 34⅛   (d) 34¼   (e) 34⅛

the trades labeled (b) & (d) would be plus tick.

Zero plus tick A zero plus tick is a price showing no change from a previous plus tick transaction. The trade labeled (c) above is a zero plus tick.

Minus tick (or down tick) The minus tick is a downward movement. In the example above, (e) is the down tick.

■ **NOTE**

Under SEC rules, a short sale can only be made on a plus tick or a zero plus tick.

Exceptions to the rule

The plus tick rule does not apply to U.S. government and municipal securities or to over the counter short sales. Some odd lot orders are also exempt.

Identification of sell orders as short

SEC rules also require that all orders to sell securities be clearly identified as either long or short. Thus, any order for a short transaction must be so labeled.

CALCULATIONS IN SHORT SALES ACCOUNTS

Decrease in market value

When selling short, a decline in market value means a gain for the customer.

Assume PSM, in the previous example, falls to $80 per share on the market. The account now looks like:

Credit Balance	$15,000
Debit Balance	$ 8,000
Equity	$ 7,000

The credit balance stays the same, similar to the debit balance in a long account, and the margin goes up. It is now 87.5% ($7,000 ÷ $8,000). In a short account, too, the difference between actual equity and required equity is excess equity, and this can be part of an SMA. In the above example:

	ACTUAL	REQUIRED (AT 50%)
Credit Balance	$15,000	$12,000
Market Value	$ 8,000	$ 8,000
Equity	$ 7,000	$ 4,000

so excess equity is $3,000.

As with any margin account, the excess equity may be allowed to stand, or taken in cash. If the customer takes cash, then the credit balance and equity are reduced accordingly. In the examples, if the client takes the SMA in cash, the account would look like:

Credit Balance	$12,000
Debit Balance	$ 8,000
Equity	$ 4,000

Buying power of SMA balance

If the customer with excess equity wishes to sell additional securities short or to buy securities, it is possible to calculate buying power. As in a long margin account, buying power is determined by:

Buying Power = SMA ÷ Margin Requirement.

In the above example, $3,000 ÷ 50% = $6,000; thus the buying power is $6,000.

If a client chooses such a course, the account would look like:

Credit Balance	$12,000 + $9,000 = $21,000
Market Value	$ 8,000 + $6,000 = $14,000
Equity	$ 4,000 + $3,000 = $ 7,000 (50% margin)

Effect on SMA of increase or decrease in short market value

Increase in short market value Should the market price of shares sold short increase in value, the customer loses. Although the credit balance is unchanged, equity in the account decreases. Recall the original account:

Market Value	$10,000
Credit Balance	$15,000
Equity	$ 5,000

and assume market value increases to $11,000:

Market Value	$11,000
Credit Balance	$15,000
Equity	$ 4,000

thus producing a margin of about 36% ($4,000 ÷ $11,000). The maintenance margin is 30%, and the level at which maintenance will be reached can be found as a function of the credit balance as follows:

Credit Balance ÷ 130% = Market Value.

In the example above:

$15,000 ÷ 130% = $11,538

an equity of $3,462 remains. Since the credit balance remains unchanged, the maintenance level is reached when the credit balance is 130% of market value. This then implies that the equity is 30% of the market value since equity + market value = credit balance.

As with long accounts, should the margin in a short account fall below the 50% requirement but remain above the maintenance level, the account is restricted. The computations for restricted short accounts are similar to those for long accounts. The obvious difference is that purchasing stock (covering short positions) frees cash while selling stock short encumbers cash.

For example, assume that the account now looks like:

Credit Balance	$60,000 SMA $5,000
Market Value	$42,000
Equity	$18,000

The client could sell short $10,000 in stock,

Credit Balance	$70,000 SMA 0
Market Value	$52,000
Equity	$18,000

and the margin would be reduced from 42.86% ($18,000 ÷ $42,000) to 34.62%. Of course the client could also deposit the additional $5,000 in margin leaving the SMA at $5,000. In which case:

Credit Balance	$75,000	SMA	$5,000
Market Value	$52,000		
Equity	$23,000		

and the margin would be 44.23% ($23,000 ÷ $52,000).

Or the client could take the $5,000 from the account:

Credit Balance	$55,000	SMA	0
Market Value	$42,000		
Equity	$13,000		

and the margin would now be 30.95% ($13,000 ÷ $42,000).

Or the client could repurchase $10,000 of securities.

Credit Balance	$45,000	SMA	$10,000
Market Value	$32,000		
Equity	$13,000		

The important requirements are the 30% maintenance level and the $2,000 minimum balance. These restrictions apply in all cases, except for low-priced stocks where the requirement is more stringent.

Combination long and short accounts

An account will often contain both long and short positions. The requirements on such accounts treat these positions separately. That is, each position must separately conform to the appropriate requirements.

For example, if an account is long 200 ACI at $50 and short 100 CAI at 80, the initial margin requirements (assuming 50% Reg T) would look like:

	LONG	SHORT
Market Value	$10,000	$ 8,000
Debit (Credit)	$ 5,000	$12,000
Equity	$ 5,000	$ 4,000

In fact, the $4,000 in equity in the short account would be applied to the debit balance thereby reducing the outstanding loan to $1,000. Maintenance margin would be computed separately as 25% of the long market value and 30% of the short market value. Here it would be,

$$25\% \times \$10,000 + 30\% \times \$8,000 = \$4,900.$$

If the equity fell below this amount, there would be a margin call.

TERMS

Margins

Margin accounts Customer puts up only a percentage of the amount required to purchase securities, broker/dealer extends credit for balance

Securities bought on margin are registered in firm's name (street name), firm is nominee, customer is beneficial owner

Margin Percentage of sales price customer must deposit

Margin requirements Set by Federal Reserve Board under law; currently 50%, can be changed; NYSE, NASD, and brokerage firms can set their own requirements

Hypothecation Pledging securities as collateral for loans

Rehypothecation When broker pledges customer's pledged securities for loan

Loan value Reciprocal of margin requirement; *i.e.*, percentage of market value lent by broker to customer (if margin requirement is 50%, loan value is 50%)

Applicable FRB regulations

Reg U Limits amount banks can lend brokers who pledge securities

Reg G Limits amount nonbank lenders can lend brokers who pledge customer securities

Reg T Limits amount brokers can lend customers on securities; specifies different types of accounts

Special requirements on margin accounts

Opening account Customer must sign margin agreement in addition to new accounts form

Approval

RR may not open margin account without branch manager's approval

Ineligible

Accounts held under Uniform Gifts to Minors Act (UGMA), fiduciary accounts absent specific authorization

□ Eligible securities: any listed securities, securities traded OTC must be on OTC margin list

□ Ineligible securities: all OTC stocks not on the list

Reg T initial margin requirement Customer who buys on margin must provide initial amount equal to stated requirements, termed the call or initial call

Terms used in calculations

□ Long market value: customer's gross cost on trade date for purposes of calculating initial margin requirement; after this, current market price

□ Debit balance: amount lent customer by brokerage firm (reciprocal of margin requirement)

□ Equity: margin customer's net worth in account

□ Market value: Debit balance + Equity

□ Buying power: leverage offered in margin transaction

$$\text{Buying power} = \text{cash available/margin \%}$$

□ Loan value: amount broker can loan to customer (reciprocal of margin requirement)

Buying power of deposited securities Customer may purchase on margin by depositing fully paid securities with broker

$$\text{Fully paid securities deposit} = \text{amount of purchase} \times \text{margin \%} \div (100\% - \text{margin \%})$$

Excess equity If market value of securities in margin account increases, equity in the account increases correspondingly, "excess equity"

Customer with excess equity can

□ Withdraw cash, increases debit balance, *i.e.*, loan value increases, interest is charged on higher amount

□ Purchase stock

□ Let account stand

Restricted accounts

□ If market value of securities in an account declines, margin declines correspondingly and it is a restricted account, and certain rules dictate how much customer must retain if anything is withdrawn (retention requirement)

Industry requirements

NYSE/NASD initial requirements for new accounts, customer must put up $2,000 equity; 100% of cost of securities if total purchase below $2,000, or full purchase price whichever is less (when-issued securities subject to same rules)

Industry maintenance requirements in a long account, customer must maintain equity of 25% or $2,000, whichever is greater; although no more than full cost of securities

□ Many brokerage firms demand even higher minimums (house requirement)

□ If market value of shares in long account falls below 25% minimum, firm sends maintenance call, must be met immediately (usually 48 hours); if not, broker may sell shares from account

□ Customer may meet call by depositing cash or additional securities or by liquidating some securities

Differences between maintenance call and a Reg T call

□ Meeting maintenance call brings equity up to 25% level, not 50%

□ Reg T call must be met in seven business days, maintenance call on demand

□ Reg T call must be met by customer payment, maintenance call may be met by market action

Calculating maintenance calls

To determine market value at which NYSE and NASD maintenance call must be issued,

$\frac{4}{3}$ × Debit balance = minimum maintenance level market value

or, Equity = $\frac{1}{3}$ of debit balance

Meeting maintenance calls

□ Deposit cash, *i.e.*, increase equity, decrease credit balance

□ Deposit fully paid securities under the formula,

$\frac{4}{3}$ Maintenance call = securities required,

□ Liquidate securities under the formula

4 × Maintenance call = value of securities to be liquidated

Special Memorandum Account (SMA)

□ Amounts kept on basis of "memorandum" entry

□ Customer who uses money in SMA increases debit balance in margin account, pays interest on amount withdrawn

□ Created in margin account when there is excess equity; customer can purchase new securities or withdraw cash without violating margin requirements

□ Not affected by drop in value of securities in account

□ Can be created by rise in value of securities in a margin account

□ Deposit of cash

□ Marginable securities (loan value goes into SMA), etc. add to SMA and withdrawing securities reduce SMA

□ Customers may also combine SMA and cash; or withdraw securities by replacing them with other marginable securities

Short sales

Short sale Any sale of a security which the seller does not own, or owns but chooses not to deliver; thus any sale consummated by delivery of a borrowed security by, or for the account of, the seller

□ To make delivery, broker borrows subject stock; customer does not own the stock, but must buy or deliver it at some future date

□ Reg T requirement on short sales currently 50%

□ Short-sellers expect security to decline in value

□ Short sales may only be transacted in margin accounts

Short sales do not involve creating debit balances, but creating credit balances (market value of securities sold + required margin deposit):

Equity = credit balance − market value of securities

Purpose of short sales:

□ Speculation

□ As one part of a hedging strategy

□ For tax purposes (sales against the box)

□ To delay delivery

□ In market arbitrage (trading the same stocks in different markets)

□ In arbitrage between equivalent securities (*e.g.*, buying convertible bond and simultaneously selling short the equivalent stock)

Rights of lenders

□ Broker must have stock to deliver to buyer, can supply from its own stock

□ If broker borrows from another firm, must deposit total market value of securities in cash with lender

□ Lender can lend and earn interest on those funds

Closing out short sales

□ Normally, short-seller covers by buying requisite securities and delivering shares to lender; special rules apply to these transactions

Margin requirements for short sales

□ In a short sale customer's account is credited with proceeds from sale of the securities

Credit balance = market value + equity

□ NYSE rules $2,000 initial deposit even if initial transaction is for less than $2,000

□ Minimum maintenance (NYSE and NASD) $2,000 or 30% of market value, whichever is greater

Regulations

□ Firm's directors, officers, and principal shareholders may not sell stock short in that firm

□ Plus-tick rule: no individual may make a short sale on any national security exchange except at a price higher than the last change in price

□ Identification: all orders to sell securities must be clearly identified as either long or short

Calculations

□ Decrease in market value means a gain for the customer

Credit balance − market value = equity

□ Excess equity: difference between actual equity and required equity; can be part of SMA; can be let stand or taken in cash

□ Buying power of SMA balance in short account (to sell additional securities short or buy securities)

Buying power = SMA/margin requirement

REVIEW QUESTIONS

1. Which of the following are exempt securities?

   (A) convertible bonds
   (B) municipal bonds
   (C) listed stocks
   (D) OTC stocks

2. After placing an order to buy 200 shares of ACI an investor informs the registered rep that he cannot pay for the stock. The registered rep should:

   (A) liquidate the position and freeze the account for 90 days
   (B) notify the NASD to freeze all other accounts
   (C) liquidate all other positions of this customer
   (D) bar any future trading by this customer

3. If an account is frozen which of the following is true?

   I.   all purchases must be paid in advance
   II. all sales require previous delivery of the securities
   III. no activity is allowed without NASD approval

   (A) I only
   (B) I and II
   (C) III only
   (D) I and III

The following information is to be used in connection with Questions 4–7: With margin set at 50% by Reg T, an investor's margin account has the following positions:

Security	Market Price
200 ACI	40
300 CAI	20
100 ATT	60
Market value	$20,000
Debit	$ 8,000
Customer's Equity	$12,000

4. What is the customer's excess equity?

   (A) $2,000
   (B) $4,000
   (C) $6,000
   (D) $8,000

5. How much buying power does the account have?

   (A) $2,000
   (B) $4,000
   (C) $6,000
   (D) $8,000

6. If the customer wished to add 200 shares of ACI at its current price to his holdings, how much cash would he need to deposit?

   (A) $0
   (B) $2,000
   (C) $4,000
   (D) $8,000

7. If he wished to deposit fully marginable securities to meet the requirement, how much would he need to deposit?

   (A) $2,000
   (B) $4,000
   (C) $6,000
   (D) $8,000

8. Which of the following are true of a maintenance call?

   I.   it is due within 7 days
   II. it is set by the FRB
   III. it can be met by market action
   IV. it is at least 25% of market value

   (A) I and III only
   (B) II and IV only
   (C) II and III only
   (D) III and IV only

9. An investor sells 100 shares of CAI at 30. If he does not already own these shares we say his position is:

   (A) hedged
   (B) short
   (C) short against the box
   (D) arbitraged

10. If this sale was in a new account his margin call would be for:

   (A) $1,000
   (B) $1,500
   (C) $2,000
   (D) $3,000

11. All of the following have set regulations regarding margin requirements EXCEPT
the:

(A) Federal Reserve
(B) NYSE
(C) SEC
(D) broker/dealer

12. Maintenance requirements on margin accounts are set by the:

(A) Federal Reserve
(B) NYSE
(C) SEC
(D) broker

13. The pledging of a customer's securities as
collateral for a debit balance is called:

(A) hypothecation
(B) rehypothecation
(C) intermediation
(D) disintermediation

14. The only account in which a short sale can
take place is a:

(A) cash account
(B) margin account
(C) special account
(D) short account

15. If an investor is short against the box and
wishes to liquidate the long side of the position only, what notations should appear on
the order ticket?

(A) none since it is liquidating a long position
(B) short sale, with the normal up or zero
plus-tick
(C) short sale with no tick requirement
(D) none, but with the up or zero plus-tick
requirement

16. All of the following could open a margin
account EXCEPT:

(A) two brothers in a joint tenant account
(B) a corporation
(C) the custodian under the Uniform Gifts
to Minors Act
(D) a married couple in a common tenancy
account

17. With Regulation T at 75%, an investor sells
100 ACI short at 30. How much would she
need to deposit to meet the margin requirement?

(A) $1,500
(B) $2,000
(C) $2,250
(D) $3,000

18. All of the following may grant an extension
under the Reg T requirement EXCEPT
the:

(A) NASD
(B) American Stock Exchange
(C) SEC
(D) NYSE

19. What is the maximum amount that can be
waived under the Reg T requirement?

(A) $0
(B) $250
(C) $500
(D) $1,000

20. An investor buys $20,000 of ACI which is
marginable and sells $15,000 of CAI on the
same day. If he had a $1,000 SMA how
much additional margin would he have to
deposit?

(A) $1,500
(B) $2,000
(C) $2,500
(D) $3,000

21. If in the previous question the SMA had
been $2,200 what would the margin call
have been?

(A) $0
(B) $300
(C) $500
(D) $1,400

22. An investor sells short 200 shares of ACI at
40. If he makes the appropriate Reg T deposit of 50% his credit balance will read:

(A) $4,000
(B) $8,000
(C) $12,000
(D) $16,000

23. If subsequently ACI rises to 50, his credit balance will now read:

    (A) $0
    (B) $4,000
    (C) $8,000
    (D) $12,000

24. If an investor decided to withdraw $20,000 of marginable securities from his account, how much cash would have to be deposited to maintain the same buying power?

    (A) $10,000
    (B) $20,000
    (C) $40,000
    (D) it depends on his SMA account

25. All of the following are true about selling short against the box EXCEPT:

    (A) it results in locking in a profit
    (B) it can result in deferring a tax liability
    (C) it must be done on an up or zero plus-tick
    (D) it converts ordinary income to a capital gain

26. If an investor has a restricted account, his margin is:

    (A) below 25%
    (B) below 50%
    (C) at 50%
    (D) above 50% but with no cash in the account

27. All of the following can be transacted in a special cash account EXCEPT:

    (A) sell convertible bonds
    (B) sell stock short
    (C) buy common stock
    (D) buy covered calls

28. The buying power in a margin account can be described as:

    (A) cash available
    (B) the cash available times the Reg T requirement
    (C) the cash available divided by the Reg T requirement
    (D) the equity in the account

29. The amount of an investor's securities that a broker may pledge to a bank for a margin loan is:

    (A) 50% of the market value of the account
    (B) 140% of the debit balance
    (C) 140% of the SMA
    (D) 240% of the debit

30. An investor has an account with a market value of $40,000 and a debit of $25,000. If $10,000 of securities are sold from the account the investor may withdraw from the account up to:

    (A) $0
    (B) $2,500
    (C) $5,000
    (D) $10,000

ANSWERS TO REVIEW QUESTIONS

1. (B) All of the others are subject to Reg T except that some OTC are not marginable at all.

2. (A) See question 3.

3. (B) When an account is frozen all transactions must be done on a cash and carry basis.

4. (A) The excess equity is the amount in the account not needed for margin requirements. Here, $20,000 of market value requires $10,000 of margin.

5. (B) The excess equity can be used for margin at 50%.

6. (B) 200 shares would cost $8,000 or $4,000 in margin of which $2,000 are already in the account. Alternatively, $8,000 would bring the market value to $28,000, requiring $14,000 in margin of which $12,000 are in the account.

7. (B) To purchase, with marginable securities, the $4,000 of securities not yet covered he needs $4,000 × 50% ÷ (100% − 50%) or $4,000.

8. (D) I and II are not true since it is due as soon as possible and it is set by NASD, NYSE, and individual firms.

9. (B) By definition.

10. (C) The minimum deposit in a new account even though it exceeds the Reg T requirement.

11. (C) The Fed sets initial margin requirements, the NYSE establishes maintenance requirements, and brokers set house rules which are often more stringent than the NYSE.

12. (A) See question 11.

13. (A) Rehypothecation is the pledging of the customer's securities to the bank for margin loans.

14. (B) A short sale always involves margin.

15. (A) This is not a short sale.

16. (C) These are not allowed under UGMA.

17. (C) $3,000 × 75% = $2,250.

18. (C) The SEC has nothing to do with this requirement.

19. (C) This is at the discretion of the brokerage house.

20. (A) In same day transaction only the difference need be margined. Here the $5,000 of new securities requires $2,500 of margin of which $1,000 were in the account.

21. (A) The $300 required, however, would not have to be met.

22. (C) The credit balance is the sum of the market value $8,000 and the margin $4,000 (equity).

23. (D) The credit balance would not change, the market value would rise and the equity would fall.

24. (A) With Reg T at 50%, cash has twice the buying power of fully paid securities.

25. (D) The transactions all result in capital gains (or losses).

26. (B) An account is restricted if it falls below initial requirements.

27. (B) Short sales take place in a margin account.

28. (C) By definition.

29. (B)

30. (C) Although this account is restricted, the client may withdraw up to 50% of the proceeds of the sale.

CHAPTER TWELVE

Analyses

PART ONE   ECONOMIC ANALYSIS

All activity involving securities takes place in the context of the economy as a whole. For this reason, the registered representative must have some ongoing knowledge of the broader economic picture, and in particular of how general trends and government actions are conventionally thought to affect securities markets.

NATIONAL INCOME AND GNP

The broadest measure of the overall economy is the "Gross National Product," or GNP. This figure is the total value (Gross) of all goods and services produced (Product) in the nation (National) in a year. GNP measures final use. For example, the leather sold to a shoe factory is not counted; its price is included in the price of the shoes sold to consumers. Therefore, adding the leather into GNP would mean counting it twice.

In short, GNP is the sum of all individual consumer spending, all government spending (except for interest payments and "transfer payments" like pensions), and all private sector capital-forming investment (*i.e.*, in facilities needed to create jobs and products).

GNP can be expressed in current dollars, *i.e.*, the actual amounts paid for all its constituents, or in terms of some base year's dollars, such as 1977 dollars. The latter eliminates the effects of inflation since the same yardstick is used to compare two years. The Commerce Department publishes its estimate of GNP once every quarter.

Components of GNP

Analysts break the GNP figure into several components.

Net National Product (NNP) The NNP is the GNP less depreciation, the amount used to replace plant and equipment worn out over the year.

National Income (NI) The NI is wages, rents, interest, and profits paid to all those who produce goods and services; it is calculated by subtracting business taxes paid from the NNP.

Personal Income (PI) The PI is the consumer's pre-tax income; it is derived by subtracting business profits from the NI.

Disposable Income (DPI) The DPI is reported quarterly and reflects what people have after taxes, including transfer payments; it is calculated by NNP less taxes and retained corporate earnings, but plus transfer payments.

Generally speaking, the GNP is viewed as the most complete measure of economic activity and is watched closely.

BUSINESS CYCLES

In general, GNP has gone up over time, but the growth is uneven and there have been periods of decline. The economy has experienced cycles of growth and decline of varying length and varying levels of height and depth.

There is a general growth period called expansion which, at some point, reaches a peak and is then followed by decline. This decline reaches bottom at the trough, or low point, after which expansion begins again.

Recession

Periods of decline are called recessions. A recession is commonly defined as two successive quarters of decline in GNP. In terms of investment strategies, a recession is conventionally thought to hurt first and most firms that produce durable goods (items like automobiles, major appliances, and goods involved in home-building). This is because recession is almost certainly accompanied by increasing unemployment, which in turn means fewer people are able to make nonessential purchases.

Since durable goods last for a long time, the decision to purchase them can often be postponed until economic conditions are better. Similarly, purchase of any items which are considered non-essential may be postponed; however, this analysis for non-essential goods should be used with caution as sales of some non-essential goods do not obey this logic.

Affected industries are often called cyclical industries. By contrast, producers of staple items, like foods and drugs which are essential at all times, are called noncyclical industries precisely because they are usually less affected by the business cycle.

Business cycle indicators

No one can precisely predict business cycles, but analysts do look at indicators, especially "leading indicators," for clues to the turning points in the cycle. The U.S. Department of Commerce has constructed three composite indices of indicators, called the index of leading indicators (12), of coincident indicators (4) and lagging indicators (6). These have been somewhat useful, though as one economist joked, "The index of leading indicators has predicted eleven of the last six turns in the economy."

As their name implies, leading indicators are supposed to change direction before the GNP does, so they draw the most attention from those interested in predicting what the economy will do. The list includes:

1 Average work week for production workers

2 Average weekly initial claims for unemployment insurance

3 Index of new orders for consumer goods

4 Vendor performance; percentage of companies receiving slow deliveries

5 Index of new business formations

6 Index of contracts for plant and equipment

7 Index of new building permits

8 Net change in inventory

9 Change in sensitive materials prices

10 Stock price index of the S&P 500

11 Money supply (M-2)

12 Change in credit outstanding

Inflation

Inflation occurs when the dollar price of a fixed "basket of goods" rises over an extended period of time. This is not to be confused with a one-time rise in prices caused, perhaps, by a natural disaster or the exercise of monopoly power by an economic entity.

Inflation is measured in several ways. The most familiar is the "consumer price index" (CPI), published monthly by the U.S. Department of Labor. This gauges the price of a market basket of goods deemed necessary for a hypothetical average family in the United States.

Explaining inflation

There are several theories which purport to explain inflation. Primarily an indication of their proposers' economic biases, these theories merely start at different points in the cycle of spiraling prices and then say the same thing.

Demand-pull theory One popular theory is called "demand-pull." If the amount of money available to buy goods and services increases faster than the amount of goods and services produced (real GNP), then prices will move up as more money chases fewer goods in the marketplace. That is, since demand outstrips supply, prices rise.

A classic example of demand exceeding supply is wartime. The productive capacity is used to produce goods which are only available for purchase by the government. Since everyone is working, more money is available to purchase what few consumer goods are around. However, if taxes are raised, this extra cash is not available, *i.e.*, because the government is paying for its purchases.

Cost-push theory Another popular theory is called "cost-push." When prices begin to rise (for example, because of demand-pull) the cost of producing goods also rises. In particular, workers will want higher wages to continue buying the same amount of goods. To maintain required profit levels, producers add these new costs into their prices. This leads into a spiral: the new higher prices bring demands for higher pay, which brings higher prices, and so on. In short, increased demand increases inflation.

Other pressures Expectations about continuing inflation, or the fear of future inflation, can also contribute inflationary pressures. Consumers then tend to buy more, fearing that if they wait, they will be forced to pay higher prices. This increasing demand can also contribute to inflation.

Effects of inflation

There is, however, a sort of brake built into the spiral itself. As demand for goods increases, so does the demand for money. If the money supply is not increased, interest rates will rise. As these rates increase, less and less economic activity is profitable, thus applying the brake to the entire economy. Workers are laid off, and those still employed tend to reduce or forego goods and wage increases, which in theory breaks the cycle. The Federal Reserve's policies from 1979 to 1982 led to a classic example of this kind of action.

While some inflation is necessary—some even say healthy—rapid inflation can have harmful effects, especially on those whose income is fixed, such as pensioners. However, real economic activity rarely follows any neat rules for long. For example, though most recessions have been times of very low inflation, in the recession of 1978 inflation stayed quite high (about 8%). This led analysts to coin the word "stagflation" to describe a situation where inflation persists, even though the economy is stagnant or actually declining.

CONTROLLING THE CYCLES—THE MONETARY APPROACH

Attempts to smooth the business cycle and slow inflation have taken two paths—broadly defined as "monetary" and "fiscal."

Briefly, monetary policies attempt to smooth the business cycle by smoothing the growth of the money supply.

The Federal Reserve System

In the U.S., the flow of money and credit is the concern of the Federal Reserve System (the "Fed") and particularly of its board of governors, seven members appointed by the President and confirmed by the Senate. This board directly controls 12 government-owned Federal Reserve Banks around the country. In addition, most commercial banks are Fed members and must abide by its rules.

In general, the Fed tries to keep the money supply growing at the same rate as real GNP is growing.

Measuring the money supply

The supply of money is measured in several ways. The most closely watched, although not necessarily the most important, is called "M-l."

M-l This includes currency in circulation plus the balances in all demand deposits, *i.e.,* accounts from which funds can be drawn by writing a check. A second important figure is "M-2."

M-2 This includes all funds in M-1, plus deposits in regular savings accounts, all time deposits under $100,000 (where the depositor has agreed to leave money in an account for a period of time), money market mutual funds, and IRAs. M-2 also includes overnight repos and non-institutional money market deposit accounts.

M-3 This is M-2 plus large time deposits, term (not overnight) repos at banks and savings and loans, and institutional money funds.

These figures are followed closely by those concerned with securities on the understanding that the Fed's mechanisms for changing growth rates (if that is deemed necessary) may lead to changes in interest rates which in turn affect investors' decisions on the relative attractiveness of stocks and bonds.

Changing the money supply

When the Fed wishes to change the growth rate of the money supply, it does so by acting in one (or more) of several ways. The most immediate method of affecting the money supply, and the easiest to reverse, involves "open market operations."

Open market operations Every month, the Fed's "Open Market Committee" (FOMC) meets to look at the most recent money supply figures in light of the Fed's own guidelines. The committee works to exert short-term control by buying or selling government securities in the open market. If the FOMC feels the money supply is growing too fast, it will sell U.S. government obligations (such as T-bills) in the market. This will draw funds out of commercial banks, thereby reducing the amount of money they have available for loans.

Conversely, if the Fed thinks money supply growth is too slow, it buys government securities on the open market and these funds soon end up in commercial banks. This generally increases the amount of funds banks have available, and in effect, puts more money into the system.

Other methods open to the Fed involve discount rates, reserve requirements, and margin requirements.

Discount rate Banks that are temporarily unable to meet their reserve requirements have the "privilege" of borrowing at the "discount window" of their regional Federal Reserve Bank. The rate at which they may borrow is called the "discount rate" and is set by the Fed. The discount window should be considered as a fall-back resource, and continuous use of this window is thought inappropriate.

If the Fed raises this rate, banks tend to borrow less (or be less inclined to let their reserves fall to the point where they need to borrow). If the discount rate is cut, they tend to borrow more. Thus, a higher discount rate tends to constrict the money supply and vice versa.

Reserve requirements Banks in the Federal Reserve system are required to retain a certain stated reserve, that is, to hold aside a certain percentage of their deposits of all types (though the requirement is higher for demand deposits). This money cannot be lent out to customers.

The reserve requirement is of particular importance because banks, in effect, create money. If a bank lends a client $10,000, it credits the client's checking account with $10,000, "creating" money for the client to spend. The client's checks are in turn deposited and lent again. This is called the "multiplier effect," and it explains why the Fed's reserve requirement is particularly powerful.

For example, assume the requirement is 20% and Bank A has deposits of $1,000. With a 20% reserve requirement, the bank must keep $200, but can lend $800. These funds are eventually deposited in Bank B. Bank B must then keep $160 but can lend $640 and so forth until there is nothing left to lend.

Mathematically, the multiplier effect is derived from the reserve requirement by the formula:

$$\text{Multiplier} = 1 \div (\text{Reserve Requirement})$$

In this example the multiplier is $1 \div .2 = 5$. Thus, the actual supply available to banks for loans is five times the amount deposited. A relatively minor change in reserve requirements can change the money supply considerably. For example, if there is a 25% requirement, then the multiplier effect is only 4. For this reason, the Fed makes such a change infrequently.

Margin requirements Since the Fed sets margin requirements under Reg T (see page 219), it can also affect the supply of money by adjusting this figure. Again, a tighter policy—higher requirements—drives the money supply down; a looser policy brings the money supply up. This can curb speculation, but it is the least powerful of the Fed's tools as it affects only the securities market.

Moral suasion Finally, the Fed can use "moral suasion," asking member banks, often through statements in the media, to pursue a more or less tight policy. Since the banks are dependent on the Federal Reserve Bank, they are not likely to ignore this "jawboning."

Effects of Fed's actions on securities markets

The Fed's monetary actions can strongly affect stock markets. For example, if the Fed perceives a threat of inflation, it uses one or more of the tools described to reduce the amount of money available for loans. Thus interest rates are pushed up. Consequently, companies reduce the amount they invest (as their cost of acquiring money goes up); as investment drops, output and employment go down, which tends to slow the entire economy. In general, corporate securities will offer lower returns and investors will tend to turn away from stocks toward bonds or other instruments which offer a better return.

Other money supply rates and measures

Here are other regularly published monetary figures analysts watch.

Prime rate The prime rate is a nominal rate which commercial banks charge their best customers, although they often lend these customers money at lower rates.

Federal funds rate A commercial bank with deposits in excess of its reserve requirements may loan to other banks which are temporarily unable to meet the requirements. These are called "federal funds," and are negotiable money market instruments (see Chapter 3). This rate is set by the supply and demand for funds, and it is highly volatile. Many other short-term rates are keyed to it.

Call loan rate The rate banks charge brokers for margin loans also may change daily.

CONTROLLING THE CYCLES—FISCAL POLICIES

Economic policies other than monetary are usually called "fiscal policies." Until recently, these policies have been based on the Full Employment Act of 1946 which charges the government with:

- □ minimizing the impact of business cycles
- □ working to promote a growing, high employment economy
- □ keeping prices as stable as possible

To meet these goals, the government uses its basic powers to tax and spend. In very simplified terms, the government increases taxes and reduces spending in an inflationary period; it lowers taxes and increases spending in a downturn.

Automatic responses

Some government responses to excessive swings in the business cycle are in effect built in or "automatic," and work opposite the direction of the cycle. For instance, some transfer payments (government funds which go directly to individuals, like unemployment insurance) are automatic under certain conditions. They work to mute the effects of a downturn by helping limit the decline in consumption. Conversely, when the economy is expanding, more people are working and contributing to these programs and thus have that much less disposable income.

Saving is another automatic response. When the economy dwindles, people are forced to rely more on their savings. This provides additional demand beyond that generated by income, and so consumption does not fall as sharply. Conversely, when the economy booms, people save more of their income, and consumption does not grow as rapidly.

Discretionary policies

In addition to automatic stabilizers, the federal government can take deliberate actions to boost employment and/or modify the business cycle.

Perhaps the most familiar of these discretionary tools is simply spending. When the economy is moving downward, the government tends to spend more (on defense, public works, etc.); when the economy seems to be expanding too quickly, the government tends to spend less.

Another familiar discretionary tool is changing tax rates and structures. Lowering tax rates should increase the amount of disposable income and consumption, while raising them should have the opposite effect. The 1986 tax reform bill, while revenue neutral, was designed to stimulate the economy by providing lower rates.

Federal budgets and income policies

In theory, the government's funds come from the taxes it collects. In fact, it is possible for the government to spend less than it takes in (and have a surplus) or to spend more (and have a deficit).

Partly because it has pursued policies designed to stimulate the economy, the U.S. government has spent, for many years, more than it receives in taxes. Recently, deficits have become so large that many economists feel they threaten the long-term economic health of the country. In theory, expenditures could be cut, but in fact political and social pressures have made such a move very difficult to achieve.

INTERNATIONAL FACTORS

Just as securities markets operate within the economy as a whole, so the U.S. economy must operate within the context of a world economy. Of prime importance in understanding the international economy is understanding the relative value of a country's currency. Generally, a currency moves up or down (appreciates or depreciates) relative to other currencies and a complex series of relative strengths and weaknesses.

The underlying idea here is that of supply and demand. It is measured by the "balance of payments."

Balance of payments

This is the term used to denote the net flow of money in or out of a country. If inflow exceeds outflow there is a surplus; if outflow exceeds inflow there is a deficit. In the U.S., the balance of payments has shown a deficit every year since 1949, although these have never approached the figures for 1984-1988.

Balance of payments figures are calculated in two ways.

Current account This is the up-to-date figure for exports and imports of merchandise, tourist expenditures, shipping, military spending, investments by U.S. firms, and bank loans.

Capital account This is U.S. money invested abroad on the debit side; foreign investments within the U.S. are on the credit side.

Factors affecting the balance of payments

The direction of these flows is affected by many things such as:

□ if interest rates are higher in one country, then investors will tend to buy debt in that country,

□ if inflation is higher in one country, holders of that country's currency will try to exchange it for another,

□ if there is a trade imbalance, then the country with the surplus trade will have the stronger currency. For example, if more German goods are bought in the U.S. than U.S. goods in Germany, more D marks will be needed by dollar holders than vice versa.

□ finally, if the climate for investment in securities, or industry, or real estate is attractive in a country, then a demand for the currency of that country increases.

Recent economic history suggests that these relationships are very complex. From 1981 to 1985 the value of the U.S. dollar gained against all major currencies yet the U.S. continued to experience larger and larger trade deficits. From 1985 to early 1987, the value of the dollar fell sharply relative to most major currencies. The fall was welcomed by many in the U.S., as it was expected to lead to a correction of trade imbalances as U.S. goods became cheaper and foreign goods more expensive.

After more than a year, however, that expectation had not been fulfilled. In fact the opposite continued to occur: the trade deficit continued to grow while the dollar fell. More recently, the dollar has risen and the trade deficit, although still large, has begun to shrink. The conflicting arguments put forth to explain this seemingly anomalous behavior suggest that these complexities are not well understood.

What is clear, however, is that these factors do dramatically affect the economy, individual industries, and individual firms within those industries. To this extent at least, an analyst—and in fact the registered representative—should keep these various factors in mind when trying to determine a course of investment action.

PART TWO   TECHNICAL AND FUNDAMENTAL ANALYSIS

Attempts to analyze the behavior of securities markets are generally called either "technical" or "fundamental," although in practice, most analysts use elements of both.

Technical analysts look at price movements in the market for clues as to when to buy or sell. They pay particular attention to indexes and averages, such as the Dow Jones or S & P, and to "charting" price movements of individual stocks.

Fundamental analysts are more concerned with basic economic factors and with measuring the soundness of particular industries and companies.

In other words, technical analysts think they can learn all they need to know about a security's future price movements by examining data on past price movements and the movement of relevant indicators. These analysts claim they do not need information such as a company's earnings or a particular industry's strength or weakness. Fundamental analysts disagree. They say that only basic economic data can provide the information necessary for buy and sell decisions.

Technical Analysis

Averages and indexes

Technical analysts pay much attention to stock averages and indexes. An "average" can be just that—the sum of market prices of all stocks in a group divided by the number of stocks in that group. A securities "index" tends to be broader and more sophisticated; it is weighted to account for some firms' outstanding shares having considerably greater dollar value than others. Depending on the elements considered, different indexes can show different results, especially in chart form. Yet over the long term, most popular market indexes show remarkable similarity.

Dow Jones Average By far the most widely quoted (and the oldest) stock average is the Dow Jones, or simply "The Dow." In fact, it is four averages:

- 30 industrial stocks, principally manufacturers (the "industrial average" or DJIA),
- 20 transportation stocks including airlines, trucking, railroads (the transportation average),
- 15 utilities (the utilities average),
- 65 stocks, total of all those above (the composite average).

Stocks are included in the averages because they are large, actively traded issues, and account for nearly 30% of the value of all listed stocks.

Thus, a Dow quote does not represent dollars and cents, although it is sometimes described in terms such as "the Dow gained $5 today," or "it lost $12.50 today." Also, dramatic numeric moves can represent very small percentages. If the Dow is reported "up 27 points" when it is at 3000, a rise of only 0.9% has occurred.

Standard & Poor's 500 This is a composite index of 500 stocks: 400 industrials, 20 transportation, 40 financial, and 40 public utilities. It includes a larger and broader selection than the Dow, representing 75% to 80% of the value of all issues listed on the NYSE. S&P's 500 is also more refined: each stock is weighted to reflect the value of its outstanding shares. For example, a company with $100,000,000 in shares outstanding will have 10 times the weight of a firm with $10,000,000 outstanding.

NYSE index This figure represents the average price per share of all common stocks traded on the NYSE. It is weighted, like the S&P 500, by the total value of outstanding shares. Sub-indexes cover industrials, transportation, utilities, and finance. Preferred stocks are not included.

Figure 12.1-a.   Rising Support Line

Figure 12.1-b.   Declining Resistance Line

**Piercing the resistance line at A will often
lead to the line becoming a support line B.**

Wilshire 5000 Stock Index   The broadest popular stock index, the "Wilshire 5000" includes 5,000 stocks from the New York and American Exchanges and the OTC market. It, too, is dollar-weighted.

NASDAQ-OTC price indexes   These indexes include a composite index for the 2,000 plus stocks listed on NASDAQ; and sub-indexes for industrial, transportation, utilities, banks, insurance, and "other finance." It is prepared by the NASD. Mutual funds, though traded OTC, are not included.

Market theories

Technical analysts consider averages and indexes in judging overall market strength or weakness, and in discerning a "bullish" or "bearish" market. When technical factors show a strong market, they recommend investors buy; when the market looks weak, they recommend selling or selling short.

In making these determinations, technicians use one or more of several theories. Keep in mind that these theories are supposed to show general trends in the market, not the worth or attractiveness of an individual security.

Dow theory   This oldest of the technical theories is supposed to indicate when a major, long-term trend in the market is about to change either up or down. Dow theory distinguishes these "primary trends" (lasting a year or more) from "secondary reactions," lasting a few weeks to a few months, and "fluctuations," which last some hours or days.

These distinctions are important because stocks rarely move in a straight line; there are almost always corrections in the other direction. Dow theorists say these smaller moves can point to a primary trend: a rising market when the chart shows each secondary low is higher than the preceding low (and each high is higher) or a falling market if the lows (and highs) show a descending pattern. (See Figure 12.1)

Indeed, such changes at the secondary level—lows starting to fall below previous levels in a rising market and vice-versa—may signal a new trend.

Both the Industrial and Transportation indexes must be rising to show an upward trend; a rise in only one is considered a false signal, especially if the other is falling. The reasoning here is that an increase in industrial production cannot be sustained unless the means to distribute (transportation) grows accordingly. Conversely, if both industrials and transportation are down, a downtrend is indicated. (Note this is more of an economic argument and, hence, more in keeping with fundamental analysis than with technical analysis.)

Once the Dow theorist determines that a primary trend exists, investors are urged to go with the trend, *i.e.*, to buy in a bull market and sell short in a bear market.

There have been many challenges to the Dow's validity as a measure of the market, but, perhaps because of its age, the Dow's popularity continues. Like the Dow index itself, Dow Theory has been criticized as imprecise, slow to show changes, and often (some studies say half the time) simply wrong; but like the Dow, it is still widely used.

Advance-decline ("breadth of market") theory This theory counts the number of traded issues moving up in price (advanced), less the number moving down (declined), to arrive at a net figure. For example, if 2,200 different securities trade, with 1,200 up, 800 down, and 200 unchanged, the advance-decline figure would be plus 400. If, over time, the figure is positive (advances exceed declines), the situation is bullish; a negative number signals a bearish market.

The time period measured can vary; the important indicator is a net change in either direction. This figure can be negative, even when a stock index is rising, since the net change measures numbers of different shares only, while indexes are weighted averages. In fact, many advance-decline theorists look for such a disparity, and think a noticeable rise or fall in the advance-decline line presages a movement up or down in the market as a whole.

As the advance-decline theory considers all traded issues, this approach provides a broader measure of securities prices than Dow theory. It is usually employed in conjunction with other theories.

Volume of trading Here the number of shares traded (the volume) is compared with changes in market price. High volume in a rising market is generally considered a bullish sign, low volume a bearish one; the idea here is that low volume means an absence of buyers, as sellers are always present.

Specifically, this theory holds that volume tends to fall before a major turn in price averages; in other words, declining volume indicates the end of a bull market and is a "sell" signal. By the same token, a surge of volume after an extended decline suggests stocks have "bottomed out" and a reversal is due; this is a "buy" signal.

Those who follow this indicator hold that volume and price must move together. They consider a price rise with low volume, or high volume with no increase in price, as signs of a technically weak market.

Odd lot theory This theory suggests that small investors always move in the wrong direction, that they act on poor or late information, so they buy or sell incorrectly or too late.

To gauge small investor sentiment, this theory examines the number of transactions for odd lots (less than 100-share units which small investors prefer). This is usually translated into an index, showing odd lot sales as a percentage of all sales. If the number is high (*i.e.*, if more odd lots are being bought, this is considered a sell signal; if the number falls, it is a buy signal).

Short interest theory "Short interest" refers to the number of outstanding shares sold short. Technicians usually calculate short interest in proportion to average daily volume or some other volume figure; this is the "short interest ratio."

Here, the underlying premise is that short-sellers, since they must eventually enter the market and buy to cover their positions, will tend to act as a brake in a declining market. Thus, a high short interest ratio (more short-sellers) is considered bullish; a low ratio is bearish.

Confidence index This index attempts to measure how confident investors are that markets will go up or down. It looks to the bond market, since bond holdings often reflect the judgement of those who manage portfolios for large institutions. If they are pessimistic, the theory holds, they will tend to move strongly toward the highest-rated bonds; if optimistic, toward lower-rated but higher-yielding bonds.

To measure the relative attraction of the two, the technician might use a ratio derived by comparing the yield on Barron's high grade 10-bond average with the yield on the Dow Jones 40-bond average, which includes some lower-rated bonds. If lower-grade bond yields are improving this is a bullish signal.

Charting—the technical analysis of individual securities

In deciding whether to buy a particular security, a technical analyst usually turns to "charting." (In fact, technicians are often also called "chartists.") Charting means plotting the stock's price movement over time on a graph.

The "levels" Here, dozens of different methods are in use, but almost all recognize "support" and "resistance" levels, "head and shoulders" formations, and "trendlines." If, in the time period covered by the chart (see Figure 12.2), the security being tracked has moved up and down in price, but has remained within a band bounded by the line LL below and the line HH above, then LL is called a "support level" and HH a "resistance level."

Figure 12.2   Rising Channel

Chartists think that once a stock "breaks through" such a level, *e.g.*, falls below LL, then it is likely to decline considerably further. Similarly, if the price were to penetrate above HH, it would be an indication that the price will continue to rise.

Example of a Head and Shoulders

Figure 12.3   After breaking the neckline at F the neckline becomes a resistance line.

One strategy is to buy securities near LL and to sell them near HH; another is to wait until such a level has been penetrated and then to "ride that trend." It should be noted that, since there are many chartists, any time a clearly defined band exists, the theory will tend to be self-fulfilling since the chartists will all act as if it were true.

Reading such a chart (or any of the others that are in use) to discover the correct pattern is something of an art, and hence, provides many opportunities for chartists to disagree.

The patterns There are many chart patterns which are believed to be significant. Without attempting to be exhaustive, we note the popular chart formation called a "head and shoulders" pattern. (see Figure 12.3)

Some chartists think such a formation indicates that a stock has peaked (top form) and will start to fall; an inversion of this pattern would indicate that a stock has bottomed out and is ready to rise.

■ **NOTE**

With the arrival of substantial computational and graphic tools, analysts have been using more and more sophisticated mathematical forms to model the price movements of securities. These include moving averages, exponential smoothings, and other more complex techniques. The goal of all of these tools is the same: to predict the future price of a security based upon information about past prices and volumes. This distinguishes them from fundamental analyses.

FUNDAMENTAL ANALYSIS

While technical analysts look at price movements in the market, the fundamental analyst looks at underlying economic factors: basic conditions in the economy itself, in a particular industry, and in particular companies within that industry. An "industry" can be more or less broadly defined, *e.g.*, electronics or microchips, rubber or tires.

Industry categories

Analysts often group industries into three broad categories.

Noncyclical industries These are relatively resistant to business cycle ups and downs, and can be considered "defensive investments." Examples are the food and drug producers and utilities. In general, investments in these firms tend to be less risky, but therefore often bring relatively low returns.

Cyclical industries The opposite of the above, cyclical industries are most affected by downturns and recoveries. Examples are producers of "durable goods," such as automobiles, heavy equipment, housing materials, etc. When the economy slows, or inflation is rising rapidly, individual consumers and businesses both tend to delay purchases of such goods.

Growth industries This grouping is less influenced by business cycles than by investors' expectations that these producers will grow faster than the economy as a whole. Such firms often concentrate heavily on research (recent examples include lasers and biotechnology).

Industry life cycles

Of course, no industry can grow forever. Recognizing this, the fundamental analyst may also look at an industry in terms of its "life cycle," and speak of phases like:

Pioneering This is a period of strong and rapid expansion, because the industry is relatively new (exploiting a technological innovation, perhaps). This is also often a period of keen competition as many firms rush to enter the market. Those that succeed reward their investors handsomely, but, of course, most firms will not succeed, with unhappy consequences for the investors. Genetic engineering is an industry in the pioneering stage. At this writing, it is not clear which of the many firms in the industry will ultimately be its leaders.

Growth In this phase, the industry expands rapidly. This tends to be a period of only modest consolidation; many firms sell their products to this growing market. Minicomputers have been an example of a growth industry.

Maturity A time of slower growth, stagnation, or even actual decline, with a few surviving firms accounting for nearly all the industry's output. The automobile industry in this country is certainly mature. As companies move through this cycle, the potential for further growth, and hence rapid price appreciation, goes down; investors look for higher dividends to compensate for this lower capital appreciation.

Other factors considered by fundamental analysts

In addition to examining broad measures, the fundamental analyst will explore a number of specific quantitative factors concerning an industry, relying on both government sources (such as the Federal Reserve Banks and the Department of Commerce) and commercial, trade, and financial publications.

Items of concern include statistics on sales (both raw figures and changes over time as compared to GNP); production and inventory levels;

industry wage rates, price levels, and profit margins; information about the financial health of an industry; and chances for industry growth.

The fundamental analyst tends to specialize in an industry or even a single company. This analyst looks at quantitative and qualitative indicators of a company's position within its industry, as well as its current financial position, stability, and expected growth.

PART THREE　SECURITIES ANALYSIS

A registered representative is often called on to analyze an individual firm, either to select a promising investment or to evaluate continuing performance. Financial statement analysis is the "window" into a company's operations.

This analysis requires a great deal of skill and experience, and the registered representative will usually rely on the research of professionals who have acquired this experience. However, the rep needs training to put this research into practice, and should be able to read financial statements.

This part explains how to read these statements and outlines measures used to gauge a firm's overall performance, its profitability, and the soundness of its financial position. The closing sections deal with investment risks as they relate to assembling an investment portfolio.

The two fundamental financial statements are the balance sheet and the income statement.

THE BALANCE SHEET

This is perhaps the most familiar form of financial statement. It provides a snapshot, usually taken at the end of the fiscal year, which shows the company's monetary position at that moment in time.

The two elements which must balance are usually displayed side by side: on one side, assets; on the other, liabilities and shareholder equity (sometimes called net worth). The idea is that the assets of the firm minus its liabilities belong to the owners or shareholders. The equation of balance is written:

Total Assets = Total Liabilities + Shareholders' Equity

Each side will be examined in turn.

Assets

Anything the corporation owns is considered an asset. These are listed on the left side of the balance sheet in decreasing order of liquidity, *i.e.*, beginning with those that are most easily converted into cash. Further, they are separated into:

Figure 12.4   AMALGAMATED CONSOLIDATED
INCORPORATED
BALANCE SHEET
DECEMBER 31, 1990

Assets			Liabilities		
Cash		$ 400,000	Accounts Payable		$ 250,000
Marketable Securities		100,000	Notes Payable		100,000
Accounts Receivable		300,000	Income Taxes Payable		100,000
Inventory		200,000	Dividends Payable		50,000
Total Current Assets		1,000,000	Total Current Liabilities		500,000
Plant & Equipment	$2,500,000		10% Bonds Payable		
Less: Accumulated			due in 1999		1,000,000
Depreciation	(600,000)		Total Liabilities		1,500,000
Net Plant & Equipment		1,900,000	Shareholders Equity		
Patents		100,000	Preferred Stock (5%)	$200,000	
			(100 par value)		
			Common Stock ($2 par)	400,000	
			Additional Paid-in		
			Capital	600,000	
			Retained Earnings	300,000	
			Total Shareholder's		
			Equity		1,500,000
			Total Liabilities and		
Total Assets		$3,000,000	Shareholder's Equity		$3,000,000

Current assets These are assets which normally would be convertible into cash within the accounting cycle, usually one year. They are:

- ◻ **Cash** The actual total, not an estimate.
- ◻ **Marketable securities** These are short-term investments in marketable instruments.
- ◻ **Accounts receivable** Items for which payment is due within a year.
- ◻ **Inventories** All goods on hand which will be converted into cash within 12 months.
- ◻ **Prepaid expenses** Expenditures for goods and services not yet received.

Fixed assets (or long-term assets) This category, sometimes called plant and equipment, includes:

- ◻ **land,**
- ◻ **plant** (buildings, machinery, other equipment), *less*
- ◻ **accumulated depreciation** or the allowance made for amortization of costs over the assumed useful life of the asset. This deduction applies to most fixed assets other than land.

Intangible assets These are non-physical items, such as trademarks, patents and copyrights, good will, and so on.

Liabilities

Anything the corporation owes is considered a liability. Liabilities are also divided into two categories: current and long-term.

Current liabilities These include obligations payable in cash within one year, such as:

- □ accounts payable, or bills not yet paid,
- □ notes payable, or money owed for loans,
- □ taxes payable, or federal or other taxes due,
- □ dividends payable, or dividends declared but not yet paid.

Long-term liabilities Debt not due within the next 12 months: bonds, mortgages, and long term loans.

Total Liabilities = Current Liabilities + Long-Term Liabilities

Shareholders' Equity or Net Worth

This is the third element of the balance sheet; in fact, the balance equation is often written as:

Shareholders' Equity = Total Assets − Total Liabilities

It includes shareholders' original contribution plus any earnings retained over the years. It represents the shareholders' residual claims against the assets of the firm. For both accounting and legal purposes, it is divided as follows.

Capital Stock This includes both preferred and common stock valued at par. Recall that preferred stock takes precedence over common stock both in the payment of dividends and in the return of their original investment on the dissolution of the corporation. Preferred stock usually has a par value of $100 per share.

Retained earnings or earned surplus Retained earnings are net earnings still held. Thus,

Retained earnings = Total profits − Total paid out dividends

Paid-in surplus or paid-in capital This is the difference between the actual issued price and par. It is the surplus amount that shareholders have paid for issued common stock.

Footnotes to the balance sheet

Reading the fine print, in this case the footnotes, can be critical. On a balance sheet, these often describe such important matters as the accounting methods used. Figure 12.4 is an example of a balance sheet.

THE INCOME STATEMENT

This provides a summary of all revenues and expenditures for a given period, usually the company's fiscal year. Unlike the "freeze frame" of the balance sheet, the income statement shows activity over the most recent period. It summarizes the profit (or loss) over that period from the sale of goods and services, minus the expenses incurred. For this reason, the income statement is often a better indicator of future performance. Figure 12.5 is the hypothetical income statement for Amalgamated Consolidated Inc.

The items in the income statement can be interpreted as follows:

Gross sales Total sales of products to customers, less:

Returns Returns from customers equal:

Net sales Gross sales minus returns.

Cost of goods sold Includes raw materials, manufacturing costs, utilities, etc.

General operating expenses Not directly connected with manufacture, *e.g.*, for sales, staff, administration, advertising, research and development.

Depreciation Amortization of plant and equipment used to produce revenues over the productive lifetime of this plant and equipment.

Operating income *i.e.*, net sales less cost of goods, general operating expense, and depreciation.

Nonoperating income (income from other sources) Royalties, earnings from subsidiaries, rents, interest, or income from investments.

Total income The sum of operating and nonoperating income, often called earnings before interest and taxes (EBIT).

Interest and other nonoperating expenses Most often this is interest on long-term debt.

Taxable income (earnings before taxes, EBIT) less:

Taxes leaves:

Net income before preferred dividends.

Preferred dividends Paid to holders of preferred stock leaves:

Net income The famous "bottom line"; the difference between revenue and expenditure for the period. Any dividends for common must be based on this figure.

Figure 12.5   AMALGAMATED CONSOLIDATED INCORPORATED
INCOME STATEMENT
FOR THE YEAR ENDED DECEMBER 31, 1990

Gross Sales	$1,100,000
Less: Returns	100,000
Net Sales	1,000,000
Less: Cost of Goods Sold	400,000
Gross Profit on Sales	600,000
Less: Operating Expenses	200,000
Less: Depreciation	100,000
Operating Income	300,000
Other Income	50,000
Operating Income (Earnings Before Interest & Taxes)	350,000
Interest Expenses	100,000
Taxable Income	250,000
Taxes	100,000
Net Income	150,000
Preferred Dividends	10,000
Net Income Available for Common	140,000
(Earnings per Share of Common $.70)	
Dividends for Common Stock ($.30 per share)	60,000
Additions (Losses) to Retained Earnings	$ 80,000

Earnings per share of common Net income divided by the number of shares of common outstanding.

Dividends for common The amount of earnings actually paid out in dividends to common stock holders.

Additions to retained earnings As defined, the residual funds that are retained and can now be added to previously retained earnings.

Footnotes As with balance sheets, footnotes on the income statement can include crucial information, *e.g.*, one-time events, such as the sale of a subsidiary or a plant. SEC regulations require registered firms to report such items separately.

STATEMENT OF CHANGES IN FINANCIAL CONDITION

A third financial statement is called the Statement of Changes in Financial Condition, or Funds Statement. While the balance sheet shows net working capital (defined as current assets less current liabilities) at a given moment, this form shows changes over the fiscal year and, more importantly, how these changes have arisen, the sources and uses of working capital.

The Statement of Changes is derived from the two balance sheets which bracket the income statement. In our illustrations, then, we would need to

1990 STATEMENT OF CHANGES FOR AMALGAMATED CONSOLIDATED INC. (SOURCES AND USES OF FUNDS STATEMENT)

SOURCES		USES	
Net Income	$150,000	Dividends for Preferred	$ 10,000
Depreciation	100,000	Dividends for Common	60,000
Increase in Acc. Pay.	40,000	Increase in Inventory	50,000
Decrease in Market. Sec.	20,000	Increase in Acc. Rec.	60,000
	$310,000	Increase in Plant & Eqp.	50,000
		Increase in Ret. Earn.	80,000
			$310,000

Figure 12.6

compare the balance sheet for Dec. 31,1989 with the one shown. The 1990 Statement of Changes might look like the example on this page. As the illustration shows, this statement is usually divided into two parts, showing funds coming in and funds going out.

Items that are sources

- □ net income (from operations) or profits

- □ depreciation (a noncash expense); it has the effect of increasing working capital since it is deducted when figuring net income, thus reducing taxes paid.

- □ sale of securities, or of noncurrent assets; this increases capital although it does not affect total assets.

Items that are uses

- □ net operating losses (cash outflow)

- □ purchase of noncurrent assets, *e.g.*, land, plant, patents; decreases capital, although it does not affect total assets

- □ cash dividends; even the declaration of a dividend creates a current liability and so reduces working capital

- □ repayment of debt

Within the Funds Statement, those items that increase current assets or decrease current liabilities lead to working capital increases and vice versa.

VALUATION PRACTICES

Different accounting methods can produce different values for the same assets or liabilities, so it is important to know which approach is being used.

Inventories

Most assets are valued at original cost. In a period of consistent inflation, such a figure could be very different for two identical items of inventory, especially if one were long-held. The cost of goods sold then depends on which item from inventory has been liquidated. There are two accounting methods in general use for valuing inventories.

FIFO (first in, first out) This assumes the first items bought (*i.e.*, the items held the longest) are the first items sold. In practice, this is usually the case; but in an inflationary period, this method will cause the cost of goods to be low, thus raising earnings and hence taxes. It also causes the inventory to be highly valued since only the new, more expensive inventory remains, thus raising the value of current assets.

LIFO (last in, first out) This assumes the last items bought (*i.e.*, the newest items) are the first sold. This has the opposite effect, lowering taxable earnings and current assets.

Depreciation

Fixed assets are depreciated using one of two accounting methods, "straight-line" or "accelerated."

Straight line This method simply divides the cost of the asset by its expected useful life. Thus a $100,000 stamping press with a usable life of 10 years is depreciated at $10,000 per year. The formula is:

   Original Cost − Salvage Value ÷ Years of Life = Annual Depreciation

Accelerated This method permits the firm to depreciate an asset more quickly and to use large depreciation allowances in the early years of an asset's life and relatively smaller ones in later years. Accelerated methods will tend to lower a firm's earnings, and hence its taxes, in early years.

EFFECTS OF CORPORATE CHANGES

Some actions by a corporation's board of directors, in particular those changing the number of outstanding shares, have a significant effect on financial statements.

New issue of stocks or bonds

The issue of new securities increases both assets (working capital) and shareholders' equity (if stocks) or long-term liabilities (if bonds).

■ **EXAMPLE**

If Amalgamated Consolidated Inc. were to issue 50,000 new shares at $10, then Working Capital and Shareholder's Equity (SE) would be increased by $500,000. Note that the original 200,000 shares would now be increased to 250,000 with the accompanying dilutions of voting rights, dividends, etc.

   If the firm had sold the same amount of bonds, long-term liabilities would have increased instead of SE, and there would not be any dilution. However, in this case, the debt to asset ratio (see page 271) would be increased.

Exercise of rights and warrants

This also raises capital. When right or warrant-holders exercise their privileges, the issuing firm must sell them shares at the specified price. This is, in effect, like issuing new shares, and, as above, increases equity and capital surplus while diluting ownership.

Conversion of convertible securities

When the holder of a convertible bond or convertible preferred stock exercises the right to convert, there is an increase in the entries for common stock at par and a decrease in bond amount or preferred stock outstanding.

■ EXAMPLE

If in the above example there had been no new issue but rather the conversion of $500,000 of bonds to 50,000 shares of common stock, then there would be no change in Working Capital. The dilution would still occur and the debt to asset ratio would be decreased.

Stock splits

A decision to split stock is usually taken to lower the market price, and thereby attract more investors. Such an action reduces par value and increases the number of shares proportionately (*e.g.*, a 2-for-1 split doubles the number of shares but cuts par value in half), but has no effect on total Stockholders' Equity. A reverse split (*e.g.*, 1-for-2), has the opposite effects on par and number of shares but, again, no effect on stockholders' equity.

Dividends

Cash dividends, when declared, are taken from retained earnings to become current liabilities; when they are paid, cash and dividends payable are both reduced. With stock dividends, though, there is a resemblance to a split, the value of the dividend is taken from retained earnings and added to Stockholders' Equity on the balance sheet, divided between common stock and capital surplus.

■ EXAMPLE

A company with SE (Stockholders' Equity) of $20 (stock at 1, capital surplus 9, retained earnings 10) declares 10% stock dividend. It still has $20 SE, but now 1.1 stock, 9.9 surplus, 9 retained.

Other actions

Other actions can affect the balance sheet. For example, if cash is used to buy new equipment, current assets are decreased and fixed assets are increased although total assets remain unchanged. On the other hand, if a current liability is paid from cash, then both current assets and current liabilities are decreased. In either case, however, the balance in the balance sheet is preserved.

PART FOUR   FINANCIAL RATIOS AND INVESTMENT POLICIES

Using information revealed by financial statements as raw material, more sophisticated analyses concerning a firm's liquidity, operating efficiency, profitability, and the value of its shares can be performed. This analysis is based on a series of measures usually expressed as the ratio of two amounts.

As mentioned above, accurate analysis requires skill and experience. Bearing this in mind, one can use the ratios discussed below to track a company's performance over time (*e.g.*, are profit margins increasing?), or to compare one firm with another. Much data on the average values for these measures for different industries as well as individual companies has been published.

In what follows, these ratios will be described and illustrated with the financial statements of Amalgamated Consolidated Inc. (see Figure 12.4). The first group of measures describes the firm's liquidity. These are primarily of interest to short-term lenders since they describe the firm's ability to meet short-term obligations.

LIQUIDITY RATIOS

The difference between current assets and current liabilities is:

Net Working Capital = Current Assets − Current Liabilities

This describes the resources available over the coming year—literally, capital to work with. At ACI, the Net Working Capital is $1,000,000 − $500,000 = $500,000. This figure is an absolute number, and as such it is hard to judge its significance.

The next measure uses the same two numbers to form a ratio, which can be used to compare firms of different sizes.

Current Ratio = Current Assets ÷ Current Liabilities

The higher the ratio, the greater the liquidity. At ACI,

Current Ratio = $1,000,000 ÷ $500,000 = 2

A more rigorous measure of liquidity, the acid test ratio, does not include inventories because they cannot be converted quickly to cash.

Acid Test Ratio (Quick Ratio) = (Current Assets − Inventories) ÷ Current Liabilities

At ACI, then:

Acid Test Ratio = ($1,000,000 − $200,000)/$500,000 = 1.6.

The most rigorous of all liquidity ratios is called a Cash Assets Ratio:

Cash Assets Ratio = (Cash + Marketable Securities) / Current Liabilities

At ACI:

Cash Assets Ratio = ($400,000 + $100,000) / $5,000,000 = 1

DEBT RATIOS

The second group of ratios is of interest to long-term debt holders.

Debt to Asset Ratio = Long-term Debt ÷ Total Assets

The ratio of long-term debt to total capitalization. At ACI,

Debt to Asset Ratio $1,000,000 ÷ $3,000,000 = ⅓

As the firm must pay interest on this debt (or face bankruptcy), too high a ratio can signal a potentially unsound situation. Accordingly, the firm's ability to cover its interest expense should also be considered.

Times Interest Earned = Income Before Interest and Taxes ÷ Interest

At ACI,

Times Interest Earned = $350,000 ÷ $100,000 (10% of $1,000,000) = 3.5.

Similarly this coverage can be considered for preferred stockholders. The significant difference is that since preferred stock dividends are paid after taxes, the numerator of this ratio is After Tax Income; the denominator is dividends for preferred stockholders.

Preferred Dividend Coverage = After Tax Income ÷ Preferred Dividends

At ACI,

Preferred Dividend Coverage = $150,000 ÷ $10,000 = 15.

CAPITALIZATION RATIOS

This group of ratios describes the manner in which a firm has capitalized itself. It compares the components of long-term capitalization—long term liabilities, preferred stock, common stock—to the total of this capitalization (TC):

Bond Ratio = long-term liabilities / TC

Preferred Stock Ratio = Par value preferred stock / TC

Common Stock Ratio = Total Value of Common Stock / TC

For ACI these are:

Bond Ratio = $1,000,000 / $2,500,000 = 0.4

Preferred Stock Ratio = $200,000 / $2,500,000 = 0.08

Common Stock Ratio = ($400,000 + $600,000 + $300,000) / $2,500,000 = 0.52

ASSET UTILIZATION RATIOS

The next set of ratios is often called asset utilization ratios. They describe some aspects of how well a firm is using its assets. The first equation measures the ability to convert inventory to sales. A high ratio is better as rapid turnover cuts the cost of storage and the risk of obsolescence.

Inventory Turnover Ratio = Net Sales ÷ Inventory

At ACI,

Inventory Turnover = $1,000,000 ÷ $200,000 = 5

Another measure of asset use is:

Receivables Turnover = Net Sales ÷ Accounts Receivable

This ratio describes the firm's ability to convert its receivables into cash. It is useful in assessing a firm's use of credit to enhance sales and its general control over its operations. Here again, a high value is good since it says that receivable collections are achieved in a timely fashion.
At ACI,

Receivables Turnover = $1,000,000 ÷ $300,000 = 3.3

PROFITABILITY RATIOS

The first profitability ratio is net profit margin; it usually would only consider operating income. Its interpretation is obvious.

Net Profit Margin (before taxes) = Net Operating Profit ÷ Net Sales

At ACI,

Net Profit Margin = $300,000 ÷ $1,000,000 = 30%

Two other profitability ratios are:

Return on Assets = Net (after tax) Profit ÷ Total Assets

and

Return on Common Equity = Earnings for Common ÷ Common Equity

At ACI,

Return on Assets = $150,000 ÷ $3,000,000 = 5%

and

Return on Common = $140,000 ÷ ($1,500,000 − $200,000) = 10.77%

CASH FLOW

Another important measure is a company's cash flow. It describes the actual amount of cash generated by the firm. As such, cash flow is in many ways more important than net income; it differs from net income primarily in that cash flow includes depreciation.

Thus, the use of accelerated depreciation has a twofold effect. On the one hand, income for the year is decreased because taxes are lowered; on the other hand, cash flow is increased since depreciation is added back in. This is illustrated below using ACI.

Cash Flow = Net Income + Current Depreciation

At ACI,

Cash Flow = $150,000 + $100,000 = $250,000.

If for example an accelerated method for depreciation yields a current depreciation of $150,000, the income statement would reflect this larger depreciation by showing

Taxable Income	= $250,000 − $50,000 (additional depreciation)
	= $200,000
Taxes (at 40%)	= $ 80,000
Net Income	= $120,000
and	
Cash Flow	= $120,000 + $150,000 = $270,000.

Thus, while income has decreased, cash flow has increased. It follows that firms which need to show earnings currently are less likely to avail themselves of the benefits of accelerated depreciation. Conversely, for firms which desire additional cash flow, net income may appear to be unduly depressed.

VALUATION RATIOS

Valuation ratios describe ways to value a company. By comparing these values to the market value, the price for which one can actually buy the company (more realistically, the shares of the company), one can judge the desirability of such an investment. The most common valuation ratio is book value.

Book value per common share

This shows the "theoretical" liquid value—"theoretical" because it is unlikely assets could actually be liquidated at their listed value—of each common stock share. A stock with a market price below book value is often said to be undervalued.

$$\text{Book Value of Common} = \frac{(\text{Common Equity} - \text{Intangible Assets})}{\text{Common Shares Outstanding}}$$

This ratio is sometimes called "tangible asset" value per share because only tangible assets are included in the valuation. Also, Common Equity means that both liabilities and preferred equity have been subtracted from the book value.

Since this ratio's denominator is shares of common stock, one must be alert to the possibility that this number could change. This is especially true for firms with convertible securities outstanding. If they are converted, the value is diluted. However, to the extent that bonds (debt) are converted, Liabilities are decreased and Common Equity is increased. A similar analysis applies to the conversion of preferred stock.

EARNINGS RATIOS

Finally, ratios which compare earnings, dividends, and stock prices are examined. The first is

(1) Earnings Per Share = Earnings for Common ÷ Common Shares Outstanding

This excludes treasury stock. At ACI,

Earnings Per Share = $140,000 ÷ 200,000 shares = $.70 per share.

Here again, this figure does not provide an accurate picture when a firm has any convertible securities, rights, options or warrants outstanding. If these are converted into, or used to buy, common shares, the number of outstanding shares will increase and earnings per share would decline.

In such a situation, it is necessary to report "earnings after dilution" or "fully diluted earnings." To arrive at this figure, one increases the number of shares outstanding by the number of shares that would be issued if options, warrants, and rights were exercised. The calculation also requires that earnings be chan____ ____ __flect reduced interest (or preferred dividend) on those issues ___

Another ratio of i___

(2) Dividend Payo___   ___arnings Per Share

At ACI,

Dividend Payout Ratio ___

As noted in Chapter 1, this figure ten__ __ __ lower for growth (usually newer) firms which keep earnings to aid in expansion, and higher for firms (usually more mature) where investors expect less growth but higher returns.

Finally, two widely used ratios are:

(3) Current Yield = Dividends per Share ÷ Share Price

and

(4) Price Earnings (P/E) Ratio = Share Price ÷ Earnings Per Share

The first measures the current return on a share of stock. It specifically does not consider the possibility of appreciation in share price. The second expresses a stock's price as a multiple of earnings. Other considerations being equal, a higher P/E Ratio reflects expectations of higher future growth.

INVESTMENT RISKS

All investment in securities involves some risk. On the simplest level, the investor risks losing some or all of the amount invested. Investors expect rewards to be commensurate with risks, that is, the greater the risk, the greater the return. This concept is at the heart of all investment decisions.

Risks are conventionally divided into several categories.

Financial risk, or business risk

Investors are concerned about the safety of their principal and of their return (dividends or interest payments).

Market risk

The market price of a company's securities can change even if there has been no material change in the company's condition or prospects. This happens, for example, when the stock market as a whole moves strongly in response to news.

Purchasing power risk

This is simply the risk that the invested dollar will not grow at the same pace as overall inflation, *i.e.*, that returns will actually buy less (have less real purchasing power).

Interest rate risk

If interest rates rise, the value of an investment, particularly a long-term investment, may fall.

Marketability, or liquidity risk

A security should be readily tradeable. If it is not, the investor may not be able to sell or buy it at the most advantageous time. Marketability risk occurs principally when the securities are thinly traded, either because the total number of outstanding shares is quite small or because the shares are closely held, *i.e.*, most outstanding shares are held by a few individuals.

Thus, low volume can indicate a security carries this risk. Another indicator is a large spread between bid and asked prices.

Call risk

Holders of bonds or preferred issues with a call provision face the risk that the issue will be called. As noted earlier, most issues pay a premium when calling and provide time limits on calling, both of which provide additional return in exchange for the risk.

PORTFOLIO POLICIES

No two individual investors have precisely the same resources or goals. It is the task of the registered representative to design a program tailored to each client, *i.e.*, to build a portfolio meeting that client's needs with the lowest possible risk.

Investment objectives

The first step involves determining the client's goals and resources. In other words, what does the client expect? How much money is or will be involved? An important task here is to project retirement needs. The careful representative will try to offer all available services suitable to the client's total situation, even though the plan may contain elements (insurance, estate planning) which will require advice from other professionals.

Financial position

The current and expected future financial status should be taken into account to help choose appropriate investment objectives. This should involve some of the steps used in examining a corporation: drawing up a personal balance sheet, perhaps even an income statement. This will help determine the present or future assets available for investment.

Constraints on investment

Once the registered representative has some idea of a client's goals and resources, it is important to know preferences that might limit investment options. For example,

- is the client able and willing to risk loss of principal?
- is the client able and willing to risk loss of income?
- can the client assume purchasing power risk?
- can the client hold investments for a long period?
- what is the client's tax status?

Building the portfolio

Portfolios should suit the investor's needs, resources, and willingness to assume risk. Portfolio strategies are usually divided into three categories: aggressive, defensive, and mixed.

Aggressive For those (often younger) investors who seek high returns and are willing to take the higher risks associated with such returns. Such a portfolio tends to include speculative securities and margin and options purchases since leverage is an important ingredient of an aggressive strategy. It might also have relatively little diversification.

Trading strategy for such a portfolio might call for moving between stocks and bonds, and "timing" transactions, *i.e.*, buying and selling to take advantage of expected fluctuations in the market.

Defensive For those (often older) investors most concerned with the safety of their principal and income, and less inclined to take risks. Such portfolios are characterized by:

- high-rated bonds, blue chips, and/or other quality common stocks.
- broad diversification, thereby spreading the risk among different types of issues.
- both long- and short-term bonds, the former for steady, predictable income, even though changing interest rates lead to fluctuations in the principal value; the latter to protect the principal, although changing interest rates mean different rates of return when funds are reinvested.
- an investment plan which controls amounts invested over time, for example, dollar cost averaging or constant dollar plans (see page 77).
- holding securities for relatively long periods.

Mixed These combine aggressive and defensive strategies to meet the needs (and temperament) of the individual client.

PART FIVE   MATHEMATICAL MARKET THEORY

There are a number of ideas about the operation of markets that employ sophisticated mathematical techniques. They begin with a basic premise: investors behave rationally. Rational investor behavior requires that riskier investments have larger expected returns. It follows then that given a choice between two investments with identical risks but differing returns, investors would prefer the one with higher return. And, that given a choice between investments with identical expected returns and differing risks, investors would choose the less risky one. No judgement is made about investments with differing risks and returns except the one stated above, *i.e.*, that higher risk requires higher return.

Defining return

By expected return, we mean the average return one should expect over time from this investment. This formulation recognizes that the return for any investment is not constant, but rather that it fluctuates. One can, however, find an average (historical) return for any investment and that is the

Distribution of Returns for Amalgamated Consolidated, Inc.

Risk: The standard deviation of Returns

$$r = \left[\sum_{i=1}^{n} = (r_i - E(r))^2 \right]^{1/2}$$

Figure 12.7   Risk: The standard deviation of returns

expected return. This theory includes an implicit assumption that the *future* expected return is equal to the *past* average return.

Defining risk

Risk is defined as deviation (technically, the "standard deviation") from the expected return. Figure 12.7 shows a chart plotting return against the probability of that return.

Characteristic line

Using a complex set of assumptions and rationales, detailed explanations of which are beyond the scope of this book, one arrives at the idea of a *characteristic line* for each security.

In Figure 12.8, this line is fitted to data which plots the return on ACI against the return on the market over some time period. (In practice, the S & P 500 is usually used as a surrogate for the market as a whole.) The slope of this line is called *beta*. It describes the return for a security in terms of the return for the market.

■ **EXAMPLE**

Investment A has a beta = 2, B has beta = 1, C has beta = .5, and D has beta = −1. If the market has a return of 10% for some period, A would be expected to return 2 × 10% or 20%, B to return 1 × 10% (the same as the market on the whole), C to return .5 × 10% or 5%, and D to return −1 × 10% or −10%.

The point on the characteristic line where it crosses the Y-axis is called *alpha*, which represents the expected return for this security when the expected return for the market as a whole is 0.

Using the characteristic line

One uses this set of ideas in two ways.

1 For an individual security—The beta of an individual security describes the volatility of its return relative to the market as a whole. An investor who is *confident* the market will rise might seek a security with a high positive beta to get a high return; at another time, he might choose a less volatile performer. In fact, if he felt the market was likely to fall,

The Characteristic Line for Amalgamated Consolidated, Inc.

The slope of this line is the beta for Amalgamated Consolidated, Inc.

Figure 12.8 The Characteristic Line for Amalgamated Consolidated, Inc.

he would seek a security with a negative beta. This can be thought of as the quantification of the ideas of cyclical and counter-cyclical securities.

2 For a portfolio—The second way in which these concepts are employed is in constructing a portfolio of securities. For instance, by combining investments with the same expected return and with betas of opposite sign, one can construct a portfolio with an equivalent return but with lower risk.

In light of an earlier observation about investor behavior, this implies the combination of these two investments is preferable to either one alone. Extensions of this reasoning are used to construct portfolios of investments that lower risk for a given expected return.

Efficient market hypothesis or EMH

The term "efficient market" means one where new information is quickly and broadly disseminated and is immediately reflected in the market price. Conceptually, then, this hypothesis implies that no information, whether technical, fundamental, or even "insider," is useful in predicting future price movements.

In fact, the three generally accepted versions of this hypothesis—the "weak form," the "semi strong form," and the "strong form"—respectively deny the usefulness of technical, fundamental, and insider information for predicting future price movements.

Random walk hypothesis

One version of the EMH is the random walk hypothesis. This asserts that price fluctuations occur randomly in the short run. The implications of this hypothesis are that there is no correlation between the return in one period and the return in the next period, and that for any time period the chances of any particular return—say a gain of 10% or a loss of 30%—are the same as they are for any other time period.

Not surprisingly, the efficient market hypothesis, which was developed by theoreticians at universities, is not too well accepted by market practitioners. It is true that larger portfolios, especially some mutual funds, strive to mirror the performance of the market at the lowest possible transaction cost, effectively admitting that they cannot "beat the market." Nevertheless, most professionals believe that some form of analysis—technical or fundamental, or both combined—is worthwhile, and that professionals can help a client achieve investment objectives with such an approach.

TERMS

Economic analysis

Gross National Product (GNP) Total value of all goods and services produced in the nation in a year; can be in current or fixed dollars

GNP components

Net National Product (NNP) GNP less depreciation

National Income (NI) NNP less business taxes

Personal Income (PI) NI less business profits

Disposable Income (DPI) NNP less taxes, retained corporate earnings, but less transfer payments

Business cycles

Expansion Time of general growth

Recession Usually defined as two consecutive quarters of decline in GNP

Cyclical industries Those most likely to be adversely affected by recession (*e.g.*, durable goods)

Noncyclical industries Usually less affected by the business cycle (*e.g.*, staples)

Leading Indicators Point to changes in the business cycle

Inflation Continuous rise in dollar price of fixed basket of goods over extended time

Consumer Price Index (CPI) Monthly price of basket of goods deemed necessary for average family

Demand-pull theory of inflation If amount of money available increases faster than amount of goods and services, producer prices will move up

Cost-push theory When prices begin to rise, cost of producing goods also rises, leading into a spiral

Stagflation Persistent inflation when economy is stagnant or actually declining

Monetary policies

Attempts to smooth business cycle by smoothing growth of money supply

M-1 Currency in circulation plus balances in all demand deposits

M-2 M-1 plus deposits in regular savings accounts, time deposits under $100,000, some money market funds, IRAs, repos

M-3 M-2 plus large time deposits, term repos, institutional money funds

Federal Reserve System Tries to keep the money supply growing at same rate as real GNP

Open market operations Fed's Open Market Committee (FOMC) exerts short-term control by buying or selling government securities in the open market

Reserve requirements Banks in Fed System must retain a certain percentage of their deposits; changing this requirement has a multiplier effect

Multiplier = 1 ÷ Reserve Requirement

Discount rate To meet reserve requirements banks borrow from Fed; Fed can raise or lower interest on these loans (discount rate)

Margin requirements Set by Fed

Moral suasion Asking member banks to pursue a policy that is more or less tight

Effects on securities markets If Fed tightens, interest rates rise, investors tend to turn away from stocks

Prime rate Rate commercial banks nominally charge their best customers

Federal funds rate Rate charged by commercial banks for loans needed by other banks to meet their reserve requirements

Call loan rate Rate banks charge brokers for margin loans

Fiscal policies

Government Increase taxes and reduce spending in inflationary period, lower taxes and increase spending during downturn

Automatic responses Built-in correctives to cyclical changes

International factors

Balance of payments Net flow of money in and out of the country

Current account Exports and imports of merchandise, tourist expenditures, shipping, military spending, investments by U.S. firms, bank loans

Capital account Money spent by U.S. corporations abroad, U.S. purchases of foreign bonds and securities on debit side; foreign investments in the U.S. on credit side

Technical and fundamental analysis

Technical analysts Look at historical data about price movements, particularly indexes and averages

Fundamental analysts Look at basic economic factors and soundness of industries or companies

Averages Can be simple arithmetic average

Indexes Usually weighted to consider relative value of constituents

Dow Jones Averages (weighted total market price of the stocks is divided by a constant)

Standard & Poor's 500 Weighted to reflect value of shares

NYSE Index Average price per share of all common stocks traded on the NYSE weighted, like the S&P 500

Wilshire 5000 Stock Index Broadest popular index, includes 5,000 stocks, is dollar-weighted

NASDAQ-OTC Price Indexes Composite index and subindexes; mutual funds not included

Market theories

Dow theory Indicates when a major trend is about to change either up or down

Advance-decline (breadth of market) theory Counts number of issues increasing in price less those that decreased

Volume of trading Compares number of shares traded with changes in market price

Odd-lot theory Examines number of odd lot transactions, usually as a percentage of all sales

Confidence Index Measures yield on high grade *vs* lower grade bonds; bullish if index is up, bearish if down

Charting Graphing stock's price movement over time

Fundamental analysis

Noncyclical industries Relatively resistant to ups and downs of business cycle

Cyclical industries Most affected by ups and downs

Growth industries Often concentrate on research and development

Securities analysis

Balance sheet Snapshot picture of company's monetary position

Total assets = Total liabilities
                    + Shareholders' equity

Income Statement Summary of all revenues and expenditures for a given period

Statement of Changes in Financial Condition Shows changes over the fiscal year, and sources and uses of working capital

Mathematical market theory

Investors behave rationally, riskier investments must have larger expected returns

Return Average return expected over time, historical return

Risk Deviation from expected return

Diversifiable risk Represents risk which can be eliminated by diversifying a portfolio

Market risk Measures how much of a stock's price changes reflects moves in overall market

Characteristic line Relates return available from the security to the return available from market as a whole

Beta Slope of characteristic line

Alpha Represents expected return for the security when expected return for market as a whole is 0

Efficient market hypothesis (EMH) Says new information is reflected in market price immediately, and implies that information is not useful for predicting price movements

Random walk Holds there is no correlation between present and future returns; and the probability of any particular return is the same in each period

REVIEW QUESTIONS

1. Which of the following are part of the index of leading indicators?

   I. housing starts
   II. new unemployment insurance claims
   III. orders for plant and equipment
   IV. prices of the S&P 500

   (A) I and II only
   (B) I and IV only
   (C) II and III only
   (D) I, II, III, and IV

2. The "Odd Lot Theory" suggests that:

   (A) sophisticated investors spread their purchases
   (B) mutual funds allow one to take advantage of pooled buying
   (C) investors who trade in odd lots are usually right
   (D) investors who trade in odd lots are usually wrong

3. On a balance sheet, retained earnings are part of:

   (A) shareholders' equity
   (B) assets
   (C) liabilities
   (D) income

4. A fundamental analyst would be likely to use which of the following information?

   I. the advance-decline ratio
   II. projected earnings
   III. trading volume
   IV. industrial production

   (A) I and II
   (B) II and IV
   (C) I and III
   (D) II and III

5. All of the following are likely EXCEPT:

   (A) a growth company would pay high cash dividends
   (B) investors might buy stocks as a source of income
   (C) a high P/E ratio suggests high expectations about future growth
   (D) a blue chip stock pays dividends regularly

6. A stable P/E ratio of 14 and a projected price of $35 for the next year suggest that next year's earnings will be:

   (A) $2.00
   (B) $2.50
   (C) $5.00
   (D) impossible to estimate

7. If a corporation has total assets of $1,000,000 and short term liabilities of $600,000 and no long term debt, then the shareholders' equity is:

   (A) $ 400,000
   (B) $ 600,000
   (C) $1,000,000
   (D) impossible to determine

8. A breakout from a "Head and Shoulders" pattern would indicate to a technical analyst that the price was:

   (A) likely to move downward
   (B) likely to drift sideways
   (C) likely to move up
   (D) pointing to a resistance line

9. "Disintermediation" is the name for which of the following?

   (A) the withdrawal of time deposits from banks
   (B) the analysis of future moves by the FOMC
   (C) the depositing of a customer's stock in a bank
   (D) the effect of raising margin requirements

10. The "Dow Industrials" is comprised of:

    (A) all NYSE stocks
    (B) 65 industrial stocks
    (C) 30 industrial stocks
    (D) all NYSE industrial stocks

11. A highly leveraged company has only a small portion of its assets in the form of:

    (A) bonds
    (B) convertible debentures
    (C) common stock
    (D) liabilities

12. A technical analyst would be likely to enter a sell stop at which of the following points?

(A) above a resistance line
(B) at new highs for the security
(C) when a support line was penetrated
(D) when potential profit can be maximized

13. The totality of goods and services produced by the U.S. is called:

(A) total savings
(B) Gross National Product
(C) total income
(D) accumulated wealth

14. The conversion of convertible bonds to common stock would result in a(n):

I. increase in debt
II. decrease in leverage
III. increase in stockholder's equity
IV. increase in total assets

(A) I and II
(B) II and III
(C) II and IV
(D) I, II, and III

15. The tangible assets of a corporation would correspond most closely with:

(A) par value
(B) market value
(C) book value
(D) working capital

16. If the Fed acted to increase the money supply by buying securities, the rate which would reflect this first is:

(A) prime rate
(B) discount rate
(C) Fed funds rate
(D) commercial paper rate

17. The rate which commercial banks usually charge their best customers is called the:

(A) bank rate
(B) Fed funds rate
(C) discount rate
(D) prime rate

18. Money can be drained by the Fed if it:

(A) increases the discount rate
(B) decreases the discount rate
(C) sells government securities
(D) does less "jawboning"

19. Typically the most highly leveraged companies are:

(A) utility companies
(B) growth companies
(C) automobile companies
(D) computer companies

20. An index which includes 500 securities is known as the:

(A) Value Line index
(B) Dow Industrials
(C) S and P index
(D) Dow composite

21. The CAI corporation earned $2.50 per share last year. If they paid $1.50 in dividends the dividend payout ratio was:

(A) 40%
(B) 50%
(C) 60%
(D) impossible to determine

22. A recession is:

(A) one qurter of decline in the GNP
(B) two consecutive quarters of decline in the GNP
(C) one year of decline in the GNP
(D) whatever the Council of Economic Advisors decides

23. The acid test ratio is:

(A) current assets $\div$ current liabilities
(B) total assets $\div$ total liabilities
(C) (current assets $-$ inventory) $\div$ current liabilities
(D) current assets $-$ current liabilities

24. If the Federal Reserve Board lowers reserve requirements all of the following would occur EXCEPT:

(A) the multiplier would increase
(B) the multiplier would decrease
(C) money would become easier
(D) banks would have more money to lend

25. The rationale for the treatment of depreciation in financial statements is to:

   (A) amortize the cost of equipment over its useful life
   (B) increase taxes
   (C) increase the firm's income
   (D) lower cash flow

26. The declaration of a cash dividend results in:

   (A) increase in long-term liabilities
   (B) increase in current liabilities
   (C) decrease in current liabilities
   (D) decrease in total assets

27. If prices remain constant and costs are decreasing, which method of inventory valuation will show the best earnings picture for the period?

   (A) FIFO
   (B) LIFO
   (C) replace as needed
   (D) don't replace inventory

28. All of the following would be defensive stocks EXCEPT:

   (A) utility stocks
   (B) supermarket stocks
   (C) computer stocks
   (D) generic drug stocks

29. The book value of a corporation could be affected by which of the following?

   I.   a decrease in market price of the stock
   II. an increase in the market price of the stock
   III. the sale of an asset at a loss
   IV. an increase in retained earnings

   (A) I and II
   (B) II and III
   (C) III and IV
   (D) I and IV

Questions 30–32 are based on the following information:

Amalgamated Consolidated Incorporated, ACI, was capitalized at $50 million. This consisted of $30 million in common stock with 1 million shares issued and $20 million in 9% long term bonds. ACI earned $5 million before interest and taxes (at 25%) and paid a dividend of $.60 per share.

30. What were the earnings per share?

   (A) $1.80
   (B) $2.40
   (C) $3.00
   (D) $5.00

31. What is the return on investment (ROI)?

   (A) 8%
   (B) 24%
   (C) 48%
   (D) 56%

32. What was the dividend payout ratio?

   (A) 20%
   (B) 25%
   (C) 50%
   (D) 60%

33. A stock with a beta of −1 would perform best during a period when the market:

   (A) went down by 10%
   (B) went down by 5%
   (C) was unchanged
   (D) went up by 10%

34. One form of the efficient market hypothesis implies:

   (A) prices increase at a random rate over time
   (B) technical analysis is better than fundamental analysis
   (C) fundamental analysis is randomly applied
   (D) current prices reflect all useful information

35. The FOMC is:

   (A) Federal Reserve Open Market Committee
   (B) Federal Oversight Management Committee
   (C) Fair, Open Markets Committee
   (D) Federal [regulation] On Making Commitments

ANSWERS TO REVIEW QUESTIONS

1. (D) All of these are leading indicators.

2. (D) The little investor is least likely to be right.

3. (A) The retained earnings are what is left after all required payments like bond interest and dividends; thus they belong to the stockholders.

4. (B) A fundamental analyst would be interested in the economic condition of the firm.

5. (A) A growth firm would want to keep its earnings for investment in expansion.

6. (B) If the price to earnings ratio is 14, then $35/earnings = 14 or earnings = $2.50

7. (A) Total assets = Debt + Shareholder's equity.

8. (A) With a "Head and Shoulders," a breakout would be downward. An inverted one would have an upward breakout.

9. (A) A bank intermediates by aggregating deposits and lending them. When funds are withdrawn this is disintermediation.

10. (C) The 65 Dow stocks are 30 industrials, 20 transports, and 15 utilities.

11. (C) The firm is leveraged because its assets are a large multiple of its equity.

12. (C) A sell stop would be used to protect a profit or limit a loss. A technician would use a support line as a signal point and enter a sell stop below it.

13. (B) By definition.

14. (B) Converting debt to equity would reduce debt and increase equity. The ratio of debt to equity (leverage) would thus be reduced.

15. (C) The market value is what the outstanding stock is worth, the par value is relatively meaningless now, and working capital only refers to current assets and liabilities.

16. (C) This is the most volatile of the rates.

17. (D) Of the others, discount rate is charged by the Fed to member banks and the Fed funds rate is the rate between banks for overnight loans of excess reserves.

18. (C) By selling securities it collects money thereby draining money.

19. (A) The cash flow of utilities is very stable since customers pay these bills regularly. This makes utilities less vulnerable to business risk and allows a highly leveraged structure.

20. (B) The Value Line has 1,500 stocks and the Dow 65.

21. (C) The ratio of dividends to earnings.

22. (B) By definition.

23. (C) The acid test is more stringent than the current ratio because it recognizes that inventory is not always liquid.

24. (A) By lowering reserve requirements, a smaller percentage of each dollar is set aside. In addition, the number of times each dollar is loaned increases. Thus, the multiplier also increases.

25. (A) The equipment is used to produce revenues over its useful life, hence its cost should be spread over that life.

26. (B) When a dividend is declared it must be paid and thus becomes a current liability.

27. (B) By charging the most recent inventory (last in first out), when costs are declining the profit margin increases.

28. (C) The others have stable sales and therefore earnings do not fluctuate as much.

29. (C) I and II do not affect the intrinsic value of the firm.

30. (B) Earnings are after interest and taxes. The former is $1.8 million leaving $3.2 million. After taxes this is $2.4 million and with 1 million shares outstanding this gives $2.40 per share.

31. (A) With an investment of $30 million the return of $2.4 million represents 8%.

32. (B) $.60 is 25% of $2.40 earnings per share.

33. (A) A beta of −1 means that it does exactly the opposite of the market and would do best when the market did worst.

34. (D) If "useful" includes insider information then this is the strong form of the hypothesis.

35. (A) By definition.

CHAPTER THIRTEEN

Taxation

The Tax Reform Act of 1986 dictated radical changes in the tax treatment of investment income. Actual writing, implementation, and interpretation of specific rules needed to meet the requirements of the legislation is now underway and will occupy the Internal Revenue Service, and the investment industry, for many years to come. For that reason, this chapter is concerned principally with broad tax considerations affecting investment decisions. (Note, too, that taxation is discussed in many particular instances throughout this text.)

GENERAL INFORMATION

Progressive and regressive taxes

Taxation schemes are conventionally divided into two categories: "progressive" and "regressive." A progressive tax takes a larger proportion of individual income as earnings increase; for example, in 1986 U.S. taxpayers were taxed at 15 different rates, ranging from 11% to 50% depending on their income. A regressive tax, on the other hand, does not consider income. Examples include sales or excise taxes.

The Tax Reform Act of 1986 considerably reduced the progressive nature of income tax. Starting in 1988, most taxpayers paid either 15% or 28% of their incomes.

While it generally eased the tax burden of those with the highest incomes, the 1986 law tightened the alternative minimum tax (A.M.T.). This rule, first introduced in 1979, provides both an alternative method of figuring one's tax liability and a minimum amount of tax (21% in 1991) that must be paid. It is directed particularly at those who take large deductions known as "preference items." Those affected must calculate both the minimum and regular taxes, and pay the higher amount.

Many of these preference items were eliminated by the 1986 law (especially those for long-term gains), but new ones appeared: examples include untaxed appreciation of real property, charitable donations, and most municipal bond income.

Types of income

For many years, the Internal Revenue Code separated "ordinary income," which included all types of earnings, interest, and dividends, from "capital gains income," *i.e.*, any gains (or losses) realized from the sale of an asset. Capital gains income was further separated into "short-term" gains (or losses) which accrued from sales of assets held for usually no more than six months and "long-term" gains (or losses), which resulted from sales of assets held for a longer time. These different types of income were taxed at different rates, which led to a number of investment strategies, some quite complex, to ensure that income was of the right kind. (In general, one wanted long-term gains and short-term or ordinary losses.)

Under the Tax Reform Act of 1986, these are distinctions without a difference: "capital gains" still exist as an accounting category, and the drafters of the legislation suggest that the differences may reappear; for the time being, however, all gains are taxed like ordinary income.

One important distinction still exists with respect to net capital losses. Up to $3,000 of such losses may be charged against income in any tax year. Any additional net capital losses may be carried forward to future years and again charged against capital gains; any resulting net capital loss can then again be charged against income with a $3,000 limit. This process can be continued until such losses have been exhausted.

■ **EXAMPLE**

Mrs. Y sells some assets and experiences a loss of $10,000 in 1992. She may deduct $3,000 of that from her 1992 income; the remaining $7,000 is carried forward. If, in 1993, she realizes a capital gain of $2,000, she may deduct the $7,000 thus showing a net loss of $5,000. Again, $3,000 of this may be charged against income; the remaining $2,000 can be carried forward.

Note that this is different from ordinary losses or expenses, which can be used to offset income with no annual dollar limitation, though they cannot exceed the amount of income.

TREATMENT OF INCOME FROM SECURITIES

Dividend income

In general, all dividends on investments, including cash distributions that are automatically reinvested, are treated as ordinary income. There are two exceptions to this rule: stock dividends where the investor is not offered the option of accepting cash payment, and dividends treated as "return of capital." In these cases, the dividend is considered to reduce the "cost basis" of the asset.

Corporate dividend income

For corporations, dividends on domestic equity securities are subject to a 70% exclusion. This exclusion does not apply to interest payments; thus, a corporation receiving "dividends" from holdings in a mutual fund that is distributing interest income from debt securities would not be eligible for this exclusion from dividend income.

Interest income

Interest income is taxable with the distinctions noted in the chapter on bonds. For instance, interest income on municipal securities is generally exempt from federal taxes and in some cases from state and local taxes as well. However, under the 1986 Tax Reform Act, certain industrial development bonds issued by municipalities that are deemed to be for "nonessential purposes" are no longer tax exempt.

Interest expense

In general, a taxpayer can deduct interest expenses incurred in making an investment from income, but the amount deducted cannot exceed net investment income. Any interest expense in excess of that amount can be carried forward and charged against net investment income in subsequent years. There is one notable exception: interest paid on loans obtained to purchase tax-exempt instruments is not deductible.

Capital gains and losses—determining "cost basis"

A capital gain (or loss) is simply the profit (or loss) realized when an asset held for investment purposes is sold or exchanged. As noted above, these are no longer differentiated from regular income, so the host of rules on determining the holding period is no longer germane.

In the simplest case, of course, the gain (or loss) realized from the sale of an asset is simply the difference between the selling price and the purchase price. But with securities held over time, a number of things can change the per-share cost, such as the issuing of dividends or rights. Thus there are a number of rules that apply to the problem of determining the "cost basis" of an investor's holdings.

Stock dividends and rights When a stock dividend is issued, a new cost basis is determined. This is the out-of-pocket cost (the total of the purchase price plus any commissions and taxes) divided by the new total number of shares.

■ **EXAMPLE**   A client buys 100 shares of PSM at $42, then receives a stock dividend of 5 shares. Ignoring commissions, the out-of-pocket cost was $4,200; the new cost basis per share is:

$$\$4,200 \div 105 \text{ shares} = \$40 \text{ per share}$$

Gifts (or inheritance) of securities The recipient of a gift of securities assumes the donor's cost basis if the current value or the eventual sale price exceeds the donor's cost. If the value drops between the time of gift and the time of sale, the cost basis is the market value at the time of gift.

Selling part of a position A client wishing to sell part of a portfolio that contains securities which have different cost bases can choose to sell certain items and thereby enjoy some tax advantage. The IRA assumes a FIFO method (first in, first out), but the investor may choose LIFO (last in, first out).

Additionally, an investor can sell "identified shares" by (a) delivering those certificates or (b) by instructing the broker to deliver those shares if they are held in a street name.

Wash sales An exception to these general rules concerns a "wash sale." A wash sale involves the sale and purchase of a security so as to create a loss. Such a loss will generally not be recognized by the IRS if the repurchase takes place within thirty days of the sale that creates the loss. Specifically, the investor cannot deduct the loss if he or she buys or has an option to buy the sold stock at any time between thirty days before and thirty days after the sale that creates the loss.

For example, if a client sells 100 shares of ACI at a loss on Dec. 15, 1992 and buys the same shares after November 15 or before January 14, 1993, then the loss may not be deducted for 1992.

■ **NOTE**

A loss can be reported only for the year of the trade date, but a gain may be reported as of the trade date or the settlement date. Thus, a gain realized from a sale during the last five trading days of the year can be reported in either year.

TREATMENT OF DEBT INSTRUMENTS

Cost basis

The cost basis for a debt instrument varies depending on whether it is purchased at issuance or in the market, and on whether it is purchased at par, a discount, or a premium.

At par A bond issued at par, or purchased in the market at par, has par as its cost basis.

At a premium With a bond issued at, or subsequently purchased at, a premium, the premium amount is amortized over the life of the bond.

■ **EXAMPLE**

A client buys a 10-year bond at $1,100 and sells it four years later for $1,150. The cost basis is computed as follows: the amortized premium of $10 per year ($1,100 − $1,000 = $100 ÷ 10 = $10 per year) is multiplied by the four years that it was held and then subtracted from his cost to yield $1,100 − $40 = $1,060. His capital gain is therefore $1,150 − $1,060 = $90.

Purchased at a discount With a bond issued at or subsequently purchased at a discount, that discount is treated as interest income rather than gain; the exception is that a government or municipal bond purchased at a discount after issuance has that purchase price as the cost basis. The interest income is accreted on an "economic accrual" basis, with the accretion treated as interest income that year. The cost basis grows by the amount of the accreted income.

■ **EXAMPLE**

The client buys a 10-year bond at issue for $800. Two years later, it is sold for $900. What is the capital gain (or loss)?

On an economic accrual basis, using compound interest, the $200 discount represents an additional 2.2% annual return over the 10 years.

Thus two years later, the cost basis is

$$\$800 \times 1.022 \times 1.022 = \$835.59$$

and capital gain is $900 − $835.59 = $64.41.

Accrued interest

As noted in Chapter 2, a bond transaction that takes place between the dates when interest is paid involves the buyer paying and the seller receiving interest accrued until the trade date. This accrued interest is not part of the cost basis of the bond.

MUTUAL FUNDS

Dividends and capital gains distributions are treated as described above. It is important to remember that reinvesting these distributions does not alter the tax liabilities.

OPTIONS

Tax consequences of options transactions and positions are covered in Chapter 9. A key point to remember is that the cost basis for stocks bought in conjunction with the purchase of an option includes the price of the option. For example, an investor who bought 100 shares of ACI at 50 and also bought 1 ACI Nov 50 Put at 3 would be considered to have a cost basis of 53 for the stock.

GIFTS AND ESTATES

Assets acquired as gifts are subject to the gift tax in lieu of income tax. There is a $10,000 per person per annum income exemption from this tax. For example, a couple could give a total of $20,000 to each of their children each year without any gift tax being levied. This allows one to begin transferring an estate without incurring estate taxes. (There is no gift tax on a spousal gift).

For gift tax purposes, the amount of a gift is its fair market value at the time of the gift. This is different from the basis for determining a capital gain (or loss).

Gifts to minors

Gifts made under the Uniform Gifts to Minors Act (UGMA) are irrevocable; hence, the income and resulting tax liability (if any) are always the responsibility of the minor.

TAX-ADVANTAGED INVESTMENTS

These are described in Chapter 5; since these instruments are designed in terms of their tax consequences, some key points are summarized here, and some additional points are included.

□ Income and loss flow through to limited partners of direct participation programs and for REITs

□ Losses for passive investors are now limited to the amount of their investment

□ For qualified deferred income plans, 401(k) contributions by employers are deductible when made. Voluntary employee contributions are limited to $7,000 annually. Eligibility requirements cannot be more strict than one year's employment for all employees who work over 1,000 hours per annum

□ Individuals may set up Individual Retirement Accounts (IRAs). The maximum contribution is $2,000 per annum; this can be deducted from income only by individuals who are not covered by a qualified pension plan or whose adjusted gross income is less than $25,000 ($40,000 for joint returns). This deductibility is phased out as income rises and ceases when income reaches $35,000 ($50,000 for joint returns). Individuals who do not qualify for the deduction may still contribute up to $2,000 to an IRA. In all cases, IRA income accrues on a tax-deferred basis. (A $250 contribution for a spouse with no income is allowed.)

□ Self-employed individuals may contribute no more than 25% of their income to Keogh Plans, up to a maximum of $30,000. Note that individuals who are employed by others but have income from self-employment may make contributions from that income

□ Certain uniform distribution rules apply to all tax-favored retirement plans. Distribution may begin at age 59½ and must begin by age 70½. Premature distributions are subject to a 10% excise tax except in the case of death or disability, for deductible medical expenses, or for certain persons aged 55 who have met early retirement provisions

□ Taxpayers who receive lump sum distributions from a plan can, after age 59½, use five-year income averaging once.

TERMS

Progressive tax Takes a larger proportion of income as earnings increase

Regressive tax Does not consider income

Tax Reform Act of 1986 All taxpayers pay either 15% or 28% of their income; tightens the alternative minimum tax (A.M.T); eliminates many "preference items" (especially long-term gains)

Types of income Ordinary income (all earnings, dividends); capital gains (realized from sale of an asset)

Capital gains Taxed as ordinary income starting 1988

Net capital losses Up to $3,000 may be charged against income in tax year; any over $3,000 may carry forward and charge against capital gain

Ordinary losses Expenses can be offset up to 100% of income, no dollar limitation

Dividends to individuals Taxed as ordinary income, except dividends paid exclusively in stock or as return of capital reduce "cost basis"

Dividends to corporations On domestic stocks, 70% excluded

Interest income Generally taxable

Calculating capital gain (loss) Difference between selling price and purchase price or cost of an asset

Wash sales Sale and purchase of a security to create a loss generally not recognized by IRS if stock repurchased within 30 days of sale

Year of loss (gain) Can report loss only at time of trade; gain at trade or settlement date

Gift and estate taxes $10,000 per person per annum exempt; spousal gift exempt; gift value = fair market value at time of gift

Gifts to minors Tax liability to minor

Tax-advantaged investments See Chapter 5

REVIEW QUESTIONS

1. An investor with a self-directed IRA would be least likely to choose which of the following?

   (A) common stocks
   (B) corporate bonds
   (C) municipal bonds
   (D) growth fund

2. An investor in the 28% bracket has a capital gain of $10,000. The tax liability for this will be:

   (A) $1,120
   (B) $1,400
   (C) $2,000
   (D) $2,800

3. A tax shelter specifically designed for self-employed individuals is a(n):

   (A) IRA
   (B) limited partnership
   (C) Keogh plan
   (D) qualified pension plan

4. To escape tax liability the moving of an IRA from one investment to another must be accomplished within:

   (A) 15 days
   (B) 30 days
   (C) 60 days
   (D) 90 days

5. For estate tax purposes assets are valued at the time of death and at:

   (A) six months prior to death
   (B) six months after death
   (C) one year prior to death
   (D) one year after death

6. An investor buys a 10% coupon $10,000 face value municipal bond in the secondary market for $8,800. If it is held to maturity, the federal tax liability will be based on:

   (A) $0 income
   (B) $1,200 interest income
   (C) $1,200 capital gains
   (D) $1,200 capital gains + annual coupon interest

7. For an investor in the 28% bracket, a municipal bond with a 10% coupon is equivalent to a corporate bond with a coupon of:

   (A) 7.2%
   (B) 10%
   (C) 12.8%
   (D) 13.9%

8. The taxable portion of ACI's $100,000 of dividend income from other U.S. corporations is:

   (A) 0
   (B) $15,000
   (C) $30,000
   (D) $80,000

9. An investor buys a $100,000 T-bond with six years to maturity at 106. If he sells it four years later for 102 his capital gain (or loss) is:

   (A) 0
   (B) $2,000 gain
   (C) $2,000 loss
   (D) $4,000 loss

10. An investor buys an original issue municipal with a 20-year maturity at a discount price of $8,000. He sells it after 10 years for $9,500. His gain is approximately:

    (A) 0
    (B) $500
    (C) $1,500
    (D) $9,500

11. A divorced couple wish to give their child a cash gift. The maximum this child can recive from them in one year without incurring gift tax is:

    (A) $5,000
    (B) $10,000
    (C) $20,000
    (D) $40,000

12. An investor reinvests the capital gains distribution from a mutual fund. The tax consequences are:

    (A) taxed as income when sold
    (B) taxed as capital gain when sold
    (C) taxed as income when received
    (D) taxed as capital gain when received

13. An investor is given the choice of a 5% stock dividend or its cash equivalent. If he chooses the stock he is taxed:

    (A) as capital gain when received
    (B) as income when received
    (C) as capital gain when stock is sold
    (D) as income when stock is sold

14. A lump sum distribution from a qualified pension plan is eligible for forward averaging of:

    (A) only one year
    (B) three years
    (C) five years
    (D) ten years

15. The following describes the tax consequences for transactions in the last five business days of the year:

    (A) gain or loss on trade date
    (B) gain or loss on settlement date
    (C) gain on trade date, loss on settlement or trade date
    (D) gain on settlement or trade date, loss on trade date

16. An investor has a $14,000 capital loss for 1991. With no other capital transactions the investor will have deductions until:

    (A) 1991
    (B) 1992
    (C) 1994
    (D) 1995

17. Which of the following are exempt from all taxes for residents of New York State?

    I.   New York State bonds
    II. New Jersey bonds
    III. U.S. bonds
    IV. Puerto Rico bonds

        (A) I and III
        (B) II and IV

    (C) I and IV
    (D) I, II, and IV

18. An investor buys a 10-year $1,000 corporate bond at an original issue discount of $100. If he holds it to maturity the total taxable income is:

    (A) interest each year + $100 interest income at maturity
    (B) interest each year + $100 capital gain at maturity
    (C) interest + accrual interest each year
    (D) interest + accrual capital gain each year

19. An investor sold a municipal bond for $18,000 + $300 of accrued interest. For U.S. tax purposes he experienced:

    (A) sale price of $18,000 + $300 interest income
    (B) sale price of $17,700
    (C) sale price of $18,000
    (D) sale price of $18,300

20. An investor bought 1 ACI Dec 70 Call at 4. If ACI went to 80 and he exercised the call and sold the stock, he would have a capital gain (ignoring transaction costs) of:

    (A) $0
    (B) $400
    (C) $600
    (D) $1,000

21. The income from a custodian account under the Uniform Gifts to Minors Act is the responsibility of the:

    (A) minor
    (B) donor
    (C) custodian
    (D) depends on whether the gift is more than $10,000 or not

22. An employee of an advertising agency with a qualified pension plan has a freelance business as well. His contribution to a Keogh is limited to:

    (A) $0
    (B) $7,000 less the contribution to the pension plan
    (C) $30,000 less the contribution to the pension plan
    (D) $30,000

23. A T-bill bought in 1991 is held to maturity in 1992. For tax purposes there is:

   (A) capital gain pro rated between 1991–1992
   (B) interest income pro rated between 1991–1992
   (C) capital gain in 1992
   (D) interest income in 1992

24. An investor bought 100 shares of CAI at $100. Subsequently, a 25% stock dividend was declared. If he eventually sold his shares for $90, he would realize a:

   (A) $15-per-share loss
   (B) $10-per-share loss
   (C) $10-per-share gain
   (D) $25-per-share gain

25. For gift tax purposes, fair market value is determined:

   (A) when gift is given
   (B) when gift is sold
   (C) at donor's cost
   (D) average of donor's cost and sale price

ANSWERS TO REVIEW QUESTIONS

1. (C) The IRA income is already tax deferred. One is less likely to choose the lower return of a municipal.

2. (D) The new act does away with the distinction between capital gain and income. The tax is 28% of the income.

3. (C) By definition. Keoghs (HR10) were specifically set up for self-employed individuals.

4. (C) This rollover applies to any amount of money, not just the $2,000 of a particular year.

5. (B) The more beneficial of these values may then be chosen.

6. (C) Municipal bonds bought in the secondary market are treated as an asset. This asset appreciated by $1,200.

7. (D) The equivalent yield is computed from the formula

EQ. Y. = coupon ÷ (1 − tax rate)
         = 10% ÷ (1 − .28)

8. (C) The Tax Reform Act of 1986 changed the dividend exclusion from 85% to 70%.

9. (A) The T-bond purchased at a premium has that premium amortized over the remaining life to find that adjusted cost.

10. (B) An original issue municipal purchased at a discount has the discount accrued (on an economic basis) over time. The accrual on a straight line basis would yield $9,000 after 10 of the 20 years to maturity. Thus, at $9,500 the investor realized a $500 gain. The accrual on an economic basis would be slightly different, but $500 would still be the closest answer.

11. (C) The law allows up to $10,000 per person per year. Their marital status is irrelevant.

12. (D) A dividend would be taxed as income when it is received.

13. (B) The stock dividend is treated as income when received, because the investor had a choice. If there had been no choice and a 5% stock dividend had been received it would have resulted in changing the cost basis for the stock.

14. (C) This is a change from the ten years previously available.

15. (D) The investor has a choice for the gain but no choice for the loss.

16. (D) The investor can take up to $3,000 each year beginning in 1991. The $14,000 would be exhausted in 1995.

17. (C) Generally residents of a state are exempt from taxes on that state's municipals. Bonds from Puerto Rico are exempt from all federal, state and local income taxes.

18. (C) The bond purchased at a discount is assumed to accrue additional interest on an annual basis.

19. (C) The municipal does not generate interest income.

20. (C) The $400 cost of the Call is added to his $7,000 cost basis, leaving a gain of $600.

21. (A) The gift is irrevocable and the assets and the income belong to the minor.

22. (D) The Keogh is independent of any pension plan as long as it comes from self-employment monies. The maximum allowable contribution is 25% of income up to $30,000.

23. (D) T-bills although sold at a discount are treated as interest income payable when the bill matures or is sold.

24. (C) The 25% stock dividend gives him 125 shares for which he paid $10,000, for a reduced cost basis of $80 per share.

25. (A) This is different from the basis for income tax purposes.

CHAPTER FOURTEEN

Reading the financial news

Every day, the registered representative must read the financial press. Although stock market quotations and other reports always cover past events, they contain information essential to this day's investment decisions.

This chapter is a guide to the major items on the financial pages: reports of trading in securities on the exchanges and over the counter, corporate reports and announcements, government and municipal bond listings, etc.

NEW YORK STOCK EXCHANGE ISSUES

This is called Consolidated or Composite because it includes all trading in listed stocks on all exchanges and over the counter.

Reading from left to right:

Figure 14.1

CONSOLIDATED TRADING

52-Week High	Low	Stock	Div	Yld %	PE Ratio	Sales 100s	High	Low	Last	Chg.
25⅝	24⅝	FFB pfF	...	...	...	172	25½	25¾	25½	...
7¼	4	FFinFd	.12	1.7	...	349	7¼	6¾	7⅛	+ ⅜
38¾	14¼	FtFnMg	.10b	.3	13	1849	37¾	36⅞	37½	+ ⅞
42½	15⅝	FIntste	3.00	9.7	10	1822	31½	30¾	30⅞	− ⅛
25¾	16¾	FIntsl pf	2.37	9.5	...	10	25	24	25	+ 1½
1⅜	¼	FinstA	...	...	...	2234	11/16	9/16	⅝	...
35⅛	20	FIIn pfB	3.57e	11.1	...	24	32½	32	32¼	...
12⅝	7¾	FtMiss	.30	2.6	42	127	11⅞	11¾	11¾	...
9¼	5⅞	FIPhil	.59e	7.6	...	80	7⅞	7¾	7¾	...
24⅞	13½	FstUC	1.12	4.5	10	3645u	25¼	24¼	25	+ ¾
49	38¾	FIUC pf	4.81e	10.0	...	59	48⅜	47⅞	48⅛	+ ¼
15½	6½	FUnRI	1.00b	10.1	9	45	10	9⅞	9⅞	− ⅛
33½	16⅞	FIVaBk	1.36	4.2	10	150	32⅜	32¼	32⅛	+ ⅛
30⅜	13⅜	FstFed	...	...	9	54	29½	28⅝	29¼	+ ¼
37⅞	22	Firstar	1.44	3.8	9	903u	38½	37½	37⅝	− ¼
89	73½	Fstar pf	8.39e	9.5	...	7	88¾	88¾	88¾	...
25⅜	22	FishPr wi	...	...	...	920	25⅛	24¾	24⅞	− ¼
25⅞	8⅞	FItNors	.80	3.1	82	1455	25½	24⅞	25½	− ⅛
34	20⅛	FItN pf	3.00	9.0	...	13	33½	33⅛	33½	− ⅛
34	20¼	FINr pfA	3.10	9.2	...	31	33⅞	33¾	33¾	+ ¼
26⅛	24¾	FItNr pfB	...	...	...	173	26⅛	25⅞	26	− ⅛
33⅝	15¾	FleetEn	.88	2.7	24	717	33	31½	32⅞	+ ⅜

52-Week High	Low	Stock	Div	Yld %	PE Ratio	Sales 100s	High	Low	Last	Chg.
38⅝	30⅜	Houlnd	2.96	7.9	12	1313	37⅜	37	37⅜	+ ⅜
16	9⅞	HowlCp	.32	2.7	10	35	12	12	12	+ ⅛
11⅜	6½	HudFd	.12	1.3	17	258	9⅜	9	9¼	− ⅛
17⅜	8⅜	Huffy s	.30	1.7	12	290	17⅜	17⅛	17¼	− ⅛
14⅞	9¾	HughSp	.36	3.0	...	43	12¼	12	12⅛	...
52⅝	37¾	Human	1.35	2.8	15	2360	48⅛	46¾	48	+ 1⅛
35	25⅛	Human wi	...	...	...	4	31⅞	31¾	31⅞	− ⅛
17¼	10¼	HuntMf	.32	1.9	26	101	16¾	16⅜	16¾	+ ½
34¼	22	Hntgln	.33e	1.4	15	98	23⅛	22¾	23	...
9¾	2	Huntwy	...	...	...	75	4⅞	4⅞	4⅞	...
11¼	9⅜	Hyprn	1.20	10.9	...	338	11⅛	11	11	...

I J K L

52-Week High	Low	Stock	Div	Yld %	PE Ratio	Sales 100s	High	Low	Last	Chg.
26¼	14¾	IBP	.60	3.4	44	3179	17¾	16¾	17¾	+ ⅞
7¾	3⅛	ICM	.12i	...	...	41	3⅜	3¼	3¼	...
8	2½	ICN Ph	...	...	...	1664	7½	6⅜	7½	+ ⅝
28¾	23	IES	2.10	8.1	6	157	26⅛	25⅞	26	+ ⅛
47½	30⅜	IMC Frt	1.08	2.3	14	380	47½	46⅞	46⅞	− ½
17	14	INAln	1.52a	9.1	...	18	16⅞	16⅜	16⅝	− ¼
22	14¾	IPTimb	2.88	13.5	7	247	21⅜	21	21⅜	+ ⅛
11¾	6¾	IRT	.80	8.8	10	10	9⅛	9⅛	9⅛	...

52-Week High-Low This is the range of prices over the preceding year, not including the current day. Prices are given in dollars and fractions of a dollar.

Stock Name of the company issuing the stock (usually an abbreviation or initials); "pf" is added for preferred stocks, an "s" if there has been a stock split.

Div. Last regular (usually quarterly or semi-annual) dividend paid per share in dollars and cents.

Yield % This is current yield, *i.e.*, annualized dividend divided by the closing market price.

P/E ratio The ratio of price to earnings over the last 12 months, *i.e.*, market price divided by earnings per share (actual or indicated).

Sales in 100s Round lots traded during the day.

High Highest price trade during the day.

Low Lowest price trade during the day.

Last Closing price for the day (this may be from the Pacific Exchange, which closes 3 hours after New York).

Change Difference between the closing price on the reported day and the close at end of trading the previous day.

Symbols and abbreviations scattered throughout the table are explained in accompanying text.

NYSE BOND TRADING

Bonds are quoted in terms of a percentage of the par or face value, with 100 equaling par. Current yield is the annual percentage return at the current price. As with stocks, fluctuations are expressed in fractions. The High, Low, Last, and Net Change figures are also derived as with the NYSE stock table.

This table does not cover most bond trading, which is conducted over the counter, nor does it include any municipal bonds.

Figure 14.2   NEW YORK STOCK EXCHANGE BOND TRADING

OVER THE COUNTER QUOTATIONS (NASDAQ NATIONAL MARKET)

Over the counter trading is recorded in two different tables. The NASDAQ National Market, or National List, includes those issues which meet certain SEC requirements (for trading volume, market value, etc.) and others that have asked to be included.

Entries in this table are like those in the NYSE stock table, but do not include Yield % or P/E Ratio.

Other over the counter quotes are shown in the NASDAQ Supplemental List. This includes only the name of the stock and dividend; the Bid (*i.e.*, the price dealers are willing to pay), and Ask (or Offer the price at which a dealer is willing to sell). Net Change shows any movement from the previous day's last reported bid price.

These quotations do not necessarily represent actual trades.

Figure 14.3   NASDAQ NATIONAL MARKET

TREASURY BILLS, BONDS AND NOTES

T-bills are issued regularly, and are purchased at a discount, with the difference between discount and face determining the yield. (The higher the purchase price, the lower the yield.)

In Figure 14.4, the date shown is the maturity date. Bid and Ask prices are quoted in terms of yield to maturity. Change is quoted in basis points. Yield is annual return at the current price, also quoted in basis points as T-bills have a $10,000 face value.

Bonds and notes are treated somewhat differently. Again, maturity date is shown first, followed by an "n" for a note (those with no symbol are bonds). Here the next column shows the coupon rate. Bid, Ask, and Change, however, are quoted in 32nds, and Yield is yield to maturity.

Figure 14.4

TREASURY BILLS, BONDS AND NOTES

Prices in 32d of a point, bill yields in basis points.

TREASURY BILLS Date -1991-	Bid	Ask	Chg.	Yield
Jul 25	5.11	5.06	+0.01	5.15
Aug 1	5.46	5.41	+0.09	5.51
Aug 8	5.48	5.41	+0.11	5.51
Aug 15	5.37	5.34	+0.06	5.45
Aug 29	5.45	5.41		5.53
Aug 22	5.42	5.38	+0.06	5.49
Sep 26	5.56	5.53	—0.02	5.68
Sep 5	5.49	5.47	—0.05	5.60
Sep 12	5.52	5.50	—0.03	5.64
Sep 19	5.55	5.53	+0.02	5.68
Oct 3	5.58	5.56	—0.01	5.72
Oct 10	5.57	5.53	—0.01	5.70
Oct 17	5.61	5.59	—0.01	5.77
Oct 24	5.62	5.59		5.77
Nov 21	5.67	5.63	—0.01	5.83
Nov 7	5.61	5.59	—0.01	5.79
Nov 14	5.63	5.59	—0.03	5.79
Oct 31	5.62	5.59	+0.01	5.78
Nov 29	5.69	5.66	+0.01	5.87
Dec 5	5.67	5.63	—0.02	5.85
Dec 12	5.69	5.66	—0.02	5.89
Dec 19	5.68	5.66	—0.01	5.89

BONDS & NOTES Date	Rate	Bid	Ask	Chg	Yield
Dec 92 p	$9\frac{1}{8}$	103-05	103-09—	01	6.70
Jan 93 p	7	100-08	100-11		6.76
Jan 93 p	$8\frac{3}{4}$	102-23	102-27		6.71
Feb 88-93	4	96-11	96-13+	01	6.43
Feb 93	$6\frac{3}{4}$	99-25	99-31		6.77
Feb 93 p	$6\frac{3}{4}$	99-26	99-30		6.78
Feb 93	$7\frac{7}{8}$	101-18	101-24+	01	6.68
Feb 93 p	$8\frac{1}{4}$	102-01	102-05		6.78
Feb 93 p	$8\frac{3}{8}$	102-06	102-10		6.80
Feb 93 n	$10\frac{7}{8}$	105-27	105-31—	01	6.81
Mar 93 p	$7\frac{1}{8}$	100-12	100-16+	01	6.80
Mar 93 p	$9\frac{3}{8}$	104-08	104-12		6.84
Apr 93 p	$7\frac{3}{8}$	100-23	100-27—	01	6.84
Apr 93 p	7	100-12	100-15		6.71
May 93 p	$7\frac{5}{8}$	101-01	101-05		6.93
May 93 n	$10\frac{1}{8}$	105-06	105-10—	01	6.96
May 93 p	$8\frac{5}{8}$	102-22	102-26		6.95
May 93 p	$6\frac{3}{4}$	99-25	99-28+	01	6.82
Jun 93 p	$8\frac{1}{8}$	102	102-04		6.94
Jun 93 p	7	100-06	100-09+	02	6.84
Jul 93 p	$7\frac{1}{4}$	100-14	100-18—	01	6.94
Aug 88-93	$7\frac{1}{2}$	100-20	100-26		6.03

BONDS & NOTES Date	Rate	Bid	Ask	Chg	Yield
Jan 97 p	8	99-27	99-31+	01	8.01
Apr 97 p	$8\frac{1}{2}$	101-26	101-30—	02	8.07
May 97 p	$8\frac{1}{2}$	101-27	101-31		8.07
Jul 97 p	$8\frac{1}{2}$	101-26	101-30		8.09
Aug 97 p	$8\frac{3}{8}$	102-12	102-16—	01	8.09
Oct 97 p	$8\frac{3}{4}$	102-29	103-01—	01	8.12
Nov 97 p	$8\frac{7}{8}$	103-17	103-21—	01	8.12
Jan 98 p	$7\frac{7}{8}$	98-20	98-24		8.13
Feb 98 p	$8\frac{1}{8}$	99-27	99-31—	02	8.13
Apr 98 p	$7\frac{7}{8}$	98-13	98-16		8.16
May 98 p	9	104-03	104-07—	02	8.18
Jul 98 p	$8\frac{1}{4}$	100-12	100-15—	01	8.16
Aug 98 p	$9\frac{1}{4}$	105-11	105-15—	02	8.21
May 93-98	7	93-20	94-17—	01	8.05
Nov 98	$3\frac{1}{2}$	95-03	96-04		4.12
Nov 98 -p	$8\frac{7}{8}$	103-12	103-16		8.23
Feb 99 p	$8\frac{7}{8}$	103-10	103-14—	02	8.25
May 94-99	$8\frac{1}{2}$	101-02	101-10+	01	7.96
May 99 p	$9\frac{1}{8}$	104-20	104-24—	01	8.28
May 99 p	8	98-12	98-17—	01	8.25
Nov 99 p	$7\frac{7}{8}$	97-14	97-18—	01	8.28
Feb 00 p	$8\frac{1}{2}$	101-01	101-05—	02	8.31

GOVERNMENT AGENCY BONDS

These are bonds issued by government agencies but not guaranteed by the federal government. They are listed like government bonds: maturity date, coupon rate, Bid, Ask and Change in 32nds; and yield to maturity.

GOVERNMENT AGENCY BONDS

Prices in 32d of a point.

FEDERAL HOME LOAN Date	Rate	Bid	Ask	Chg	Yield
Jul 91	$7\frac{1}{2}$	100	100-03		1.81
Jul 91	8.15	100-01	100-04		0.00
Aug 91	6.17	99-31	100-02—	01	5.42
Aug 91	7.20	100-04	100-07		4.92
Aug 91	8.60	100-09	100-12+	01	4.77
Aug 91	11.10	100-16	100-20		4.78
Sep 91	7.40	100-06	100-09—	01	5.72
Sep 91	7.90	100-10	100-13		5.52
Sep 91	8.80	100-15	100-18+	01	5.55
Sep 91	$11\frac{3}{4}$	100-31	101-03—	01	5.52
Oct 91	7.80	100-14	100-18		5.56
Oct 91	8.70	100-22	100-25		5.61
Oct 91	9.95	101	101-03		5.66
Nov 91	7.15	100-11	100-15		5.72
Dec 91	7	100-12	100-15		5.87
Dec 91	11.40	102-07	102-10		5.92
Jan 92	7	100-13	100-16—	01	6.01
Feb 92	$6\frac{1}{4}$	99-31	100-02—	01	6.13
Feb 92	8.35	101-06	101-10		6.07
Feb 92	11.45	102-31	103-02—	01	6.15
Mar 92	7.10	100-16	100-19		6.18

FEDERAL HOME LOAN Date	Rate	Bid	Ask	Chg	Yield
Nov 98	$9\frac{1}{4}$	104-21	104-27—	02	8.35
Jan 99	9.30	105-01	105-07		8.35
Jun 99	8.60	101-12	101-18—	01	8.33
Jul 99	8.45	100-13	100-19+	03	8.35
Aug 99	8.60	101-07	101-13+	01	8.36
Oct 99	$8\frac{3}{8}$	99-25	100-03+	02	8.36
Jan 00	8.60	100-29	101-03		8.42
Feb 04	$9\frac{1}{2}$	107-15	107-25+	05	8.48
Source—	Bloomberg	L.P.			

FEDERAL FARM CREDIT Date	Rate	Bid	Ask	Chg	Yield
Jul 91	9.10	100-01	100-04		0.00
Jul 91	14.70	100-06	100-10		3.22
Aug 91	6.60	100	100-03		3.67
Aug 91	8	100-02	100-05		3.19
Sep 91	8.05	100-08	100-11		5.07
Oct 91	8.05	100-12	100-15		5.55
Oct 91	10.60	101-04	101-07—	01	5.62
Nov 91	7.70	100-14	100-17		5.70

Figure 14.5

STOCK OPTIONS

Listed options are shown in Figure 14.6, which is broken up by the active exchanges. The terms below are fully explained in Chapter 9.

◻ name (of the option) and close (closing price of the stock on the NYSE),

◻ strike price is usually quoted in $5 increments if the price is less than $100; in $10 increments if the price is between $100 and $200; in $20 increments if over $200,

◻ shows the closing premiums paid for calls which expire in the three named months,

◻ shows the closing premiums paid for puts which expire in the three named months.

CHICAGO BOARD
OPTIONS EXCHANGE

Option & Strike NY Close Price		Calls-Last Jul Aug Sep			Puts-Last Jul Aug Sep		
AplMag	10	r	r	5/8	r	r	r
Baybks	15	1½	r	r	r	r	r
16¾	17½	r	r	1	r	r	r
BergBr	25	r	r	3	r	r	r
Blkbst	7½	2¾	3	2⅞	r	r	r
10¼	10	5/16	13/16	1¼	3/16	5/8	15/16
10¼	11¼	s	s	7/8	s	s	17/16
10¼	12½	r	¼	7/16	1⅜	113/16	2⅝
10¼	15	s	s	3/16	s	s	r
10¼	17½	s	s	⅛	s	s	7⅛
BrMSq	60	s	s	22¼	s	s	¼
81⅞	70	s	s	r	s	s	¼
81⅞	75	7½	r	8⅝	r	r	r
81⅞	80	2	3½	4¾	1/16	1	1⅞
81⅞	85	1/16	1	2⅛	3⅜	1	...
Bruns	12½ 2¼	r21 11/16			r	r	r
15⅛	15	⅛	5/8	1	3/16	r	r

Figure 14.6

MUTUAL FUNDS

These tables are usually quite abbreviated. More elaborate tables are discussed in Chapter 4.

Name of the fund If a sponsor offers several funds, they are listed separately under the sponsor's name.

NAV The Net Asset Value per share, or the amount a shareholder receives on redeeming a share (redemption value).

Buy (or Offer) NAV plus maximum sales charge. If there is no sales charge, the initials "NL" appear, indicating No Load.

Change Difference between the reported NAV and previous day's NAV.

Figure 14.7

MUTUAL FUNDS

	N.A.V.	Buy	Chg.
AARP Invst:			
CapGr	20.77	NL	-.07
GinlIM	15.10	NL	-.04
GenBd	14.82	NL	-.04
GthInc	20.93	NL	-.01
TxFBd	15.32	NL	+.03
TxFSh	15.26	NL	...
ABT Midwest:			
Emrg	7.33	7.70	...
Fl Govt	9.99	10.41	-.03
Fl Gth	13.63	14.31	-.03
Gthinc	11.63	12.21	...
IntGv	10.19	10.40	-.03
SecInc	8.52	8.94	-.01
TFLtd.	10.05	10.26	...
UtilInc	13.50	14.17	-.08
AdsnCo	13.09	13.49	+.02
ADTEK	9.57	NL	+.01
AdvnlGv	9.49	9.91	-.02
AIM Funds:			
Chart	6.78	7.12	-.01
Constl	10.49	11.01	+.01
CvYid	8.80	9.24	-.05
Grnwy	9.53	10.05	-.02
HiYld	8.75	9.19	+.01
Sumit	6.39	...	...
Weing	9.19	9.65	...
A M A Funds:			
ClasGl	9.96	NL	+.03
Clasin	8.74	NL	...
EMT	17.03	11.58	-.04

	N.A.V.	Buy	Chg.
Tg2000	32.67	NL	-.03
Tg2005	20.83	NL	-.03
Tg2010	14.55	NL	-.09
Berger Group:			
100	17.87	NL	...
101	12.56	NL	...
BingSGr	9.51	NL	+.03
Boston Co:			
CapAp	31.28	NL	-.09
GNMA	11.65	NL	-.02
Mgdl	11.24	NL	-.02
SpGth	14.06	NL	-.05
BosGri	10.34	NL	-.01
Bowser	1.44	NL	-.03
Brndywn	10.82	NL	-.02
Bruce r	86.91	NL	-.30
Bull & Bear Gp:			
CapGr	9.92	NL	-.01
EqInc	10.23	NL	-.02
Gold	16.60	NL	+.01
HiYld	11.34	NL	-.01
TxFre	16.70	NL	-.01
USGvt	14.37	NL	-.01
Calamos	10.15	NL	+.02
CalMun	8.44	NL	...
CalTrst	10.82	NL	-.02
CalUSGv	9.50	NL	-.03
Calvert Group:			
Arial	16.03	16.78	+.08
Equity	14.97	NL	+.07
Inco	15.41	16.13	...

	N.A.V.	Buy	Chg.
TxFU	10.57	11.01	-.02
DIT Funds:			
CaGth	12.17	NL	-.03
Curnt	9.33	NL	+.01
GvtSc	9.75	NL	-.02
OTCGr	22.03	NL	-.02
Deslinyl	10.47	NL	-.02
Desfll	14.83	...	-.06
DG Div	22.27	NL	-.13
DadCx BL	30.90	NL	-.04
DadCx St	33.21	NL	-.03
DblExC	10.17	10.40	...
DbleTx	11.12	11.58	...
Drexel Burnham:			
Burnh	19.64	20.35	-.02
DS BD r	10.51	NL	-.01
DS CV r	8.49	NL	-.01
DS E r	10.53	NL	-.04
DS Gv r	9.47	NL	-.02
DS Gr r	11.08	NL	+.04
DS Op r	8.92	NL	+.03
DS PS r	9.97	NL	-.01
Fenrn r	9.67	NL	-.01
TFLtd	10.36	10.52	-.01
FTLng	8.98	9.38	...
Dreyfus Grp:			
A Bnd	13.22	NL	-.10
CalTx	14.00	NL	-.03
CapVl	24.85	26.05	-.13
CySec	7.89	NL	+.02
Dreyf	12.54	13.70	...

	N.A.V.	Buy	Chg.
SIEnS r	7.34	7.49	-.08
SIFnS r x	24.77	25.28	-.08
SIFd r x	14.60	14.90	+.02
SIHlth r	31.33	31.97	+.06
SIMD r x	6.54	6.67	+.06
SIMou r	9.21	9.40	+.02
SIIndl r x	12.24	12.49	+.11
SILesr r	18.93	19.32	-.03
SIMethr x	14.84	15.14	+.04
SIPap r x	11.61	11.85	+.04
SIPrp r x	9.50	9.69	-.05
SIReg r	7.99	8.15	-.03
SIReil r x 9.15	9.36	-.04	
SISL r	7.97	8.13	+.05
SISoft r	13.03	13.36	-.03
SITec r	17.08	17.43	+.06
SITele r	14.79	15.28	-.01
SIUtil r x	23.44	23.92	-.08
FiduCap	12.86	NL	-.08
Financial Prog:			
Dyha	6.57	NL	-.02
FSB Gv	6.99	NL	-.02
FSP Eg	8.04	NL	+.05
FSP Ep	8.22	NL	+.05
FSP Fin	6.36	NL	...
FSP U	7.83	NL	-.04
FeciTx	13.24	NL	-.03
Gold	6.04	NL	+.01
HISci	12.07	NL	-.03
HiYld	7.77	NL	-.02
Indust	3.41	NL	+.01

	N.A.V.	Buy	Chg.
Growth	8.33	8.75	+.02
TotRel	6.76	7.10	+.02
US Gvt	9.95	10.45	...
Hor Mart	22.66	NL	-.01
Hummer	13.84	NL	+.08
Hutton Group:			
Bond r	10.43	NL	-.05
Calif	9.95	10.36	-.02
CvSec	8.84	9.21	+.01
Gwth r	13.33	NL	-.07
Optin r	8.03	NL	+.02
GvtScr	8.06	NL	-.03
Basic r	11.62	NL	-.01
Natl	10.28	10.71	-.02
NY Mu	10.090	10.51	-.02
PrcM r	10.27	NL	+.06
SpEq r	11.25	NL	-.09
IRI Stck	8.27	8.66	-.01
IAI Funds:			
Apollo	10.96	NL	...
Bond	9.69	NL	-.01
IntFd r	9.21	NL	+.15
Region	17.82	NL	+.09
Reserv	10.19	NL	...
Stock	15.78	NL	-.01
IDS Mutual:			
IDSAp r	8.90	NL	-.03
IDS Bd	4.55	4.71	...
IDS Ca	4.58	4.82	...
IDS Dis	5.71	6.01	-.04
IDSEq r	7.08	NL	...

■ **NOTE** Only open-end funds are included; closed-end funds are listed in stock tables.

CORPORATE SALES AND EARNINGS REPORTS

These are very brief summaries, often footnoted.

They usually (though not always) cover a quarterly period, and often offer figures for a six-month period or for a year, permitting a reader to derive several important ratios. Customarily, these show sales or revenues, net income, earnings per share, and average number of shares outstanding.

Figure 14.8   ## COMPANY EARNINGS

For periods shown, (N) indicates stock is listed on the New York Stock Exchange, (A) the American Stock Exchange and (O) Over-the-Counter.

American Brands Inc.(N)

Qtr to June 30	1991	1990
Revenue $	2,937,000,000	2,952,400,000
Net inc	181,600,000	158,400,000
Share earns	.88	.81
Shares outst	202,000,000	191,800,000
6mo rev	6,794,200,000	6,156,100,000
Net inc	398,300,000	353,800,000
Share earns	1.94	1.81
Shares outst	201,600,000	191,700,000

The company said all share earnings and shares outstanding reflected a 2-for-1 stock split in the form of a 100 percent dividend, which became effective in October 1990.

American Cyanamid Co. (N)

Qtr to June 30	1991	1990
Sales $	1,420,400,000	1,228,300,000
Net inc	131,800,000	b111,400,000
Share earns	1.41	1.16
6mo sales	2,733,200,000	2,380,800,000
Net inc	236,600,000	b202,300,000
Share earns	2.53	2.11

b-Included income of $3,000,000, or 3 cents a share, in the quarter and a loss of $3,000,000 in the 6 months, both from discontinued operations.

The company said the discontinued operations were related to the Shulton Group, the company's divested consumer products business.

Arco Chemical (N)

Qtr to June 30	1991	1990
Revenue $	703,000,000	705,000,000
Net inc	33,000,000	102,000,000
Share earns	.34	1.06
6mo rev	1,385,000,000	1,390,000,000
Net inc	85,000,000	b227,000,000
Share earns	.89	2.37

b-Included gain of $43 million from cumulative effect of change in accounting principle.

The company said second-quarter results include a $12 million pre-tax favorable adjustment for property and casualty liability costs recorded in 1990 related to the plant incident and shutdown in Channelview, Texas.

Black & Decker (N)

Qtr to June 30	1991	1990
Revenue $	1,106,500,000	1,224,600,000
Net inc	7,300,000	16,100,000
Share earns	.11	.26
6mo rev	2,194,100,000	2,228,000,000
Net inc	11,400,000	26,100,000
Share earns	.18	.43

Burlington Northern Inc.(N)

Qtr to June 30	1991	1990
Revenue $	1,080,000,000	1,172,000,000
Net loss	b420,000,000	c71,000,000
Share earns	—	.92
Shares outst	76,396,000	76,794,000
6mo rev	2,212,000,000	2,355,000,000
Net loss	b428,000,000	c134,000,000
Share earns	—	1.74
Shares outst	76,315,000	76,664,000

Central & South West Corp.(N)

Qtr to June 30	1991	1990
Revenue $	717,000,000	649,000,000
Net inc	94,000,000	59,000,000
Share earns	.93	.54
6mo rev	1,365,000,000	1,208,000,000
Net inc	157,000,000	191,000,000
Share earns	3.44	1.87

Colgate Palmolive (N)

Qtr to June 30	1991	1990
Revenue $	1,516,400,000	1,452,900,000
Net inc	93,300,000	81,900,000
Share earns	.66	.58
Shares outst	133,533,000	131,966,000
6mo rev	2,978,200,000	2,754,100,000
Net inc	184,600,000	163,100,000
Share earns	1.31	1.16
Shares outst	133,441,000	131,958,000

Dana Corp.(N)

Qtr to June 30	1991	1990
Sales $	1,134,300,000	1,323,700,000
Net inc	4,600,000	31,600,000
Share earns	.11	.78
6mo sales	2,185,500,000	2,590,600,000
Net inc	6,700,000	54,700,000
Share earns	.16	1.34

The company said 1991 second quarter net income included a gain of $5.9 million from the sale of a subsidiary. First quarter 1991 net income includes a $6 million gain on sales of subsidiaries net of additional reserves.

CORPORATE DIVIDEND REPORTS

These brief announcements of regular dividends show the company's name, payment frequency (*e.g.*, quarterly), dollar amount per share, date the dividend will be paid, and record date (date on which a shareholder must own the share to receive the dividend).

Irregular dividends are similarly reported when announced (usually at the end of a fiscal year), as are stock dividends (showing percentage rather than a dollar amount). Notices will show when a dividend has increased or has been omitted.

Figure 14.9   ## DIVIDENDS DECLARED

	Period rate	Stk of record	Payable
IRREGULAR			
FutureGermany Fd	Q .02	9-5	9-13
Germany Fund	.10	9-5	9-13
Merrimac Ind	x .075	9-5	9-19
x-commences quarterly			
New Germany Fd	.07	9-5	9-13
INCREASED			
Am Filtrona	Q .235	8-9	8-25
Consol Rail	Q .45	8-30	9-16
Golden Corral	Q .27	7-31	8-14
Metro Bnchsrs	Q .15	7-29	8-13
Omni Capital	Q .11	7-29	8-12
Schwab,Charles	Q .05	8-1	8-15
Unifi Inc	Q .15	8-19	8-26
OMITTED			
Baltek Corp			
CalFed Inc			
SPECIAL			
FstFdlSv Charlotte	.20	7-31	8-9
REGULAR			
AmericusTr Xerox	x .6475	8-2	8-16
x-payable on prime & units.			
Ashland Oil	q .25	8-22	9-15
Athlone Ind	q .25	8-2	8-16
Barnett Bks	Q .33	9-9	10-1
Burlington Nth	Q .30	9-9	10-1

	Period rate	Stk of record	Payable
REGULAR			
CA Water Svc	Q .45	8-1	8-15
CIM Hi YldSecur	M .07	7-26	8-5
Charter Pwr	Q .0275	8-6	8-14
Chase Manhattan	Q .30	8-1	8-15
Cinn G&E,	Q .62	7-29	8-15
Coca Cola Co	Q .24	9-15	10-1
CommerceBncp NJ	.1125	-31	8-15
Constar Intl	Q .16	8-13	9-3
Core Ind	Q .12	-30	9-23
Crompton Knowles	Q .13	8-2	8-23
DF Stheastern	Q .05	7-31	8-9
Dreyfus Corp	Q .13	8-5	8-14
FstFed FinclSvc	.14	8-2	8-22
FstFedS&L Lenawee	Q .22	7-30	8-15
FstFdlSv Charlotte	Q .15	7-31	8-9
FstFidel Bncptn	Q .30	7-29	8-6
Firstar Corp	Q .36	7-29	8-15
Ft Wayne Ntl	Q .27	9-13	10-1
Fuller HB,	Q .155	8-1	9-5
Fulton Fincl	Q .20	9-20	10-15
Gillette Co	Q .155	8-1	9-5
Gorman Rupp	Q .25	8-9	9-10
Hawaiian El	Q .55	8-12	9-10
Heritage Fin	Q .14	7-29	8-9
Hewlett Packard	Q .125	9-25	10-16
Horizon Ind	Q .02	8-1	8-15
Iowa NtlBkshrs	Q .38	7-31	8-7

	Period rate	Stk of record	Payable
REGULAR			
Kansas P&L,	Q .465	9-4	10-1
Massbank Corp	Q .11	7-31	8-16
NY Times	Q .14	9-6	9-25
Newhall Land	Q .20	8-2	9-9
Nthwst NaturGas	Q .42	7-31	8-15
ONEOK Inc	Q .21	7-31	8-15
Occidntl Petrol	Q .25	9-10	10-15
Oppenheimr MulGv	M .076	7-26	8-9
PPG Indust	Q .42	8-12	9-12
Pacific G&E,	Q .41	-16	10-15
Provident Bkshrs	Q .05	7-29	8-9
RMI Titanium	Q .025	8-1	9-1
Safecard Svcs	S .075	7-31	9-16
Skyline Corp	Q .12	9-12	10-1
Sonoco Prod	Q .23	8-16	9-10
Sthwstn Ntl	Q .24	8-10	9-10
Summit Bncp	Q .20	9-1	9-15
Summit Bncp adjpf	.3781	9-1	9-15
Time Warner	Q .25	8-23	9-10
Tultex Corp	Q .09	9-6	10-1
United Mobile	Q .05	8-15	9-15
Valero Energy	Q .09	7-30	9-6
ValliCorp Hold	Q .05	8-1	9-1
Village Fincl	Q .05	7-29	8-12
WPL Holdings	Q .45	7-31	8-15
West One Bncp	Q .24	9-30	10-17
g-Payable in Canadian Funds.			

This announcement is not an offer to sell or a solicitation of an offer to buy any of these securities. The offering is made only by the Prospectus, copies of which may be obtained in any State in which this announcement is circulated only from underwriters qualified to act as dealers in securities in such State.

<u>NEW ISSUE</u>   May 26, 1988

2,666,400 Shares

CAROLCO PICTURES INC.

Common Stock

Price $9.375 Per Share

PaineWebber Incorporated

Bear, Stearns & Co. Inc.

Furman Selz Mager Dietz & Birney
Incorporated

Alex. Brown & Sons Incorporated	The First Boston Corporation	Donaldson, Lufkin & Jenrette Securities Corporation
Drexel Burnham Lambert Incorporated	A. G. Edwards & Sons, Inc.	Goldman, Sachs & Co.
Lazard Frères & Co.	Montgomery Securities	Morgan Stanley & Co. Incorporated
Prudential–Bache Capital Funding		Shearson Lehman Hutton Inc.
Smith Barney, Harris Upham & Co. Incorporated		Crowell, Weedon & Co.

Advest, Inc. Bateman Eichler, Hill Richards William Blair & Company Blunt Ellis & Loewi
                        Incorporated   Incorporated

Cowen & Co.   First Albany Corporation   Ladenburg, Thalmann & Co. Inc.

Neuberger & Berman Oppenheimer & Co., Inc. Stifel, Nicolaus & Company Sutro & Co.
                                                        Incorporated   Incorporated

Thomson McKinnon Securities Inc.   Wheat, First Securities, Inc.

Arnhold and S. Bleichroeder, Inc.   First Manhattan Co.   Gruntal & Co., Incorporated

Josephthal & Co.   Mabon, Nugent & Co.   Newhard, Cook & Co.
Incorporated   Incorporated
Rowland, Simon & Co.   Wedbush Securities, Inc.

Figure 14.10   Tombstone

TOMBSTONE ANNOUNCEMENTS

It is important to note that these are announcements, not advertisements, as, under SEC regulations, sales cannot be made from the announcement.

A firm is not legally required to publish this announcement; if it does, it can only include:

1 the name of the security (A date can be included showing when a primary offering is issued, or simply the date on which the announcement appears.)

2 number of shares being offered (or number of bonds)

3 offering price

4 managing underwriter (the seller)

5 members of the underwriting syndicate. Usually arranged in order of the size of their commitment, and alphabetically within each group. Members of the selling group are not shown.

■ **NOTE**

The disclaimers must be included because the SEC holds that an investor cannot buy shares without a copy of the prospectus.

BLUE LIST (SECONDARY MARKET FOR MUNICIPALS)

The *Blue List* contains secondary market municipal bond listings. Included are

- □ name of issuing agency
- □ coupon rate
- □ maturity date
- □ bid price, expressed as a percentage of par (considered to be $1000)
- □ asked price, as a percentage of par
- □ change in price from previous day
- □ yield to maturity

■ **NOTE**

The "f" indicates the bond is trading flat, *i.e.*, without accrued interest.

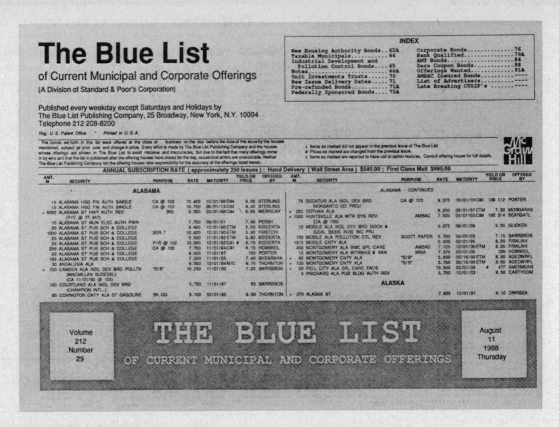

Figure 14.11   Blue List

Reprinted with permission of Standard & Poor's Corporation.

MUNICIPAL BOND OFFICIAL NOTICE OF SALE

These include the following:

- □ name of issuing agency
- □ total amount of issue
- □ date, time, and place of sale
- □ maturity(ies) of bonds
- □ call features
- □ type of bond (G.O. or revenue, etc.)
- □ denomination(s)
- □ dates on which interest will be paid
- □ bidding instructions (minimum bid, amount of good faith deposit required, bidding procedure, bid form)
- □ name of bond counsel
- □ method and place of settlement
- □ person authorizing sale

This announcement is not an offer to sell or a solicitation of an offer to buy any of these securities.
The offering is made only by the Prospectus.

NEW ISSUE   September 30, 1986

2,148,315 Shares

M. A. Hanna Company

$2.125 Convertible Exchangeable Preferred Stock

The shares of $2.125 Convertible Exchangeable Preferred Stock, with a liquidation preference of $25 per share, of the Company are convertible at the option of the holder at any time, unless previously redeemed, into shares of the Common Stock of the Company at a conversion price of $24.875 per share, subject to adjustment under certain conditions.

The Preferred Stock also is exchangeable in whole at the option of the Company on any dividend payment date beginning December 30, 1989, for the 8.50% Convertible Subordinated Debentures Due December 30, 2016 of the Company at the rate of $25 principal amount of Debentures for each share of Preferred Stock. The Debentures, if issued, will be convertible at the option of the holder at any time, unless previously redeemed, into shares of Common Stock at a price equivalent to the conversion price applicable to the Preferred Stock for which the Debentures were exchanged.

Price $25 Per Share
plus accrued dividends, if any, from date of issuance.

Copies of the Prospectus may be obtained in any State in which
this announcement is circulated only from such of the Underwriters as are qualified to act as dealers in securities in such State.

| PaineWebber | | The First Boston Corporation |
| Incorporated | | |

Bear, Stearns & Co. Inc.	Alex. Brown & Sons	Dillon, Read & Co. Inc.
	Incorporated	
Donaldson, Lufkin & Jenrette	Drexel Burnham Lambert	A. G. Edwards & Sons, Inc.
Securities Corporation	Incorporated	
Goldman, Sachs & Co.	Hambrecht & Quist	E. F. Hutton & Company Inc.
	Incorporated	
Kidder, Peabody & Co.	Lazard Frères & Co.	Merrill Lynch Capital Markets
Incorporated		
Montgomery Securities	Morgan Stanley & Co.	Prudential–Bache
	Incorporated	Securities
L. F. Rothschild, Unterberg, Towbin, Inc.	Salomon Brothers Inc	Shearson Lehman Brothers Inc.
Smith Barney, Harris Upham & Co.	Wertheim & Co., Inc.	Dean Witter Reynolds Inc.
Incorporated		

Figure 14.12   Tombstone

MUNICIPAL BOND BUYER INDEX

This is an index of investment grade long-term tax exempt bonds. It shows the average yield for such bonds by category within the classes revenue bonds and general obligation bonds.

BOND BUYER INDEXES

AVERAGE MUNICIPAL BOND YIELDS—COMPILED WEEKLY

	20 G.O. BONDS (1)	11 G.O. BONDS (1)	25 REV. BONDS (2)	TREASURY BONDS (3)
May 21	8.31	8.17	8.68	9.00
May 14	7.82	7.70	8.20	8.72
May 7	7.86	7.74	8.20	8.64
Apr. 30	7.85	7.72	8.13	8.44
Apr. 23	7.82	7.69	8.16	8.53
Apr. 15	7.90	7.77	8.28	8.27
Apr. 9	7.27	7.14	7.54	8.07
Apr. 2	6.93	6.80	7.26	7.91
Mar. 26	6.79	6.67	7.11	7.55
Mar. 19	6.68	6.55	7.08	7.50
Mar. 12	6.61	6.48	7.02	7.51
Mar. 5	6.54	6.40	6.92	7.44
Feb. 26	6.59	6.45	7.01	7.49
Feb. 19	6.62	6.49	7.05	7.53
Feb. 12	6.67	6.53	7.09	7.58
Feb. 5	6.57	6.43	6.98	7.46
Jan. 29	6.56	6.43	6.98	7.44
Jan. 22	6.54	6.40	6.92	7.36
Jan. 15	6.65	6.51	7.04	7.37
Jan. 8	6.70	6.57	7.01	7.31

Figure 14.13

20 GO Bond Index: the average yield of 20 general obligation bonds with 20-year maturities. The average rating for the 20 bonds is "A".

11 GO Bond Index: the average yield on 11 of the 20 bonds in the 20 Bond Index. The average rating for the 11 bonds is "Aa".

Revenue Bond Index: the average yield on 25 revenue bonds with 30-year maturities.

VISIBLE SUPPLY OF MUNIS

SAMPLE OF DATA FROM THE VISIBLE SUPPLY

The 30-day visible supply is compiled daily from the Bond Buyers Guide. It shows the total dollar volume expected to come to the market during the next 30 days. Along with the total there is also a breakdown into competitive and negotiated offerings.

1987	Competitive	Negotiated	Total
10/30	1,113,865,950	1,305,275,000	2,419,140,950
10/23	1,104,170,000	750,410,000	1,809,580,000
10/16	1,362,092,000	360,715,000	1,722,807,000

Figure 14.14

MUNICIPAL BOND INDEX
MERRILL LYNCH 500

Week ended Wednesday, July 23, 1986

The following index is based on yields that about 500 major issuers, mainly of investment grade, would pay on new ? long term tax-exempt securities. The securities are presumed to be issued at par; general obligation bonds have a 20-year maturity and revenue bonds a 30-year maturity. The index is prepared by Merrill Lynch, Pierce, Fenner & Smith Inc., based on data supplied by Kenny Information Systems, a unit of J.J. Kenny & Co.

–OVERALL INDEX–

7.83 –0.63

–REVENUE BONDS–

Sub-index 7.97 –0.85

	2-23-88	Change in Week
AAA-Guaranteed	7.77	–0.00
Airport	7.00	–0.00
Electric-Retail	7.00	–0.00
Electric-Wholesale	8.10	–0.00
Hospital	7.00	–0.00
Housing	8.00	–0.00
Miscellaneous	7.81	–0.00
Pollution Control/ Ind. Dev.	8.15	–0.00
Transportation	7.90	–0.00
Utility	7.92	–0.00

–GENERAL OBLIGATIONS–
Sub-index 7:40 –0.00

	2-23-88	Change in Week
Cities	7.51	–0.00
Counties	7.11	–0.00
States	7.27	–0.00
Other Districts	7.68	–0.00

The transportation category airport utility includes electrics. The transportation category each airport utility includes electrics.

Figure 14.15

MUNICIPAL BONDS TOMBSTONE

Information in this announcement includes:

1 Name of bond counsel.

2 Description of the denomination and type(s) of bonds. All municipal bonds must be registered, but both serial and term bonds can be combined in one issue.

3 For serial bonds, a listing of the amount, due date, interest rate, and price. This is called the "scale;" those which mature over a longer term pay a higher rate of interest. The price quoted is a percent of par.

4 The date on which interest begins to accrue (the "dated date").

5 Class of bond (revenue or G.O., etc.).

6 Dates on which interest will be paid.

7 Names of managing underwriter(s) and of firms in the underwriting syndicate, arranged as with a corporate tombstone.

STANDARD & POOR'S STOCK GUIDE

A much more complete view of securities activity is provided by the Standard & Poor's Stock Guide, which gives up to date information on some 4,000 stocks. Reading from left to right, it includes:

□ ticker symbol and name of the issue

□ market(s) where stock is traded

□ Standard & Poor's rating of the issue

□ par value

□ institutional holdings

□ brief description of the firm's business

□ high and low prices for the issue for several past periods

□ average number of shares sold and high, low, and last prices for most recent month

□ current dividend yield and P/E ratio

□ past dividend payment record, and current dividend

□ financial position and capitalization from most recent balance sheet

□ earnings per share for the preceding five years, the current year, and interim earnings, if any

Standard & Poor's Stock Guide also includes the Mutual Fund Data Sheet.

Agency Rent-A-Car   3033

NASDAQ Symbol AGNC   (Incl. in Nat'l Market; marginable)

Price	Range	P-E Ratio	Dividend	Yield	S&P Ranking	Beta
Mar. 28'88	1988					
19	21–17	19	2---	2---	B+	NA

Summary

Agency believes it is the nation's largest company specializing in the insurance replacement automobile rental market. With a fleet of about 32,500 vehicles, Agency conducts its business through more than 500 offices in the U.S. and Canada. Growth in the rental fleet, increased fleet utilization and higher rental rates aided earnings in recent periods. Nearly 60% of the shares are closely held.

Business Summary

Agency Rent-A-Car, Inc., rents automobiles on a short-term basis, primarily to customers whose insurance coverage entitles them to a replacement vehicle in the event that their own car is damaged, stolen or requires major repairs. Based on its fleet of about 32,500 vehicles, Agency believes that it is the largest firm in its specialized segment of the U.S. car rental market. Wholly owned TransAutomotive Insurance Co. is a multi-line insurance company chartered in Texas. The unit had been writing long-haul motor carrier excess liability, physical damage, and general liability and cargo reinsurance coverage, but it ceased underwriting operations in 1982 pending improvement in the commercial casualty insurance business.

As of 1987–8 year-end, Agency was operating 510 car rental offices in the U.S. and Canada. Generally, an insured requiring a replacement vehicle is referred to the company by the insurance adjuster or agent handling his claim. Insurance replacement rental rates range from $15 to $18.50 and business and vacation rentals are approximately $24 a day. Approximately 8% of revenues were derived from car rentals to business or vacation travelers. The company acquires its fleet through two wholly owned automobile agencies.

The rates charged for insurance replacement rentals are usually substantially lower than those charged by the large business and vacation automobile rental companies because business and vacation travelers demand a wide selection of automobiles and often rent for high mileage travel resulting in considerable wear and tear on the automobile. Insurance replacement rentals are usually used as a family car replacement for

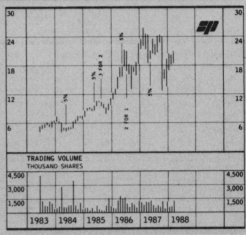

routine, low mileage, local use. The business and vacation rental companies also have to locate in expensive space in airport locations to be competitive, while the insurance replacement rental company operates in suburban locations so it can deliver the customer's car directly to their home or business.

Important Developments

Mar. '88—The company reported that at 1987–8 year-end it was operating 510 offices in 41 states and 2 Canadian provinces and expected to add 75 offices in 1988–9. Since becoming a public company in 1983, Agency has opened 320 new offices.

Next earnings report due in June.

Per Share Data ($)

Yr. End Jan. 31	1988	1987	1986	1985	1984	1983	1982	1981	1980	1979
Book Value	NA	3.38	2.65	2.01	1.47	1.06	0.82	0.55	0.35	0.25
Earnings	1.01	0.82	0.64	0.54	0.41	0.24	0.28	0.21	0.10	0.08
Dividends[1]	Nil	Nil	Nil	Nil	Nil	0.00¼	0.00⅛	0.00¼	Nil	Nil
Payout Ratio	Nil	Nil	Nil	Nil	Nil	1%	1%	1%	Nil	Nil
Calendar Years	1987	1986	1985	1984	1983	1982	1981	1980	1979	1978
Prices—High	26	22⅝	11¼	7⅝	6⅝	NA	NA	NA	NA	NA
Low	12⅞	10⅞	7⅜	4¼	4⅜	NA	NA	NA	NA	NA
P/E Ratio—	26–13	28–13	18–12	14–8	16–11	NA	NA	NA	NA	NA

Data as orig. reptd. Adj. for stk. divs. of 5% May 1987, 100% Jul. 1986, 5% May 1986, 50% Aug. 1985, 5% May 1985, and 5% May 1984. 1. Paid prior to public offering. 2. Pays stk. (see Dividend Data). NA-Not Available.

Standard OTC Stock Reports   April 6, 1988   Standard & Poor's Corp.
Vol. 54/No. 39/Sec. 2   Copyright © 1988 Standard & Poor's Corp. All Rights Reserved   25 Broadway, NY, NY 10004

Figure 14.16   Standard & Poor's Stock Guide

Reprinted with permission of Standard & Poor's Corporation.

CHAPTER FIFTEEN

Federal and state regulations

This chapter covers federal and state laws and regulations concerning the issuance of, and trading in, securities. Much of this information has already been presented in earlier chapters; however, it is discussed here in depth because a registered representative must be familiar with the legislation itself.

Note that this text refers to certain rules by number (usually assigned by the SEC or NSDA) for convenience, but test questions concern only the content of rules and not their numbers.

PART ONE   THE SECURITIES ACT OF 1933

The Securities Act of 1933 was the first federal legislation designed to regulate interstate activities in securities. It affects only new issues (primary or secondary distributions); it is basically designed to ensure that investors receive complete, accurate information. The act is administered and enforced by the Securities and Exchange Commission (SEC).

Although the act contains many provisions and definitions, its aim is to require full and fair public disclosure of important elements of new issues, and to prevent fraud.

REGISTRATION REQUIREMENTS

Under the act, all newly-issued securities sold through interstate commerce must be registered with the SEC. Registration is accomplished by filing an "S-1" statement, which gives detailed information about both the issuing entity and the issue. The S-1 statement must be accompanied by a prospectus. The prospectus is an abbreviated version of the registration: it contains the same information but omits supporting documentation.

The S-1 statement

The S-1 statement includes:

□ nature of issuer's business

□ information about corporate officers and directors (name and address, business history, etc.)

□ specific description of how proceeds of the new issue will be used

□ financial statements, including balance sheet and income accounts, showing capitalization and funded debt for preceding three years

□ amount of corporate securities held by officers, directors, and beneficial owners holding 10% or more of these securities

□ statement describing any legal action pending against the company

□ cost of promoting the new issue

□ legal opinion

□ articles of incorporation

□ underwriter's spread

Penalties for misleading statements

If the S-1 statement proves to be misleading, either because it contains false statements or omits important information, all those who have signed it can be prosecuted for fraud. Maximum criminal penalties, if convicted of this crime, are three years in prison or $5,000 fine for each count. Civil remedies are also available. Within three years of the offering, or within one year of the time the fraud is discovered, a purchaser has the "right of recovery" from all those who are named in, or have signed, the registration statement. This includes not only corporate partners and directors, but underwriters, attorneys, accountants, and appraisers, anyone, in fact, who signs a report supporting facts in the statement.

SEC review process

As discussed in Chapter 6, the SEC must review the registration before the new issue can be sold to the public. Once registration is filed (the "filing date"), the law calls for a 20-day "cooling-off" period. This period allows the SEC time to review and dampens the effect news of a new issue may have on the market. When the review is complete, sales can begin; this is called the "effective date."

Deficiency letters In practice, the cooling-off period is often longer than 20 days. The SEC may need more information; if this is the case, it will issue one or more "deficiency letters" asking for certain specific amendments. Once these are received, 20 days can again pass before the effective date.

■ **NOTE**

The SEC has the power to lengthen or shorten the cooling-off period.

Stop orders If the SEC thinks the registration statement contains misstatements or omits important facts it can suspend the entire registration process with a "stop order." The issuer is then entitled to a hearing before such an order is promulgated.

■ **NOTE**

The SEC cannot be said to "approve" a new issue. It makes no judgement on the accuracy of the registration statement or on the quality of the issue itself, but simply reviews for completeness. The prospectus must include wording explaining this "nonapproval."

The preliminary prospectus

While SEC review is in progress, no sales of the new issue are allowed, but the issuer can produce and circulate a preliminary prospectus to get indications of interest from prospective purchasers. This is similar to the final prospectus, but lacks the final price, date certificates will be ready for delivery, or the underwriters' spread.
   On its face, the preliminary prospectus must say that:

□ registration has been filed but is not yet effective,
□ the information is subject to change,
□ this is not an offer to sell or a solicitation to buy.

This material must be printed in red (and the preliminary prospectus is often called a "red herring").
   In addition, during the waiting period the underwriter cannot make any predictions about the issuer's performance, though it is proper to answer unsolicited inquiries about the new issue.
   As noted in Chapter 6, the offering price and underwriters' spread are the last amendments to be filed with the SEC.

Selling the new issue

As soon as the registration is effective, but not before, the new issue may be sold, subject to the following regulations:

Primary distribution Anyone who purchases the new issue within 90 days of the effective date must receive the prospectus.

Secondary distribution When the issuer already has shares outstanding, anyone who purchases the new issue within 40 days of the effective date must receive the prospectus.

■ **NOTE**

In all cases, the prospectus must be delivered to the buyer before, or no later than, confirmation of the sale.

Advertising Dealers cannot advertise the new issue for 90 days after the effective date, except by delivering the prospectus. Tombstone ads (see Figure 14.12) are allowed.

Mutual funds If the prospectus is used more than nine months after the effective date (as with mutual funds), the information it contains must be no more than 16 months old.

EXEMPT SECURITIES

Under the Act, certain securities are exempt from the registration requirements (though not from the fraud provisions). These include:

1 Securities issued or guaranteed by the U. S. government, or by U.S. government agencies.

2 Obligations issued by any state or other political subdivision (thus municipals are exempt).

3 Commercial paper (corporate debt) or bankers' acceptances with maturities of less than 270 days.

4 Instruments issued by common carriers (railroads, trucking companies, airlines) which are regulated by the Interstate Commerce Act.

5 Domestic banks or trust companies, savings and loans associations, building and loan societies, co-op banks are all exempt.

6 Nonprofit groups (churches, schools, etc.).

7 Private placements (see below).

8 Intrastate issues.

9 "Regulation A" filings, *i.e.*, issues of $1.5 million or less (see page 318).

10 Fixed annuity contracts and insurance policies.

EXEMPT TRANSACTIONS

Even with those securities that are not exempt, some transactions are not subject to the requirements of the act. These include:

1 Transactions between "private individuals" (*i.e.*, not the issuer, underwriter or a dealer).

2 Private placements (*i.e.*, where the issuer makes no public offering, see below.)

3 Unsolicited broker transactions.

PRIVATE PLACEMENT
(REGULATION D)

Securities placed with selected investors, and never offered to the public, are exempt from registration and prospectus requirements. However, they are still subject to the anti-fraud provisions of the Act, and must meet some standards: they may not be advertised, there must be disclosure in some cases, the securities' price must be negotiated.

Further, the issuer may not sell to an underwriter, and cannot sell to more than 35 people in any 12-month period. Securities sold in this fashion may be resold only in accordance with Rule 144 (see below) or if they are registered with the SEC.

Regulation D governs private placements. The conditions for a private placement include:

□ issuer must have reason to think the buyer is a sophisticated investor and that the buyer will not resell the securities quickly. The buyer usually furnishes an "investment letter."

□ buyer must be provided with an "offering memorandum," which gives the same financial information as a prospectus.

Rule 501

This regulation defines "accredited investors." Such investors are not included in the limit of 35 purchasers of private placements. Accredited investors include:

□ any financial institution (banks, insurance companies, and employee benefit plans)

□ any individual with net worth of over $1,000,000 (including joint net worth with spouse)

□ any individual with an income of over $200,000 in each of the preceding two years and a "reasonable expectation" of continuing to earn such an income

□ directors, executives and general partners of the issuer

Additionally, the regulation spells out the conditions under which a security would be exempt from SEC regulations.

Other rules

Other rules under Regulation D require:

□ an issuer claiming exemption must file a "notice of sale" with the SEC

□ purchasers, for the most part, must have access to the same information as in a registration statement

□ any company not required to report to the SEC or any investment company can issue up to $500,000 of securities without registering them. There is no limit on the number of investors, but general solicitation is prohibited.

□ any non-investment company (including partnerships) is exempt from registration requirements on issues of $5,000,000 or less to no more than 35 unaccredited investors (there is no limit on the number of accredited investors)

□ any issue to 35 or fewer "sophisticated" investors (again, accredited investors don't count toward this total). This rule does allow others to participate if they act through a "purchaser's representative" who is "sophisticated."

SALE OF RESTRICTED AND CONTROL SECURITIES (RULE 145)

Securities acquired through a Reg. D transaction (private placement), or through an employee stock option plan, are "restricted" or unregistered. Securities held by a person in control (a corporate officer or director, or a major shareholder) are called "control securities." Rule 145 applies to stock acquired through merger or acquisition only.

Restricted or unregistered securities

These provisions apply to the sale of securities that have never been registered (*e.g.*, acquired through a private placement or a merger).

Ownership The seller must have owned (fully paid for) the securities for at least two years. This period excludes any time in which the seller has a short position or owned puts in this stock. If ownership of the new securities is transferred, a new two-year period begins, unless they are a gift.

Broker's role The securities can only be sold by the broker on an agency basis. That is, the broker can execute a sell order, but cannot solicit an order to buy.

SEC notification The seller of restricted securities must file a notice of intention to sell (Form 144) with the SEC, and act within 90 days of filing (or file a new form). This requirement does not apply if the transaction involves 500 or fewer shares and does not exceed $10,000.

Limits on quantity A seller may sell only 1% of the total number of shares currently outstanding, or an amount equal to the weekly average number of shares sold during the four weeks prior to the SEC filing—whichever is greater.

Such a sale may be made only once in a three-month period.

Control securities

A number of rules cover securities transactions involving corporate officers, directors or those who own at least 10% of any class of outstanding securities. In addition,

Public information Control securities can be sold only if certain information is available to the buyer, either the annual or quarterly reports filed with the SEC (which include income statements and balance sheets), or equivalent information from firms which do not file ("non-reporting companies").

Holding period Same as for restricted securities, including the exemption on a smaller issue. However, if the control securities are registered the two-year wait does not apply.

Limits on quantity These limits are the same as for restricted securities; the Rule includes all members of the control person's immediate family.

"Nonaffiliated persons"

A person who is not in a position of control but holds restricted securities is called "nonaffiliated." He may sell all his holdings after three years and is exempt from the filing and information requirements of Rule 144.

INTRASTATE TRANSACTIONS (RULE 147)

Under Rule 147, securities sold only to residents of the state in which the issuer is also a resident and operates a business are exempt from registration requirements. The rule stipulates:

Residence The issuer must reside in and do business within the state at the time of the offering.

Doing business "Doing business" means: the issuer's main office is located in that state, has at least 80% of its assets within that state, and derives 80% of gross revenues from operations within that state.

Use of proceeds Issuer will be using at least 80% of the proceeds from the Rule 147 transaction for operations within that state.

Resale For nine months after the issuer's last sale, these securities can be resold only to residents of that state.

Purchaser's residence All purchasers must live within the state (an individual's main residence or a corporation's main office must be within the state) and provide written proof of that to the issuer.

Certificate The issuer must place, on each certificate, a legend stating that the security is not registered under the Act and describing the resale restrictions.

Transfer The issuer must give its transfer agent "stop transfer" instructions to prevent illegal transactions in the after-market.

REGULATION A OFFERINGS

Certain small-scale and limited offerings are exempt from the Act's registration and prospectus requirements. Regulation A sets qualifying conditions for these exemptions.

Size Reg A offerings cannot exceed $1,500,000 in total value in a 12-month period.

Filing The issuer must file a notification form at a regional SEC office within 10 days before the initial offering. Filing alone is not sufficient; the SEC must review the information and decide whether the issue qualifies.

Time limits The offering must take place within 90 days of the filing date or the SEC will consider that the issuer has "abandoned" the matter.

"Offering circular" Reg A issues of more than $100,000 must be accompanied by an offering statement describing the issue. A copy of this statement must be filed with the SEC within 10 business days prior to its public distribution; purchasers must receive a copy at least 48 hours before the confirmation of sale is mailed.

The only advertising permitted is a tombstone containing basic information (name of issuer; name, amount, and price of the offered securities).

ADVERTISING

Regulations govern the amount and kind of information that may be released to the public during the "cooling-off" period, *i.e.*, after the registration statement is filed but before the issue is registered. It provides a guide for the underwriters of a proposed distribution.

Advertisements *must* include:

□ wording to the effect that the registration statement has been filed with the SEC but has not yet become effective

□ a statement as to whether the security is offered in connection with a distribution by the issuer or by a security holder, or both; and whether this represents new financing or refunding, or both

□ name and address of a person who can provide a written prospectus

□ notice that securities may not yet be sold

□ a statement that the communication is not an offer to sell nor a solicitation of an offer to buy

Advertisements or other communications during the "cooling-off" period *may* include:

□ identification of the issuer

□ title and amount of securities to be offered

□ some indication of the issuer's general type of business (if an investment company, its classification)

□ the price of the security, or method of determining its probable price range

□ names of underwriters

□ whether the security is a legal investment in the opinion of counsel

PART TWO   THE SECURITIES EXCHANGE ACT OF 1934

The purpose of this act is to bar unfair practices once securities have been issued. It regulates exchanges and over the counter markets, brokers, dealers, and is, in general, designed to ensure that the market is fair and orderly.

■ **NOTE**   The Securities Act of 1933 concerns new issues; the Securities Exchange Act of 1934 regulates trading of issued securities in the secondary market.

Perhaps the most significant feature of the 1934 Act is the creation of the Securities and Exchange Commission (SEC) as an enforcing authority for the securities industry. Its five commissioners are appointed by the President, approved by the Senate for five-year terms, and are barred from any business or stock activity when they are serving.

The SEC is specifically charged with establishing rules regulating credit, brokers' treatment of customers' securities, etc., all detailed below. The Act also defines terms like "broker" and "dealer," and includes provisions for regulating exchanges.

RULES GOVERNING REGISTRATION

The 1934 Act calls on exchanges to regulate themselves, but all national securities exchanges must register with the SEC, agree to abide by the law, supply up-to-date information about the organization's rules and membership, including its provisions for dealing with members who conduct business in ways which violate the principles of the Act.

Others who must register with, and are regulated by, the SEC are individuals or firms engaged in securities transactions in interstate commerce. These include exchange members who deal with the public, such as specialists, brokers or dealers who engage in over the counter transactions, members of national securities associations. Also, securities themselves must be registered with the SEC.

Exempted from registration requirements are small local exchanges, brokers/dealers who do not do business with the public or who work only intrastate (though anyone who uses the mail is subject to the Act), and issues that are exempt (government, intrastate, and some smaller issues).

CREDIT REGULATIONS

Under the 1934 Act, the Federal Reserve Board is given authority to control the amount of credit "initially extended and subsequently maintained" on securities (see page 217). The board does this by restricting the borrowing of members, brokers, and dealers under its Regulation T, which is enforced by the SEC.

It is unlawful for any member of a national securities exchange, or any broker/dealer who transacts business through such a member, to borrow on any listed security except through a FRB member bank, or to have a total indebtedness in excess of 15 times its net capital. These requirements do not apply to exempt securities (direct federal government obligations, or government-guaranteed obligations).

HYPOTHECATION AND COMMINGLING OF CUSTOMERS' SECURITIES

No member of a national exchange or broker or dealer may:

☐ pledge a customer's securities (hypothecate) to a bank as security for a loan without the customer's written consent

☐ commingle a customer's securities with those of other customers or of the firm without written permission

When the firm does have permission to commingle and hypothecate customer's securities, it may not pledge them for an amount in excess of the debit balance in the customer's account.

MANIPULATION AND DECEPTION

SEC regulations prohibit fraud and/or the manipulation of securities' prices.

Manipulative devices

It is unlawful to act so as to give a false appearance of active trading in a security; any device(s) used to manipulate markets is prohibited. These include:

"Wash sales" One person buys and sells to create the misleading appearance of active trading.

"Matching orders" Two or more individuals act together and enter identical (or almost identical) orders simultaneously, so the transaction appears on the tape although there has been no true change of ownership.

False information For example, urging a transaction in a particular security by saying some person is going to move in a way that will affect its price.

Short sales

Another way in which the Act guards against manipulation is with rules concerning short-selling. The specific intent here is to prevent an investor from cornering the market by continually selling short and driving a security's price down, then buying the securities back cheaply.

Thus, the basic rule is the "plus tick" rule: no short sales are permitted at a price lower than the last reported regular-way sale. In other words, selling short is only allowed at a price higher than the last reported sale (a plus tick), or at a price which is the same as the last reported sale but higher than the last reported sale at a different price. (See Chapter 11.)

With odd lots, the plus tick rule is applied in terms of the last reported round lot sale price.

Someone who holds a short position in a security may not tender that security in response to a tender offer.

Other prohibited activities

Solicitation Because it is possible to manipulate prices by soliciting purchases on an exchange, the law prohibits distributors of securities (underwriters) to solicit trade in those securities. There are some exceptions, including:

- unsolicited customer orders
- bids offered for the purpose of stabilizing the issue by managing underwriters
- "market making" transactions which take place 10 business days before distribution

Tenders To prevent those who make a tender offer from purchasing in the market, the rules prohibit anyone who makes a tender (or exchange) offer for a particular security from purchasing that security except under the terms of that offer.

Credit disclosure To guard against deception, credit terms must be disclosed in margin transactions. This means a customer must receive a written statement of rates and charges at the time a margin account is opened. No credit can be extended on the purchase of new issues.

■ **NOTE**

All these rules are issued pursuant to the anti-fraud provisions of the 1934 Act. While some particular transactions are exempted from requirements of the Act, as noted, none are exempt from anti-fraud provisions.

STABILIZATION

As noted in Chapter 6, the 1934 Act permits stabilization of a new issue, provided it:

- takes place prior to the effective date of the issue
- is disclosed in the prospectus
- is not used to raise the price of the offered security (stabilization can only be used to prevent a drop in the market price during distribution)
- is not performed by anyone other than the managing underwriter
- does not involve a bid higher than the current offering price

INSIDER RULES

The act restricts the activities of "insiders." An insider is defined as:

☐ an officer or director of a corporation

☐ anyone holding 10% or more of the shares (of any class of equity security) issued by the corporation

☐ anyone who has information about the corporation not available to the public

Basically, insiders are not allowed to profit from their information by trading in a stock before that information is public. For that reason, those who become insiders must file a personal statement with the SEC.

If an insider makes a profit on the corporation's stock in a period of less than six months, the corporation can legally recover that profit. Insiders must report all personal transactions in securities of their corporations no later than 10 days after the end of the calendar month in which they occur. Generally, insiders are barred from any short selling.

PROXIES

Solicitation of proxies is also regulated by the SEC under the Act. A shareholder can give someone power to vote in his or her behalf through a proxy. The regulations state that companies which solicit proxies must provide shareholders with accurate, detailed information about any proposals up for vote; this information must also be submitted to the SEC for review.

In a situation where control of a company is at stake, usually called a "proxy contest" (*e.g.*, where another firm is trying to acquire a company), those involved in soliciting proxies must register with the SEC as "participants." This does not include anyone (such as a broker) who is asked for advice; the key concept is "unsolicited advice." Those who fail to register can face criminal penalties.

RECORD-KEEPING AND REPORT-FILING REQUIREMENTS

Every broker or dealer, and every national securities exchange must keep detailed records; copies must be filed with the SEC as that agency deems necessary to protect investors. A representative of the SEC or the NASD may examine such records at any time without warning.

All registered brokers or dealers must annually file an income statement and balance sheet, certified by an independent accountant, with the SEC. Copies of these reports must go to the firm's customers.

All individuals involved—partners, officers, directors, or employees—in a listed exchange, brokerage, or dealership must submit their fingerprints to the U.S. Attorney General.

OTC REGULATIONS

Under Section 15A of the 1934 Act (The Maloney Amendment), the National Association of Securities Dealers (NASD) is established to regulate the over the counter market. The NASD itself must be registered with the

SEC; any nonmember broker/dealer whose business involves any interstate commerce or transactions involving national securities exchanges is directly regulated by the SEC.

Recommendations In recommending any security to a customer, registered brokers and dealers must be sure it is reasonable and suitable for the particular customer. (NASD bylaws are set forth on pages 330-339.)

Supervision The Act requires close supervision of all "associated persons" (employees) of a broker or dealer. Thus, all member firms must have on file written procedures for such supervision. Duties of a designated supervisor include:

- reviewing and approving (in writing) each new customer account and conducting frequent examinations of established accounts
- reviewing and approving (in writing) all security transactions and correspondence by associated persons
- reviewing customer complaints

Customer accounts Member firms are required to:

- establish a particular form for new accounts
- maintain current records on each customer
- keep detailed records on discretionary accounts to show that transactions in the account are not excessive
- maintain current information about the companies, especially with respect to dividends, splits, rights subscriptions, etc.
- keep all customer complaints on file

CAPITAL REQUIREMENTS

Net capital requirements: SEC Rule 15c3-1

To ensure that brokers or dealers remain solvent, the law limits the total indebtedness of member firms to a specific percentage of net capital. The rule sets the requirements for various categories of brokers and stipulates the elements which must be considered as debt or capital.

Use of customer free credit balance: SEC 15c3-2

"Free credit balance" effectively refers to cash in the customer's account; *i.e.*, any liability payable to the customer on demand. The rule holds that the broker/dealer can use these amounts for its business operations if the customer is advised in writing every three months:

- the amount of the free credit balance
- that funds are not segregated and may be used by the broker/dealer for its own business
- the funds are payable to the customer on demand

Customer protection: Rule 15c3-3

Essentially, this rule holds that the broker must keep physical control over all customers' fully-paid securities (*i.e.*, not including those pledged for a bank loan).

In addition, every broker or dealer must maintain a "special reserve bank account for the exclusive benefit of customers" separate from any other bank account, containing an amount worked out according to a formula provided (basically, the amount by which the firm's obligation to customers exceed customer obligations to the firms).

PART THREE   OTHER REGULATIONS

INVESTMENT COMPANY ACT OF 1940 (ICA 1940)

Most of the provisions of the Investment Company Act of 1940 are presented in Chapter 4, Mutual Funds, so this will be only a very brief review.

This Act defines the three principal types of investment companies: face amount certificate companies, unit investment trusts, and management companies including diversified, nondiversified, open-end, and closed-end companies. Like the 1933 and 1934 Acts, this legislation is enforced by the SEC, and extends the requirements of those acts to investment companies, especially those ensuring a fair and equitable issuance of securities. A related law, the Investment Advisers Act of 1940, requires all investment advisers to register with the SEC.

Various provisions of the act require registration of investment companies, restrict the choice of directors, prohibit certain types of transactions, outline shareholders' rights, and so on. All are covered in Chapter 4.

Two amendments to the Securities Exchange Act of 1934 are the Maloney Act of 1938 and the Securities Acts Amendments of 1975. The first gave OTC markets the power of self-regulation and led to the creation of the NASD. The second extended self-regulation to municipal securities and led to the creation of the MSRB.

FEDERAL RESERVE BOARD REGULATIONS

As noted above, the SEC authorized the Federal Reserve Board to regulate credit involved in securities purchases. Two regulations govern such matters.

Regulation U

Banks are limited in the amount of credit they may extend for the purchase of listed stocks or bonds. Customers who borrow under the Regulation must file a statement indicating the purpose of the loan, and banks must keep this statement for three years after the loan is repaid. Loans made for other purposes are called "non-purpose loans."

Regulation T

Reg T sets rules on extending credit in securities transactions; these apply to all securities broker/dealers and members of national securities exchanges.

Basically, the regulation limits the amount of credit a broker/dealer may extend to clients who are purchasing securities on margin (not including municipal or U.S. government or commodity transactions).

SECURITIES INVESTOR PROTECTION CORPORATION (SIPC)

In 1970, Congress created the Securities Investor Protection Corporation (SIPC) to provide limited protection to customers of securities firms that are forced to liquidate, and to promote confidence in the securities industry. In effect, it protects an investor's cash and securities (but not commodity accounts) up to $500,000.

SIPC membership

SIPC is not an agency of the government, but a nonprofit membership corporation composed of members: all broker/dealers registered under the 1934 Act, all members of national securities exchanges, and most NASD members. It is financed by an assessment on members' securities-related business, and can receive emergency funding from the Treasury with SEC approval.

Liquidation procedures

When it is determined that a member must liquidate, the SIPC may ask a federal court to appoint a trustee to supervise the liquidation. The trustee must:

1 Notify customers of the liquidation.

2 See that customers receive securities registered in their name, or those in the process of being registered (*i.e.*, any securities that can be identified as belonging to a specific client). There is no limit on the value of the returned property.

3 See that customers receive all other "customer property" (cash and securities) held by the firm, divided on a pro-rata basis. Again, there is no limit on the value of the returned property.

4 Remaining claims are satisfied by the SIPC, subject to certain limitations.

Limits on Customer Claims

The SIPC covers claims of up to $500,000 per separate customer, of which not more than $100,000 may be in cash. This is not coverage "per account." Under the SIPC Act, when a single customer holds accounts in different forms, each account is considered separate. For example, consider an investor who has an individual account, a joint account with his or her spouse, and acts as trustee in yet a third account, all with the same broker/dealer. In liquidation, these would be considered three "separate customers."

However, a person who has one or more individual accounts (say, a cash and a margin account) with one firm is considered a single customer, and will be covered for only $500,000 in liquidation.

Clients must file claims directly with the SIPC trustee. Claims are valued as of the date the trustee begins liquidation. Reimbursement is "in kind," *i.e.*, claims for securities are satisfied by delivery of those securities. Customers are not protected if securities rise or fall in value between the time of filing and date of delivery.

Trust Indenture Act of 1939

Requirements of this act are covered in Chapter 2. Basically, it concerns all corporate bonds issued to the public interstate and requires that a trustee be appointed to safeguard the rights of bondholders; it also mandates full disclosure of information in the written agreement between the corporation and its creditors (the trust indenture), etc.

State Regulations

Although the securities industry is also regulated at the state level, it is not possible to discuss each state's particular regulations in detail. However, some general similarities do exist. For example, the Uniform Securities Act is actually a model followed by many states in formulating their own laws.

State "blue sky laws," discussed in Chapter 6, provide protection in securities transactions similar to that provided by federal legislation. Most states also require the regulation and registration of securities, of broker/dealers, and of individual agents; many impose capital requirements for those active in the securities industry. In addition, many states have antifraud regulations.

Uniform gifts to minors

This, too, is a model act; it has been adopted by most states. It is discussed in some detail in Chapter 10.

Prudent man rule

In many states, some version of this rule applies to the investment-related activities of fiduciaries or trustees. In essence, it holds that people acting on behalf of another can only invest in those securities which a reasonably prudent man who is seeking reasonable income and preservation of capital would choose.

Legal lists

These are published by the banking departments of some states. They list securities that institutions (*e.g.*, banks, insurance companies) may purchase. Its purpose, like that of the prudent man rule, is to prevent speculative activity with funds belonging to others. In some states which lack the prudent man rule, the list also governs the behavior of trustees and fiduciaries.

Law of agency

This stipulates that a registered representative acts on behalf of his or her employer as an agent, and may not:

- □ act on behalf of a third party whose interests conflict with the employer's
- □ acquire private interests which conflict with the employer's
- □ work for another firm in the same business, except with the employer's permission

Questions on federal and state regulations follow Chapter 16.

CHAPTER SIXTEEN

Industry regulations

PART ONE   NASD REGULATIONS

The National Association of Securities Dealers, Inc. (NASD) is a self-regulating body which sets standards for the over-the-counter securities market. It was established as a "national securities association" under the Maloney Act, which became law in 1938. That law is now Section 15A of the Securities Exchange Act of 1934.

A set of by-laws, printed in the NASD Manual, concerns requirements for qualifying and registering as a member. Other important units are the:

□ Rules of Fair Practice, which concern member firms' dealings with the public

□ Uniform Practice Code, which covers dealings between brokerage firms

□ Code of Procedure, which deals with violations of NASD rules

□ Code of Arbitration, which deals with settling disputes between members, and between members and the public

PURPOSES

In its Certificate of Incorporation, the NASD declares its purposes. These include:

1 To promote the investment banking and securities business, standardize its principles and practices, promote high standards of commercial honor, and encourage observance of applicable laws.

2 To provide a medium which enables members to work with government and other agencies on problems affecting investors, the public, and those engaged in the investment banking and securities business.

3 Adopting and enforcing rules of fair practice and rules preventing fraud and manipulation; to promote just and equitable principles of trade for the protection of investors.

4 Promote self-discipline among members, deal with grievances between members and between members and the public.

BY-LAWS: MEMBERSHIP

Eligibility

NASD by-laws say that any broker or dealer or securities underwriter legally authorized (under federal or state law) to transact business in the investment banking or securities field, who actually transacts such business in the United States, and who pledges to abide by NASD rules, is eligible for membership.

Commercial banks are specifically excluded. Under certain conditions, individuals can be disqualified from membership or from seeking membership. These include:

1 Anyone suspended or expelled from a self-regulatory organization (such as the NASD or any national securities exchange).

2 Anyone who has been subject to an SEC order suspending or revoking broker or dealer registration.

3 Anyone who has been convicted of a felony or misdemeanor involving securities trading, perjury, bribery, embezzlement, and so on, in the preceding 10 years.

Registration of members

Under the by-laws, members must register as principals or representatives. Principals are those actively engaged in the investment banking or securities activities of a member firm, including officers, directors, partners, and supervising managers. Representatives are those who engage in such activities as an employee of a member.

Branch offices Every member firm is required to register its branch offices and inform the board of governors of any branch opening or closing.

Exemptions No registration is required for:

- □ those who deal exclusively in exempt securities, commodities, or listed securities (those traded on a national exchange)
- □ clerical or administrative personnel

      □ persons who provide capital but are not directly engaged in the member firm's activities

Conditions Both principals and representatives must pass a qualifying exam. For registered representatives, registration is nontransferable. If they change employers, they must re-register in the new position. If more than two years elapse, the former members may have to requalify.

    Those who wish to terminate their registration must submit a written resignation to the NASD.

Advantages Although NASD membership is voluntary, it does carry certain benefits. Member firms receive preference when they underwrite and trade in the over-the-counter market; members may deal with nonmembers only on the same basis as the general public and members cannot join in an underwriting with nonmembers.

Operations

Under the by-laws, a 27-member Board of Governors, the governing body of the NASD, is responsible for administering its affairs. This board divides the country into 13 geographical districts. In each, a District Committee functions to provide administration on the local level. At times, this becomes the District Business Conduct Committee and acts as a disciplinary body (see page 339).

Assessments

The Board of Governors draws up a budget annually, and imposes assessments on members to meet financial needs. Charges include: a basic membership fee, plus a percentage of gross income, and a fee for each registered representative, principal, and branch office, and fees for registration and membership applications and exams.

RULES OF FAIR PRACTICE

As noted, these rules principally concern relations between members and their customers. They are intended to ensure just and equitable charges and customs in retail transactions, and to prevent fraud and manipulation.

    Perhaps the most general (and most important) rule is entitled Business Conduct of Members. It simply states that members "shall observe high standards of commercial honor and just and equitable principles of trade."

Executing retail transactions in the OTC market

When buying or selling for a customer, a member must find the best interdealer market for the securities; *i.e.*, must get the best price possible in the current market.

    A member may not turn to a third party, *i.e.*, channel the transaction through another broker/dealer, unless it will demonstrably reduce the cost to the customer.

Prompt receipt and delivery of securities

Purchases No member may accept a purchase order for securities from a customer unless he is certain the customer agrees to pay for them promptly (in seven business days) and to receive securities against payment, even for executions that represent only part of a larger order.

Sales A member cannot execute a customer's sell order unless:

1 The member has possession of the security; or

2 The customer is long in that security in his account with the member; or

3 The member has reasonable assurance (a) the customer will deliver the security within five business days of the execution of the order; or (b) the security is on deposit with a qualified institution which has been instructed to deliver the securities against payment.

Forwarding of proxy and other materials

Members must forward proxy materials, annual reports, and other legally required information to each beneficial owner of shares held by the member (in a street name). This material is furnished by the issuer, which also pays the cost of distributing it.

"Free riding and withholding"

Members must make a bona fide public distribution at the public offering price for securities which trade at a premium in the secondary market ("hot issues"). Failure to do so is termed "free riding and withholding"; this rule is designed to prevent a broker/dealer from artificially raising prices by holding securities off the market in the face of considerable demand. It applies no matter how the member acquired the securities: as underwriter, as selling group member, or from an underwriter or selling group member.

More specifically, the rules say a member:

1 Cannot hold any such securities in the member firm's account.

2 Cannot sell such securities to any officer, director, employee, agent or associate, of the member (or of another broker/dealer) or to members of any such person's immediate family. (This includes parents, children, brother or sister, spouse, and father-, mother-, brother- and sister-in-law as well as any other person materially supported by the member.)

3 Cannot sell such securities to a finder or anyone acting in fiduciary capacity to the managing underwriter, or to members of his or her immediate family.

4 Cannot sell such securities to senior officers of institutions (*e.g.*, banks, savings and loans, insurance companies) or to employees of such institutions whose work involves securities transactions, or to members of their immediate families.

Exceptions

A member may sell securities to those described in items 3 and 4 above, and to family members of those described in item 2 above, or to any account in which those persons have a beneficial interest, provided:

1 The member can demonstrate the securities were sold in accordance with those persons' normal investment practices; *i.e.,* that it reflects a customary—in terms of frequency and amount—purchase from the member; a consistent policy of purchasing only hot issues would not be likely to qualify as "normal" *and*

2 That the total amount of securities sold is insubstantial and not disproportionate to total public sales. (Insubstantial is not defined in any fixed way, but applies to both aggregate sales and sales to any one individual. As for disproportionate, this obviously depends on the size and price of the issue; the Manual suggests, as a guideline only, 10% of the member's total participation in the issue.)

A member cannot sell these securities at or above the public offering price to another broker/dealer; however, he may sell all or part of these securities to another member broker/dealer if that member provides written assurance that the purchase is for public customers.

Recommendations to customers ("fair dealing")

In recommending a security transaction to a customer, a registered representative must have reasonable grounds to believe that it is suitable in terms of the customer's other holdings, resources, and needs. More specifically, this means members:

1 Cannot recommend speculative, low-priced securities without attempting to get information about the customer's financial situation.

2 Cannot engage in excessive trading or "churning."

3 Cannot trade in mutual fund shares, as these are not considered suitable for short term trades.

Also, members cannot engage in fraudulent conduct, specifically:

4 Establish fictitious accounts, to execute prohibited transactions (*e.g.,* purchase of hot issues), or to disguise actions contrary to a firm's policy.

5 Conduct transactions in discretionary accounts without the customer's written permission.

6 Execute transactions without customer authorization, or to send confirmations to customers, thereby making them accept transactions not agreed to.

7 Borrowing customer's funds or securities without written authorization.

8 Engage in any illegal fraudulent activity, such as forgery, misstatement or manipulation.

Members are also advised that recommending purchase of securities beyond a customer's financial ability is an unfair practice.

Charges for services performed

A member is allowed to charge for such services as collection of dividends and interest due, transfer of securities, appraisals, safekeeping, etc. Such charges must be reasonable and fair (not discriminatory between customers).

Fair prices and commissions

In all over the counter securities transactions, a member must buy or sell at a price which is fair and reasonable, considering all relevant factors; if the member is acting as an agent, any commission or service charge must be similarly fair and reasonable. The guiding interpretation here is the "5% markup policy." It is important to note that this is a guide, not a rule: greater (or smaller) markups may be considered fair under certain circumstances including:

- the type of security (common stocks tend to have a higher markup than bonds, for example)
- market conditions for the security (if market activity is slow, the markup may be higher than in a more active market)
- price of the security (lower price securities might warrant a higher percentage markup)
- size of transaction (handling expenses may be less in percentage terms on a larger transaction)
- expenses involved in obtaining the security
- services rendered in completing the transaction

However, excessive expenses (such as high salaries or high rent) are not considered to justify a higher markup. Markups must be based on current market value. This guideline applies to transactions in which a member:

- buys a security to fill an order received from a customer for that security ("riskless" or "simultaneous" transactions)
- sells a security to a customer from inventory (markup should be based on current market price, not the broker/dealers' cost)
- buys a security from a client (here the rule applies to markdown, not a markup)
- acts as agent
- participates in a "proceeds transaction" (In these trades, a customer sells securities to or through a broker/dealer, and the proceeds are used to pay for other securities purchased from or through that broker/dealer at or about the same time. This is considered a single transaction.)

■ NOTE
NASD markup policy is not applicable to securities where a prospectus is required, and securities are sold at a public offering price. This effectively excludes new issues and mutual fund shares.

Publication of transactions and quotations

Members cannot publish any communication (advertisement, circular, etc.) that reports a security transaction unless the member believes it represents a bona fide sale or purchase. Similarly, members cannot report a bid or asked price unless they believe it represents a bona fide bid or offer (a firm quote). Nominal (approximate) quotes can be used, but they must be clearly identified.

This rule also explicitly prohibits publishing a figure as a firm quote unless a bona fide transaction took place at that price. Using false or misleading quotations to induce a customer to purchase securities is considered manipulation and fraud.

Offers at stated prices

Members cannot offer to buy or sell securities at a stated price unless they are prepared to trade at that price. In short, quotations should be firm; the action of refusing to honor an offered quotation is called "backing away." Although the rules acknowledge that "subject" quotes are sometimes necessary, a member making a "firm trading market" in a security is expected to buy or sell a normal unit at the quoted price.

Disclosure of price in selling agreements

Selling group agreements must state the public price of the securities involved. They must also stipulate who gets concessions (if any) and under what circumstances.

Securities taken in trade

The term "taken in trade" refers to a transaction in which a member purchases (as agent or principal) a security from a customer as part of an agreement that the customer will purchase securities which are part of a fixed price offering from the member. The rule holds that such securities must be purchased at a fair market price, *i.e.*, what a dealer in that security would normally pay. If the member is acting as agent, a normal commission must be charged.

Use of information obtained in fiduciary capacity

A member acting as paying agent, transfer agent, trustee, or the like, may not use any information received in that capacity to solicit trades, unless asked to do so by the issuer.

Influencing or rewarding employees of others

No member or associated person shall give anything of value worth more than $50 in any year to any person (or any agent or employee of any person) if the gift is in relation to that person's (or employer's) business (*e.g.*, bribing another firm's order clerk to channel orders to a member). This does not, however, prohibit business-related expenses, such as meals or theater tickets.

Payment designed to influence market prices

Members cannot give anything of value to induce anyone to publish information which could affect the market price of a security (*e.g.*, paying a market letter publisher or journalist for favorable comment). This rule explicitly excepts clearly-defined paid advertising.

Disclosure on confirmation

At or before the time a transaction with a customer is completed, members must provide written confirmation showing whether the member acted as broker or dealer; if the member acted as a broker, the member must report, or offer to report, the identity of the other party and other details of the trade.

■ NOTE

Commission amounts must be disclosed (but not markups except on riskless transactions) and a broker or dealer member cannot act as both principal and agent in the same transaction.

Disclosure of control

A member controlled by or controlling the issuer of a security or in a "control position" must so inform customers prior to entering into a contract for purchase or sale of such security. This disclosure must be delivered in writing at or before the completion of any transaction.

This would include, for example, a situation in which officers of the issuing company are also officers of the member firm, or when the shares offered are in a company which owns interest in the member firm.

Disclosure of participation or interest in primary or secondary distribution

This echoes the preceding rule: a member who participates in distribution of a security as broker or as dealer must inform customers in writing of that involvement at or before the completion of any transaction involving that security.

Discretionary accounts

This reinforces the "fair dealing" rule mentioned above, and forbids a member or registered representative from exercising any authority over a customer's account without written authorization. All such activity must be approved in writing by the member, especially with regard to avoiding excessive transactions (churning).

Offerings "at the market"

A member who is in any way financially involved in the primary or secondary distribution of a security not traded on a national exchange may not tell a customer it is being offered "at the market," unless the member has reason to believe there is another market other than the one made or controlled by the member.

Solicitation of purchases on an exchange to facilitate a distribution of securities

It is prohibited for a member who has a financial interest in the distribution of a security to pay someone to buy any security of that same issuer on an exchange, or to pay someone to solicit another person to buy such a security, unless the purchase is for that member's own account. This rule is intended to avoid creating false trading activity.

Use of fraudulent devices

This catchall rule simply prohibits members from using manipulation, deception, or fraud to effect any transaction.

Customers' securities or funds

In holding that a member may not make "improper use" of funds or securities belonging to a customer, this rule specifically incorporates the provisions of Rule 15c3-3 (see page 325). In addition, members or associated persons are forbidden to:

1 Lend securities carried for any customer's account without that customer's written authorization (a "loan consent agreement").

2 Lend securities carried for any customer's account which are fully paid for, or are excess margin securities (*i.e.*, which exceed the customer's indebtedness) without written authorization. Such securities must be segregated and clearly identified.

3 Guarantee a customer against loss.

4 Share directly or indirectly in the profits or losses of any customer's account without prior written authorization. Any such sharing must be in direct proportion to the financial contributions made to the account by each person. (Note that this provision on proportion does not apply to the accounts of the immediate family of the member or associated person.)

Installment or partial payment sales

Basically, a member cannot transact business for or with a customer on an installment plan.

Books and records

Members are required to keep all records and books in compliance with applicable laws and NASD regulations. In particular, complete customer account forms must be on file. Written complaints from customers, and actions taken in response, must be recorded in a separate file.

Disclosure of financial condition

Members must provide a copy of the firm's most recent balance sheet to any bona fide customer who requests it.

Net prices to persons not in investment banking or securities business

Members may not offer any concession, discount or other allowance in a securities transaction to any person outside the securities industry. Trades with the general public must be at the net price.

Selling concessions

A member may pay or receive selling concessions only for services rendered; these can only be paid to brokers or dealers actually involved in the investment banking or securities business. Members are prohibited from granting concessions to nonmembers who are not involved in a distribution or to the general public.

Dealing with nonmembers

This rule repeats the strictures on dealing with nonmembers in an underwriting, and also forbids transactions with nonmembers on any terms or for any charges other than those offered the general public. An exception is made for nonmember broker/dealers trading in a foreign country and ineligible for membership in a registered securities association. If the transaction involves some allowance, however, the foreign firm must agree to abide by this rule.

Investment companies

Much of the contents of this rule is covered in Chapter 4. It defines terms associated with investment company offerings, and includes the following provisions:

Underwriters Members who are underwriters of an investment company may not sell its shares to any broker/dealer except at the public offering price, unless a sales agreement between the parties is in effect.

Sales charge Members are barred from offering or selling shares in an open end investment company, or "single payment" plans of a registered unit investment trust, if the public offering price is excessive. Basically, this means any sales charges in excess of 8.5% of the offering price; lower rates are stipulated if dividend reinvestment is not available or if "rights of accumulation" or quantity discounts are not offered.

Other provisions Members are prohibited from "selling dividends," or withholding orders so as to make a profit. Members may not purchase these securities from an underwriter (or as an underwriter from the issuer) except to cover purchase orders already received or for their own investment.

Favoring In selling or distributing shares, members may not favor or disfavor any particular company on the basis of sales commissions or sales incentives.

Supervision

Each member must establish and enforce written procedures which allow proper supervision of each registered representative and associated person to assure they comply with all applicable laws and rules.

Members are responsible for proper supervision, and must designate a partner, officer or manager in each office of supervisory jurisdiction, including the main office, to carry out the written procedures. An office of supervisory jurisdiction is one designated as responsible for the review of activities of registered representatives in that office or any other office of the member.

In addition, members must periodically review securities transactions and correspondence, customer accounts, etc.

Transactions for personnel of another member

A member who knowingly executes a securities transaction for the employee of another member should try to determine that the transaction will not have an adverse effect on that member's employer. In these cases, the member that executes the order must notify the employer in writing, and provide duplicate confirmation to that firm if requested. Notification is not required with investment companies' securities.

A person employed by a member who transacts securities business with another member should notify the employing member of that fact.

Variable contracts of an insurance company

This rule defines variable contracts, sets limits on sales charges and lists procedures for handling (see page 101).

Margin accounts

Members are prohibited from effecting margin transactions in any manner that does not meet NASD requirements (see page 225). Particulars are set forth in Appendix A to the Rules.

THE UNIFORM PRACTICE CODE

These are rules governing delivery of securities, and other practices connected with securities transactions described in Chapter 10.

CODE OF PROCEDURE

This code applies to all proceedings relating to disciplining members, eligibility requirements, and limiting or denying services. As noted above, each of the 13 NASD district committees becomes a District Business Conduct Committee for these purposes.

The District Business Conduct Committee This committee may issue a complaint itself (for example, if a routine inspection reveals some violation of laws or rules), or can act when it receives a complaint. In either case, the complaint must be detailed in writing; a copy must be sent to the party or parties named in the complaint.

The party(ies) named in the complaint must answer in writing; when the answer is filed, any of those involved (complainant, respondent, or the committee) may request a hearing. The entire committee may sit as a hearing panel, or appoint a hearing panel. At a hearing, both complainant and respondent are entitled to testify and be represented by counsel; documentary evidence, if any, must be submitted before the hearing.

Decisions may be appealed to the NASD Board of Governors, which may uphold the decision and/or reduce or increase any penalty or sanction. Further appeals can be made to the SEC, which can uphold or reverse penalties or sanctions. The SEC may lower, but cannot increase, penalties or sanctions.

CODE OF ARBITRATION

This covers disputes between members and: other members; associated persons; public customers; and registered clearing agencies. The NASD board of governors appoints a national arbitration committee, including representatives from the public, which sets rules for arbitration and establishes a pool of arbitrators. A director of arbitration appoints panels from this pool.

Under the code, disputes are arbitrated at the instance of a member against another member, a member against an associated person (or vice versa), an associated person against another associated person, and with any dispute involving a registered clearing agency.

PART TWO   NYSE REGULATIONS

The rules and regulations of the New York Stock Exchange, set out in its Constitution, serve as a model for other, smaller, national exchanges. Details about operation of the exchange are covered in Chapter 8; some of these reflect exchange rules and will be recapitulated here.

THE REGISTERED REPRESENTATIVE

A registered representative is an employee of a NYSE- or NASD-member firm, licensed to operate as a broker/dealer, and who has passed the qualifying ("Series 7") exam. Acting on behalf of that employer, the registered representative is an agent who solicits business (including orders for securities trades) and provides information on investments. The representative must deal fairly with clients.

■ NOTE

The term "registered representative" does not apply to those who act only as securities traders or arbitrageurs, or who only solicit commodities contracts. A person who sells only government or municipal issues (exempt securities) for a NASD member firm would not be required to take the exam. This exception does not apply to those employed by a NYSE member firm.

Qualifications

Passing the Series 7 Exam is only one step in the registration process. Registered representatives must also be registered with and approved by the exchange itself (employers are responsible for verifying an employee's work record). Candidates must have reached legal majority in the state in which they are working, and usually are required to register with that state's securities department.

The registered representative's agreement

All registered representative candidates are required to sign a statement agreeing to abide by the constitution and rules of the NYSE. They must agree to notify their firm in the case of arrest, personal bankruptcy, or involvement in any investigation or litigation involving the securities industry. The firm, in turn, notifies the NYSE. A person confined in a mental institution must also notify his employer, although in this case the employer does not necessarily have to inform the exchange.

In addition, prospective registered representatives agree:

☐ not to agree to pay or actually pay a customer's debit balance without the written consent of the NYSE

☐ not to guarantee a customer against loss or guarantee a profit

☐ not to share in the profits or losses of a customer's account

☐ not to rebate any part of commissions or any other compensation to a customer

☐ not to keep a personal account except with a member firm or a bank, and that with employer's consent

☐ not to accept any sort of compensation for a transaction except from the employer without written permission from the NYSE

Fixed duties of registered representative

Full time The registered representative must devote full time to the job (unless explicitly hired as a part-time employee).

Other work A representative may accept an after-hours position in another business only with the permission of the employer and the NYSE.

Leave A registered representative may take leave for up to one year, with the employer's permission (NYSE permission is not required) provided he or she accepts no other employment during that time; the rep may not enter the employer's premises while on leave.

Teaching A registered representative may teach evening classes on a financial subject for a reasonable fee with an employer's permission.

Termination Whenever a registered representative or officer leaves a firm, or is transferred to another office, the NYSE Department of Member Firms must be notified of that fact and of the reasons for termination. Registration is not transferable: the representative who joins a new firm must reregister with that firm.

PUBLIC COMMUNICATIONS
(ADVERTISING AND SPEAKING)

Published material All advertising, for use in any medium, and all other communications (research reports, brochures, market letters, etc.) must meet standards of truthfulness and good taste. Members are expected to avoid exaggerated claims or statements; recommendations must be reasonably based and supported by factual information—including the current market price.

Other rules reflect NASD regulations. For example, if a firm recommends a security in which it has some interest, that interest must be disclosed. If testimonials are used, it must be clear that they may not indicate future performance or be said to reflect all customers' experience; any projections must be explicitly identified as estimates.

All literature must be approved by the member firm (usually by an authorized person in the firm); research reports must be approved by a supervisory analyst.

Speaking The registered representative must get permission from the employer for each speech or lecture course he or she offers. The firm assumes responsibility for the content of any speech or lecture, and must keep a record for three years showing:

- □ sponsoring group's name and the name and address of the person who chaired the program
- □ topic(s) discussed
- □ approximate number of people in attendance
- □ speaker's name

CONDUCT OF ACCOUNTS

A number of rules deal specifically with the handling of customer accounts.

"Know your customer" rule

Every member firm must know the essential facts about every one of its customers, every new or continuing cash or margin account, and every order.

Accordingly, one person in the firm (a general partner, principal executive, or other designated supervisor) is responsible for seeing that essential facts about each customer are recorded, and for diligently supervising all the registered representatives' accounts. When a new account is opened, it must be specifically approved before or just after the first transaction is executed. This may be done by a branch manager who determines all essential facts pertaining to the customer are on record. But the account must still be approved by the firm's designated principal.

Corporate accounts Special rules apply to dealings with corporations. Member firms cannot open a corporate margin account without determining the corporation's charter and by-laws permit such transactions. With either a cash or margin account, the member firm must ensure that the individual conducting business in that account is authorized to do so by the corporation.

Other rules When an account is opened for someone acting as an agent, members must have on file the name of the principal, and written proof of the agent's authority. The registered representative is responsible for obtaining certain information about new accounts (see pages 202–203).

It is never permissible to open an account for a third party (though customers can grant power of attorney or open accounts in trust for minors).

Designation of accounts

Accounts carried on a member firm's books must be in the customer's own full name. Customers who wish to transact business through a numbered account may do so, but the firm must have on file a written statement, signed by the customer, attesting to ownership of the account.

"Street name" accounts

When customer-owned securities are held in the name of the broker/dealer this is called "in street name." The firm is then the "owner of record"; the actual owner is "the beneficial owner."

Voting rights stay with the beneficial owner, who must tell the owner of record how to vote. However, if there is nothing of importance to be voted on, and the firm has mailed proxies 15 days prior to the meeting and received no answer within five days, "in street name" stock may be voted by the firm. This rule was established to make it easier for a corporation to reach a legal quorum at stockholders' meetings.

Accounts of members and allied members in other member firms

Member firms cannot have the account of a member or allied member of another member firm without prior written consent from that firm. This must be signed by a general partner or principal executive, and all transactions must be reported to the person who granted approval.

Accounts of employees of other member firms

Cash accounts Individuals employed by the NYSE, or a corporation in which the NYSE has majority holdings, or by any member organization, cannot open a cash account at another member firm without written permission from their employers.

Margin accounts NYSE and member firm employees, as well as employees of banks, trust companies, insurance companies or of any firm that deals in securities, cannot open a margin account at a member firm without written permission from their employers.

Discretionary accounts

Some accounts (see page 207) give the registered representative power to act on the customer's behalf in choosing securities, and deciding when and how much to buy or sell. All such accounts activity is valid only if there is prior written authorization from the customer giving discretionary power to a third party. (This is not required when the customer simply asks the registered representative to decide when to enter an order, or to get, *e.g.*, the "best price.")

Member firms must review such accounts frequently to be sure there is no churning, or excessive trading.

Statements of account

Member firms must send their customers statements showing securities and cash positions at least quarterly. If the customer so instructs the firm in writing, originals of these statements, as well as confirmations of particular transactions, may be sent to a person holding power of attorney, with a duplicate going to the customer.

Designation on orders

No order can be executed on the exchange floor unless the customer's name (or some information designating an account) is on the order. Any change in this designation must be authorized, and approved in writing on the order itself.

Records

Member firms are required to keep records of all orders sent to the floor for at least three years.

Errors

The actual price at which an order is executed is binding, even though the price is erroneously reported to the customer verbally or in writing on the confirmation.

Audit

Member firms must be audited by an independent public accountant annually.

ARBITRATION

Disputes

All disputes involving members—for example, between a registered representative and a firm, between two firms, etc.—are handled by the arbitration board of the NYSE. Findings in the arbitration are compulsory and binding; there is no appeal.

Disputes involving non-members, such as customers, may also be handled through arbitration if the non-member agrees to this process. Customers are usually asked to sign an agreement to arbitrate when opening a new account. Arbitrators are chosen from a panel of experienced and knowledgeable individuals. Panels consist of three or four except in disputes involving large sums of money, when there are five arbitrators.

Discipline

Accusations against a NYSE member's employee must be detailed in writing and signed. The accused has 15 days in which to answer in writing. He is entitled to counsel and to cross examine any witnesses before the panel convened to consider the charge(s). That panel's findings may be appealed to the exchange board of directors, but no further. Unlike NASD rules,

NYSE rules do not permit appeals to the SEC or the courts. The exchange must keep a record of the proceedings and the findings.

LISTING

Chapter 8 gives details of current standards for listing on the NYSE. To recapitulate, a corporation must have at least:

- 2,000 owners of 100 shares or more
- 1.1 million shares publicly held
- monthly trading volume of 100,000 shares
- market value of $18,000,000, or net tangible assets of $18,000,000
- earnings of $2.5 million for the last fiscal year and $2 million for the two previous fiscal years to be eligible for listing.

These standards are altered occasionally.

PART THREE   MSRB REGULATIONS

Because the courts have ruled the Constitution bars direct federal regulation of other governmental entities (states, cities, municipal agencies, etc.), municipal securities are not subject to the Securities Act of 1933 mandating registration of new issues, nor do the issuers of such securities have to meet the reporting requirements of the Securities Exchange Act of 1934.

For these reasons, trading in municipals was for years generally unregulated until 1975, when the Municipal Securities Rulemaking Board (MSRB) was created as part of the Securities Acts Amendments. The 15-member board has five representatives each from banks, brokerage firms, and the public.

While the 1975 legislation could not extend SEC jurisdiction to municipals or their issuers, it could and did effectively extend the provisions of the 1934 Act to those who work professionally in the municipals market—securities firms and banks. The federal anti-fraud provisions and some further rules now apply to transactions involving municipals; in particular, the underwriting of municipal bonds is now subject to federal regulation.

Thus, the MSRB, though it owes its existence to an act of Congress, is not a government agency. It is a self-regulatory organization, the principal rule-maker for the municipal securities industry, financed solely by private firms and banks operating in that industry.

Although MSRB rules have the force of law, *i.e.*, they are issued in compliance with SEC regulations, the board itself does not have the authority to enforce those laws or to inspect industry activities.

Instead, under the 1975 Amendments, authority in the municipal securities industry is delegated to the SEC, NASD, and federal bank regulatory agencies. The 1975 Act assigns these functions as follows:

- MSRB has rulemaking authority only
- SEC has primary enforcement, inspection, and rulemaking authority
- NASD has inspection and enforcement authority for those NASD members who are subject to MSRB rules

Three bank regulatory agencies have the authority to enforce MSRB rules for bank dealers: Comptroller of the Currency (enforces rules governing national banks), Federal Reserve Board (enforces rules governing non-national banks that are members of the Federal Reserve System), and Federal Deposit Insurance Corporation (FDIC) for all other banks.

■ **NOTE**

NASD member firms that are not members of a national exchange must maintain a fidelity bond. Non-NASD member firms face the same requirement—but these rules do not apply to bank dealers. Hence, the three bank regulatory agencies enforce the appropriate rules for such dealers.

RULES

MSRB Rules are often referred to by number (G1 to G35). It is not possible to discuss each one in detail.

Standards of professional qualification, G2, G3

Representatives can qualify by passing the general securities exam or the municipal securities representative exam. Only registered representatives may effect transactions.

In addition, each firm must have at least two principals (firms with 10 or fewer employees need only have one) who passed the municipal securities principal's qualifying exam.

Brokers, G4-7

- Anyone expelled or suspended from any exchange or securities association is disqualified from working as a municipal securities broker.
- A fidelity bond is required for every municipal securities broker.
- A prospective municipal securities broker must furnish an employment record of at least 10 years including any disciplinary action taken against him.

Keeping of records, G8-10

Municipal securities brokers must keep current books and records. Some records must be kept for six years:

- blotter entries (records of original entries)
- customer accounts
- all positions held in each security

□ syndicate transactions

□ customer complaints

In addition, other records must be kept for at least three years:

□ transactions in progress (transfers, validations, etc.)

□ confirmations

□ customer information

Municipal underwriting, G11

Describes the requirements for the underwriting agreements (see page 116).

Settlement and delivery, G12

G12 describes the details of delivery and settlement including settlement date, conditions for good delivery and information required on confirmations.

Quotations, G13

Published quotations must be bona fide bids or offers; nominal quotations, *i.e.*, quotes provided for information, are only allowed if they are so identified.

Reports of purchase and sale, G14

Any reported transaction must represent an actual trade—fictitious or deceptive reports are not permitted.

Customer confirmations, G15

A municipal securities broker or dealer must send a customer written confirmation at or before the completion of a transaction. This must describe the transaction in detail. It must also indicate (among other things):

□ a description of the securities

□ whether or not the firm acted as principal or agent

□ if the securities are callable

Periodic examinations, G16

Every municipal securities firm must be examined by the NASD at least every two years.

Customer treatment, G17, 18

A municipal securities broker/dealer must deal with customers in a fair and honest way. He must try to get the best possible price when executing trades for a customer.

Know your customer, G19

As in the NASD Rules of Fair Practice, municipal securities broker/dealers must believe their recommendations are suitable for the customer; excessive trading (churning) is prohibited.

Gifts, G20

No municipal securities broker/dealer or sales representative may receive (or give) business-related gratuities or gifts to or from one person valued at more than $100 in any one year. This does not include business expenses allowable under the IRS rules, *e.g.*, business dinners or entertainment.

Advertising, G21

False and misleading communications are prohibited. All advertising (including new issue tombstones) and other literature must have prior written approval from a principal of the firm.

Control relationships, G22

Any control relationship between the issuer and the municipal securities professional must be disclosed. Examples would include situations where the professional works for the municipality, or where the broker/dealer has financial interest in a firm affected by industrial revenue bonds.

Financial advisors, G23

When a municipal securities firm acts as financial advisor to an issuer, the terms of the relationship (including compensation) must be set out in writing. If the firm sells shares of the issue to its customer, the relationship must be disclosed.

If the firm wishes to participate in an underwriting it:

☐ may be required to terminate its relationship
☐ must get written permission from the issuer
☐ must disclose the details of the previous arrangement

Ownership information obtained in fiduciary capacity, G24

This prohibits anyone in the municipal securities industry from using "inside" information in trading except with the issuer's consent.

Improper use of assets, G25

A municipal securities broker/dealer may not misuse municipal securities or funds held on another person's behalf, may not guarantee a customer against loss, and may not share in a customer's profits or losses.

Administration of discretionary accounts, G26

As with other rules governing discretionary accounts (see page 207), this requires the customer's written approval for such accounts. In addition, each transaction must be reviewed and approved in writing by a municipal securities principal of the firm.

Supervision, G27

Sales must be supervised: each firm is required to designate a municipal securities principal and a financial and operations principal; further, each firm must establish and maintain written supervisory procedures in conformance with MSRB rules, including procedures for opening new accounts, for all transactions and related correspondence, for handling customer complaints, and for periodic examination of accounts.

Transactions with employees of other firms, G28

Again, as with NASD rules, no account may be opened for an employee of another municipal securities broker/dealer without prior written notice to the employer; that firm must also receive a duplicate of every confirmation of a trade in the account.

Availability of board rules, G29

All municipal securities broker/dealers must keep a copy of MSRB Rules, and make them available to any customer who requests them.

Prices and commissions, G30

When a broker/dealer acts as a principal, he must buy or sell at a price that is fair and reasonable, including the markup or markdown; when acting as an agent, commissions charged must also be fair and reasonable. While this echoes the NASD rule, there is no 5% guideline policy.

Reciprocal dealings with municipal securities investment companies, G31

A broker who sells for an investment company may not accept any compensation from that company except the normal sales charge, or make any other special deals.

New issue disclosure, G32, 33

Customers who purchase a new municipal issue must receive a final copy of the official statement (or offering circular) either with or prior to final confirmation of the transaction.

In addition, if the new issue involves a negotiated underwriting (see page 116), the customer must also be advised of:

- the amount of the underwriting spread
- the amount of the commission received by the firm
- the offering price for each maturity in the issue

Rule G33 sets out the computations for accrued interest—a 360-day year comprised of twelve 30-day months.

An underwriter may not publish an announcement offering new issues unless they are available at the end of the pre-sale period, although such an announcement may indicate certain maturities are available.

CUSIP numbers, G34

A municipal broker or dealer who is the managing underwriter of a new municipal securities issue must apply for a CUSIP (Committee Uniform Securities Identification Procedure) number for the issue, and ensure that the number appears on all certificates. This rule took effect July 8, 1983, for all municipal securities that have:

- □ a par value of at least $500,000, or
- □ a par value of $250,000 or more, where the issuer's outstanding debt exceeds $250,000, or
- □ where the issuer's outstanding debt exceeds $500,000 (in these cases, an issue of any amount must have a CUSIP number.)

Local assessment bonds or notes with maturities of one year or less are exempt from this requirement.

Dispute and arbitration, G35

Disputes within the municipal securities industry are handled with the MRSB code of arbitration. It provides a board of arbitration that is similar to the one used at NASD. There is a six-year statute of limitations of issues brought to the board.

TERMS

Securities act of 1933

Purpose of act To ensure investors receive complete, accurate information on new issues

Registration All newly issued securities sold interstate must be registered by filing S-1 statement, includes detailed information about issuer and issue

Review process SEC must review registration before new issue can be sold to public

Cooling-off period Renewable 20-day interval set aside for review

Effective date When review completed and sales can begin

Deficiency letters Sent by SEC asking for more information

Stop orders Issued if SEC thinks registration statement contains misstatements or omissions

Note SEC does not approve issue, simply reviews for completeness

Preliminary prospectus Can be issued during review, omits final price, delivery date or underwriters' spread, must state that this is not an offer to sell or a solicitation to buy

Selling the new issue

Prospectus Registration data without documentation, must be delivered to purchasers

Advertising Dealers cannot advertise new issue for 90 days after effective date, except by prospectus or tombstone ads

Mutual funds If prospectus used more than nine months after effective date, information must be no more than 16 months old

Exempt securities (not subject to registration requirements, subject to anti-fraud provisions)

government securities

municipals

commercial paper or bankers' acceptances with maturities less than 270 days

instruments issued by common carriers; domestic banks, trust companies, savings and loans, building and loan societies, co-op banks; non-profit groups

private placements

intrastate issues

Regulation A filings

fixed annuity contracts and insurance policies

Exempt transactions

between private individuals

unsolicited broker transactions

private placement, subject to Reg D

Restricted or unregistered securities Acquired through Reg D transaction or through an employee stock-option plan; governed by Rule 144

Control securities Those held by a person in control (corporate officers, directors or owners of at least 10% of any class of outstanding securities); also governed by special rules

Intrastate Transactions (Rule 147) Securities sold only intrastate (strictly defined) may be exempt from registration requirements

Reg A offerings

□ cannot exceed $1,500,000 in total value in a 12-month period

□ issuer must file a notification; offering must take place within 90 days

□ if for more than $100,000, must be accompanied by an offering statement

□ only advertising permitted is a tombstone

Advertising Regulates any communication after statement filed but before issue registered

Securities and Exchange Act of 1934

Purpose To bar unfair practices once securities have been issued; regulates exchanges, over the counter markets, brokers, dealers; creates SEC as enforcing authority

Registration All national securities exchanges; any individual or firm engaged in interstate securities transactions must register with (and be regulated by) the SEC

Exemptions Small local exchanges, brokers who do no business with the public

Prohibited activities

Hypothecation and commingling Forbidden without written permission

Manipulation and deception Prohibited, specifically including wash sales, matching orders, false information

Short sales (plus tick rule) No short sales at a price lower than last reported regular way sale

Solicitation Firms may not trade in securities they are underwriting except to stabilize, or market making transactions 10 business days before distribution

Tender offer Anyone who makes tender (or exchange) offer may not purchase that security except under terms of that offer

Credit disclosure Credit terms must be disclosed in writing in margin transactions

Note No transactions are exempt from Act's antifraud provisions

Records

Every broker or dealer, every national securities exchange must keep detailed records

Registered brokers or dealers Must file income statement and balance sheet annually

Over the counter transactions

NASD Established by Section 15A of 1934 Act to regulate OTC market

Recommendation Recommendations must be reasonable and suitable for customer

Supervision Employees of a broker or dealer must be closely supervised

Designated supervisor Must approve each new account, all security transactions, correspondence, review customer complaints

Capital requirements

Set by SEC Rules

Investment Company Act of 1940 Defines principal types of investment companies, extends requirements of 1933 and 1934 Acts to them

Investment Advisers Act of 1940 All investment advisers must register with SEC; Amendments (1970 and 1975) govern sales charges

Federal Reserve Board Regulations

Reg U Limits credit banks may extend for purchase of listed stocks or bonds

Reg T Covers extending credit in securities transactions

Securities Investor Protection Corporation (SIPC)

Claim limits Up to $500,000 per separate customer, not per account, of which not more than $100,000 in cash

Trust Indenture Act of 1939

Concerns corporate bonds, requires appointment of trustee, trust indenture

State regulations

Uniform Securities Act Model followed by many states

Blue sky laws Provide protection similar to federal legislation

Uniform Gifts to Minors Act Model adopted by most states

Prudent man rule State rule governing fiduciaries' actions

Legal lists List of securities institutions may purchase

NASD regulations

Rules of fair practice Concerns member firms' dealings with the public

Uniform practice code Covers dealings between brokerage firms

Code of procedure Deals with violations of rules

NASD code of arbitration For disputes

Eligibility for membership Any broker, dealer or securities underwriter

Ineligible Commercial banks, anyone suspended or expelled from a self-regulatory organization or by SEC, convicted of certain crimes in preceding 10 years

Registration Member must register as principal or representative

Exemptions Those who deal exclusively in exempt securities, commodities, listed securities, clerical or administrative personnel, persons who only provide capital

Conditions Principals and representatives must pass qualifying exam, RR's registration is non-transferable

Investment companies

Investment company underwriters may not sell its shares to any broker except at public offering price, unless sales agreement is in effect. Sales charge cannot be in excess of 8.5% of the offering price

Members may not

- sell dividends or withhold orders to make a profit
- purchase these securities from underwriter (or from issuer) except to cover purchase orders or for own investment
- favor or disfavor any particular company on the basis of sales commissions or sales incentives

Supervision Members must establish and enforce written procedures of supervising of each RR and associated persons

Transactions for personnel of another member In executing transaction for employee of another member, should determine transaction will not adversely affect that member's employer, must notify employer in writing

NYSE regs

Registered representative (RR) Employee of NYSE- or NASD-member firm licensed to operate as a broker

Qualifications Must pass Series 7 Exam, be registered with and approved by exchange, agree to abide by NYSE Rules; generally must devote full time to job; after-hours work, leave of absence, etc. restricted

Termination If RR or officer leaves firm or is transferred, NYSE must be notified

Public communications All published communications must be truthful, in good taste, approved by member firm

Speeches or lectures RR must get employer permission, firm assumes responsibility for content

Arbitration Disputes involving members handled by NYSE arbitration committee, findings compulsory and binding, no appeal

MSRB Regs

Municipal securities rulemaking board Extends provisions of 1934 Act to professionals in municipals market, rulemaking authority only

Professional qualification Any broker or dealer who conducts transactions in municipal securities must be qualified

Records Municipal securities broker must keep current books and records

Rules on published quotations, confirmations, execution, recommendations, etc. Like NASD Rules of Fair Practice

Gifts No business related gratuities or gifts to or from one person worth more than $100 in any year

Advertising Like rules covering other securities

Control relationships Between issuer and municipal securities professional must be disclosed

Information obtained as fiduciary; use of assets, discretionary accounts, supervision, transactions with employees of other firms All as with NASD rules

Prices and commissions Must be fair and reasonable, no 5% guideline policy, special deals not allowed

New Issue Purchasers of new municipal issue receive copy of Official Statement

CUSIP Numbers Managing underwriter of new municipals issue must apply for CUSIP numbers and ensure number appears on all certificates

REVIEW QUESTIONS

1. All of the following are subject to MSRB regulation EXCEPT:

   (A) municipal bond department of a NYSE member firm
   (B) the issuing municipalities
   (C) underwriters of municipal bonds
   (D) municipal bond sales personnel

2. The financial statement of a broker-dealer would contain all of the following EXCEPT:

   (A) the firm's balance sheet
   (B) any loans outstanding
   (C) the firm's trading record
   (D) the firm's income statement

3. If a new issue is considered "hot," the rules of fair practice forbid "free riding." Which of the following would fall into that category?

   I. allocating stock to a member of the underwriting firm
   II. allocating stock to partners of other brokerage firms
   III. allocating stock to partners of the underwriting firm

       (A) III only
       (B) I and III only
       (C) II and III only
       (D) I, II, and III

4. Form 144 remains in effect for:

   (A) 30 days
   (B) 45 days
   (C) 60 days
   (D) 90 days

5. The length of time covered by a single registration under Rule 145 is:

   (A) 1 year
   (B) 2 years
   (C) 5 years
   (D) 7 years

6. Which of the following requires full disclosure for public offerings?

   (A) Securities and Exchange Act of 1934
   (B) The Trust Indenture Act of 1939
   (C) The Securities Act of 1933
   (D) The Holding Company Act of 1935

7. The Trust Indenture Act of 1939 applies to all of the following EXCEPT:

   (A) municipal bonds
   (B) revenue bonds
   (C) corporate debentures
   (D) T-bonds

8. All of the following are prohibited under SEC Rule 144 EXCEPT:

   (A) adding a special commission to the seller's cost
   (B) selling before notification to the SEC
   (C) selling on an exchange without announcing that it is 144 stock
   (D) soliciting orders from the broker's customers

9. The maximum size of a Reg A offering is:

   (A) $1 million
   (B) $1.5 million
   (C) $2 million
   (D) $3 million

10. On distributing a "hot issue" one may allocate stock to which of the following provided it is part of their normal pattern of investment and it is not a substantial part of the total offering?

    I. a registered rep of the member firm
    II. the father of an employee of the member firm
    III. the member firm for its account
    IV. an officer of an insurance company

        (A) I and II
        (B) II and III
        (C) II, III, and IV
        (D) II and IV

11. The rules on withholding and "free riding" apply to which of the following?

    (A) a new issue selling at a discount
    (B) a new issue selling at a premium
    (C) any listed security
    (D) any security

12. Which of the following new issue debt instruments is most likely to be purchased through competitive bidding?

    (A) corporate debentures
    (B) corporate adjustment bonds
    (C) municipal general obligation bonds
    (D) municipal water and sewer bonds

13. The bidding procedure on a new municipal bond issue coming out under competitive bidding would be described in:

    (A) Official Notice of Sale
    (B) Preliminary Prospectus
    (C) Blue List
    (D) Official Statement

14. Under NASD rules, a mutual fund underwriter may give an account executive which of the following?

    (A) two $40 tickets to a Broadway show
    (B) a $75 gift certificate
    (C) a discount from the price listed in the prospectus
    (D) a commission added to the one listed in the prospectus

15. How long after the effective date for a new issue is it before a firm can accept orders for a margin account?

    (A) 30 days
    (B) 45 days
    (C) 60 days
    (D) 90 days

16. The decision to allow an over the counter stock to be bought on margin is made by the:

    (A) NASD
    (B) Federal Reserve Board
    (C) SEC
    (D) market makers

17. An investor enters an order to sell short 100 ACI at $45\frac{1}{2}$ on a stop limit. The last recorded round lot sale was at $45\frac{7}{8}$. Subsequently there are round lot sales at $45\frac{3}{8}$, $45\frac{3}{8}$, $45\frac{5}{8}$ and $45\frac{1}{2}$. The sale which triggers this order is at:

    (A) $45\frac{3}{8}$
    (B) $45\frac{1}{2}$
    (C) $45\frac{5}{8}$
    (D) $45\frac{7}{8}$

18. The sale which causes this order to be executed is at:

    (A) $45\frac{3}{8}$
    (B) $45\frac{1}{2}$
    (C) $45\frac{5}{8}$
    (D) $45\frac{7}{8}$

19. If a registered representative and a firm agree to an arbitration proceedings in some dispute, NYSE rules say that the decision:

    (A) may never be appealed
    (B) may be appealed to the NYSE
    (C) may be appealed to the NASD
    (D) may be appealed to the SEC

20. What is the margin account value of listed long call options?

    (A) the same as the premium
    (B) the premium minus the out of the moneyness
    (C) the in the moneyness minus the premium
    (D) they have no value for margin account uses

21. Trading volume in ACI over the past six weeks was:

last week	20,000 shares
two weeks ago	25,000 shares
three weeks ago	20,000 shares
four weeks ago	24,000 shares
five weeks ago	20,000 shares
six weeks ago	15,000 shares

If there are 2 million shares outstanding, and an investor owns 100,000 shares of restricted stock, what is the maximum number he could sell under Rule 144?

    (A) 20,000
    (B) 25,000
    (C) 22,250
    (D) 24,250

22. Which legislation empowered the Federal Reserve to set margin requirements?

(A) The Securities Act of 1933
(B) The Securities and Exchange Act of 1934
(C) The Banking Act of 1937
(D) The Trust Indenture Act of 1940

23. The amount banks may loan on rehypothecated securities is regulated by:

(A) Reg T
(B) Reg U
(C) SEC rules
(D) what the bank feels is prudent

24. The Securities Act Amendments of 1975 set enforcement responsibility of MSRB rules with all of the following EXCEPT:

(A) NASD
(B) NYSE
(C) SEC
(D) Comptroller of the Currency

25. All of the following are represented on the MSRB EXCEPT:

(A) banks
(B) bond attorneys
(C) brokerage firms
(D) the general public

ANSWERS TO REVIEW QUESTIONS

1. (B) MSRB rules do not regulate the issuer.

2. (C) The trading record of the broker is not part of the firm's financial statement.

3. (D) All of these are forbidden.

4. (D) After this period a new notification to the SEC is required.

5. (B) Rules for disposing of the stock mirror those of rule 144. The difference is in how the stock was acquired.

6. (C) This was the first major legislation regulating securities. It was designed to prevent fraud in the issuance of new securities.

7. (D) U.S. government securities are specifically exempt from the provisions of the act.

8. (A) Such a fee may be allowed. It takes into account the potentially more difficult task of selling such stock.

9. (B) By definition.

10. (D) The others are forbidden to receive stock under any circumstances.

11. (B) The rules apply to hot issues. Only choice B fits that description.

12. (C) Municipal general obligation bonds usually must be sold through competitive bidding.

13. (A) This is usually published in the daily Bond Buyer's Guide.

14. (A) Gifts are limited to $50. The other two choices are not allowed.

15. (D) The Fed decides which securities are marginable.

16. (B) In general, listed stocks are marginable and some OTC stocks are after designation by the Fed.

17. (A) A sell stop is a stop below the market. Hence 45⅜ triggers the stop.

18. (C) This is an up tick and satisfies the 45½ limit.

19. (A) There is no appeal from NYSE arbitration.

20. (D) Long options have no margin value since they expire after some time. If an option is exercised the stock received may have margin value.

21. (C) The average for the past four weeks is 22,250 and 1% of 2 million shares is 20,000. Under Rule 144 the larger of these two amounts may be sold.

22. (C) This act empowers the Fed to set margin requirements and to regulate exchanges and brokers.

23. (B) The amount of stock the broker may use as collateral is restricted to 140% of the debit balance.

24. (B) Other bank regulatory agencies (FDIC, FRB) also have enforcement responsibility.

25. (B) The fifteen members of the board are chosen five each from the other three groups.

Two practice examinations

PRACTICE
EXAMINATION
ONE

Practice Examination One
Answer Sheet
Part 1

1 Ⓐ Ⓑ Ⓒ Ⓓ	26 Ⓐ Ⓑ Ⓒ Ⓓ	51 Ⓐ Ⓑ Ⓒ Ⓓ	76 Ⓐ Ⓑ Ⓒ Ⓓ	101 Ⓐ Ⓑ Ⓒ Ⓓ
2 Ⓐ Ⓑ Ⓒ Ⓓ	27 Ⓐ Ⓑ Ⓒ Ⓓ	52 Ⓐ Ⓑ Ⓒ Ⓓ	77 Ⓐ Ⓑ Ⓒ Ⓓ	102 Ⓐ Ⓑ Ⓒ Ⓓ
3 Ⓐ Ⓑ Ⓒ Ⓓ	28 Ⓐ Ⓑ Ⓒ Ⓓ	53 Ⓐ Ⓑ Ⓒ Ⓓ	78 Ⓐ Ⓑ Ⓒ Ⓓ	103 Ⓐ Ⓑ Ⓒ Ⓓ
4 Ⓐ Ⓑ Ⓒ Ⓓ	29 Ⓐ Ⓑ Ⓒ Ⓓ	54 Ⓐ Ⓑ Ⓒ Ⓓ	79 Ⓐ Ⓑ Ⓒ Ⓓ	104 Ⓐ Ⓑ Ⓒ Ⓓ
5 Ⓐ Ⓑ Ⓒ Ⓓ	30 Ⓐ Ⓑ Ⓒ Ⓓ	55 Ⓐ Ⓑ Ⓒ Ⓓ	80 Ⓐ Ⓑ Ⓒ Ⓓ	105 Ⓐ Ⓑ Ⓒ Ⓓ
6 Ⓐ Ⓑ Ⓒ Ⓓ	31 Ⓐ Ⓑ Ⓒ Ⓓ	56 Ⓐ Ⓑ Ⓒ Ⓓ	81 Ⓐ Ⓑ Ⓒ Ⓓ	106 Ⓐ Ⓑ Ⓒ Ⓓ
7 Ⓐ Ⓑ Ⓒ Ⓓ	32 Ⓐ Ⓑ Ⓒ Ⓓ	57 Ⓐ Ⓑ Ⓒ Ⓓ	82 Ⓐ Ⓑ Ⓒ Ⓓ	107 Ⓐ Ⓑ Ⓒ Ⓓ
8 Ⓐ Ⓑ Ⓒ Ⓓ	33 Ⓐ Ⓑ Ⓒ Ⓓ	58 Ⓐ Ⓑ Ⓒ Ⓓ	83 Ⓐ Ⓑ Ⓒ Ⓓ	108 Ⓐ Ⓑ Ⓒ Ⓓ
9 Ⓐ Ⓑ Ⓒ Ⓓ	34 Ⓐ Ⓑ Ⓒ Ⓓ	59 Ⓐ Ⓑ Ⓒ Ⓓ	84 Ⓐ Ⓑ Ⓒ Ⓓ	109 Ⓐ Ⓑ Ⓒ Ⓓ
10 Ⓐ Ⓑ Ⓒ Ⓓ	35 Ⓐ Ⓑ Ⓒ Ⓓ	60 Ⓐ Ⓑ Ⓒ Ⓓ	85 Ⓐ Ⓑ Ⓒ Ⓓ	110 Ⓐ Ⓑ Ⓒ Ⓓ
11 Ⓐ Ⓑ Ⓒ Ⓓ	36 Ⓐ Ⓑ Ⓒ Ⓓ	61 Ⓐ Ⓑ Ⓒ Ⓓ	86 Ⓐ Ⓑ Ⓒ Ⓓ	111 Ⓐ Ⓑ Ⓒ Ⓓ
12 Ⓐ Ⓑ Ⓒ Ⓓ	37 Ⓐ Ⓑ Ⓒ Ⓓ	62 Ⓐ Ⓑ Ⓒ Ⓓ	87 Ⓐ Ⓑ Ⓒ Ⓓ	112 Ⓐ Ⓑ Ⓒ Ⓓ
13 Ⓐ Ⓑ Ⓒ Ⓓ	38 Ⓐ Ⓑ Ⓒ Ⓓ	63 Ⓐ Ⓑ Ⓒ Ⓓ	88 Ⓐ Ⓑ Ⓒ Ⓓ	113 Ⓐ Ⓑ Ⓒ Ⓓ
14 Ⓐ Ⓑ Ⓒ Ⓓ	39 Ⓐ Ⓑ Ⓒ Ⓓ	64 Ⓐ Ⓑ Ⓒ Ⓓ	89 Ⓐ Ⓑ Ⓒ Ⓓ	114 Ⓐ Ⓑ Ⓒ Ⓓ
15 Ⓐ Ⓑ Ⓒ Ⓓ	40 Ⓐ Ⓑ Ⓒ Ⓓ	65 Ⓐ Ⓑ Ⓒ Ⓓ	90 Ⓐ Ⓑ Ⓒ Ⓓ	115 Ⓐ Ⓑ Ⓒ Ⓓ
16 Ⓐ Ⓑ Ⓒ Ⓓ	41 Ⓐ Ⓑ Ⓒ Ⓓ	66 Ⓐ Ⓑ Ⓒ Ⓓ	91 Ⓐ Ⓑ Ⓒ Ⓓ	116 Ⓐ Ⓑ Ⓒ Ⓓ
17 Ⓐ Ⓑ Ⓒ Ⓓ	42 Ⓐ Ⓑ Ⓒ Ⓓ	67 Ⓐ Ⓑ Ⓒ Ⓓ	92 Ⓐ Ⓑ Ⓒ Ⓓ	117 Ⓐ Ⓑ Ⓒ Ⓓ
18 Ⓐ Ⓑ Ⓒ Ⓓ	43 Ⓐ Ⓑ Ⓒ Ⓓ	68 Ⓐ Ⓑ Ⓒ Ⓓ	93 Ⓐ Ⓑ Ⓒ Ⓓ	118 Ⓐ Ⓑ Ⓒ Ⓓ
19 Ⓐ Ⓑ Ⓒ Ⓓ	44 Ⓐ Ⓑ Ⓒ Ⓓ	69 Ⓐ Ⓑ Ⓒ Ⓓ	94 Ⓐ Ⓑ Ⓒ Ⓓ	119 Ⓐ Ⓑ Ⓒ Ⓓ
20 Ⓐ Ⓑ Ⓒ Ⓓ	45 Ⓐ Ⓑ Ⓒ Ⓓ	70 Ⓐ Ⓑ Ⓒ Ⓓ	95 Ⓐ Ⓑ Ⓒ Ⓓ	120 Ⓐ Ⓑ Ⓒ Ⓓ
21 Ⓐ Ⓑ Ⓒ Ⓓ	46 Ⓐ Ⓑ Ⓒ Ⓓ	71 Ⓐ Ⓑ Ⓒ Ⓓ	96 Ⓐ Ⓑ Ⓒ Ⓓ	121 Ⓐ Ⓑ Ⓒ Ⓓ
22 Ⓐ Ⓑ Ⓒ Ⓓ	47 Ⓐ Ⓑ Ⓒ Ⓓ	72 Ⓐ Ⓑ Ⓒ Ⓓ	97 Ⓐ Ⓑ Ⓒ Ⓓ	122 Ⓐ Ⓑ Ⓒ Ⓓ
23 Ⓐ Ⓑ Ⓒ Ⓓ	48 Ⓐ Ⓑ Ⓒ Ⓓ	73 Ⓐ Ⓑ Ⓒ Ⓓ	98 Ⓐ Ⓑ Ⓒ Ⓓ	123 Ⓐ Ⓑ Ⓒ Ⓓ
24 Ⓐ Ⓑ Ⓒ Ⓓ	49 Ⓐ Ⓑ Ⓒ Ⓓ	74 Ⓐ Ⓑ Ⓒ Ⓓ	99 Ⓐ Ⓑ Ⓒ Ⓓ	124 Ⓐ Ⓑ Ⓒ Ⓓ
25 Ⓐ Ⓑ Ⓒ Ⓓ	50 Ⓐ Ⓑ Ⓒ Ⓓ	75 Ⓐ Ⓑ Ⓒ Ⓓ	100 Ⓐ Ⓑ Ⓒ Ⓓ	125 Ⓐ Ⓑ Ⓒ Ⓓ

Practice Examination One
Answer Sheet
Part 2

126 Ⓐ Ⓑ Ⓒ Ⓓ	151 Ⓐ Ⓑ Ⓒ Ⓓ	176 Ⓐ Ⓑ Ⓒ Ⓓ	201 Ⓐ Ⓑ Ⓒ Ⓓ	226 Ⓐ Ⓑ Ⓒ Ⓓ
127 Ⓐ Ⓑ Ⓒ Ⓓ	152 Ⓐ Ⓑ Ⓒ Ⓓ	177 Ⓐ Ⓑ Ⓒ Ⓓ	202 Ⓐ Ⓑ Ⓒ Ⓓ	227 Ⓐ Ⓑ Ⓒ Ⓓ
128 Ⓐ Ⓑ Ⓒ Ⓓ	153 Ⓐ Ⓑ Ⓒ Ⓓ	178 Ⓐ Ⓑ Ⓒ Ⓓ	203 Ⓐ Ⓑ Ⓒ Ⓓ	228 Ⓐ Ⓑ Ⓒ Ⓓ
129 Ⓐ Ⓑ Ⓒ Ⓓ	154 Ⓐ Ⓑ Ⓒ Ⓓ	179 Ⓐ Ⓑ Ⓒ Ⓓ	204 Ⓐ Ⓑ Ⓒ Ⓓ	229 Ⓐ Ⓑ Ⓒ Ⓓ
130 Ⓐ Ⓑ Ⓒ Ⓓ	155 Ⓐ Ⓑ Ⓒ Ⓓ	180 Ⓐ Ⓑ Ⓒ Ⓓ	205 Ⓐ Ⓑ Ⓒ Ⓓ	230 Ⓐ Ⓑ Ⓒ Ⓓ
131 Ⓐ Ⓑ Ⓒ Ⓓ	156 Ⓐ Ⓑ Ⓒ Ⓓ	181 Ⓐ Ⓑ Ⓒ Ⓓ	206 Ⓐ Ⓑ Ⓒ Ⓓ	231 Ⓐ Ⓑ Ⓒ Ⓓ
132 Ⓐ Ⓑ Ⓒ Ⓓ	157 Ⓐ Ⓑ Ⓒ Ⓓ	182 Ⓐ Ⓑ Ⓒ Ⓓ	207 Ⓐ Ⓑ Ⓒ Ⓓ	232 Ⓐ Ⓑ Ⓒ Ⓓ
133 Ⓐ Ⓑ Ⓒ Ⓓ	158 Ⓐ Ⓑ Ⓒ Ⓓ	183 Ⓐ Ⓑ Ⓒ Ⓓ	208 Ⓐ Ⓑ Ⓒ Ⓓ	233 Ⓐ Ⓑ Ⓒ Ⓓ
134 Ⓐ Ⓑ Ⓒ Ⓓ	159 Ⓐ Ⓑ Ⓒ Ⓓ	184 Ⓐ Ⓑ Ⓒ Ⓓ	209 Ⓐ Ⓑ Ⓒ Ⓓ	234 Ⓐ Ⓑ Ⓒ Ⓓ
135 Ⓐ Ⓑ Ⓒ Ⓓ	160 Ⓐ Ⓑ Ⓒ Ⓓ	185 Ⓐ Ⓑ Ⓒ Ⓓ	210 Ⓐ Ⓑ Ⓒ Ⓓ	235 Ⓐ Ⓑ Ⓒ Ⓓ
136 Ⓐ Ⓑ Ⓒ Ⓓ	161 Ⓐ Ⓑ Ⓒ Ⓓ	186 Ⓐ Ⓑ Ⓒ Ⓓ	211 Ⓐ Ⓑ Ⓒ Ⓓ	236 Ⓐ Ⓑ Ⓒ Ⓓ
137 Ⓐ Ⓑ Ⓒ Ⓓ	162 Ⓐ Ⓑ Ⓒ Ⓓ	187 Ⓐ Ⓑ Ⓒ Ⓓ	212 Ⓐ Ⓑ Ⓒ Ⓓ	237 Ⓐ Ⓑ Ⓒ Ⓓ
138 Ⓐ Ⓑ Ⓒ Ⓓ	163 Ⓐ Ⓑ Ⓒ Ⓓ	188 Ⓐ Ⓑ Ⓒ Ⓓ	213 Ⓐ Ⓑ Ⓒ Ⓓ	238 Ⓐ Ⓑ Ⓒ Ⓓ
139 Ⓐ Ⓑ Ⓒ Ⓓ	164 Ⓐ Ⓑ Ⓒ Ⓓ	189 Ⓐ Ⓑ Ⓒ Ⓓ	214 Ⓐ Ⓑ Ⓒ Ⓓ	239 Ⓐ Ⓑ Ⓒ Ⓓ
140 Ⓐ Ⓑ Ⓒ Ⓓ	165 Ⓐ Ⓑ Ⓒ Ⓓ	190 Ⓐ Ⓑ Ⓒ Ⓓ	215 Ⓐ Ⓑ Ⓒ Ⓓ	240 Ⓐ Ⓑ Ⓒ Ⓓ
141 Ⓐ Ⓑ Ⓒ Ⓓ	166 Ⓐ Ⓑ Ⓒ Ⓓ	191 Ⓐ Ⓑ Ⓒ Ⓓ	216 Ⓐ Ⓑ Ⓒ Ⓓ	241 Ⓐ Ⓑ Ⓒ Ⓓ
142 Ⓐ Ⓑ Ⓒ Ⓓ	167 Ⓐ Ⓑ Ⓒ Ⓓ	192 Ⓐ Ⓑ Ⓒ Ⓓ	217 Ⓐ Ⓑ Ⓒ Ⓓ	242 Ⓐ Ⓑ Ⓒ Ⓓ
143 Ⓐ Ⓑ Ⓒ Ⓓ	168 Ⓐ Ⓑ Ⓒ Ⓓ	193 Ⓐ Ⓑ Ⓒ Ⓓ	218 Ⓐ Ⓑ Ⓒ Ⓓ	243 Ⓐ Ⓑ Ⓒ Ⓓ
144 Ⓐ Ⓑ Ⓒ Ⓓ	169 Ⓐ Ⓑ Ⓒ Ⓓ	194 Ⓐ Ⓑ Ⓒ Ⓓ	219 Ⓐ Ⓑ Ⓒ Ⓓ	244 Ⓐ Ⓑ Ⓒ Ⓓ
145 Ⓐ Ⓑ Ⓒ Ⓓ	170 Ⓐ Ⓑ Ⓒ Ⓓ	195 Ⓐ Ⓑ Ⓒ Ⓓ	220 Ⓐ Ⓑ Ⓒ Ⓓ	245 Ⓐ Ⓑ Ⓒ Ⓓ
146 Ⓐ Ⓑ Ⓒ Ⓓ	171 Ⓐ Ⓑ Ⓒ Ⓓ	196 Ⓐ Ⓑ Ⓒ Ⓓ	221 Ⓐ Ⓑ Ⓒ Ⓓ	246 Ⓐ Ⓑ Ⓒ Ⓓ
147 Ⓐ Ⓑ Ⓒ Ⓓ	172 Ⓐ Ⓑ Ⓒ Ⓓ	197 Ⓐ Ⓑ Ⓒ Ⓓ	222 Ⓐ Ⓑ Ⓒ Ⓓ	247 Ⓐ Ⓑ Ⓒ Ⓓ
148 Ⓐ Ⓑ Ⓒ Ⓓ	173 Ⓐ Ⓑ Ⓒ Ⓓ	198 Ⓐ Ⓑ Ⓒ Ⓓ	223 Ⓐ Ⓑ Ⓒ Ⓓ	248 Ⓐ Ⓑ Ⓒ Ⓓ
149 Ⓐ Ⓑ Ⓒ Ⓓ	174 Ⓐ Ⓑ Ⓒ Ⓓ	199 Ⓐ Ⓑ Ⓒ Ⓓ	224 Ⓐ Ⓑ Ⓒ Ⓓ	249 Ⓐ Ⓑ Ⓒ Ⓓ
150 Ⓐ Ⓑ Ⓒ Ⓓ	175 Ⓐ Ⓑ Ⓒ Ⓓ	200 Ⓐ Ⓑ Ⓒ Ⓓ	225 Ⓐ Ⓑ Ⓒ Ⓓ	250 Ⓐ Ⓑ Ⓒ Ⓓ

PART ONE

TIME 3 HOURS
QUESTIONS 1-125

DIRECTIONS

Each of the questions or incomplete statements below is followed by four suggested answer options. Choose the best answer and then blacken the corresponding space on the answer sheet.

1. An investor opens an account by selling short 200 shares of a listed stock at 18. What is the initial margin requirement?

   (A) $400
   (B) $800
   (C) $1,600
   (D) $2,000

2. Options expire at:

   (A) 3:00 P.M. Central Time on the third Friday of the expiration month.
   (B) 4:30 P.M. Central Time on the third Friday of the expiration month.
   (C) 4:30 P.M. Central Time on the third Saturday of the expiration month.
   (D) 10:59 P.M. Central Time on the third Saturday of the expiration month.

3. An out of the money option has a premium of $400. This premium reflects:

   (A) $400 of intrinsic value.
   (B) $400 of time value.
   (C) $200 of intrinsic and $200 of time value.
   (D) Some undeterminable mix of intrinsic and time value.

4. Under which of the following circumstances may a registered representative purchase a hot issue from his own firm?

   (A) Never
   (B) If it is part of his regular trading pattern.
   (C) For family members, if it is in their regular pattern.
   (D) If the purchase represents a small part of the total issue.

5. A mutual fund bid at $9.30 has a 7% load. What is the offer price?

   (A) $8.65
   (B) $9.30
   (C) $10.00
   (D) $10.70

6. Registering an offering with the SEC ensures that the:

   (A) SEC has examined the registration statement.
   (B) SEC has approved this investment.
   (C) statement has the relevant facts about the issue.
   (D) issue is suitable for investment by the public.

7. Under NASD rules, a guilty finding by the District Business Conduct Committee may be appealed first to:

   (A) NASD Board of Arbitration.
   (B) NASD Board of Governors.
   (C) SEC.
   (D) courts in the state where the alleged infraction takes place.

8. Listings of available corporate bonds and the names of dealers are found in:

   (A) pink sheets.
   (B) *Blue List*.
   (C) yellow sheets.
   (D) bond book.

9. A customer buys an ACI Sep 45 call at 6½. She exercises when ACI reaches 60. Assuming Reg T at 50%, how much must she deposit in her margin account to complete this transaction?

   (A) $2,250
   (B) $2,900
   (C) $3,000
   (D) $3,650

10. Which of the following trades would appear on the Consolidated Tape?

    I.   Exchange Market
    II.   Primary Market
    III. Options Market
    IV. Third Market

    (A) I and II
    (B) II and IV
    (C) I and III
    (D) I and IV

11. Bonds issued by the territory of Guam are taxed by:

    (A) only states and municipalities.
    (B) only the federal government.
    (C) neither federal nor state governments.
    (D) both federal and state governments.

12. All of the following change the terms of a listed option EXCEPT:

    (A) a 2% stock dividend.
    (B) a 1 for 3 reverse split.
    (C) a $.10 cash dividend.
    (D) a rights distribution.

13. A fund with NAV of $10 sells at $9.50. It is:

    (A) a closed-end fund.
    (B) an open-end fund.
    (C) a front-end load fund.
    (D) a no-load fund.

14. A depreciation deduction would be available on each of the following EXCEPT:

    (A) subsidized housing.
    (B) a shopping center.
    (C) developable acreage.
    (D) single-family homes.

Questions 15 and 16 can be answered using the following information:

An investor sells 200 shares of ACI short at 45. Simultaneously she buys 2 ACI Sep 50 Calls at ¾.

15. If ACI goes to 41 at expiration and she covers, her net profit (or loss) will be:

    (A) $400.
    (B) $650.
    (C) $800.
    (D) $800 loss.

16. At expiration, what is the maximum loss she can incur?

    (A) $800.
    (B) $950.
    (C) $1,000.
    (D) $1,150.

17. A customer has $300,000 in cash and $300,000 in securities in his account. Under SIPC, he would receive a maximum of:

    (A) $100,000 for the cash.
    (B) $300,000 for the securities.
    (C) $400,000 for the cash and securities.
    (D) $500,000 for the cash and securities.

18. A quote of 101.08 for a $100,000 T-Bond would mean a dollar amount of:

    (A) $100,108.
    (B) $100,250.
    (C) $101,080.
    (D) $101,250.

19. Stocks with a high negative beta could be characterized as being:

    (A) defensive.
    (B) aggressive.
    (C) low volatility.
    (D) blue chip.

20. The purchaser of an index option call would be hoping for:

    (A) a decline in the stock market.
    (B) a rise in the stock market.
    (C) a rise in the bond index.
    (D) a decline in the bond index.

21. After tax income is maximized for someone in the 28% tax bracket by purchasing a:

    (A) 7% T-Bill.
    (B) 8% corporate bond.
    (C) 6% tax-exempt municipal bond.
    (D) 7½% T-Bond.

22. A broker might be disqualified by the MSRB for all of the following reasons EXCEPT:

(A) conviction on an attempt to defraud a customer.
(B) expulsion from the NASD.
(C) conviction of a failure to make full disclosure of a conflict of interest on a transaction.
(D) conviction on a moving traffic violation.

23. Dollar cost averaging results in:

(A) buying the same number of shares each time.
(B) buying more shares when the price is high.
(C) buying more shares when the price is low.
(D) buying an average number of shares each year.

Questions 24 and 25 refer to the following:

Write 2 ACI Mar 40 Calls @ 6
Buy 2 ACI Mar 50 Calls @ 1½

24. The maximum possible profit on these trades is:

(A) $900.
(B) $1,200.
(C) $1,400.
(D) $2,300.

25. The maximum loss would occur if, at expiration, ACI is:

(A) 40.
(B) 41½.
(C) 46.
(D) 50.

26. An investor buys a $10,000 par value municipal bond in the market for $8,800. Assume he is in the 28% tax bracket. If he holds it to maturity, his taxable income is:

(A) none.
(B) $1,200 of ordinary income.
(C) $1,200 of capital gain.
(D) $600 ordinary and $600 capital gain.

27. An investor's SMA balance is $3,500. If he buys 500 shares of ACI at $40, how much in fully paid marginable securities will he

have to deposit to meet a 50% Regulation T requirement?

(A) $6,500.
(B) $10,000.
(C) $13,000.
(D) $16,500.

28. Each of the following is true of series EE bonds EXCEPT:

(A) they are non-negotiable.
(B) they can be used as collateral.
(C) they are a direct debt of the United States government.
(D) they are sold at a discount.

29. Which of the following is most likely to generate large current deductions and possible future cash flow?

(A) Oil and gas development programs
(B) Buying triple net leasebacks
(C) Undeveloped land
(D) Oil and gas exploratory programs

30. All of the following are quoted in 32nds EXCEPT:

(A) T-Bonds.
(B) T-Bills.
(C) GNMAs.
(D) T-Notes.

31. To get the most complete financial information about a new issue of municipal securities, one should consult the:

(A) prospectus.
(B) official statement.
(C) registration statement.
(D) tombstone.

32. The yield on a common stock is determined from:

(A) earnings and P/E (price/earnings) ratio.
(B) dividends and P/E.
(C) dividends and price.
(D) earnings and assets.

33. Regulations for municipal securities are issued by all of the following EXCEPT:

(A) SIPC.
(B) MSRB.
(C) NASD.
(D) SEC.

34. Which of the following is an advantage for limited partners?

(A) Voting power on partnership investments
(B) Flow through of income and losses
(C) Liquidity of investment
(D) All of the above

35. Under the Investment Company Act, which of the following are considered investment companies?

I. A face amount certificate company
II. An insurance company
III. A "management company" fund
IV. A company with mineral leaseholds

   (A) I and II
   (B) I and III
   (C) II and III
   (D) II and IV

36. What are Fannie Mae securities?

(A) Packages of commercial mortgages
(B) Short term discount notes and debentures
(C) Packages of FHA and VA mortgages
(D) Industrial development bonds

Choose from among the following choices to answer questions 37–39:

(A) Spread
(B) Takedown concession
(C) Takedown
(D) Manager's expense

37. The portion of the municipal bond offering price that is the difference between the public offering price and what the issuer receives is:

38. The amount that a member of the syndicate receives if it sells the security is:

39. The amount that a member of the selling group receives is:

40. The coverage on revenue bonds refers to the ratio of:

(A) gross revenue to operating expenses.
(B) gross revenue to interest expenses.
(C) net revenue to debt service.
(D) net revenue to annual interest expense.

Questions 41–43 refer to the information below:

An investor's margin account has the following information:

Long Market Value	Debit Record	SMA
$40,000	$23,000	$1,500

41. What is the buying power in the account?

(A) $0
(B) $750
(C) $1,500
(D) $3,000

42. How much equity does the investor have?

(A) $1,500
(B) $17,000
(C) $23,000
(D) $40,000

43. If the investor sold $5,000 from this account, what is the total amount the investor could remove?

(A) $0
(B) $1,500
(C) $2,500
(D) $4,000

44. According to MSRB rules, all of the following would be an acceptable gift from one registered representative to another EXCEPT:

(A) two $40 tickets to the theater.
(B) video tapes worth $75.
(C) a $200 business dinner.
(D) a gift certificate for $50.

45. A customer sells short 200 shares of ACI at 50 and deposits the appropriate margin with Regulation T at 50%. If the price of ACI drops to 40, how much excess cash can the customer remove from the account?

(A) $1,000
(B) $2,000
(C) $3,000
(D) $5,000

The following information should be used to answer questions 46 and 47:

An investor writes an ACI Nov 60 straddle at 4. The put is exercised at expiration when the market price is 50. The investor resells 100 shares of ACI for $5,000.

46. His net for these transactions is:

(A) $400 profit.
(B) $600 profit.
(C) $600 loss.
(D) $1,000 loss.

47. If prior to being exercised, the investor had bought the same straddle at 9, he would realize:

(A) $900 capital loss.
(B) $900 ordinary loss.
(C) $500 capital loss.
(D) $500 ordinary loss.

Questions 48–50 refer to the following choices:

(A) Balanced fund
(B) Income fund
(C) Growth fund
(D) Load fund

Choose the type of fund that best describes the funds listed in the questions below:

48. AAA Fund invests primarily in money market instruments.

49. BBB Fund is loaded up with equities of firms that reinvest most earnings.

50. CCC Fund has a portfolio of stocks, bonds, and preferred stocks.

51. An investor would like to find a large inventory of New York City general obligation bonds. He should consult the:

(A) pink sheets.
(B) yellow sheets.
(C) *Blue List*.
(D) *Bond Buyer Index*.

52. A put option is out of the money if the strike price is:

(A) below the market price.
(B) at the market price.
(C) above the market price.
(D) below the exercise price.

53. One of two partners in a partnership account dies. The registered representative should:

(A) close the account.
(B) freeze the account.
(C) liquidate all short positions.
(D) accept only cash orders.

Questions 54–56 are based on the following combination of trades:

Mr. Smith buys 1 ACI Nov 50 Call at 7 and 1 ACI Nov 50 Put at 3.

54. What is the maximum possible loss on these trades?

(A) Unlimited
(B) $300
(C) $700
(D) $1,000

55. What is the maximum possible gain on these trades?

(A) Unlimited
(B) $300
(C) $700
(D) $1,000

56. If ACI goes to 30 at expiration and the investor has not exercised beforehand, his profit (or loss) would be:

(A) $1,000.
(B) $1,300.
(C) $1,700.
(D) $2,000.

57. The effective return on a municipal bond with a coupon of 8% for an investor in the 28% bracket is:

(A) 8%.
(B) 10.8%.
(C) 11.1%.
(D) 12.8%.

Questions 58–61 make use of the following information:

An investor buys $100,000 of a real estate program. For 1991, his portion generates revenues of $200,000 and expenses of $150,000. Additionally, there are $50,000 of interest payments and $25,000 of depreciation.

58. What net gain (loss) is passed through to this investor for 1991?

    (A) $25,000 gain
    (B) $0
    (C) $25,000 loss
    (D) $50,000 loss

59. How much operating income is generated?

    (A) $25,000 loss
    (B) $0
    (C) $25,000 gain
    (D) $50,000 gain

60. What is the cash flow for his portion of the program?

    (A) $0
    (B) $15,000
    (C) $25,000
    (D) $40,000

61. If the investor is in the 31% tax bracket and has $40,000 of other passive income, this program will result in a:

    (A) net tax saving of $12,300.
    (B) net tax saving of $7,750.
    (C) total tax bill for passive income of $12,300.
    (D) total tax bill for passive income of $7,750.

62. Which of the following is true of T-bonds?

    (A) They have little inflation risk.
    (B) They have little interest rate risk.
    (C) They have little credit risk.
    (D) They are not widely available.

63. Which of the following are on the same side of the market?

    I.   Long Calls and Long Puts
    II. Long Calls and Short Puts
    III. Short Calls and Long Puts
    IV. Short Calls and Short Puts

        (A) I and II
        (B) I and IV
        (C) II and III
        (D) III and IV

Questions 64 and 65 can be answered with the following information:

ACI sells at $40 per share. Last year, it had earnings of $4 per share and a dividend payout ratio of 60%.

64. ACI's P/E is:

    (A) 1/10.
    (B) 4.
    (C) 6.
    (D) 10.

65. ACI's dividend for last year (was):

    (A) $1.60.
    (B) $2.40.
    (C) $4.00.
    (D) cannot be determined

66. An option is purchased and expires unexercised. For income tax purposes, the premium would be treated as:

    (A) a capital loss at the time of purchase.
    (B) a capital loss at the time of expiration.
    (C) an ordinary loss at the time of purchase.
    (D) an ordinary loss at the time of expiration.

67. A stockholder with 200 shares of ACI must vote to fill three positions on the board of directors. If voting rights are cumulative, he may use his votes in any of the following ways EXCEPT:

    (A) 200 votes for each of three candidates.
    (B) 300 votes for each of two candidates.
    (C) 600 votes for each of three candidates.
    (D) 600 votes for one candidate.

68. MSRB rules apply to all of the following EXCEPT:

    (A) municipal bond salesmen.
    (B) municipal bond underwriters.
    (C) municipal bond issuers.
    (D) municipal bond dealers.

Questions 69 and 70 refer to the following information:

ACI has a convertible bond with a conversion price of $50 per share.

69. The conversion ratio for these bonds is:

   (A) 2 to 1.
   (B) 5 to 1.
   (C) 20 to 1.
   (D) 50 to 1.

70. If the bond is currently selling at $1,100 and is at parity, the stock is selling at:

   (A) $22.
   (B) $55.
   (C) $220.
   (D) $550.

Questions 71–73 are answerable with the following information:

An investor writes one CAI Dec 40 Call. CAI is selling at 44, and he collects a premium of $5.

71. At what price for CAI would the writer break even?

   (A) $40
   (B) $45
   (C) $49
   (D) $50

72. The writer's loss is limited to:

   (A) $100.
   (B) $400.
   (C) $600.
   (D) Unlimited

73. What is the writer's maximum possible gain?

   (A) $100
   (B) $500
   (C) $600
   (D) $1,000

74. Which of the following is used by a technical trader?

   (A) Head and shoulders pattern
   (B) P/E
   (C) Quick Ratio
   (D) Leverage

75. The "visible supply" refers to:

   (A) the supply of corporate bonds becoming available.
   (B) the supply of T-bonds becoming available.
   (C) the supply of new equities becoming available.
   (D) the supply of municipal bonds becoming available.

76. Which of the following positions requires maintenance margin?

   (A) A covered call
   (B) A covered put
   (C) An uncovered call
   (D) A long straddle

77. A customer buying an OTC stock from a firm that is a market-maker in that stock, pays a price that:

   (A) includes a mark-up.
   (B) does not include a mark-up.
   (C) includes a commission.
   (D) includes a commission and a mark-up.

78. If a municipal bond is purchased at a discount, and sold before maturity, the capital gain (loss) is measured from:

   I. cost basis for an original issue purchase.
   II. cost basis for an aftermarket purchase.
   III. accreted cost basis for an original issue purchase.
   IV. accreted cost basis for an aftermarket purchase.

   (A) I and III
   (B) I and IV
   (C) II and III
   (D) II and IV

79. The municipal issue most likely to require a sinking fund is a:

   (A) balloon issue.
   (B) serial issue.
   (C) term issue.
   (D) revenue issue.

80. What kind of investment company pays out 90% of its net investment income to its shareholders?

(A) Registered
(B) Diversified
(C) Regulated
(D) Balanced

81. An options contract for British pounds is for 25,000 BPs. If the strike price is $150, the value of the contract is:

(A) $2,500.
(B) $3,750.
(C) $25,000.
(D) $37,500.

82. An Equipment Trust Certificate is likely to be issued by a(n):

(A) bank.
(B) airline.
(C) electric company.
(D) accounting firm.

83. Which of the following is true of a Put option?

(A) It would be bought by someone who is bearish.
(B) It would be sold by someone who is bearish.
(C) It is out of the money when the market price is larger than the strike price.
(D) It has unlimited risk for the writer.

84. A refunding is likely to occur for which of the following issues if all of them are selling at a current basis of 6.50?

(A) 5% coupon callable in 1991 at 102
(B) 6% coupon callable at par in 2001
(C) 6.5% coupon maturing in 1999
(D) 7% coupon maturing in 1994

85. The face value of an order for 5M bonds is equal to:

(A) $5.
(B) $50.
(C) $500.
(D) $5,000.

86. If the board of directors declare a stock split, all of the following are true EXCEPT:

(A) liquidity increases.
(B) it is easier for the public to buy the stock.
(C) the stock price rises.
(D) the stock price falls.

87. An investor buys 3 New York State revenue bonds at 106. If the bonds mature in 6 years and she sells them after 4 years at 104, with respect to taxes she has a:

(A) $60 capital loss.
(B) $60 capital gain.
(C) $20 interest income gain.
(D) None of the above

88. In an underwriting of a municipal bond issue, the additional takedown was ½ and the concession was ¼. If the manager's fee was ¹/₁₆, then, for each bond sold, a member of the syndicate would receive:

(A) ¼.
(B) ⁵/₁₆.
(C) ⁹/₁₆.
(D) ¾.

89. If a municipality redeems outstanding bonds with the proceeds from a new bond issue, this is called:

(A) calling the bonds.
(B) refunding the bonds.
(C) sinking the bonds.
(D) defending the bonds.

90. In trying to sell shares in a mutual fund, the registered representative may:

(A) offer quantity discounts for large purchases arranged over an 18-month period.
(B) compute yield based on all distributions made over the preceding five-year period.
(C) consolidate income and capital gains distributions.
(D) show net asset value at the beginning and end of the period discussed.

91. An investor bought a 6.5% Ohio general obligation bond regular way on April 10. The last coupon date was February 15.

How many days of interest must he add to the purchase price?

(A) 54
(B) 55
(C) 61
(D) 62

92. Having won a competitive bidding to underwrite a municipal bond, a syndicate now finds that rates have fallen as they are about to bring the issue to market. The syndicate would probably:

(A) sell the bonds at a discount.
(B) sell the bonds at a premium.
(C) reduce the amount given to the municipality.
(D) not bring the issue to market.

Questions 93 and 94 refer to the following types of securities:

(A) double-barreled bonds.
(B) special tax bonds.
(C) revenue bonds.
(D) special assessment bonds.

Choose the type of security that best describes the bonds listed below.

93. A bond issued to build a new toll bridge with tolls paying off the bond.

94. A bond issued by a municipality backed by proceeds from assessments and further guaranteed by a state agency.

95. A trade made directly between an investment company and a bank is a:

(A) first market trade.
(B) second market trade.
(C) third market trade.
(D) fourth market trade.

96. The NASD mark-up policy for customer over-the-counter transactions requires:

(A) prices to be reasonably related to the current market price of the security.
(B) prices to be reasonably related to dealer's cost.
(C) a mark-up to be based on the volume of business in that customer's account.
(D) the mark-up not to exceed 5% of the current offering price.

Questions 97 and 98 are based on the following investments:

Long 1 ACI Feb 50 Call at 6
Short 1 ACI Feb 60 Call at 5

97. What is the maximum possible gain if the position is held to expiration?

(A) $500
(B) $900
(C) $1,100
(D) Unlimited

98. At what price would an investor break even?

(A) 51
(B) 56
(C) 61
(D) 65

99. Which type of investment company may not issue long-term debt instruments?

(A) An open end investment company
(B) A face amount certificate company
(C) A unit investment trust company
(D) A closed end management company

100. Defaulted bearer municipal bonds are traded:

(A) flat and stripped of coupons.
(B) flat and with unpaid past-due coupons attached.
(C) with accrued interest to the date of delivery added to the price.
(D) with accrued interest to the date of delivery added to the price and with the unpaid coupons attached.

101. If a corporation is conservatively capitalized, it will raise most of its capital by selling:

(A) preferred stock.
(B) common stock.
(C) convertible bonds.
(D) bonds.

102. All of the following are true of Federal Funds EXCEPT:

    (A) they represent funds in excess of reserve requirements.
    (B) they are overnight loans.
    (C) they are very sensitive indicators of rates.
    (D) they are loans from the Fed to member banks.

103. Under the UGMA, which of the following is true?

    (A) A donor may not be a custodian.
    (B) Twins may have a single account.
    (C) Trading in a margin account is not allowed.
    (D) Parents may be joint custodians.

104. A serial issue of municipals has maturities from 1993 to 2002 with the latter offering a 7% coupon to yield 7.50%. If the bonds are callable in 1994 at 103, in 1995 at 102 and at par thereafter, the bonds maturing in 2002 should be priced to the:

    (A) 1994 date.
    (B) 1995 date.
    (C) 1996 date.
    (D) maturity date.

105. The coupon rate on a municipal is:

    I.   the nominal rate.
    II. the current rate.
    III. the yield to maturity.
    IV. the rate stated on the bond.

        (A) I and II
        (B) II and III
        (C) III and IV
        (D) I and IV

106. All of the following characterize variable annuities EXCEPT:

    (A) they often invest in mutual funds.
    (B) they are professionally managed.
    (C) they have a fixed minimum payout.
    (D) their returns are based on market performance.

107. An OTC dealer buys 100,000 shares of ACI at 20 and sells 1,000 immediately.

Which of the following is closest to being fair and reasonable?

    (A) A markup of 7%
    (B) A sale at 22
    (C) A sale at 21 plus $.50 commission
    (D) The maximum suggested NASD markup

108. Compared to a bond without this feature, a bond with a call feature would:

    (A) be cheaper.
    (B) be more expensive.
    (C) be more attractive to investors.
    (D) require lower coupon rates.

109. All of the following should be determined about a new customer by a registered representative EXCEPT:

    (A) investment objectives.
    (B) financial resources.
    (C) financial requirements.
    (D) prior investment results.

110. To include a second dealer in a transaction unnecessarily is a violation of NASD Rules, and is known as:

    (A) disintermediation.
    (B) churning.
    (C) twisting.
    (D) interpositioning.

111. Which of the following would be considered a fair and reasonable reoffering price for 7% municipals purchased at a 7% basis?

    I.   101
    II. 107
    III. 6.75
    IV. 5.50

        (A) I and IV
        (B) II and III
        (C) I and III
        (D) II and IV

112. What is the dollar value of a ⅞ change in an option's premium price?

    (A) $7.80
    (B) $8.75
    (C) $78.00
    (D) $87.50

113. Selling new corporate securities to a small group of sophisticated investors without registering the securities is called:

(A) secondary placement.
(B) exchange placement.
(C) private placement.
(D) Regulation A placement.

114. When must advertisements for mutual fund shares be submitted to the NASD for review?

(A) Prior to publication
(B) Within three days of publication
(C) Within five days of publication
(D) Within ten days of publication

115. A customer without a position writes 1 ACI Nov 60 Put and writes 1 ACI Nov 60 Call. The position established is a:

(A) long combination.
(B) short combination.
(C) short straddle.
(D) long straddle.

116. Before issuing revenue bonds, a municipal authority would probably do all of the following EXCEPT:

(A) have a ballot referendum.
(B) do a feasibility study.
(C) publish a notice of sale.
(D) get a bond attorney.

117. Tax-sheltered investments provide all of the following advantages to limited partners EXCEPT:

(A) opportunities to limit risk.
(B) liquid investment.
(C) opportunities to defer taxes.
(D) opportunities to reduce taxes.

118. An investor wishes to swap one municipal bond holding for another one. Which of the following would not enter into consideration of this transaction?

(A) Maturity
(B) Coupon
(C) Accrued interest
(D) Quality

119. With regard to NASD arbitration proceedings, which of the following is true:

(A) Non-members may not request their use in controversies involving members.
(B) Members may not demand their use in controversies with other members.
(C) The finding must be accepted by a member in controversy with a non-member.
(D) Members may demand their use in controversies with non-members.

120. Securities sold at "seller's option" can be delivered at the option of the seller if he gives written notice of:

(A) one day.
(B) five weeks.
(C) seven days.
(D) ten days.

121. A short straddle would be profitable if:

(A) the market price differs from the strike price by more than the sum of the premiums.
(B) the market price differs from the strike price by less than the sum of the premiums.
(C) the premiums are large.
(D) the strike price is more than two times the larger premium.

122. Written authority to enter orders in the client's account and to withdraw money and securities from the account without consulting the client is known as a:

(A) hypothecation agreement.
(B) rehypothecation agreement.
(C) limited trading authorization.
(D) full trading authorization.

123. Under SEC regulations, who among the following may be restricted in their use of non-public information about a public corporation?

(A) Financial printers
(B) Officers and directors
(C) Underwriters
(D) All of the above

124. A T-bill is characterized by all of the following EXCEPT:

    (A) it is issued at a discount.
    (B) it has a $10,000 minimum denomination.
    (C) it matures in no more than two years.
    (D) it is in book entry form.

125. In executing an order for a public customer, a member asks the specialist in the stock to guarantee him a price while giving the customer an opportunity to obtain a better price. This is known as:

    (A) floor protection.
    (B) a special deal.
    (C) a stop order.
    (D) stopping stock.

PART TWO

TIME 3 HOURS
QUESTIONS 126-250

DIRECTIONS

Each of the questions or incomplete statements below is followed by four suggested answer options. Choose the best answer and then blacken the corresponding space on the answer sheet.

Questions 126 and 127 use the following information.

An investor bought $150,000 of a DPP and was also responsible for a $100,000 recourse loan.

126. The investor's basis in this program is:

    (A) $50,000.
    (B) $100,000.
    (C) $150,000.
    (D) $250,000.

127. Assume the investor had passive income of $300,000. What is the minimum possible passive income for this investor for the year?

    (A) $300,000
    (B) $200,000
    (C) $150,000
    (D) $50,000

128. A basis point on a corporate bond ($1,000 par) would be worth:

    (A) $.10.
    (B) $1.00.
    (C) $10.00.
    (D) $100.00.

Questions 129–131 refer to the following page from a specialist's book:

BUY		CAI		SELL
300	MERRILL	45		
1,000	BACHE	$\frac{1}{8}$		
200	DWR	$\frac{1}{4}$		
		$\frac{3}{8}$		
		$\frac{1}{2}$	500	STOP DREXEL
		$\frac{5}{8}$	400	MERRILL
			100	BACHE
		$\frac{3}{4}$	500	MERRILL
			200	DREXEL
		$\frac{7}{8}$	1,000	DWR
			500	BACHE

129. The current quote and size is:

    (A) 45 - 45$\frac{7}{8}$ 1,500 - 2,800.
    (B) 45$\frac{1}{4}$ - 45$\frac{1}{2}$ 1,500 - 2,800.
    (C) 45 - 45$\frac{1}{2}$ 200 - 100.
    (D) 45$\frac{1}{4}$ - 45$\frac{5}{8}$ 200 - 500.

130. For his own account, the specialist may bid no less than:

    (A) 45$\frac{1}{4}$.
    (B) 44$\frac{3}{8}$.
    (C) 45$\frac{1}{2}$.
    (D) He may not bid for the stock.

131. If the last sale was at 45½ on a minus tick, the lowest possible offer by a short seller would be:

(A) 45¼.
(B) 45⅜.
(C) 45½.
(D) 45⅝.

Questions 132 and 133 are based on the following information:

An 8% municipal bond $10,000 par value maturing in ten years is trading at 90.

132. To the nearest .1%, what is the nominal yield?

(A) 7.2%
(B) 8.0%
(C) 8.8%
(D) 8.9%

133. To the nearest .1%, what is the current yield?

(A) 7.2%
(B) 8.0%
(C) 8.8%
(D) 8.9%

134. All of the following can be classified as money market instruments EXCEPT:

(A) federal funds
(B) American Depository Receipts.
(C) bankers' acceptances.
(D) commercial paper.

135. The Advance-Decline line used by technical analysts is intended to gauge the:

(A) direction of the market.
(B) volatility of the market.
(C) quality of the market.
(D) volume of activity in the market.

136. When does Regulation T require payment for an option bought in a margin account?

(A) On the seventh business day following the trade.
(B) On the trade date.
(C) On the next business day after the trade.
(D) On the fifth business day following the trade.

137. When depositors withdraw money from savings institutions to invest in higher yielding instruments, this is called:

(A) reverse repo.
(B) the multiplier effect.
(C) disintermediation.
(D) open market operations.

138. When revenues exceed deductions in a DPP, we say that:

(A) phantom income is generated.
(B) cash flow is positive.
(C) operating income is positive.
(D) the crossover point has been reached.

139. Which of the following types of accounts are specifically prohibited by NYSE rules?

I.   Third party accounts
II. Accounts under an alias
III. Code number accounts
IV. Limited discretion accounts

(A) II and III only
(B) I only
(C) II and IV only
(D) I and IV only

140. When interest rates on bonds rise, which of the following happens to old bonds outstanding?

I.   Dollar prices rise
II. Yields rise
III. Dollar prices decline
IV. Yields decline

(A) I and II only
(B) I and IV only
(C) II and IV only
(D) II and III only

141. Municipal security offerings of new issues of municipal securities are exempted from all but the:

(A) 1933 Securities Act.
(B) 1934 Securities Exchange Act.
(C) 1935 Holding Company Act.
(D) 1939 Trust Indenture Act.

142. Under NYSE rules, opening an account for which of the following would require prior written consent and duplicate confirmations of all transactions sent to his employer?

(A) An employee in another member organization
(B) An employee of a registered investment company
(C) An officer of a trust company
(D) An independent insurance agent

143. In a municipal bond underwriting, which of the following is the correct order of allocation?

I. Pre-sale
II. Syndicate account less concession
III. Orders at the takedown prices
IV. Designated

(A) II, I, III, IV
(B) IV, III, II, I
(C) III, II, I, IV
(D) I, II, IV, III

144. A Direct Participation Program that does not have a legitimate business purpose is called a(n):

(A) tax shelter.
(B) abusive shelter.
(C) limited partnership.
(D) passive shelter.

145. A customer learns that he bought 100 ACI at 34¼. Today he discovers the correct price to be 34½. As a result:

(A) the customer is permitted to cancel the trade.
(B) the registered representative must pay the difference.
(C) the customer is responsible for the price as executed.
(D) the firm must take the transaction into its own error account.

146. All of the following are true of most United States Government Agency bonds EXCEPT:

(A) they may have interest coupons attached.
(B) they are freely traded.
(C) they are considered relatively safe investments.
(D) they are direct obligations of the United States Government.

147. The document that stipulates the rights and obligations of the general and limited partners in a Direct Participation Program is called the:

(A) Agreement of Limited Partnership.
(B) Certificate of Incorporation.
(C) Partnership Papers.
(D) Limited Liability Agreement.

148. Option allocation assignments notices to customers may use which of the following methods?

I. Random selections
II. FIFO
III. LIFO
IV. Equitable allocation

(A) I, II, and IV only
(B) II, III, and IV only
(C) I and II only
(D) II and IV only

149. According to MSRB rules, each municipal securities dealer must keep a copy of those rules in:

(A) the main office of the firm.
(B) any office of the firm where three or more representatives conduct municipal securities business.
(C) each office of the firm.
(D) any office of the firm which does not have a municipal securities principal in residence.

150. During the "cooling-off" period in connection with an underwriting, all of the following usually take place EXCEPT:

(A) issuance of a red herring.
(B) due diligence meetings.
(C) blue sky filings.
(D) stabilization.

151. The owner of a call option is entitled to a dividend payable on the underlying stock:

(A) always.
(B) never.
(C) only if he exercises before the ex-dividend date.
(D) only if he exercises after the ex-dividend date.

152. What Act requires that municipalities file disclosures of pertinent information prior to a public offering?

(A) Securities Act of 1933
(B) Securities Exchange Act of 1934
(C) Trust Indenture Act of 1939
(D) No such law presently exists.

153. The accounting statement that presents a snapshot of a financial position of a business at a particular point in time (rather than over a period of time) is called the:

(A) balance sheet.
(B) income statement.
(C) sources and uses.
(D) earnings statement.

154. For listed options, the Options Clearing Corporation determines all but the:

(A) striking price.
(B) premium amount.
(C) contract size.
(D) expiration.

155. Municipal term bonds are usually quoted on a:

(A) discount basis.
(B) current yield basis.
(C) yield to maturity basis.
(D) dollar price basis.

The following choices apply to questions 156–158:

(A) Equity options
(B) Interest rate options
(C) Index options
(D) Foreign currency options

Select the choice that best describes the options listed below.

156. Options that would be used to hedge a portfolio of three listed stocks.

157. Options for hedging FOMC moves.

158. Options affected by the interbank rate.

159. Settlement on an index option is made by:

(A) cash.
(B) delivery of a futures contract.
(C) delivery of the underlying securities.
(D) any of the above.

160. The balance sheet equation is:

(A) assets = stockholder's equity.
(B) assets − liabilities = profits.
(C) total assets − total liabilities = profits.
(D) total assets − total liabilities = net worth.

161. Options on foreign currencies are traded on the Philadelphia Stock Exchange. Which of the following currencies have listed options contracts?

I. Japanese Yen
II. British Pounds
III. Canadian Dollars
IV. German Marks

(A) I, II, and IV only
(B) II and III only
(C) I and IV only
(D) I, II, III, and IV

162. An investor purchases 5 ($1,000 par) 15-year municipal bonds at $107.50. Three years later, he sells them at $105. This results in a:

(A) loss of $50.
(B) gain of $50.
(C) loss of $125.
(D) gain of $125.

Questions 163 and 164 refer to the choices listed below:

(A) Free riding
(B) Matched sales
(C) Wash sales
(D) Short against the box

Select the choice that best describes the activities listed below.

163. Which activity describes buying and selling of equal totals of some security at the same price using a single broker and never actually changing the true owner of the securities?

164. Which activity describes buying and selling equal totals of some security to establish two separate positions?

165. A convertible bond selling at $1,110 has been called at 110. The bond is convertible at 50 to a stock that is currently selling at 54. Ignoring transaction costs, an investor should:

(A) sell the bond.
(B) allow the bond to be called.
(C) convert and sell the stock.
(D) buy additional bonds and tender them.

166. A trade to be settled "when as and if issued" will settle:

(A) on the issue date.
(B) one day after issue.
(C) five days after issue.
(D) on a date to be assigned.

167. All of the following are true of purchases of repos EXCEPT:

(A) they are an investment in treasury instruments.
(B) they provide flexibility in the amount invested.
(C) they are a non-competitive market.
(D) they offer money market rates.

168. All of the following are part of the computation of cost depletion in a drilling program EXCEPT the:

(A) extracted crude in storage.
(B) extracted crude sold.
(C) recoverable reserves.
(D) adjusted cost basis of the property.

Questions 169 and 170 refer to the following information:

An investor buys 200 shares of CAI at 46 and sells 2 CAI Aug 50 Calls at 3.

169. With no previous exercise, her break even point at expiration would be:

(A) 40.
(B) 43.
(C) 49.
(D) 53.

170. If the Calls are exercised when CAI is at 56, she will realize a:

(A) $600 loss.
(B) $200 gain.
(C) $1,400 gain.
(D) $2,600 gain.

171. How often must an "open" order left with the specialist be reconfirmed?

(A) Daily
(B) Weekly
(C) Monthly
(D) Semi-annually

172. The Trust Indenture Act of 1939 sets forth the following:

I. the rules of the NASD.
II. the responsibilities of the trustee.
III. the rights of the stockbrokers.
IV. the obligations of the entity issuing the debt.

(A) I and II only
(B) II and IV only
(C) I and III only
(D) I, II, III, and IV

173. Which of the following industries would be most likely to be hurt by interest rates increasing rapidly?

(A) Mining companies
(B) Chemical companies
(C) Railroad companies
(D) Utility companies

174. Who is the beneficial owner of stock registered in "street" name?

(A) The broker/dealer
(B) The transfer agent
(C) The registrar
(D) The customer

175. When do listed equity options cease to trade?

(A) 3:00 P.M. Eastern Time on the expiration date
(B) 10:59 A.M. Eastern Time on the business day prior to the expiration date
(C) 4:00 P.M. Eastern Time on the business day prior to the expiration date
(D) 10:59 P.M. Eastern Time on the business day prior to the expiration date

176. The writer of an option that has been exercised:

  (A) may retender this obligation.
  (B) must make good on his obligation.
  (C) may buy an option to balance the position.
  (D) all of the above.

177. A municipal bond is purchased at a premium. Order the yields from lowest to highest.

  I. Nominal yield
  II. Yield to maturity
  III. Current yield

    (A) I, II, III
    (B) III, II, I
    (C) I, III, II
    (D) III, I, II

178. All of the following are prohibited under SEC Rule #144 EXCEPT:

  (A) selling shares without notifying the SEC.
  (B) sales on an exchange without advising purchasers they are acquiring 144 stock.
  (C) solicitation of purchase orders from customers of the firm.
  (D) charging the seller a special commission to compensate the firm for its extra distribution effort.

179. *The New York Times* reported that Amalgamated Consolidated Incorporated announced a quarterly dividend of $1.20 with a record date of January 20. The dividend is payable February 28. An investor who purchased ACI on February 23 would:

  (A) receive the dividend.
  (B) not receive the dividend.
  (C) receive it if the trade had been for "cash."
  (D) receive $1 of dividend.

180. The name for a written consent signed by all limited partners permitting the general partner to act outside the partnership agreement is a:

  (A) Partnership Democracy.
  (B) Flip Flop Agreement.
  (C) Partnership Agreement.
  (D) Certificate Amendment.

Questions 181–183 refer to the following customer margin account:

Long Market $60,000	Short Market $20,000
Debit Record $30,000	Credit Record $30,000
SMA -0-	

181. What is the customer's equity?

  (A) $5,000
  (B) $40,000
  (C) $56,000
  (D) $80,000

182. If the market value of the short position falls to $10,000, what is the customer's equity?

  (A) $15,000
  (B) $40,000
  (C) $46,000
  (D) $50,000

183. What is the new SMA?

  (A) $5,000
  (B) $10,000
  (C) $15,000
  (D) $20,000

184. An investor purchases a 9% corporate bond in February at par. If she pays $30 in accrued interest and collects two semi-annual interest payments on the bond, her tax liability is:

  (A) $0.
  (B) $30.
  (C) $60.
  (D) $90.

185. The length of time covered by a single SEC notification under Rule #144 is:

  (A) 60 days.
  (B) 90 days.
  (C) 180 days.
  (D) 360 days.

186. Free-riding and withholding are violations of the:

(A) Securities Exchange Act of 1934.
(B) NYSE Constitution.
(C) NASD Rules of Fair Practice.
(D) Securities Act of 1933.

187. All of the following oil and gas programs involve producing wells EXCEPT:

(A) developmental.
(B) balanced.
(C) exploratory.
(D) income.

188. A Regulation A offering cannot exceed:

(A) $1,000,000.
(B) $1,500,000.
(C) $2,500,000.
(D) $3,000,000.

189. To qualify as an "intra-state" offering under Rule 147, an offer must have:

(A) 80% of the corporation's assets located in that state.
(B) 80% of the proceeds of the offering used in that state.
(C) 80% of the corporate revenues earned in that state.
(D) all of the above.

190. An investor exercises an index option at noon on Tuesday. The exercise value used to determine his profit or loss is:

(A) Monday's close.
(B) Tuesday's opening.
(C) Tuesday's noon value.
(D) Tuesday's close.

191. Which of the following is true for qualified profit sharing plans?

(A) Contributions from the corporation are taxable.
(B) Employee benefits are predetermined.
(C) Contributions are mandatory whether the firm is profitable or not.
(D) All income from the plan's assets are not taxed until received.

192. Which of the following options is "in the money"?

(A) CAI Nov 40 Puts   CAI stock at 45
(B) ACI Nov 50 Calls   ACI stock at 55
(C) ACI Feb 55 Calls   ACI stock at 55
(D) CAI Feb 50 Puts   CAI stock at 45

193. A T-bill was purchased at $9,500 in November 1992. If it matures at $10,000 in February 1993, the tax consequences are:

(A) $500 capital gains 1993.
(B) $500 interest income 1993.
(C) $500 interest income divided proportionately between 1992 and 1993.
(D) $500 capital gains divided proportionately between 1992 and 1993.

194. If a mutual fund had a portfolio consisting of a wide variety of biotechnology firms, it would best be characterized as a:

(A) Specialized fund.
(B) Growth fund.
(C) Closed-end fund.
(D) Open-end fund.

195. If federal funds rates decline over time, all of the following are likely EXCEPT:

(A) the federal government is encouraging expansion.
(B) short rates are decreasing.
(C) the prime is decreasing.
(D) reserves are decreasing.

196. An offering of $20,000,000 of 7% New York State highway bonds would pay semiannual interest totaling:

(A) $350,000.
(B) $700,000.
(C) $1,000,000.
(D) $3,500,000.

197. Customers with inactive accounts must receive statements at least:

(A) monthly.
(B) every three months.
(C) every six months.
(D) annually.

198. When a variable annuity contract is to begin payout, which of the following is true?

(A) The monthly dollars of payout is fixed.
(B) The number of units of payout is fixed.
(C) The value of each unit is fixed.
(D) The securities are liquidated.

199. For tax purposes, the first cash distributions from a depreciation in previous years must be added as taxable income. This is called:

(A) recapture.
(B) return on equity.
(C) limited partner costing.
(D) reverse depreciation.

Questions 200–202 refer to the following types of debt issues:

(A) T-bills
(B) Federal funds
(C) Commercial paper
(D) Banker's acceptances

Which choice is best described in the following questions? (Remember that a choice might be used more than once.)

200. They are used to promote foreign trade.

201. They are quoted as an interest rate.

202. They are exempt from state and local taxes.

203. If a United States corporation owns common stock of another United States corporation, dividend payments received are:

(A) taxed as capital gains.
(B) taxed as ordinary income.
(C) effectively taxed at 30% of their normal rate.
(D) taxed at 70% of the normal rate.

204. Which method of payment yields the largest monthly payment from an annuity contract?

(A) Lump sum
(B) 15 year certain
(C) Life annuity
(D) Life annuity plus one survivor

205. ACI declares a 20% stock dividend. When ACI goes ex-dividend, an ACI Jun 60 Call would become:

(A) ACI Jun 60 Call for 120 shares.
(B) ACI Jun 50 Call for 120 shares.
(C) ACI Jun 60 Call for 100 shares.
(D) ACI Jun 50 Call for 100 shares.

206. If a margin account is restricted but has a positive SMA, how much may an investor withdraw from the account?

(A) No funds may be withdrawn from a restricted account.
(B) Fifty percent of the SMA may be withdrawn.
(C) All of the SMA may be withdrawn.
(D) All of the SMA up to an amount that leaves the account with 25% margin.

207. Which of the following transactions cannot be performed in a cash account?

(A) Sell an ACI Call; buy ACI stock.
(B) Buy an ACI Put; buy ACI stock.
(C) Buy an ACI Call; buy ACI stock.
(D) Sell an ACI Put; sell Short ACI stock.

208. The margin requirement for an investor who owned $100,000 of 6% T-notes that mature on 1/1/96 and wrote a T-note call at 6 for notes maturing in January 1996 is:

(A) 15% of market value plus the premium.
(B) 20% of market value minus the premium.
(C) 0.
(D) 20% of market value minus out of the moneyness.

209. A certificate of limited partnership would need to be amended if any of the following occurred EXCEPT:

(A) a new limited partner is added.
(B) a new general partner is added.
(C) a new financing arrangement is made.
(D) a new sharing arrangement is made.

210. An end-of-year statement of a real estate limited partnership contains the following information:

Rental income	$200,000
Expenses	$ 75,000
Depreciation	$ 50,000
Interest payments	$ 50,000
Principal payments	$ 50,000

The investor would report a gain (loss) on his tax return of:

(A) $25,000 loss.
(B) $25,000 gain.
(C) $75,000 gain.
(D) $125,000 gain.

211. Which of the following securities is not exempt from the Securities Act of 1933?

(A) Benevolent corporations
(B) Municipal securities
(C) Insurance companies
(D) Bank issues

212. A customer purchases 1 CAI Dec 50 Call at 1. A few months later it is out of the money by 4. What is the customer's maximum possible loss?

(A) $100
(B) $200
(C) $300
(D) $400

213. The largest expense incurred in its first year by an open-ended investment company is usually the:

(A) management fee.
(B) commission to salesmen.
(C) legal fees.
(D) accounting fees.

214. A customer places an order to sell 100 ACI at 42⅝ on a stop limit. Trades then take place as follows:

42⅝   42½   42⅜   42¼

Execution takes place at:

(A) 42¼.
(B) 42⅜.
(C) 42½.
(D) The order cannot be executed.

215. Under the NASD Uniform Practice Code, which of the following is not a good delivery for a 700 share trade?

(A) Twenty certificates of 35 shares each
(B) Seven certificates of 40 shares each and seven of 60 shares each
(C) One certificate for 200 shares and one certificate for 500 shares
(D) One certificate for 700 shares

216. An investor has a $10,000 long term loss in 1992 with no offsetting gains. What is the last year in which he has a carry forward loss?

(A) 1992
(B) 1993
(C) 1994
(D) 1995

217. Under Rule 144 every 90 days one may sell:

(A) an average of the past four weeks' trading volume.
(B) an average of the past six weeks' trading volume.
(C) one percent of the outstanding shares.
(D) whichever is greater of (A) or (C).

218. ACI closes at 45 on an uptick on the NYSE and goes ex-dividend $.40 the next day. The lowest possible price for a short sale on the opening the next day is:

(A) 44⅜.
(B) 44½.
(C) 44⅝.
(D) 45.

219. For a mutual fund, net investment income is derived from:

(A) dividend income.
(B) interest and dividend income.
(C) capital gains.
(D) interest and dividend income plus capital gains.

220. If an OTC order is placed for 220 shares at the market on one ticket, and the mar-

ket price is 40, then the order must be executed as:

(A) 200 shares at 40 and 20 shares at 40⅛.
(B) 220 shares at 40.
(C) 220 shares at 40⅛.
(D) This cannot be placed as a single order.

221. The "dated date" is the:

(A) trade date.
(B) settlement date.
(C) date from which accrued interest starts.
(D) date from which all computations are made.

222. An investor wants preservation of capital and a minimum amount of purchasing power risk. As a registered representative, you would suggest:

(A) T-bonds.
(B) project notes.
(C) AA high-quality corporate bonds.
(D) revenue bonds.

223. Which of the following ratios provides the most stringent test of liquidity?

(A) (Current assets − inventory)/current liabilities
(B) Current assets/current liabilities
(C) Assets/liabilities
(D) Cash and marketable securities/liabilities

224. Municipalities would probably assess an ad valorem tax on:

(A) population.
(B) property.
(C) sales of goods and services.
(D) income.

225. List the following Moody's ratings in descending order:

I.   Aa
II. Aaa
III. Al
IV. Baa

    (A) II, I, III, IV
    (B) III, II, I, IV
    (C) III, IV, I, II
    (D) II, III, I, IV

226. If Total Assets are $1,000,000 and Short-term Liabilities are $600,000 for a corporation that has no long-term debt, then the Shareholder's Equity is:

(A) impossible to determine.
(B) $600,000.
(C) $400,000.
(D) $1,000,000.

227. All of the following customer records must be kept by the registered representative EXCEPT:

(A) each customer's current position.
(B) each customer's purchase and sale for the past three years.
(C) each customer's dividend income for the past three years.
(D) a cross-indexed file of his entire customer holdings.

228. An investor pays a 7.5% sales commission on the purchase of 1,000 shares of a mutual fund offered at $15. If he sells it and must pay a .5% redemption fee and the fund has not changed in value, he will receive approximately:

(A) $15,000.
(B) $14,925.
(C) $13,730.
(D) $13,800.

229. The Keogh Act would allow each of the following to set up a self-retirement fund EXCEPT:

(A) a lawyer in private practice.
(B) a municipal employee with an income from selling paintings.
(C) a broker with the funds from a Christmas bonus.
(D) a salaried plumber from freelance plumbing income.

230. The Dow Industrials is comprised of:

(A) all NYSE stocks.
(B) 65 blue chip stocks.
(C) 30 blue chip stocks.
(D) all NYSE industrial stocks.

231. Under NYSE Rules, an investor can open a numbered account if:

(A) he provides written evidence of responsibility for the account.

(B) he deposits $250,000 to cover the SIPC.

(C) he gets a bank letter of credit to cover the SIPC.

(D) it is not allowed.

232. A mutual fund pays dividends and also has a capital gains distribution. An investor has owned shares in this fund for two years. The payouts would be treated as:

(A) ordinary income.

(B) capital gains.

(C) ordinary income and capital gains.

(D) long-term capital gains.

233. The maximum allowable contribution to a Keogh plan is:

(A) $2,000.

(B) $7,500.

(C) $15,000.

(D) $30,000.

234. Under NYSE rules, which of the following require prior permission from the investor's employer?

I. A margin account for an employee of a bank

II. An account for an employee of the exchange

III. A cash account for an employee of another broker

(A) I and II

(B) II and III

(C) I and III

(D) I, II, and III

235. An investor writes 2 ACI Oct 40 Calls at 3 and at the same time writes 1 ACI Oct 40 Put at 5. If ACI goes to 44 and the Calls are exercised and the Put expires, the investor will realize:

(A) a gain of $300.

(B) a gain of $600.

(C) a gain of $1,100.

(D) a loss of $800.

236. If the manager says that the retention is 80%, an underwriter who has an allot-ment of 100,000 shares would have how many available for his customers?

(A) 20,000.

(B) 80,000.

(C) 100,000.

(D) 100,000 plus 80% of the remainder.

237. All of the following are true of the tax treatment of variable annuities EXCEPT:

(A) early withdrawals are subject to a tax penalty.

(B) payments are considered part income and part return on investment.

(C) earnings are not taxed until withdrawal.

(D) all payments are taxed as received.

238. Which of the following parties does an investor notify when he wishes to exercise an option?

(A) The writer

(B) The clearing member

(C) The OCC

(D) The AMEX or the CBOE

239. A registered representative who violates NYSE rules:

I. is subject to expulsion.

II. is subject to fine.

III. is subject to censure.

IV. is subject to suspension.

(A) II and III

(B) II and IV

(C) II, III, and IV

(D) I, II, III, and IV

240. The totality of final goods and services produced in the United States is called:

(A) Total Savings.

(B) Gross National Product.

(C) Total Income.

(D) Accumulated Wealth.

241. A general obligation bond has an official statement that says that property taxes may not rise above a certain level. This is an example of a:

(A) moral obligation bond.

(B) fixed debt service bond.

(C) limited tax bond.

(D) limited obligation bond.

242. The Revenue Bond Index is an average of:

(A) 11 bonds.
(B) 20 bonds.
(C) 25 bonds.
(D) 30 bonds.

243. The agreement between the issuer and the trustee of a municipal bond issue is written by the:

(A) trustee's attorney.
(B) underwriter's attorney.
(C) bond counsel.
(D) syndicate manager.

244. A premium of 1.20 on a T-bond option would require payment of:

(A) $1,200.
(B) $3,000.
(C) $12,000.
(D) $30,000.

245. All of the following recommendations from a registered representative would be acceptable EXCEPT:

(A) ACI has been recommended by our research department.
(B) CAI should go up by at least $10 next year.
(C) CAI earnings are estimated to be $3 next year.
(D) ACI looks good in the light of next year's projected GNP.

246. The conversion of convertible bonds to common stock would result in:

I.   an increase in debt.
II. a decrease in leverage.
III. an increase in stockholder's equity.
IV. an increase in total assets.

    (A) I and II
    (B) II and III
    (C) II and IV
    (D) I, II, and III

247. All of the following are true of SIPC EXCEPT:

(A) it is made up of broker/dealers.
(B) it is an arm of the federal government.
(C) it is a non-profit corporation.
(D) membership is compulsory for broker/dealers who carry customer accounts.

248. An underwriter in an Eastern account has a 15% participation. The underwriting is for $10 million and he has sold $1.5 million. If $1 million now remains unsold, what is his liability?

(A) Nothing
(B) $100,000
(C) $150,000
(D) $1 million

249. If an account is frozen, which of the following is true?

I.   All purchases must be paid for in advance.
II. All sales require previous delivery of the securities.
III. No activity is allowed without NASD approval.
IV. No activity is allowed without approval by a principal of the firm.

    (A) II and IV
    (B) I and II
    (C) III and IV
    (D) I and III

250. If a corporation changed its accounting from Accelerated Cost Recovery System to straight-line, which of the following would occur?

(A) Early years would show an increase in stated earnings.
(B) Later years would show an increase in stated earnings.
(C) Early years would show a decrease in stated earnings.
(D) All years would show a decrease in stated earnings.

PRACTICE EXAMINATION ONE ANSWER KEY
PART ONE

1	D	33	A	65	B	97	B
2	B	34	B	66	B	98	A
3	B	35	B	67	C	99	A
4	A	36	B	68	C	100	B
5	C	37	A	69	C	101	B
6	C	38	C	70	B	102	D
7	B	39	B	71	B	103	C
8	C	40	C	72	D	104	D
9	A	41	D	73	B	105	D
10	D	42	B	74	A	106	C
11	C	43	D	75	D	107	D
12	C	44	C	76	C	108	A
13	A	45	C	77	A	109	D
14	C	46	C	78	C	110	D
15	B	47	C	79	C	111	C
16	D	48	B	80	C	112	D
17	C	49	C	81	D	113	C
18	D	50	A	82	B	114	B
19	A	51	C	83	A	115	C
20	B	52	A	84	D	116	A
21	C	53	B	85	D	117	C
22	D	54	D	86	C	118	C
23	C	55	A	87	B	119	C
24	A	56	A	88	D	120	A
25	D	57	C	89	B	121	B
26	C	58	C	90	D	122	D
27	C	59	C	91	D	123	D
28	B	60	A	92	B	124	C
29	D	61	B	93	C	125	D
30	B	62	C	94	A		
31	B	63	C	95	D		
32	C	64	D	96	A		

PRACTICE EXAMINATION ONE ANSWER KEY
PART TWO

126	D	158	D	190	D	222	B
127	D	159	A	191	D	223	A
128	A	160	D	192	D	224	B
129	D	161	D	193	B	225	A
130	B	162	A	194	A	226	C
131	D	163	C	195	D	227	C
132	B	164	D	196	B	228	D
133	D	165	A	197	B	229	C
134	B	166	D	198	B	230	C
135	A	167	C	199	A	231	A
136	A	168	A	200	D	232	C
137	C	169	B	201	B	233	D
138	D	170	C	202	A	234	D
139	B	171	D	203	C	235	A
140	D	172	B	204	C	236	A
141	D	173	D	205	B	237	D
142	A	174	D	206	D	238	B
143	D	175	C	207	D	239	D
144	B	176	B	208	C	240	B
145	C	177	C	209	C	241	C
146	D	178	B	210	B	242	D
147	A	179	B	211	C	243	C
148	C	180	A	212	A	244	B
149	C	181	B	213	B	245	B
150	D	182	D	214	D	246	B
151	C	183	C	215	A	247	B
152	D	184	C	216	D	248	C
153	A	185	B	217	D	249	B
154	B	186	C	218	B	250	A
155	D	187	D	219	B		
156	A	188	B	220	B		
157	B	189	D	221	C		

ANSWER EXPLANATIONS
PART ONE

1. (D) The initial margin requirement is $2,000 or the maximum loss. In the case of a short sale, maximum loss is unlimited.

2. (B) Trading stops on the third Friday, and they may be exercised until 4:30 p.m. of that day.

3. (B) An out of the money option has no intrinsic value.

4. (A) Never.

5. (C) The load is charged on the offer to yield the bid. Thus $10 = $9.30/93%.

6. (C) The SEC takes no responsibility beyond this.

7. (B) Subsequently, it could be appealed to the SEC, and finally, to federal court, not state courts.

8. (C) Pink sheets are OTC stocks and *Blue List* is for municipal bonds.

9. (A) The purchase is made at 45. So the requirement is 50% of that. The premium payment has no relevance to this question.

10. (D) No options transactions are reported, nor are new issues.

11. (C) These issues as well as those of Puerto Rico and the United States Virgin Islands are triple exempt.

12. (C) All of the others change the number of shares outstanding.

13. (A) This fund is trading at a discount to NAV. No-loads trade at NAV and front-end loads trade at NAV plus sales charge. An open-end fund is sold by the fund and would not be offered for less than shares are worth.

14. (C) Undeveloped land does not depreciate.

15. (B) She earns $800 on her short sale, and the options expire worthless, costing her $150.

16. (D) At expiration at any price 50 or above will cost $1,150. At any lower price, her loss would be less.

17. (C) Maximum coverage is $500,000, but only $100,000 is covered for cash in the account. Therefore, he would receive $300,000 for his securities plus $100,000 for the cash.

18. (D) The quote is for 101 and 8/32. Each point is $1,000.

19. (A) Negative beta stocks would move in the opposite direction from the market. Incorporating them into a portfolio tends to smooth returns.

20. (B) An index option is an option on a stock index. The holder of a call would like to see stocks rise.

21. (C) All of the other securities are subject to a 28% tax. The largest of these is at

$$8\% \times (1 - .28) = 5.76\% < 6\%$$

22. (D) All of the others are sufficient grounds for disqualification.

23. (C) Dollar cost averaging requires investing the same amount each time. Thus, when the price is low, one buys more shares for the money.

24. (A) Maximum profit will occur if the 40 calls are not exercised. The writer keeps the entire premium of $1,200. If this occurs, the 50 calls also expire worthless, and he loses $300 for a net of $900.

25. (D) At 50, his calls are worthless, and he loses $400 on each call that he wrote. Below 50, he loses less on the written calls.

26. (C) For municipals purchased at a discount in the market, the increase is not interest income but capital gain.

27. (C) The total purchase is for $20,000. The buying power of the SMA is $7,000. The remaining $13,000 requires $6,500 in cash or $13,000 in fully paid securities.

28. (B) They are non-negotiable, and hence, would not be useful as collateral.

29. (D) Choices A and B would both generate cash quickly, and choice C does not generate deductions. An exploratory program could not generate cash soon and would have deductions.

30. (B) T-bills are quoted on a discount yield basis in .01s.

31. (B) Since municipal securities do not have the SEC registration requirement, neither a prospectus nor a registration statement is required. The Official Statement provides the financial information usually provided in a prospectus.

32. (C) The yield is the return on the investment in the stock. This is the dividend divided by the market price.

33. (A) The SIPC is a jointly owned investor's protective corporation.

34. (B) This is the only one which is an advantage to a limited partner.

35. (B) Mineral leaseholds do not invest in securities. Insurance companies are not covered under the act.

36. (B) These securities are issued as short-term discount notes and debentures. FNMA buys VA- and FHA-insured mortgages and packages them into bundles that provide the revenues to finance these securities.

37. (A) The difference between the offering price and what the issuer receives is called the spread. The manager takes a small fee from each share called his expense, leaving the takedown or concession. A syndicate member will reallow some portion of this to members of the selling group.

38. (C) A member of the syndicate that sells the security itself would get the takedown.

39. (B) See Question 37.

40. (C) For a revenue bond, one compares the money available (net revenue) to the money required to pay for the bond (debt service). The ratio of one to the other is called the coverage.

41. (D) The buying power is twice the amount in the SMA.

42. (B) The investor's equity is the difference between market value and the debit record.

43. (D) The sale releases 50% of the proceeds to the SMA. The total of $1,500 plus $2,500 could be removed.

44. (C) MSRB rules permit gifts with value not exceeding $100.

45. (C) Initially, the account had $10,000 market value and $5,000 equity for a credit balance of $15,000. Now market value is $8,000, so the required margin is $4,000, leaving $3,000 of the credit balance which may be taken.

46. (C) His loss is $1,000 minus the $400 of premium.

47. (C) He sold the straddle for $400 and bought it for $900 for a $500 capital loss.

48. (B) Money market instruments have little opportunity for capital appreciation. They do generate income.

49. (C) Firms that reinvest earnings are giving up current income to achieve growth.

50. (A) A balanced fund has assets in both stocks and bonds generating income and (hopefully) capital appreciation.

51. (C) The *Blue List* provides dealer offerings of outstanding municipal bonds. The Bond Buyer Index provides average yields for a group of 20 general obligation 20-year bonds. The other two do not refer to municipal bonds.

52. (A) One would have no incentive to exercise here because one could sell in the market at a higher price.

53. (B) Each partner is a general partner and when one dies the partnership is terminated. Hence the account is frozen.

54. (D) If ACI expires at 50, he loses both premiums.

55. (A) In principle, ACI can go up with no limit and hence his profit is (after subtracting $1,000 in premiums) unlimited.

56. (A) At 30, the investor realizes $2,000 minus $1,000 in premiums. The Call expires worthless.

57. (C) The effective return = coupon/(1 − Tax Rate) = .08/.72 − 11.1%.

58. (C) Both the interest and the depreciation are subtracted from the net of revenue minus expense to get net gain.

59. (C) Operating income does not include interest payments.

60. (A) The cash flow adds depreciation back into net gain.

61. (B) The $25,000 loss is deducted from his passive income. At 31% this generates a saving of $7,750.

62. (C) A and B are false because all coupon instruments rise and fall in price inversely with interest rates. There is little chance of default by the United States government, so C is true. Finally, there are many billions of dollars' worth of them available in the market.

63. (C) If you are long Calls, you want the market to go up. If you are short Puts, you have written Puts; hence, you also want the market to go up so that the Put is not exercised. If you are short Calls and long Puts, you want the market to decline.

64. (D) The P/E or price-earnings ratio is the market price ($40) divided by earnings per share ($4 = 10).

65. (B) The dividend payout ratio is the percentage of earnings paid as dividend. In this case, $4 times 60% = $2.40.

66. (B) An option is a capital asset that has tax consequences when it is disposed of. In this case, it expired worthless and the loss is realized at expiration.

67. (C) With cumulative voting rights, he can cast 600 in any way he chooses. Choice C, however, gives him 1,800 votes.

68. (C) The MSRB rules apply to individuals and firms that trade in municipal bonds and not to issuers of these securities.

69. (C) The conversion ratio is based on par. At $1,000 par, the $50 per share for common gives a ratio of 20 shares of common to 1 bond.

70. (B) With a 20 to 1 conversion and the bond selling at $1,100, each share would have to be worth $1,100/20 = $55 to have parity.

71. (B) The $500 premium just offsets the loss the writer sustains when he buys 100 shares at 45 and delivers to the holder at 40.

72. (D) He loses the difference between CAI's market price and 40. If this price increases without limit, his loss does the same.

73. (B) His maximum gain occurs if he collects the premium and the option expires unexercised.

74. (A) This is a price chart pattern. The other choices are all part of fundamental analysis.

75. (D) This information for the next thirty days is compiled and published in the *Bond Buyer*.

76. (C) There is no maintenance margin on covered options (choices A and B). A long straddle would require both premiums immediately and nothing further.

77. (A) A market maker acts as principal; hence, the customer pays a mark-up and not a commission.

78. (C) Original issue bonds have the discount treated as interest income so the basis is the accreted cost. This is not true for bonds bought in the aftermarket.

79. (C) Since all of the bonds of a term issue mature at one time, a sinking fund is usually required.

80. (C) Regulated investment companies are required to pay out a minimum of 90% of their net income annually to their shareholders.

81. (D) The strike price is given as 150 or $1.50. Hence, 25,000 BP's are worth $1.50 times 25,000 = $37,500.

82. (B) Equipment Trust Certificates are issued by firms usually with rolling stock as collateral.

83. (A) One buys a Put if one believes the market will fall (bearish). The risk to the writer is limited by the strike price since even if the market price goes to zero, the writer must buy at the strike price.

84. (D) This is the only issue with a higher coupon than current rates.

85. (D) By definition. We write 1M = $1,000.

86. (C) If the number of shares increases, the price of each share decreases.

87. (B) Municipal bonds bought at a premium in the secondary market have their cost basis adjusted over the holding period. After 4 years, the basis for these bonds is 102, so a sale of 3 bonds at 104 represents a capital gain of $60.

88. (D) If the member sold the bonds he would get the takedown, which is the additional takedown plus the concession.

89. (B) Calling bonds simply means redeeming them early. A fund is set aside for purposes of redemption.

90. (D) All other choices are incorrect. Choices B and C violate the Statement of Policy, and the maximum time span of a letter of intent is 13 months, not 18 months.

91. (D) Interest is computed from coupon date February 15 up to, but not including, delivery date April 17, on a thirty-day month basis. This yields (February) 16 plus 30 plus 16 (April) = 62.

92. (B) If rates have fallen, these bonds are now more attractive and can sell at a premium. This would increase the money going to the community.

93. (C) This is a revenue bond since it is paid from revenues of the toll bridge.

94. (A) There are two sources of payment and that describes a double-barrelled bond. Note there is no special assessment, so choices C and D are incorrect.

95. (D) Trading between institutions is termed "trading in the fourth market." The first market represents exchanges, the second market represents the OTC market, and the third represents OTC (NASD) trading of exchange listed issues.

96. (A) Mark-ups must be based upon the current market rather than inventory costs. The 5% is a guideline which may be violated in certain circumstances.

97. (B) At 60 the investor makes $400 on his long Call at 50 and keeps the entire $500 on his short Call.

98. (A) At 51, the investor loses $500 on his long Call ($100 profit − $600 premium) and earns the $500 premium on his short Call.

99. (A) By definition. Open-end management companies may only issue "voting stock." They may not issue any senior securities.

100. (B) Defaulted bonds trade "flat" (meaning without accrued interest) since interest on the bonds is not being paid by the issuer. To be a "good delivery," the defaulted bonds must have the unpaid past-due coupons attached.

101. (B) To be conservatively capitalized, the firm would avoid fixed payments whether interest or dividends.

102. (D) They are loans from banks with excess reserves to banks whose reserves are not adequate to meet federal requirements.

103. (C) This is true and none of the other statements is true.

104. (D) Since the coupon is less than the yield to maturity, the bonds are at a discount. Therefore, they are priced to maturity.

105. (D) These two terms are synonymous.

106. (C) They do not have a fixed minimum payout precisely because their return is based on performance.

107. (D) A greater-than-usual mark-up is only permissible on an extremely large or an extremely small transaction. This trade is neither. Since choice C has both mark-up and commission it is also not permitted.

108. (A) This feature is not favorable to investors. Since they cannot be sure of getting the stated return until maturity, all of the other choices describe a bond that is better for investors.

109. (D) This is not required of the registered representative, although it might be helpful to him in "knowing his customer."

110. (D) Interpositioning causes a customer to pay more or receive less on his order.

111. (C) A mark-up of 1 point or 25 basis points would be considered fair and reasonable.

112. (D) The premium is multiplied by 100 because the option is for 100 shares.

113. (C) This describes private placements.

114. (B) Other advertising must be submitted to the NASD within five business days after first use; however, mutual fund ads must be submitted within three days after first use.

115. (C) A straddle is a Put and a Call on the same stock with the same strike price and the same expiration month. Since the customer wrote both a Put and a Call, this is a short straddle.

116. (A) A referendum is not likely since no additional taxes are involved. The other choices are likely.

117. (C) Limited partnerships are usually highly liquid. The other advantages do obtain.

118. (C) The accrued interest has no bearing on a swap transaction.

119. (C) As part of the membership agreement, members are bound to accept such findings.

120. (A) With a seller's option, contract delivery can be effected if the buyer is given one day's written notice.

121. (B) A short straddle holder collects two premiums. He makes money if there is little movement in the market price. Choice B exactly describes the circumstances of his making money.

122. (D) Full trading authorization permits the agent to withdraw money and securities from the client's account. Limited trading authorization only permits the entering of orders.

123. (D) Anyone privy to material non-public information emanating from an "insider" is prohibited from making improper use of the information.

124. (C) Maximum maturity for T-bills is one year.

125. (D) This defines "stopping stock."

ANSWER EXPLANATIONS
PART TWO

126. (D) The recourse loan is his risk and, hence, part of his basis.

127. (D) If his total investment, including the recourse loan, were lost, he would be left with $50,000.

128. (A) A basis point is .01 of a point. On a $1,000 bond, each point is worth $10. Hence, a basis point is $.10.

129. (D) The volume for the highest bid and the lowest offer. Stop orders are not considered in a quotation.

130. (B) A specialist must bid more than any existing bid in a trade for his own account.

131. (D) This is the only price which would represent the plus tick necessary in a short sale.

132. (B) The nominal yield is the named yield (in this case, 8%).

133. (D) The current yield is the return available now. In this case $800/$9,000 = 8.888%.

134. (B) ADRs are depository receipts representing stock of foreign companies. The others are all money market instruments.

135. (A) The Advance/Decline ratio theory shows market direction and may indicate that a change in direction is near.

136. (A) This is the Regulation T requirement. The OCC requires dealers to pay on the next business day. Most firms have house rules that require clients to do the same.

137. (C) By definition.

138. (D) This is the definition of the crossover point.

139. (B) Third party accounts are specifically prohibited. The other choices are permitted when properly documented.

140. (D) Rates up equals prices down. Prices down equals yield up.

141. (D) This act about the trust indenture does apply to municipals.

142. (A) Prior written permission is required to open any kind of account for an employee of another member organization; also, duplicate confirmations and statements must be sent to the employer.

143. (D) The normal account procedure.

144. (B) By definition, they are subject to legal attack by the Internal Revenue Service. Losses from them may not be accepted by the IRS.

145. (C) Rule 411 of the NYSE requires that the report be corrected to the actual trade price.

146. (D) Most agency bonds are not directly guaranteed by the United States Government as to payment of principal or interest.

147. (A) The Agreement of Limited Partnership describes all of the rights, obligations, and limitations of the partners to the agreement.

148. (C) Only random selections or FIFO are allowed under OCC rules.

149. (C) This is required under MSRB Rules (G-29).

150. (D) Stabilization can occur only after the initial public offering.

151. (C) When he exercises, the shares are his, and hence he is entitled to the dividend.

152. (D) There are no requirements prior to a public offering.

153. (A) The balance sheet shows the condition of the corporation at a given point in time (usually the end of the year), while the income statement shows the result over a period of time (usually one year).

154. (B) The premium is determined in the market.

155. (D) For this reason, term bonds are often called "dollar bonds."

156. (A) Options on each individual stock would be the best hedge.

157. (B) FOMC moves are moves by the Federal Reserve that affect the money supply and, hence, interest rates.

158. (D) The interbank market is the market in foreign currencies.

159. (A) Exercise of index options is settled by payment of cash.

160. (D) By definition. It states that assets are made up of stockholder's equity plus liabilities.

161. (D) Options on all of these currencies exist.

162. (A) The premium of $75 must be amortized over 15 years or $5 per year. After three years, the adjusted price is 106, so selling for 105 represents a $10 loss per bond.

163. (C) This is a description of a wash sale used to give the appearance of activity and trading interest in some security. Simultaneous buying and selling of some security at the same price is called *a matched purchase and sale* and accomplishes the same purpose.

164. (D) One sells short (against the box) a security previously bought to lock in a profit on a long position without having the completed trade credited to the account at the time.

165. (A) This yields $110. The bond is called at $1,100 and, if converted, would give 20 shares selling at $54 each for a total of $1,080.

166. (D) This is the correct answer although the date to be assigned could be one of the other choices.

167. (C) They are, in fact, highly competitive markets.

168. (A) The cost depletion only considers the crude that has already been sold.

169. (B) She collects $600 in premiums but experiences a $600 loss on the stock purchased at $46 and currently at $43.

170. (C) Her profit is the $600 premium plus $800 on the 200 shares bought at $46 and delivered at $50.

171. (D) Under NYSE Rules open order on the specialist's book must be renewed semi-annually.

172. (B) The trust indenture does not define rights of stockholders and makes no mention of NASD regulations.

173. (D) Public utilities are usually very sensitive to interest rate changes because most of their assets are funded with debt.

174. (D) The customer is the "beneficial" owner, and the broker/dealer is the owner of "record."

175. (C) This is the same as 3:00 p.m. Central Time.

176. (B) The writer is obligated to deliver stock on a Call or buy it on a Put.

177. (C) The bond is at a premium so the current yield is lower than the nominal yield. The yield to maturity is lower still since at redemption the investor does not recover the premium.

178. (B) Under Rule #144, this is permissible. None of the other items are permissible under the rule.

179. (B) The dividend is payable to those who own the stock on the record date.

180. (A) This allows the general partner some latitude in his other activities.

181. (B) The equity is $30,000 from the long account ($60,000 − $30,000) plus $10,000 from the short account ($30,000 − $20,000) = $40,000.

182. (D) At this point, the equity in the short account has increased to $20,000 ($30,000 − $10,000), so the total is now $50,000.

183. (C) With a 50% Regulation T, the long account is fully margined. The short account now has a market value of $10,000, requiring $5,000 in margin. The additional $15,000 in customer's equity goes into the SMA.

184. (C) The $30 in accrued interest is subtracted from the $90 that she collects for the year, leaving tax due on $60 of interest income.

185. (B) After 90 days, a new notification is needed.

186. (C) The prohibition against free-riding and withholding is found in the NASD Rules of Fair Practice.

187. (D) An income program invests in producing properties. Exploratory or developmental programs drill for oil and/or gas. A balanced program is a combination of producing properties and drilling.

188. (B) The maximum value of an offering permitted under Regulation A is $1,500,000.

189. (D) All of the choices are required for an offering to qualify as "intra-state."

190. (D) The exercise value is the quote for Tuesday's close.

191. (D) Corporate contributions are deductible to the firm. The benefits depend on the firm's profitability and the profitability of the investments, and, as the name implies, if the firm has no profits, there is nothing to share (*i.e.*, the firm is not required to make contributions in years when it is not itself profitable).

192. (D) The Put gives one the right to sell at 50 when the stock is at 45. This is obviously profitable.

193. (B) T-bills are sold at a discount. The appreciation is all interest income taxable in the year of maturity.

194. (A) The fund specializes in one type of stock. Note that most biotechnology firms might be considered growth stocks but are not necessarily so.

195. (D) If federal funds rates are declining, then the supply of reserves (the funds from which federal funds loans are made) is probably increasing, making more funds available and, hence, cheaper.

196. (B) The total payment is 7% of $20,000,000 or $1,400,000. The semi-annual payment is half of that.

197. (B) They may be and often are sent monthly, but the requirement is quarterly statements.

198. (B) The number of units is fixed, but the value of each unit and, hence, the dollar amount varies with market experience. Obviously, the securities are not liquidated (or the market experience would be irrelevant).

199. (A) This is the term used by the IRS to describe the process of reclaiming as ordinary income the amounts claimed against personal income in previous years.

200. (D) These are used primarily with respect to foreign trade.

201. (B) All of the others are quoted on a discount basis.

202. (A) This is true of United States Treasury securities in general. These are exempt from state and local taxes.

203. (C) They are 70% tax-exempt, so the effective rate is 30% of the normal rate. For example, if the normal rate is 35% and dividend payments are $10,000, then $7,000 is exempt and $3,000 is taxed at 35% to yield $1,050. This is effectively a rate of 10.5% on the total, which is 3/10 (30%) of the normal rates.

204. (C) All of the others have some fixed minimum commitment from the insurer. This perforce lowers the amount available for monthly payments.

205. (B) The number of shares is raised to reflect the dividend, and, inversely, the strike price is lowered so that the total value is unchanged.

$$(100 \times \$60 = 120 \times \$50)$$

206. (D) A restricted account is margined at between 25% (maintenance) and 50% (Regulation T requirement). The account may not go below maintenance, but, otherwise, SMA funds may be withdrawn.

207. (D) The other choices can all be performed in a cash account. This one must be done in a margin account.

208. (C) This is a covered option and, hence, there is no margin required.

209. (C) The certificate of partnership would not be affected by any change in how partnership investments are financed.

210. (B) Repayment of principal is not a loss, but the other items are deducted from income to arrive at net income.

211. (C) Insurance companies' new issues are not excluded from registration under the Securities Act of 1933.

212. (A) Buying an option, one can lose no more then the premium; in this case, $100.

213. (B) Sales commissions can be as high as 8½%. Management fees are typically between ½% and 1%.

214. (D) A sell stop limit order is placed below the current market price and is used to liquidate a long position if the loss becomes too great. In this example, the first trade had gone to the "stop" price of 42⅝, so the order is activated as a limit order at 42⅝. Since the stock never trades as high as 42⅝ again, the order to sell cannot be executed.

215. (A) The rule is that shares must add up to 100 or be in round multiples of 100. Note: Since 40 + 60 = 100, choice B is good delivery. Only choice A fails the rule.

216. (D) This allows deductions of $3,000 for 1992, 1993, and 1994, and $1,000 carried forward to 1995.

217. (D) Rule #144 states that one can sell an average of the past four weeks' trading volume or 1% of the outstanding shares, whichever is greater.

218. (B) A short sale can only be made on a plus tick or zero-plus tick. ACI closed at 45 on an uptick and the next day goes ex-dividend ($.40). When a stock goes "ex-dividend," the price is reduced by the amount of the dividend or the next highest eighth if the dividend is not an amount divisible by ⅛; here the price is reduced by ½, giving an adjusted plus tick price of 44½.

219. (B) Net investment income is interest and dividends less expenses.

220. (B) The OTC requirement is that an order of at least 100 shares must be made on each order ticket at the same price. Therefore, 220 shares at 40 is allowed.

221. (C) By definition.

222. (B) Project notes are short-term debt backed by the full faith and credit of the United States Government. The short-term maturity reduces purchasing power risks.

223. (A) This is the quick ratio. It is more stringent than the current ratio, which includes inventory. The other choices have total liabilities in the denominator, and these do not reflect liquidity since they are not necessarily payable soon.

224. (B) An ad valorem (to the value) tax is another name for a property tax.

225. (A) The Moody's rating system starts with a highest rating of Aaa. The A1 rating is higher than A but lower than Aa.

226. (C) Total assets = Debt + Shareholder's equity. In this case, all of the debt is short term.

227. (C) Records of dividends are not required.

228. (D) $15 × (1 − .075) = Bid = $13.875. If a 0.5% redemption fee is charged, the investor receives approximately $13.80, which, if multiplied by 1,000 shares, gives $13,800.

229. (C) These bonus funds are not from self-employment and hence do not qualify for a Keogh.

230. (C) By definition.

231. (A) A numbered account is acceptable if the beneficial owner gives written proof of his ownership.

232. (C) The mutual fund acts as a conduit. The investors are responsible for all taxes.

233. (D) The allowable deduction is 25% of income up to a maximum of $30,000.

234. (D) For I and II this applies only to margin accounts. For III it applies to cash and margin accounts.

235. (A) He must purchase 200 shares at $44 and tender them at $40. This loss of $800 is subtracted from the $1,100 he collects in premiums.

236. (A) The retention is the amount retained by the syndicate for group sales. In this case, they retain 80% of the allotment, leaving 20% or 20,000 shares.

237. (D) Some of the payment is considered return of equity.

238. (B) When an investor wishes to exercise, he notifies his broker who in turn notifies the OCC.

239. (D) All of these are possible.

240. (B) By definition.

241. (C) A restriction on taxing power makes it a limited tax G.O. bond.

242. (D) There are also two G.O. indexes: a 20 bond index with average rating A and an 11 bond index with average rating Aa.

243. (C)

244. (B) The premium is quoted on the basis of $25 for a basis point. Hence, 1.20 or 120 points × $25 = $3,000.

245. (B) It is unacceptable to project future price increases.

246. (B) Converting debt to equity reduces leverage = (debt/equity) and obviously increases equity. Assets are unaffected.

247. (B) It is not a part of the federal government but, rather, a corporation owned by broker/dealers.

248. (C) In an Eastern account, each member has an undivided responsibility. In this case, if $1 million remains unsold and he has a 15% share, his responsibility is 15% of $1 million.

249. (B) A frozen account requires that all transactions be covered in advance.

250. (A) By changing to straight line, depreciation in early years is reduced. This increases earnings since depreciation is treated as a cost to be subtracted from revenues.

PRACTICE EXAMINATION TWO

Practice Examination Two
Answer Sheet
Part 1

#		#		#		#		#	
1	Ⓐ Ⓑ Ⓒ Ⓓ	26	Ⓐ Ⓑ Ⓒ Ⓓ	51	Ⓐ Ⓑ Ⓒ Ⓓ	76	Ⓐ Ⓑ Ⓒ Ⓓ	101	Ⓐ Ⓑ Ⓒ Ⓓ
2	Ⓐ Ⓑ Ⓒ Ⓓ	27	Ⓐ Ⓑ Ⓒ Ⓓ	52	Ⓐ Ⓑ Ⓒ Ⓓ	77	Ⓐ Ⓑ Ⓒ Ⓓ	102	Ⓐ Ⓑ Ⓒ Ⓓ
3	Ⓐ Ⓑ Ⓒ Ⓓ	28	Ⓐ Ⓑ Ⓒ Ⓓ	53	Ⓐ Ⓑ Ⓒ Ⓓ	78	Ⓐ Ⓑ Ⓒ Ⓓ	103	Ⓐ Ⓑ Ⓒ Ⓓ
4	Ⓐ Ⓑ Ⓒ Ⓓ	29	Ⓐ Ⓑ Ⓒ Ⓓ	54	Ⓐ Ⓑ Ⓒ Ⓓ	79	Ⓐ Ⓑ Ⓒ Ⓓ	104	Ⓐ Ⓑ Ⓒ Ⓓ
5	Ⓐ Ⓑ Ⓒ Ⓓ	30	Ⓐ Ⓑ Ⓒ Ⓓ	55	Ⓐ Ⓑ Ⓒ Ⓓ	80	Ⓐ Ⓑ Ⓒ Ⓓ	105	Ⓐ Ⓑ Ⓒ Ⓓ
6	Ⓐ Ⓑ Ⓒ Ⓓ	31	Ⓐ Ⓑ Ⓒ Ⓓ	56	Ⓐ Ⓑ Ⓒ Ⓓ	81	Ⓐ Ⓑ Ⓒ Ⓓ	106	Ⓐ Ⓑ Ⓒ Ⓓ
7	Ⓐ Ⓑ Ⓒ Ⓓ	32	Ⓐ Ⓑ Ⓒ Ⓓ	57	Ⓐ Ⓑ Ⓒ Ⓓ	82	Ⓐ Ⓑ Ⓒ Ⓓ	107	Ⓐ Ⓑ Ⓒ Ⓓ
8	Ⓐ Ⓑ Ⓒ Ⓓ	33	Ⓐ Ⓑ Ⓒ Ⓓ	58	Ⓐ Ⓑ Ⓒ Ⓓ	83	Ⓐ Ⓑ Ⓒ Ⓓ	108	Ⓐ Ⓑ Ⓒ Ⓓ
9	Ⓐ Ⓑ Ⓒ Ⓓ	34	Ⓐ Ⓑ Ⓒ Ⓓ	59	Ⓐ Ⓑ Ⓒ Ⓓ	84	Ⓐ Ⓑ Ⓒ Ⓓ	109	Ⓐ Ⓑ Ⓒ Ⓓ
10	Ⓐ Ⓑ Ⓒ Ⓓ	35	Ⓐ Ⓑ Ⓒ Ⓓ	60	Ⓐ Ⓑ Ⓒ Ⓓ	85	Ⓐ Ⓑ Ⓒ Ⓓ	110	Ⓐ Ⓑ Ⓒ Ⓓ
11	Ⓐ Ⓑ Ⓒ Ⓓ	36	Ⓐ Ⓑ Ⓒ Ⓓ	61	Ⓐ Ⓑ Ⓒ Ⓓ	86	Ⓐ Ⓑ Ⓒ Ⓓ	111	Ⓐ Ⓑ Ⓒ Ⓓ
12	Ⓐ Ⓑ Ⓒ Ⓓ	37	Ⓐ Ⓑ Ⓒ Ⓓ	62	Ⓐ Ⓑ Ⓒ Ⓓ	87	Ⓐ Ⓑ Ⓒ Ⓓ	112	Ⓐ Ⓑ Ⓒ Ⓓ
13	Ⓐ Ⓑ Ⓒ Ⓓ	38	Ⓐ Ⓑ Ⓒ Ⓓ	63	Ⓐ Ⓑ Ⓒ Ⓓ	88	Ⓐ Ⓑ Ⓒ Ⓓ	113	Ⓐ Ⓑ Ⓒ Ⓓ
14	Ⓐ Ⓑ Ⓒ Ⓓ	39	Ⓐ Ⓑ Ⓒ Ⓓ	64	Ⓐ Ⓑ Ⓒ Ⓓ	89	Ⓐ Ⓑ Ⓒ Ⓓ	114	Ⓐ Ⓑ Ⓒ Ⓓ
15	Ⓐ Ⓑ Ⓒ Ⓓ	40	Ⓐ Ⓑ Ⓒ Ⓓ	65	Ⓐ Ⓑ Ⓒ Ⓓ	90	Ⓐ Ⓑ Ⓒ Ⓓ	115	Ⓐ Ⓑ Ⓒ Ⓓ
16	Ⓐ Ⓑ Ⓒ Ⓓ	41	Ⓐ Ⓑ Ⓒ Ⓓ	66	Ⓐ Ⓑ Ⓒ Ⓓ	91	Ⓐ Ⓑ Ⓒ Ⓓ	116	Ⓐ Ⓑ Ⓒ Ⓓ
17	Ⓐ Ⓑ Ⓒ Ⓓ	42	Ⓐ Ⓑ Ⓒ Ⓓ	67	Ⓐ Ⓑ Ⓒ Ⓓ	92	Ⓐ Ⓑ Ⓒ Ⓓ	117	Ⓐ Ⓑ Ⓒ Ⓓ
18	Ⓐ Ⓑ Ⓒ Ⓓ	43	Ⓐ Ⓑ Ⓒ Ⓓ	68	Ⓐ Ⓑ Ⓒ Ⓓ	93	Ⓐ Ⓑ Ⓒ Ⓓ	118	Ⓐ Ⓑ Ⓒ Ⓓ
19	Ⓐ Ⓑ Ⓒ Ⓓ	44	Ⓐ Ⓑ Ⓒ Ⓓ	69	Ⓐ Ⓑ Ⓒ Ⓓ	94	Ⓐ Ⓑ Ⓒ Ⓓ	119	Ⓐ Ⓑ Ⓒ Ⓓ
20	Ⓐ Ⓑ Ⓒ Ⓓ	45	Ⓐ Ⓑ Ⓒ Ⓓ	70	Ⓐ Ⓑ Ⓒ Ⓓ	95	Ⓐ Ⓑ Ⓒ Ⓓ	120	Ⓐ Ⓑ Ⓒ Ⓓ
21	Ⓐ Ⓑ Ⓒ Ⓓ	46	Ⓐ Ⓑ Ⓒ Ⓓ	71	Ⓐ Ⓑ Ⓒ Ⓓ	96	Ⓐ Ⓑ Ⓒ Ⓓ	121	Ⓐ Ⓑ Ⓒ Ⓓ
22	Ⓐ Ⓑ Ⓒ Ⓓ	47	Ⓐ Ⓑ Ⓒ Ⓓ	72	Ⓐ Ⓑ Ⓒ Ⓓ	97	Ⓐ Ⓑ Ⓒ Ⓓ	122	Ⓐ Ⓑ Ⓒ Ⓓ
23	Ⓐ Ⓑ Ⓒ Ⓓ	48	Ⓐ Ⓑ Ⓒ Ⓓ	73	Ⓐ Ⓑ Ⓒ Ⓓ	98	Ⓐ Ⓑ Ⓒ Ⓓ	123	Ⓐ Ⓑ Ⓒ Ⓓ
24	Ⓐ Ⓑ Ⓒ Ⓓ	49	Ⓐ Ⓑ Ⓒ Ⓓ	74	Ⓐ Ⓑ Ⓒ Ⓓ	99	Ⓐ Ⓑ Ⓒ Ⓓ	124	Ⓐ Ⓑ Ⓒ Ⓓ
25	Ⓐ Ⓑ Ⓒ Ⓓ	50	Ⓐ Ⓑ Ⓒ Ⓓ	75	Ⓐ Ⓑ Ⓒ Ⓓ	100	Ⓐ Ⓑ Ⓒ Ⓓ	125	Ⓐ Ⓑ Ⓒ Ⓓ

Practice Examination Two
Answer Sheet
Part 2

126 Ⓐ Ⓑ Ⓒ Ⓓ	151 Ⓐ Ⓑ Ⓒ Ⓓ	176 Ⓐ Ⓑ Ⓒ Ⓓ	201 Ⓐ Ⓑ Ⓒ Ⓓ	226 Ⓐ Ⓑ Ⓒ Ⓓ
127 Ⓐ Ⓑ Ⓒ Ⓓ	152 Ⓐ Ⓑ Ⓒ Ⓓ	177 Ⓐ Ⓑ Ⓒ Ⓓ	202 Ⓐ Ⓑ Ⓒ Ⓓ	227 Ⓐ Ⓑ Ⓒ Ⓓ
128 Ⓐ Ⓑ Ⓒ Ⓓ	153 Ⓐ Ⓑ Ⓒ Ⓓ	178 Ⓐ Ⓑ Ⓒ Ⓓ	203 Ⓐ Ⓑ Ⓒ Ⓓ	228 Ⓐ Ⓑ Ⓒ Ⓓ
129 Ⓐ Ⓑ Ⓒ Ⓓ	154 Ⓐ Ⓑ Ⓒ Ⓓ	179 Ⓐ Ⓑ Ⓒ Ⓓ	204 Ⓐ Ⓑ Ⓒ Ⓓ	229 Ⓐ Ⓑ Ⓒ Ⓓ
130 Ⓐ Ⓑ Ⓒ Ⓓ	155 Ⓐ Ⓑ Ⓒ Ⓓ	180 Ⓐ Ⓑ Ⓒ Ⓓ	205 Ⓐ Ⓑ Ⓒ Ⓓ	230 Ⓐ Ⓑ Ⓒ Ⓓ
131 Ⓐ Ⓑ Ⓒ Ⓓ	156 Ⓐ Ⓑ Ⓒ Ⓓ	181 Ⓐ Ⓑ Ⓒ Ⓓ	206 Ⓐ Ⓑ Ⓒ Ⓓ	231 Ⓐ Ⓑ Ⓒ Ⓓ
132 Ⓐ Ⓑ Ⓒ Ⓓ	157 Ⓐ Ⓑ Ⓒ Ⓓ	182 Ⓐ Ⓑ Ⓒ Ⓓ	207 Ⓐ Ⓑ Ⓒ Ⓓ	232 Ⓐ Ⓑ Ⓒ Ⓓ
133 Ⓐ Ⓑ Ⓒ Ⓓ	158 Ⓐ Ⓑ Ⓒ Ⓓ	183 Ⓐ Ⓑ Ⓒ Ⓓ	208 Ⓐ Ⓑ Ⓒ Ⓓ	233 Ⓐ Ⓑ Ⓒ Ⓓ
134 Ⓐ Ⓑ Ⓒ Ⓓ	159 Ⓐ Ⓑ Ⓒ Ⓓ	184 Ⓐ Ⓑ Ⓒ Ⓓ	209 Ⓐ Ⓑ Ⓒ Ⓓ	234 Ⓐ Ⓑ Ⓒ Ⓓ
135 Ⓐ Ⓑ Ⓒ Ⓓ	160 Ⓐ Ⓑ Ⓒ Ⓓ	185 Ⓐ Ⓑ Ⓒ Ⓓ	210 Ⓐ Ⓑ Ⓒ Ⓓ	235 Ⓐ Ⓑ Ⓒ Ⓓ
136 Ⓐ Ⓑ Ⓒ Ⓓ	161 Ⓐ Ⓑ Ⓒ Ⓓ	186 Ⓐ Ⓑ Ⓒ Ⓓ	211 Ⓐ Ⓑ Ⓒ Ⓓ	236 Ⓐ Ⓑ Ⓒ Ⓓ
137 Ⓐ Ⓑ Ⓒ Ⓓ	162 Ⓐ Ⓑ Ⓒ Ⓓ	187 Ⓐ Ⓑ Ⓒ Ⓓ	212 Ⓐ Ⓑ Ⓒ Ⓓ	237 Ⓐ Ⓑ Ⓒ Ⓓ
138 Ⓐ Ⓑ Ⓒ Ⓓ	163 Ⓐ Ⓑ Ⓒ Ⓓ	188 Ⓐ Ⓑ Ⓒ Ⓓ	213 Ⓐ Ⓑ Ⓒ Ⓓ	238 Ⓐ Ⓑ Ⓒ Ⓓ
139 Ⓐ Ⓑ Ⓒ Ⓓ	164 Ⓐ Ⓑ Ⓒ Ⓓ	189 Ⓐ Ⓑ Ⓒ Ⓓ	214 Ⓐ Ⓑ Ⓒ Ⓓ	239 Ⓐ Ⓑ Ⓒ Ⓓ
140 Ⓐ Ⓑ Ⓒ Ⓓ	165 Ⓐ Ⓑ Ⓒ Ⓓ	190 Ⓐ Ⓑ Ⓒ Ⓓ	215 Ⓐ Ⓑ Ⓒ Ⓓ	240 Ⓐ Ⓑ Ⓒ Ⓓ
141 Ⓐ Ⓑ Ⓒ Ⓓ	166 Ⓐ Ⓑ Ⓒ Ⓓ	191 Ⓐ Ⓑ Ⓒ Ⓓ	216 Ⓐ Ⓑ Ⓒ Ⓓ	241 Ⓐ Ⓑ Ⓒ Ⓓ
142 Ⓐ Ⓑ Ⓒ Ⓓ	167 Ⓐ Ⓑ Ⓒ Ⓓ	192 Ⓐ Ⓑ Ⓒ Ⓓ	217 Ⓐ Ⓑ Ⓒ Ⓓ	242 Ⓐ Ⓑ Ⓒ Ⓓ
143 Ⓐ Ⓑ Ⓒ Ⓓ	168 Ⓐ Ⓑ Ⓒ Ⓓ	193 Ⓐ Ⓑ Ⓒ Ⓓ	218 Ⓐ Ⓑ Ⓒ Ⓓ	243 Ⓐ Ⓑ Ⓒ Ⓓ
144 Ⓐ Ⓑ Ⓒ Ⓓ	169 Ⓐ Ⓑ Ⓒ Ⓓ	194 Ⓐ Ⓑ Ⓒ Ⓓ	219 Ⓐ Ⓑ Ⓒ Ⓓ	244 Ⓐ Ⓑ Ⓒ Ⓓ
145 Ⓐ Ⓑ Ⓒ Ⓓ	170 Ⓐ Ⓑ Ⓒ Ⓓ	195 Ⓐ Ⓑ Ⓒ Ⓓ	220 Ⓐ Ⓑ Ⓒ Ⓓ	245 Ⓐ Ⓑ Ⓒ Ⓓ
146 Ⓐ Ⓑ Ⓒ Ⓓ	171 Ⓐ Ⓑ Ⓒ Ⓓ	196 Ⓐ Ⓑ Ⓒ Ⓓ	221 Ⓐ Ⓑ Ⓒ Ⓓ	246 Ⓐ Ⓑ Ⓒ Ⓓ
147 Ⓐ Ⓑ Ⓒ Ⓓ	172 Ⓐ Ⓑ Ⓒ Ⓓ	197 Ⓐ Ⓑ Ⓒ Ⓓ	222 Ⓐ Ⓑ Ⓒ Ⓓ	247 Ⓐ Ⓑ Ⓒ Ⓓ
148 Ⓐ Ⓑ Ⓒ Ⓓ	173 Ⓐ Ⓑ Ⓒ Ⓓ	198 Ⓐ Ⓑ Ⓒ Ⓓ	223 Ⓐ Ⓑ Ⓒ Ⓓ	248 Ⓐ Ⓑ Ⓒ Ⓓ
149 Ⓐ Ⓑ Ⓒ Ⓓ	174 Ⓐ Ⓑ Ⓒ Ⓓ	199 Ⓐ Ⓑ Ⓒ Ⓓ	224 Ⓐ Ⓑ Ⓒ Ⓓ	249 Ⓐ Ⓑ Ⓒ Ⓓ
150 Ⓐ Ⓑ Ⓒ Ⓓ	175 Ⓐ Ⓑ Ⓒ Ⓓ	200 Ⓐ Ⓑ Ⓒ Ⓓ	225 Ⓐ Ⓑ Ⓒ Ⓓ	250 Ⓐ Ⓑ Ⓒ Ⓓ

PART ONE

TIME 3 HOURS
QUESTIONS 1-125

DIRECTIONS

Each of the questions or incomplete statements below is followed by four suggested answer options. Choose the best answer and then blacken the corresponding space on the answer sheet.

1. ACI issued one million shares of convertible preferred (par $100). The shares are convertible at $45 and the common is currently selling at $36. If an investor paid $90 per share for 100 shares of preferred, which of the following is true?

   I.   The conversion rate is 2.22.
   II. The conversion rate is 2.50.
   III. The preferred is selling below parity.
   IV. The preferred is selling above parity.

   (A) I and III
   (B) I and IV
   (C) II and III
   (D) II and IV

2. Which act empowered the Federal Reserve Board to regulate credit in securities transactions?

   (A) The Securities Act of 1933
   (B) The Securities Exchange Act of 1934
   (C) The Maloney Act of 1938
   (D) The Investment Company Act of 1940

3. CAI had earnings of $6 per share. If it paid quarterly dividends of $.60, its dividend payout ratio was:

   (A) 10%.
   (B) 30%.
   (C) 40%.
   (D) 60%.

4. Which of the following strategies has the greatest potential risk?

   (A) Writing naked Puts
   (B) Buying naked Puts
   (C) Writing naked Calls
   (D) Buying naked Calls

5. An investor owns 100 shares of ACI at $45.00. If she writes a straddle on ACI with a $45.00 strike, which subsequent event will have the greatest potential loss for her?

   (A) ACI remains unchanged.
   (B) ACI goes to 100.
   (C) ACI goes to 0.
   (D) Neither option is exercised.

6. All of the following are on the same side EXCEPT:

   (A) long Call–short stock.
   (B) long Call–long stock.
   (C) short Call–short stock.
   (D) short Put–long stock.

7. In 1987, an investor purchased a T-note with a May 12 settlement date. If the most recent interest payment had been January 15, how many days of accrued interest must he add to the purchase price?

   (A) 116
   (B) 118
   (C) 120
   (D) 121

8. An investor purchased a corporate bond with settlement on June 5. If the most recent payment had been on March 15, how many days of accrued interest must she add to the purchase price?

   (A) 78
   (B) 79
   (C) 80
   (D) 81

9. ACI is trading at 50. What is the loan value of an ACI Jun 30 Call trading at 22?

   (A) $0
   (B) $1,000
   (C) $1,100
   (D) $2,000

Questions 10–12 are based on the following information:

Regulation T is at 50%, house maintenance margin at 30% and NYSE maintenance at 25%.

Market Value	30,000
Debit Balance	17,000
SMA	5,000

10. How much in marginable securities would Mrs. P need to deposit to remove the account from restricted status?

(A) $0
(B) $1,000
(C) $2,000
(D) $4,000

11. At what market value will this account be at NYSE minimum maintenance?

(A) $20,000
(B) $22,667
(C) $24,287
(D) $25,000

12. How much cash can she currently withdraw from the account without any other transactions?

(A) $0
(B) $3,000
(C) $4,000
(D) $5,000

13. Under which circumstances at expiration would an investor experience the largest profit from selling 1 ACI Sep 40 Call and buying 1 ACI Sep 50 Call?

(A) ACI is at $40.
(B) ACI is between $40 and $50.
(C) ACI is at $50.
(D) It cannot be determined.

14. At what expiration price would this investor experience the greatest loss?

(A) ACI is at $40.
(B) ACI is between $40 and $50.
(C) ACI is at $50.
(D) It cannot be determined.

15. Which of the following would not be considered "good delivery" in a municipal bond transaction?

(A) Callable bonds
(B) Bearer bonds in $1,000 denominations
(C) Bonds with an attached legal opinion
(D) None of the above

16. The MSRB regulates all of the following EXCEPT:

(A) banks that do municipal securities business.
(B) brokers that do municipal securities business.
(C) dealers that do municipal securities business.
(D) issuers of municipal securities.

17. A new issue of a municipal bond due to mature on July 1, 2009 is dated January 1, 1987. A customer purchases these with a settlement date of February 15. How many days of accrued interest must the customer pay?

(A) 43
(B) 44
(C) 45
(D) 46

18. All of the following are *direct* obligations of the United States government EXCEPT:

(A) FNMA.
(B) GNMA.
(C) Series EE bonds.
(D) flower bonds.

19. The moment when taxable income begins to exceed cash distributions in a direct participation program is the:

(A) real phantom income point.
(B) cross-over point.
(C) profit point.
(D) cash-flow point.

20. In a direct participation program, if there was depreciation of the asset, all of the following would be true EXCEPT:

(A) cash flow increases.
(B) income increases.
(C) taxes increase.
(D) net assets decrease.

21. A municipal security issue of revenue bonds is being analyzed for "coverage." The appropriate ratio is:

(A) net revenue to total expenses.
(B) gross revenue to operating expenses plus debt service.
(C) net revenue to debt service.
(D) gross revenue to debt service.

22. A bull spread "breaks even" when the difference between the market price and the lower strike price is equal to the:

(A) higher premium minus the lower one.
(B) higher premium minus the market price.
(C) higher premium plus the lower one.
(D) lower premium minus the market price.

23. A Put option is "in the money" if:

(A) the strike price is at market price.
(B) the strike price is above market price.
(C) the strike price is below market price.
(D) the strike price is at exercise price.

24. Federal funds are:

(A) obligations of the Federal Reserve Bank.
(B) obligations to the Federal Reserve Bank.
(C) obligations by one bank to another to meet Federal Reserve requirements.
(D) very stable interest rates.

25. All of the following are money market instruments EXCEPT:

(A) commercial paper.
(B) banker's acceptances.
(C) federal funds.
(D) ADRs.

26. All of the following are true of the pink sheets EXCEPT:

(A) they show firm quotes for one round lot.
(B) they are wholesale quotes.
(C) they are published daily.
(D) they list market makers for the quoted securities.

27. The order in which a transaction is processed is:

I.   order department
II. margin department
III. purchase and sale
IV. cashier

(A) I, III, II, IV
(B) III, I, IV, II
(C) I, II, III, IV
(D) III, IV, I, II

Questions 28–30 refer to the following strategy:

Buy 100 shares of CAI at $53. Sell one CAI Nov 50 Call at 7.

28. The investor will first experience a loss if CAI is:

(A) below $48.
(B) below $46.
(C) below $50.
(D) below $60.

29. If CAI is at $51 when the previously unexercised option expires, his profit (loss) will be:

(A) $100.
(B) $100 (loss).
(C) $400.
(D) $600.

30. The maximum profit possible during the life of the option is:

(A) $100.
(B) $300.
(C) $400.
(D) $700.

The following information is useful for answering questions 31 and 32:

A limited partner in a balanced oil and gas program has invested $50,000 and is responsible for a recourse loan of an additional $40,000.

31. The investor's basis is:

(A) $10,000.
(B) $40,000.
(C) $50,000.
(D) $90,000.

32. If the investor had passive income of $70,000, the maximum loss he could claim would be:

(A) $40,000.
(B) $50,000.
(C) $70,000.
(D) $90,000.

33. The sponsor of a functional sharing arrangement oil- and gas-drilling program would pay:

(A) all non-deductible expenses.
(B) all intangible expenses.
(C) a share of deductible expenses.
(D) a share of non-deductible expenses.

34. A preliminary prospectus can do which of the following?

(A) It can be used during the cooling-off period.
(B) It can be used to blue sky an issue.
(C) It can be used to generate orders.
(D) It can be used to get indications of interest.

Questions 35–38 refer to the following:

An investor with no other positions buys 1 ACI Mar 40 Put at 4½ and buys 1 ACI Mar 40 Call at 1½.

35. The market price at ACI is most likely to be:

(A) below $40.
(B) at $40.
(C) above $40.
(D) it cannot be determined.

36. The maximum loss this investor could experience is:

(A) $300.
(B) $450.
(C) $600.
(D) Unlimited.

37. The maximum profit he could experience is:

(A) $450.
(B) $600.
(C) $3,400.
(D) unlimited.

38. At expiration ACI was at $50. If he had not exercised up to then, he would experience:

(A) $600 loss.
(B) $400 gain.
(C) $600 gain.
(D) $1,000 gain.

39. Which of the following has the least volatile interest rate?

(A) Federal funds rate
(B) Prime rate
(C) T-bill rate
(D) Discount rate

40. Interest on new issues of municipal bonds accrues from the:

(A) previous interest payment.
(B) dated date.
(C) settlement date.
(D) purchase date.

41. All of the following provide information about proposed municipal bond issues EXCEPT:

(A) *Munifacts*.
(B) *Daily Bond Buyer*.
(C) *Blue List*.
(D) newspapers.

42. Which of the following municipal securities has the lowest price if they all mature on the same date?

(A) 7¼% coupon at 7¼%
(B) 8% coupon at 8⅜%
(C) 8% coupon at 7¾%
(D) 7¼% coupon at 7⅜%

Questions 43–45 refer to the following strategy:

An investor buys 3 ACI Jun 50 Calls at 4.

43. At what price will the investor break even?

(A) $46
(B) $50
(C) $54
(D) $62

44. His maximum possible loss on this investment is:

(A) $400.
(B) $1,200.
(C) $15,000.
(D) unlimited.

45. If he exercises these when ACI is at $60 and wishes to purchase the stock in his margin account, how much will he be required to deposit in the margin account?

(A) $7,500
(B) $8,700
(C) $9,000
(D) $10,200

46. To analyze a general obligation bond, one would consider all of the following EXCEPT the:

(A) size of the issue.
(B) size of the population base.
(C) denomination of the issue.
(D) income of the ratepayers.

47. The name of the interest rate at which member banks may borrow from the Federal Reserve Bank is:

(A) federal funds rate.
(B) discount rate.
(C) prime rate.
(D) money supply rate.

Questions 48–50 refer to the following information:

A customer has the following accounts:

Account	Market Value	Balance
Cash (with marginable securities)	$20,000	$ 5,000
Long	$30,000	$16,000 (Debit)
Short	$10,000	$14,000 (Credit)
SMA	$ 4,000	

48. What is her total equity?

(A) $43,000
(B) $60,000
(C) $65,000
(D) $69,000

49. What is the total buying power in the two margin accounts?

(A) $4,000
(B) $6,000
(C) $8,000
(D) $10,000

50. What is the total buying power of all accounts?

(A) $20,000
(B) $27,000
(C) $38,000
(D) $40,000

51. The premium on a Value Line index option is 2½. The total dollar price of this premium is:

(A) $250.
(B) $500.
(C) $625.
(D) $1,250.

Questions 52–54 refer to the following strategy:

An investor buys 100 shares of CAI at 45 and writes 1 CAI Apr 50 Call at 2.

52. At what price would she break even?

(A) $43
(B) $48
(C) $50
(D) $52

53. If the Call is exercised when CAI is at $54, she has:

(A) $200 loss.
(B) $200 gain.
(C) $500 gain.
(D) $700 gain.

54. What is the most this investor could lose?

(A) $200
(B) $4,300
(C) $4,500
(D) Unlimited

Questions 55 and 56 refer to the following information:

ACI has issued a convertible bond with a conversion price of $100 per share.

55. The conversion rate is:

  (A) 5 to 1.
  (B) 10 to 1.
  (C) 20 to 1.
  (D) 100 to 1.

56. If the bond is selling at $1,150, the parity price for the stock is:

  (A) $100.
  (B) $110.
  (C) $115.
  (D) $150.

Questions 57 and 58 refer to the following information:

CAI has ten million shares authorized. A total of eight million shares have been issued and there are currently one million shares of treasury stock. CAI has a market price of $50.

57. If the next common stock dividend is declared at $.75, the total amount to be distributed is:

  (A) $750,000.
  (B) $5,250,000.
  (C) $6,000,000.
  (D) $7,500,000.

58. If the annual dividend for CAI has been $3.00, CAI has a current yield of:

  (A) 3%.
  (B) 6%.
  (C) 7.5%.
  (D) 15%.

59. When an offering becomes effective under SEC rules, this means that the SEC has:

  (A) checked the accuracy of the registration statement.
  (B) approved the offering.
  (C) attested that the offering meets minimum investment standards.
  (D) determined that the registration statement is complete.

Questions 60–62 refer to the following investments:

Long 2 ACI Jun 50 Puts at 3½
Short 2 ACI Jun 45 Puts at ½

60. If they have not been previously exercised, at expiration what is the maximum possible profit on this trade?

  (A) $200
  (B) $300
  (C) $400
  (D) $600

61. If they have not been previously exercised, at expiration what is the maximum possible loss from this trade?

  (A) $300
  (B) $400
  (C) $600
  (D) Unlimited

62. At what market price would this investment break even?

  (A) $45.50
  (B) $47.00
  (C) $48.00
  (D) $49.50

63. Another name for the nominal rate (yield) is:

  (A) yield to maturity.
  (B) current yield.
  (C) coupon rate.
  (D) current yield-coupon rate.

64. Regular way for United States treasury securities means:

  (A) next business day payment—five business day delivery.
  (B) five business day payment—five business day delivery.
  (C) next business day payment—next business day delivery.
  (D) five business day payment—next business day delivery.

65. An investor pays $70 in accrued interest on a 9% corporate bond bought at 90. If the bond has ten years to maturity, how

much interest is reportable for this first tax year?

(A) $10
(B) $30
(C) $90
(D) $100

66. If a municipality solicits bids for an offering, the winning bid will be the one that offers to:

(A) sell it at the lowest price.
(B) sell it at the highest price.
(C) sell it at the lowest cost to the municipality.
(D) raise the most money for the municipality.

67. According to MSRB rules, a municipal securities principal must approve all of the following EXCEPT:

(A) opening new accounts.
(B) handling of customer complaints.
(C) legal opinions.
(D) every transaction.

68. According to MSRB rules, the total of gifts and gratuities that may be accepted from one person by a registered representative in one year may not exceed:

(A) $25.
(B) $50.
(C) $75.
(D) $100.

69. All of the following are true of full discretionary accounts EXCEPT:

(A) they must be reviewed regularly by a supervisory person.
(B) they must have written authorization from the customer.
(C) a father can sell securities for a son's account with verbal authorization.
(D) a registered representative can remove cash from such an account.

Questions 70–72 are based on the following:

Sell 1 CAI Apr 35 Put at 2 when CAI is at $39.

In all cases, assume that there has been no exercise prior to expiration.

70. This trade will break even if CAI is at:

(A) $33.
(B) $35.
(C) $37.
(D) $41.

71. The maximum possible profit is:

(A) $200.
(B) $400.
(C) $3,700.
(D) $4,100.

72. If CAI is at 25, the investor's profit (loss) is:

(A) $800 profit.
(B) $800 loss.
(C) $1,200 profit.
(D) $1,200 loss.

73. All of the following are true of T-bills EXCEPT:

(A) they are issued in book entry form.
(B) they are traded on a discount basis.
(C) they are less risky than T-bonds.
(D) they usually have a higher rate than the prime.

74. For information on unlisted corporate bonds, one should examine the:

(A) yellow sheets.
(B) *Blue List.*
(C) pink sheets.
(D) visible supply.

75. All of the following are required by MSRB rules for customer confirmations EXCEPT:

(A) the amount of any commission in any broker transaction.
(B) the source of any commission in any broker transaction.
(C) notification if the bonds are not in bearer form.
(D) the amount of any mark-up on a dealer transaction.

76. The Securities Act of 1933 regulates which of the following?

   (A) Securities dealer operations
   (B) Registration of securities
   (C) Management of investment companies
   (D) Securities exchange operations

77. The Securities Exchange Act of 1934 regulates all of the following EXCEPT:

   (A) capital requirements for broker/dealers.
   (B) financial reports by broker/dealers.
   (C) hypothecation of customer securities.
   (D) cooling-off period.

Questions 78–80 refer to the following strategy:

Sell short 200 shares of ACI at 50.
Buy 2 ACI Sep 55 Calls at 1½.

78. This strategy will break even if ACI is at:

   (A) $48.50.
   (B) $51.50.
   (C) $53.00.
   (D) $56.50.

79. The maximum possible profit would occur if ACI were at:

   (A) $0.
   (B) $1.50.
   (C) $50.
   (D) $55.

80. The maximum possible loss from this strategy is:

   (A) $700.
   (B) $1,300.
   (C) $9,700.
   (D) $10,000.

81. All of the following are true of GNMA's EXCEPT:

   (A) they are direct obligations of the United States government.
   (B) they usually pay a higher rate than T-bonds of comparable maturity.
   (C) they often include some return of capital before maturity.
   (D) they are exempt from state and local taxes.

Questions 82–84 refer to the following income statement:

Consolidated Amalgamated Inc.
Income Statement for year ending
December 31, 1990.

Net Sales	$20,000,000
Cost of Goods	($12,000,000)
Administrative Costs	($ 3,000,000)
Operating Profits	$ 5,000,000
Other Income	$ 500,000
(EBIT) Total Income	$ 5,500,000
Fixed Interest	($ 1,000,000)
(EBT) Income before Taxes	$ 4,500,000
Income Tax	($ 1,500,000)
Net Income	$ 3,000,000
Common Stock Dividends	($ 1,200,000)
Retained Earnings	$ 1,800,000

CAI has 1.2 million shares issued of which 200,000 are treasury stock.

82. What are the earnings per share?

   (A) $1.00
   (B) $1.20
   (C) $2.50
   (D) $3.00

83. What is the profit margin on operations?

   (A) 15%
   (B) 22.5%
   (C) 25%
   (D) 27.5%

84. What is the times interest earned?

   (A) 5.5 to 1
   (B) 4.5 to 1
   (C) 3 to 1
   (D) 1.8 to 1

85. Which of the following choices represent the same class?

   (A) All ACI options
   (B) All ACI 50 options
   (C) All ACI Calls
   (D) All ACI Jun

86. The premium on an option which is "at the money" is made up of:

    (A) all intrinsic value.
    (B) all time value.
    (C) half intrinsic value plus half time value.
    (D) some positive amounts of intrinsic and time value.

87. Which of the following is a long straddle?

    (A) Buy 1 CAI Sep 45 Call; sell 1 CAI Sep 40 Call.
    (B) Buy 1 CAI Sep 45 Put; sell 1 CAI Sep 40 Call.
    (C) Buy 1 CAI Sep 45 Put; buy 1 CAI Sep 45 Call.
    (D) Sell 1 CAI Sep 45 Call; sell 1 CAI Sep 45 Put.

Questions 88–90 refer to the following choices:

    (A) Banker's acceptances
    (B) T-bills
    (C) Repos
    (D) Commercial paper

Choose the money market instrument best described in each of the following:

88. This instrument is limited to 270-day maturity.

89. This instrument is used to foster foreign trade.

90. This instrument is traded for a fixed length of time.

91. An account where both owners have trading authority and where the tenant's portion reverts to his estate is called:

    (A) joint tenants with rights of survivorship.
    (B) tenants in entirety.
    (C) communal tenants.
    (D) joint tenants in common.

92. A client account for an investment advisor requires all of the following EXCEPT a(n):

    (A) full trading authorization.
    (B) new account forms for each account.
    (C) agreement to furnish any other forms dictated by house requirements.
    (D) disclosure form stating that the client knows that the advisor is trading other accounts.

93. Which of the following is a good delivery for a transaction of 500 shares?

    (A) Four 25 share certificates; ten 20 share certificates; one 200 share certificate
    (B) Ten 40 share certificates; one 100 share certificate
    (C) Four 50 share certificates; four 75 share certificates
    (D) Five 40 share certificates; one 300 share certificate

94. For each listed options contract the issuer is the:

    (A) exchange on which it is listed.
    (B) writer of the contract.
    (C) writer's brokerage firm.
    (D) Options Clearing Corporation.

95. Exercise notices are assigned on the basis of:

    (A) earliest written.
    (B) latest written.
    (C) largest holder.
    (D) random selection.

96. Settlement for the purchase of OCC listed options is:

    (A) same day.
    (B) next day.
    (C) five business days.
    (D) seven business days.

97. The minimum denomination for T-notes and T-bonds is:

    (A) $1,000.
    (B) $5,000.
    (C) $10,000.
    (D) $100,000.

98. All of the following are acceptable collateral by a brokerage firm EXCEPT:

(A) FNMA securities.
(B) AAA Corporates.
(C) EE bonds.
(D) T-bills.

99. Four directors are to be elected at the ACI annual meeting under cumulative voting. Mr. P owns 200 shares. He may cast no more than:

(A) 200 votes.
(B) 200 votes for any one director.
(C) 400 votes for any one director.
(D) 800 votes for any one director.

100. If any employee of an insurance company provides a letter from an officer of the insurers saying that the employee may open a margin account and that the company does not wish to receive duplicate confirmations, the registered representative may:

(A) not open the account.
(B) open the account.
(C) open the account but send duplicates anyway.
(D) open the account but inform the SEC that no duplicates are being sent.

101. All of the following would result in an adjustment of the options contract EXCEPT:

(A) 5% stock dividend.
(B) $.10 dividend.
(C) 3/2 stock split.
(D) rights distribution.

102. ACI has declared a 25% stock dividend. At the ex-dividend date, an ACI Dec 50 option will become (remain):

(A) unchanged.
(B) ACI 50 for 125 shares.
(C) ACI 40 for 100 shares.
(D) ACI 40 for 125 shares.

103. Listed options cease trading on the third Friday of expiration month at:

(A) 3:00 p.m. Eastern Time.
(B) 3:00 p.m. Central Time.
(C) 4:30 p.m. Eastern Time.
(D) 4:30 p.m. Central Time.

104. A corporation which earns no income in a particular year would not be required to pay interest on what type of bond?

(A) Equipment trust certificate
(B) Income bond
(C) Convertible debenture
(D) Subordinated debenture

105. The inclusion of a call protection provision for a bond means:

(A) the investor must pay a premium for this protection.
(B) the issuer is protected if the bonds are called.
(C) the investor is insured against loss of principal in the event of a call.
(D) the issuer may not call the bond for some period of time.

106. A 9% bond due to mature in one year trades at 10%. What is its approximate price?

(A) $900
(B) $990
(C) $1,000
(D) $1,100

107. The most risky oil and gas limited partnership is likely to be a(n):

(A) exploratory program.
(B) balanced program.
(C) drilling program.
(D) income program.

108. If a partnership borrows money from one of its limited partners, this partner:

(A) becomes a general partner.
(B) loses his limited partner status.
(C) is in violation of the partnership agreement.
(D) becomes a general creditor of the partnership.

109. To protect itself, a Japanese car manufacturer who is buying parts from the United States and is afraid that the yen will fall relative to the dollar is most likely to buy:

(A) Japanese yen Puts.
(B) Japanese yen Calls.
(C) U.S. dollar Puts.
(D) U.S. dollar Calls.

110. An investor sells 1 CAI Jul 50 Call at 7 and 1 CAI Jul 50 Put at 3. He will profit unless CAI is:

(A) above 60 or below 40.
(B) above 57 or below 43.
(C) above 54 or below 47.
(D) above 53 or below 47.

111. The writer of a put option on D-marks would like:

(A) the D-mark to decline.
(B) the D-mark to appreciate relative to the dollar.
(C) the dollar to appreciate relative to the D-mark.
(D) United States interest rates to rise relative to German rates.

112. The usual methods for underwriting municipal bonds are:

I. negotiated for revenue bonds.
II. negotiated for general obligation bonds.
III. competitive for revenue bonds.
IV. competitive for general obligation bonds.

    (A) I and II
    (B) II and IV
    (C) III and II
    (D) III and IV

113. According to MSRB, a potential customer must be told all of the following with respect to a negotiated municipal underwriting EXCEPT:

(A) amount of any fee received from the issuer by the firm.
(B) initial offering price of each maturity.
(C) membership of the underwriting syndicate.
(D) amount of the underwriting spread.

114. The advantage of writing a covered Call is that it:

(A) limits gain on the equity position.
(B) reduces possible loss on equity position.
(C) raises maximum possible gain on the equity position.
(D) prevents major loss on the equity position.

115. Which of the following is a spread?

(A) Long 1 ACI Sep 50 Call; short 1 ACI Sep 60 Call
(B) Long 1 ACI Sep 50 Call; short 1 ACI Sep 50 Put
(C) Long 1 ACI Sep 50 Call; long 1 ACI Sep 50 Put
(D) Long 1 ACI Sep 50 Call; long 1 ACI Dec 60 Call

116. Variable annuities must be registered with the SEC and:

(A) state insurance commissions.
(B) NASD.
(C) state banking commissions.
(D) ERISA governors.

117. Arrange from first to last the order in which to allocate bonds in a new municipal bond issue.

I. Syndicate orders
II. Pre-sale orders
III. Designated orders
IV. Member orders

    (A) II, I, III, IV
    (B) III, I, II, IV
    (C) II, IV, I, III
    (D) IV, II, III, I

118. An investor writes 1 CAI 40 Call at 12 when CAI is selling at $50. If this Call is uncovered, how much must she deposit to meet margin requirements?

(A) $750
(B) $1,200
(C) $1,950
(D) $2,500

119. A customer must return a signed options agreement to the brokerage firm at which he is trading:

(A) before trading begins.
(B) within five days of when trading begins.
(C) when trading begins.
(D) within 15 days of when trading begins.

120. What type of risk is assumed by the purchaser of a fixed annuity contract?

(A) Investment risk
(B) Mortality risk
(C) Purchasing power risk
(D) All of the above

121. The ratio of net debt to assessed valuation would be considered for which type of municipal bonds?

(A) Revenue bonds
(B) General obligation bonds
(C) Industrial development bonds
(D) Double-barrelled bonds

122. An investor makes fixed payments of $1,000 each to purchase shares of a mutual fund when the shares are selling at $50, $40, and $50 respectively. Her average cost per share is closest to:

(A) $43.33.
(B) $46.15.
(C) $46.67.
(D) $50.00

123. The taxable portion of a variable annuity purchased for a lump sum payment five years earlier is taxed:

(A) not at all.
(B) as ordinary income.
(C) as capital gains.
(D) as part ordinary and part capital gains.

124. An open-end mutual fund with an NAV of $46.25 has a 7.5% load. An investor who bought these shares would pay:

(A) $46.25 per share.
(B) $49.73 per share.
(C) $50.00 per share.
(D) $53.50 per share.

125. Which of the following most closely resembles a REIT with respect to method of acquisitions?

(A) Closed-end fund
(B) Open-end fund
(C) Load fund
(D) No load fund

PART TWO

TIME 3 HOURS
QUESTIONS 126-250

DIRECTIONS

Each of the questions or incomplete statements below is followed by four suggested answer options. Choose the best answer and then blacken the corresponding space on the answer sheet.

126. When an investor sells shares in a closed end fund, he receives:

(A) NAV.
(B) NAV less commission.
(C) market price.
(D) market price less commission.

127. A variable annuity has a "15 year certain" life annuity. If the annuitant lives beyond 15 years from the time payout begins:

(A) payments stop.
(B) payments decrease but continue for the recomputed life expectancy period.

(C) payments continue as before.
(D) payments continue for the recomputed life expectancy period.

128. In the secondary market, an investor buys $20,000 municipal bonds at 92 and holds them two years to maturity where he collects $20,000. His tax liability is based on:

(A) $0.
(B) $800.
(C) $1,600.
(D) $9,200.

129. Under the "know your customer" rule, a registered representative should ascertain all of the following information EXCEPT the client's:

(A) occupation.

(B) address.

(C) investment objectives.

(D) prior trade experience.

130. When an investment company buys a portfolio of municipals and doesn't trade them, thus incurring low transaction costs, and charges no management fee it is called a:

(A) closed-end investment company.

(B) unit investment trust.

(C) face amount certificate company.

(D) open-end investment company.

131. With respect to an official statement, all of the following are true EXCEPT:

(A) an official statement must be filed with the SEC.

(B) customers must get it no later than with confirmation.

(C) it contains financial information about the issue.

(D) it is not a requirement for a new municipal issue.

132. Municipal bonds are insured by which of the following?

I. SIPC

II. MBIAC

III. FDIC

IV. FGIC

(A) I only

(B) II and IV

(C) I and III

(D) I, II, III, and IV

133. An investor has a $17,000 capital loss in 1990. If he has no other capital transactions except in 1991 when he has an $8000 gain, he will be able to deduct losses until:

(A) 1990.

(B) 1991.

(C) 1992.

(D) 1993.

134. An investor withdraws money from an IRA. If he is 55 years old at the time, he can avoid taxation or penalty on this withdrawal if:

(A) he reinvests in a five-year CD.

(B) he reinvests within 60 days in another IRA.

(C) he reinvests within 90 days in another IRA.

(D) he reinvests in an accredited retirement plan.

135. The maximum allowable contribution to an IRA for a woman with an unemployed husband is:

(A) $2,000 in one account.

(B) $2,000 in two accounts.

(C) $2,250 in one account.

(D) $2,250 in two accounts.

136. $10,000 face value municipal bonds are purchased at 107.5 when there are 15 years to maturity. If they are sold in five years for 102.5, the tax consequences are:

(A) $250 loss.

(B) $250 gain.

(C) $500 gain.

(D) $500 loss.

137. The equivalent yield for an investor in the 33% bracket for a municipal bond paying 7½% is approximately:

(A) 7½%.

(B) 10%.

(C) 11.10%.

(D) 11.19%.

138. If a callable municipal security is partially recalled, which of the following is true?

(A) The remaining bonds become less attractive.

(B) The remaining bonds become more attractive.

(C) The yield on the remaining bonds goes up.

(D) This cannot happen. The issue must be called in its entirety.

139. One benefit of an oil and gas limited partnership is:

(A) rental income.

(B) depletion allowance.

(C) mortgage interest deduction.

(D) perpetual income.

140. All of the following should be considered in deciding the suitability of a limited partnership EXCEPT:

(A) the customer's objectives.
(B) the size of the partnership.
(C) the customer's tax status.
(D) the program's managers.

141. All of the following are considered insiders in a corporation under the Securities Act of 1934 EXCEPT:

(A) a clerk who has access to non-public information.
(B) a corporate director.
(C) a corporate officer.
(D) an owner of at least 1½% of stock.

142. Which of the following would result from the Federal Reserve causing a lowering of interest rates?

(A) The dollar would rise in value relative to other currencies.
(B) The dollar would fall in value relative to other currencies.
(C) Business failures would increase.
(D) The stock market would fall.

143. An investor buys $150,000 of a direct participation program. If the program generates a $30,000 loss for her share, the tax consequences for this investor are:

(A) no loss is allowed.
(B) a $15,000 loss.
(C) a $30,000 loss.
(D) a $150,000 loss.

144. All of the following are true of limited partnerships EXCEPT:

(A) all profits are distributed equally.
(B) the partnership has a limited life.
(C) the partnership interests are generally illiquid.
(D) the partnership must demontrate an intent to be profitable.

145. The sponsor of a direct participation program might be considered to have a conflict of interest if:

(A) he managed adjacent property for himself.
(B) he exchanged partnership property at fair market value.
(C) he marketed partnership shares himself.
(D) he sought partnership approval to change objectives.

146. A letter sent to syndicate members by the manager of a successful bid on a municipal bond issue contains all of the following information EXCEPT:

(A) the amount of good faith deposit required.
(B) the exact date of settlement and delivery of the bonds.
(C) a list of each member's participation.
(D) how the bonds will be advertised.

147. How many days are municipal syndicate accounts usually set up to run for?

(A) 10 days
(B) 20 days
(C) 30 days
(D) 60 days

148. Each of the following plays some role in deciding upon eligibility of municipal securities for purchase by commercial banks, EXCEPT the:

(A) Comptroller of the Currency.
(B) Federal Reserve Bank System.
(C) FDIC.
(D) MSRB.

149. Who is entitled to the "takedown" in municipal bond underwriting?

(A) A member of the syndicate
(B) A member of the selling group
(C) Any municipal securities dealer
(D) Any trust department of a commercial bank

150. New issues of municipal securities are exempted from all but the:

(A) Securities Act of 1933.
(B) Securities Exchange Act of 1934.
(C) Holding Company Act of 1935.
(D) Trust Indenture Act of 1939.

151. Under the Securities Acts Amendments of 1975, MSRB rules are enforced by the:

I.   NYSE
II. SEC
III. Federal Reserve Board
IV. NASD

    (A) II, III, and IV only
    (B) II and III only
    (C) I and II only
    (D) I, II, III, and IV

152. A "cash" transaction of municipal bonds would settle on:

(A) the same day.
(B) the next day.
(C) five business days later.
(D) on a date to be agreed to.

153. Which of the following are exempt from *all* Federal and local income taxes?

(A) Virgin Islands
(B) Puerto Rico
(C) Guam
(D) All of the above

154. The rate of return in a tombstone advertisement for a municipal serial bond is characterized as a(n):

(A) after tax yield.
(B) effective yield.
(C) nominal yield.
(D) yield to maturity.

155. The *most* significant factor in evaluating the safety of a sewer revenue bond is:

(A) population.
(B) number of users of the sewers.
(C) property taxes.
(D) debt service coverage.

156. An investor owns 4 ACI Jan 50 calls. If ACI distributes a 25% stock dividend, the investor would now hold:

(A) 4 calls of 100 shares.
(B) 5 calls of 100 shares.
(C) 4 calls of 125 shares.
(D) 5 calls of 125 shares.

157. An investor buys a Jun DM (Deutsche mark) 68 call at ½. The size of the contract is 62,500 DM. His premium would total:

(A) $312.50.
(B) $625.00.
(C) $3,125.00.
(D) $6,250.00.

158. Which of the following is exempt from compliance with Regulation T?

(A) A broker or dealer who does not handle margin accounts.
(B) A broker or dealer who handles business only in fully registered securities.
(C) A broker or dealer who transacts less than 10% of his business through the medium of a member of a national securities exchange.
(D) None of the above.

159. All of the following taxes are recognized as flat rate taxes EXCEPT:

(A) a gift tax.
(B) an excise tax.
(C) a gasoline tax.
(D) a general tax.

160. Under Regulation T of the Federal Reserve, which of the following may grant extensions of time for payment in a client's account?

(A) The NASD
(B) The New York Stock Exchange
(C) The Midwest Stock Exchange
(D) Any of the above

161. If T-note options are backed by $100,000 of face value securities, the purchase of 4 T-note options at 16 would require a premium of:

(A) $640.
(B) $2,000.
(C) $2,560.
(D) $4,000.

162. If an account is "frozen" a customer:

(A) may sell but not buy securities.
(B) must have the necessary cash or securities in the account before the order can be executed.
(C) may not trade securities under any circumstances.
(D) Must deposit sufficient cash for any transaction by the settlement date.

163. What Federal Reserve Board regulation governs the extension of securities-related credit by banks?

(A) Regulation G
(B) Regulation T
(C) Regulation U
(D) Regulation X

164. Which of the following is an acceptable deposit to answer an NYSE maintenance call?

(A) EE Bonds
(B) United States Treasury Notes
(C) SMA
(D) None of the above

165. What is the status of a customer whose account's assets exceed the SIPC coverage limits when his broker/dealer becomes insolvent?

(A) The customer becomes a general creditor of the firm.
(B) All other broker/dealers are assessed to make up the customer losses involved.
(C) He loses the excess assets.
(D) SIPC issues notes to cover payment of the deficiency.

166. A "buy-in" of a customer occurs if he has failed to deliver securities:

(A) 10 days after settlement date.
(B) 15 days after settlement date.
(C) 20 days after settlement date.
(D) 30 days after settlement date.

167. Pledging customer securities as security for debit balances is called:

(A) subordination.
(B) hypothecation.
(C) rehypothecation.
(D) intermediation.

168. An investor seeking predictable tax-sheltered cash flow should probably choose:

(A) cattle feeding programs.
(B) oil exploration programs.
(C) real estate triple net lease back programs.
(D) undeveloped land programs.

169. The United States balance of payments deficit goes down if:

(A) foreign investment in United States companies increases.
(B) foreign investment in United States companies decreases.
(C) interest rates paid on domestic savings accounts decrease.
(D) yields on foreign deposits in the United States decrease.

170. A tax shelter specifically designed for self-employed individuals is called a(n):

(A) Individual Retirement Account.
(B) Keogh Plan.
(C) variable annuity.
(D) limited partnership.

171. To maintain a fair and orderly market and to act as a broker's broker are the two functions of the:

(A) two dollar broker.
(B) specialist.
(C) odd lot broker.
(D) floor trader.

172. A concession of 1 point on the sale of a new issue of municipals is equal to:

(A) $.10.
(B) $1.
(C) $10.
(D) $100.

173. In a trade of municipal bonds, the confirmation would include all of the following EXCEPT the:

(A) bond rating.
(B) trade date.
(C) total dollar amount of the trade.
(D) description of the bond.

174. The registered representative should maintain all of the following customer records EXCEPT a record of:

 (A) each customer's current holdings.
 (B) all of his customer's securities in a cross-indexed file.
 (C) his customer's capital gains and losses for the past three years.
 (D) all of his customer's purchases and sales for the past three years.

175. Under the UGMA, all of the following are true EXCEPT:

 (A) minors cannot make gifts to other minors.
 (B) the maximum value of a gift to a minor is $10,000.
 (C) gifts given to minors cannot be reclaimed.
 (D) only one custodian for one minor at any one time.

176. In a limited partnership, the subscription agreement contains all of the following EXCEPT:

 (A) the identity of the signatories.
 (B) the recipient of the funds.
 (C) suitability standards.
 (D) the order of priority of payouts on liquidation.

177. Which of the following NYSE orders are automatically reduced in value when the underlying stock begins trading ex-dividend?

 I. Buy Stop
 II. Buy Limit
 III. Sell Stop
 IV. Sell Limit

  (A) I and III
  (B) I and IV
  (C) II and III
  (D) II and IV

178. According to NYSE rules, decisions rendered by the Board of Arbitration are:

 (A) final and binding on all parties.
 (B) not binding on all parties.
 (C) appealable.
 (D) subject to review by NASD.

179. The bond counsel takes responsibility for all of the following EXCEPT judging:

 (A) the validity of an issue.
 (B) its eligibility for federal tax exemption.
 (C) the syndicate.
 (D) the issuance procedures.

180. Which of the following is not permitted under NYSE rules?

 (A) Numbered accounts
 (B) Accounts with three tenants in common
 (C) Third party accounts
 (D) Accounts that are opened with full trading authorization

181. All of the following represent ownership of a corporation EXCEPT:

 (A) common stock.
 (B) preferred stock.
 (C) convertible debentures.
 (D) convertible preferred.

182. Exchange-listed securities traded in the over-the-counter market are traded in:

 (A) primary market.
 (B) second market.
 (C) third market.
 (D) fourth market.

183. All of the following can be used as collateral in a margin account EXCEPT:

 (A) FNMA stock.
 (B) FNMA bonds.
 (C) option contracts.
 (D) T-notes.

184. The flow-through principle applies to all of the following EXCEPT:

 (A) corporate earnings.
 (B) mutual funds.
 (C) REITs.
 (D) limited partnerships.

185. Which of the following represents ownership of a foreign company?

 (A) Banker's acceptances
 (B) ADRs
 (C) Japanese yen options
 (D) Eurobonds

186. Which of the following best describes the tax consequences of a 5% stock dividend from a U.S. corporation?

(A) Dividend income in the year of the declaration.
(B) A capital gain in the year of the declaration.
(C) A 5% increase in the cost basis.
(D) A 5% decrease in the cost basis.

187. Which of the following generally has the longest life?

(A) Stock rights
(B) Stock options
(C) T-bond options
(D) Warrants

188. A customer bought some stock 9 months ago. If there is no further activity in the account the customer should receive a statement:

(A) the next time there is activity.
(B) monthly.
(C) quarterly.
(D) annually.

189. An investor finds that she can buy ACI on the NYSE at 50 while the market for ACI on the Pacific Stock Exchange is at 52. If she bought in New York and sold on the West Coast she would be engaging in:

(A) intermediation.
(B) arbitrage.
(C) hypothecation.
(D) fast trading.

190. Investment companies must issue financial statements:

(A) monthly.
(B) quarterly.
(C) semi-annually.
(D) after each audit.

191. The Securities Exchange Act of 1934 allows the SEC to regulate:

(A) short selling.
(B) proxy solicitations.
(C) margin activities.
(D) all of the above.

192. To qualify for listing on the NASDAQ system, a security must satisfy which of the following?

I. At least two market makers
II. Assets of at least $2,000,000
III. 100,000 shares publicly held
IV. Must be owned by at least 300 investors

(A) I and II.
(B) II and IV.
(C) I, II, and IV.
(D) I, II, III, and IV.

193. Upon the formation of a municipal security syndicate account, the syndicate letter would indicate all of the following EXCEPT the:

(A) proposed members' participation.
(B) type of issue.
(C) duration of the syndicate.
(D) yield to the public.

194. ACI has 1 million shares outstanding and makes a rights offering of 200,000 shares. If the price of ACI cum rights is $52 and the subscription price is $50, then the theoretical value of a right is:

(A) $.40.
(B) $.50.
(C) $1.00.
(D) $2.00.

195. Which of the following is true of T-bills?

(A) They are riskier than T-notes.
(B) They are sometimes issued at par.
(C) They may never yield a capital gain.
(D) Their rate is usually higher than the prime rate.

196. Property has a market valuation of $25,000,000 and is assessed uniformly at 50%. If the tax rate is 10 mills, the amount to be collected is:

(A) $12,500.
(B) $25,000.
(C) $125,000.
(D) $250,000.

197. An investor in a real estate direct participation program is least likely to benefit from:

    (A) depreciation.
    (B) depletion.
    (C) appreciation.
    (D) rental income.

198. When a new issue of stock is sold to a limited number of investors without any registration statement having been filed, this is called a:

    (A) secondary distribution.
    (B) private placement.
    (C) Rule 144 distribution.
    (D) Regulation A offering.

199. The NASD 5% markup policy could apply to which of the following?

    (A) Sale of open-end mutual fund shares
    (B) Sale of shares in a secondary distribution
    (C) Sale of over-the-counter securities
    (D) Sale of a new issue of non-exempt securities

200. All of the following are risks of participation in a limited partnership EXCEPT:

    (A) illiquidity of the investment.
    (B) an unfavorable ruling on the tax status of the program.
    (C) larger than anticipated losses.
    (D) premature termination of the program.

201. Transactions from all of the following markets appear on the consolidated tape EXCEPT those of the:

    (A) primary market.
    (B) secondary market.
    (C) third market.
    (D) fourth market.

202. All of the following are part of current assets EXCEPT:

    (A) inventory.
    (B) receivables.
    (C) payables.
    (D) marketable securities.

203. An investor in a real estate limited partnership that bought raw land would primarily be seeking:

    (A) current income.
    (B) capital appreciation.
    (C) deductions for operating expenses.
    (D) intangible cost deductions.

204. An investor buys a municipal bond "regular way" on September 12. Coupon dates for this security are June 15 and December 15. How many days of accrued interest would she have to add to the purchase price?

    (A) 88
    (B) 89
    (C) 93
    (D) 94

205. Which of the following trades appears on the tape only after the trade is completed?

    (A) Special offer
    (B) Exchange distribution
    (C) Specialist block purchase
    (D) Secondary distribution

Questions 206–208 refer to the following types of mutual funds:

    (A) Balanced fund
    (B) Growth fund
    (C) Sector fund
    (D) Income fund

206. Which type of fund is subject to industry risk?

207. Which type of fund would own low yield, high P/E stocks?

208. Which type of fund would invest in money market instruments?

209. A bond that is purchased at a discount and is used for the payment of estate taxes is called a(n):

    (A) estate bond.
    (B) deep discount bond.
    (C) tax-free bond.
    (D) flower bond.

210. A municipal bond with an 8% coupon which matures in 2010 to yield 8.5% is called at par in 1999. The yield to call is:

(A) 8%.
(B) between 8% and 8.5%.
(C) 8.5%.
(D) greater than 8.5%.

211. A mutual fund's management fee is usually:

(A) included in the front-end load.
(B) based on the number of shares outstanding.
(C) based on the performance of the fund.
(D) less than 1% of the total assets managed.

212. A firm quote would cover what quantity of stock?

(A) 1 share
(B) 100 shares
(C) 500 shares
(D) Any amount of shares

213. To facilitate his efforts at explaining direct participation programs to his clients, an accountant asks to receive your offering literature automatically. Which of the following is true?

(A) This is permitted for registered investment advisors.
(B) This is always allowed.
(C) The material must be marked "not for general public."
(D) This is not permitted.

214. If municipal bonds were no longer tax-free the likely consequence would be:

(A) municipal bond prices would fall.
(B) municipal bond yields would fall.
(C) corporate bond yields would rise.
(D) there would be no significant consequence.

215. The legal opinion on a municipal bond does all of the following EXCEPT:

(A) attest to its exemption from federal tax.
(B) describe the conditions of the bond.
(C) give assurance as to the payment of interest.
(D) attest to the validity of the issue.

216. An investor's margin account is restricted by $500. If the account is credited with $1,500 of dividends, how much can the investor withdraw?

(A) $0
(B) $500
(C) $1,000
(D) $1,500

217. A technical analyst would enter a buy-stop:

(A) below a support level.
(B) below a previous low.
(C) above a resistance level.
(D) below a resistance level.

218. When the proceeds of a gasoline tax are the only source of revenue for a bond, the bond is called a:

(A) G.O. bond.
(B) revenue bond.
(C) special tax bond.
(D) equipment tax bond.

219. The discount on an original issue municipal that is held to maturity generates what tax consequence?

(A) Some non-taxable interest income
(B) An ordinary taxable income gain
(C) A long-term capital gain
(D) A short-term capital gain

220. A DPP in a drilling program would have large deductions in the first year from:

(A) depletion allowance.
(B) depreciation.
(C) tangible drilling costs.
(D) intangible drilling costs.

221. An order was entered as good for two months and placed as GTC. Who is responsible for cancelling the order after two months?

(A) The broker
(B) The customer
(C) The member firm
(D) The specialist

222. An "insider" has filed a form 144 with the SEC. How long does he have to sell these securities under this notice?

(A) 30 days
(B) 60 days
(C) 90 days
(D) 180 days

223. If a municipal securities dealer acting for a client recommends a security, according to MSRB rules, he would have to notify the client in writing:

(A) of the security's recent range of prices.
(B) of any financial interest he had in the underwriting.
(C) of the security's credit rating.
(D) None of the above

224. Which of the following is the lowest investment grade rating?

(A) BBB
(B) Ba
(C) BB
(D) B

225. The "Official Notice of Sale" would contain all of the following EXCEPT:

(A) size of the issue.
(B) type of bond.
(C) amount of good faith deposit.
(D) bond rating.

226. Which of the following describes the "dated date" on a bond?

(A) The date on which trading begins
(B) The date on which interest begins to accrue
(C) The settlement date
(D) The trade date

Questions 227–229 refer to the excerpt from the specialist's book listed below:

BUY	CAI	SELL
200 DWR	55	
100 Hutton	⅛	
300 Drexel	¼	
	⅜	
	½	
	⅝	200 Drexel
		100 Schwab
	¾	200 Merrill
	⅞	100 DWR

227. The size of the market in CAI is:

(A) 300 by 100.
(B) 300 by 200.
(C) 300 by 300.
(D) 600 by 600.

228. The specialist could bid for stock for his own account at:

(A) 55¼.
(B) 55⅜.
(C) 55½.
(D) 55⅝.

229. If both entries at 55⅝ were sell stops, the specialist could sell from his own account at:

(A) 55⅜.
(B) 55½.
(C) 55⅝.
(D) 55¾.

230. Member firms must keep a written record of all speaking engagements for at least:

(A) six months.
(B) one year.
(C) three years.
(D) five years.

231. The type of variable annuity which will result in the largest monthly checks is:

(A) lump sum.
(B) life annuity.
(C) life annuity with rights of survivorship.
(D) 10-year certain life.

232. Selling stock under Rule 144 is regulated by the:

(A) Securities Act of 1933.
(B) Securities Exchange Act of 1934.
(C) Holding Company Act of 1935.
(D) Maloney Act of 1938.

233. Short sales on the over-the-counter market can take place:

(A) never.
(B) without restriction.
(C) after a plus tick only.
(D) after a plus tick or a zero plus tick.

234. Disintermediation is not likely to occur unless:

(A) the Fed reduces the discount rate.
(B) the Fed reduces reserve requirements.
(C) the Fed does long term reverse repos.
(D) the Fed resorts to jawboning.

235. All of the following are true of variable annuities EXCEPT:

(A) annuity income is not taxed until payout begins.
(B) returns are based on portfolio performance.
(C) there is no minimum payout.
(D) performance is proportional to the movement of the Dow.

236. An escrow account for pre-refunded municipals could contain:

(A) only secured municipals.
(B) U.S. Treasury or agency securities.
(C) any revenue bond.
(D) AAA corporate bonds.

237. When transacting a municipal bond swap, you are likely to incur a wash sale ruling if you vary only the:

(A) rating.
(B) municipality.
(C) maturity.
(D) coupon.

238. The portion of net revenues set aside for replacement of major equipment in a municipal revenue issue would be placed in a:

(A) surplus fund.
(B) renewal fund.
(C) debt service fund.
(D) maintenance fund.

239. The maximum amount that an investor could be due in a margin account without generating a margin call is:

(A) $100.
(B) $500.
(C) $1,000.
(D) at the broker's discretion.

240. The security that gives the investor the longest time within which to purchase a stock is:

(A) calls.
(B) puts.
(C) rights.
(D) warrants.

241. If an investor sells short a security that she already owns she is said to have:

(A) sold short.
(B) sold out the position.
(C) sold "short against the box."
(D) done a wash sale.

242. According to MSRB rules, copies of MSRB rules must be available at which of the following locations?

(A) Each office of the firm
(B) The main office of the firm
(C) Any office where no principal of the firm is stationed.
(D) Any office where there are at least two salespersons.

243. The opening of a numbered account under NYSE Rule 406:

(A) is never allowed.
(B) is allowed for accounts not covered by SIPC.
(C) is allowed if the investor provides a "letter of credit."
(D) requires a written voucher of responsibility.

244. In a cash account, under NYSE rules, which of the following would require written consent by an employer?

   (A) An employee of a bank

   (B) An employee of an insurance company

   (C) An employee of a trust company

   (D) None of the above

245. An abusive tax shelter is one:

   (A) which has no legitimate profit-making purpose.

   (B) which allows large tax write-offs.

   (C) which takes advantage of investors.

   (D) in which the general partner has a conflict of interest.

246. The "nine-bond" rule applies to:

   (A) bonds with coupons below 9%.

   (B) trades of 9 bonds or less.

   (C) trades of 90 bonds or less.

   (D) markets that offer no more than 9 types of bonds.

247. Under Rule 147, the minimum time before securities from intra-state offerings can be sold outside the state is:

   (A) 3 months.

   (B) 6 months.

   (C) 9 months.

   (D) 1 year.

248. The maximum coverage of cash in any one account under SIPC is:

   (A) $100,000.

   (B) $300,000.

   (C) $500,000.

   (D) unlimited.

249. All of the following are true of convertible bonds EXCEPT:

   (A) they can be converted to common stock.

   (B) they can be used as collateral.

   (C) they can be used to hedge a short position.

   (D) their coupon rate is higher than that of non-convertible bonds.

250. The random walk theory is related to:

   (A) the theory of variable returns.

   (B) the diversifiability of risk.

   (C) the efficient market hypothesis.

   (D) the existence of negative betas.

PRACTICE EXAMINATION TWO ANSWER KEY
PART ONE

1	B	33	A	65	B	97	A
2	B	34	D	66	C	98	C
3	C	35	A	67	C	99	D
4	C	36	C	68	D	100	B
5	C	37	D	69	C	101	B
6	A	38	B	70	A	102	D
7	B	39	D	71	A	103	B
8	C	40	B	72	B	104	B
9	A	41	C	73	D	105	D
10	D	42	B	74	A	106	B
11	B	43	C	75	D	107	A
12	D	44	B	76	B	108	D
13	A	45	A	77	D	109	A
14	C	46	C	78	A	110	A
15	A	47	B	79	A	111	B
16	D	48	A	80	B	112	C
17	B	49	C	81	D	113	C
18	A	50	C	82	D	114	B
19	B	51	D	83	C	115	A
20	B	52	A	84	A	116	A
21	C	53	D	85	C	117	A
22	A	54	B	86	B	118	A
23	B	55	B	87	C	119	D
24	C	56	C	88	D	120	C
25	D	57	B	89	A	121	B
26	A	58	B	90	C	122	B
27	A	59	D	91	D	123	B
28	B	60	C	92	D	124	C
29	C	61	C	93	A	125	A
30	C	62	B	94	D		
31	D	63	C	95	D		
32	C	64	C	96	B		

PRACTICE EXAMINATION TWO ANSWER KEY
PART TWO

126	D	158	D	190	C	222	C
127	C	159	A	191	D	223	B
128	C	160	D	192	D	224	A
129	D	161	B	193	D	225	D
130	B	162	B	194	B	226	B
131	A	163	C	195	C	227	C
132	B	164	B	196	C	228	B
133	C	165	A	197	B	229	B
134	B	166	A	198	B	230	C
135	D	167	C	199	C	231	B
136	A	168	C	200	C	232	A
137	D	169	A	201	A	233	B
138	B	170	B	202	C	234	D
139	B	171	B	203	B	235	D
140	B	172	C	204	D	236	B
141	D	173	A	205	B	237	A
142	B	174	C	206	C	238	B
143	C	175	B	207	B	239	B
144	A	176	D	208	D	240	D
145	A	177	C	209	D	241	C
146	B	178	A	210	D	242	A
147	C	179	C	211	D	243	D
148	D	180	C	212	B	244	D
149	A	181	C	213	D	245	A
150	D	182	C	214	A	246	B
151	A	183	C	215	C	247	C
152	A	184	A	216	D	248	A
153	D	185	B	217	C	249	D
154	D	186	D	218	C	250	C
155	D	187	D	219	A		
156	C	188	C	220	D		
157	A	189	B	221	A		

ANSWER EXPLANATIONS
PART ONE

1. **(B)** The conversion rate is $100 ÷ $45 = 2.22. If one can get 2.22 shares of common for one share of preferred and common is selling at $36, then the conversion is worth 2.22 × $36 = $79.92. So, at $90, the preferred is above parity.

2. **(B)** The Securities Exchange Act regulated the operations of the exchanges and the secondary markets in general. The Securities Act of 1933 was designed to regulate new issues.

3. **(C)** Quarterly dividends of 60 give a $2.40 annual dividend. $2.40 is 40% of the $6 that was earned.

4. **(C)** If the option is uncovered (naked) the potential loss to the writer is governed by the price change in the stock. This naturally is largest on the upside (Calls) since it can never go below $0 but can go up without limit. Recall the buyer's risk is limited to the premium.

5. **(C)** If ACI goes to 100 (Choice B), the writer gives up potential gain but actually has a profit from the straddle premium collected. If it goes to $0, she actually loses $4,500 less premiums collected.

6. **(A)** To be long a Call means to buy a Call, in which case you want the stock to rise. This is the opposite of being short stock.

7. **(B)** Accrued interest is based on actual days up to and including settlement date. This gives 17 days in January, 28 days in February, 31 in March, 30 in April, and 12 in May for a total of 118.

8. **(C)** For corporates, accrued interest is based on a 30-day month and does not include the settlement date. Hence, 16 days in March, 30 in April and May, and 4 in June for a total of 80.

9. **(A)** Options have no loan value.

10. **(D)** A deposit of $4,000 in securities would bring the market value to $34,000, at which point a $17,000 debit balance would mean the account was at 50%.

11. **(B)** With maintenance margin at 25%, ⁴/₃ times the debit balance equals the market value. ⁴/₃ × $17,000 = $22,667.

12. **(D)** With house maintenance at 30%, 1/(1 − .3) times the debit record or $24,286 is maintenance margin. Hence all $5,000 can be withdrawn from the SMA.

13. **(A)** If ACI is $40, both options are worthless. The premium on the ACI Sept 40 Call is larger than the one on the ACI Sep 50 Call so the investor pockets all of that difference.

14. **(C)** At $50, the ACI Sep 40 is worth $1,000 and the other one is worthless. Above $50, both options increase in value at the same rate and the investor's loss is unchanged. Below $50, the option he sold loses value (he gains), and, since the one he bought remains worthless, his total loss decreases. Therefore, his maximum loss occurs if ACI expires at $50 (or higher).

15. **(A)** Unless otherwise specified, good delivery requires noncallable bonds.

16. **(D)** The MSRB has no jurisdiction over municipalities which are issuing securities.

17. **(B)** The municipal begins accruing interest from the dated date up to, but not including, settlement date on a 30-day month basis. Thus, we have 30 days for January plus 14 in February.

18. **(A)** Federal National Mortgage Association securities have an implied obligation from the federal government, but it is not direct. GNMA is owned by a department of the government (HUD) and is a direct obligation. The other two choices are treasury issues and, hence, certainly direct obligations.

19. **(B)** As the name implies, the program has crossed over to where taxable income exceeds cash distributions. Often a partnership will be sold or refinanced before this point.

20. (B) Since depreciation reduces the value of assets, it represents an income loss.

21. (C) The net revenue is that revenue available for debt service after expenses have been paid.

22. (A) For example, if the premiums were 9 for the ACI Sep 40 and 3 for the ACI Sep 50, then with ACI at $46, the difference between $46 and $40 market price minus lower strike price exactly equals the difference between 9 and 3.

23. (B) A Put is "in the money" if one can sell "put" stock at a higher price than one must pay for the stock. The latter is the market price and the former is the strike (or exercise) price.

24. (C) They are, in fact, cash assets over and above the requirements for federal reserves. These are lent overnight to banks which do not have sufficient reserves to meet FRB reserve requirements.

25. (D) American Depository Receipts are receipts for shares of stock in foreign corporations.

26. (A) They are not firm quotes, but rather yesterday's closing dealer-to-dealer quote.

27. (A) The order is placed from the order room. It then goes to P&S, after which it is processed for margin (if necessary), and, finally, goes to the cashier for disbursements or collection.

28. (B) At $46, the $700 premium exactly offsets the $700 loss in the value of CAI.

29. (C) If CAI is at $51, the buyer exercises at $50, which means that our investor collects $5,000. He paid $5,300 for the shares and has pocketed a $700 premium. The net of these transactions is $400.

30. (C) This is the most he can make during the life of the option since he can never get more than $5,000 plus $700 in premium no matter how high CAI goes. Of course, he can gain more after expiration if CAI was below $50 until then and rises afterwards.

31. (D) The basis consists of the total liability of the investor, which would include the value of a recourse loan.

32. (C) Losses cannot exceed the value of any passive income for the year. Of course, the investor could carry forward as much as $20,000 if the entire oil program investment, including the recourse loan, were to be lost.

33. (A) The point of a functional sharing arrangement is to allow the limited partners all of the deductible expenses.

34. (D) All of the other choices describe events that occur later.

35. (A) The premium for the Put is much larger than that for the Call. This must reflect intrinsic value, *i.e.*, the Put is in the money. Therefore, the strike price $40 for the Put is above the market price.

36. (C) If ACI is at $40, both options expire worthless and the investor loses both premiums or $600.

37. (D) If ACI goes to $0, he earns $4,000 − $600, which is the most he can make from the Put. If ACI goes to $100, he earns $6,000 − $600, and the higher ACI goes the higher is his profit. In principle, there is no upper bound on ACI's price, and, hence, his profit potential is also unlimited.

38. (B) At $50, he earns $1,000 on his Call and has paid $600 in premiums for a net profit of $400.

39. (D) The discount rate is the least volatile of these rates as it represents a conscious choice by the Fed to affect rates. Of the others, the prime rate is least volatile, but it too is now automatically readjusted as other rates move.

40. (B) There is no previous payment date on a new issue. Thus, the dated date is when interest begins to accrue.

41. (C) The *Blue List* describes already issued securities.

42. (B) The 8% coupon yielding $8\tfrac{3}{8}$% has a greater discount than the $7\tfrac{1}{4}$% coupon yielding $7\tfrac{3}{8}$%. The other two are not at a discount. It is important to remember that this might not be true if the securities had different times to maturity.

43. (C) Break-even will occur when he can realize the same amount from exercising as he has paid in premiums, in this case, if he exercises (to buy at $50) when the market price is $54.

44. (B) His maximum possible loss occurs if his investment is worthless. He paid three times $400 for this, so his loss can be as high as $1,200.

45. (A) If he exercises, he buys at $50. The total on three Calls is three times $5,000. With a 50% Regulation T, he must put up $7,500. The premiums paid earlier go to the writer and are irrelevant here.

46. (C) The denomination of the issue would not affect the ability of the municipality to service or repay the debt.

47. (B) By definition. The Federal Funds rate is the rate on funds *between* banks. The prime is the rate at which banks lend to their best customers.

48. (A) The total equity is $25,000 in the cash account + $14,000 in the long account ($30,000 − $16,000) + $4,000 in the short account ($14,000 − $10,000) for a total of $43,000.

49. (C) The buying power in the margin accounts comes from the SMA. The $4,000 there gives $8,000 in buying power with Regulation T at 50%.

50. (C) The total buying power would consist of $9,000 in cash and $20,000 in marginable securities. This comes to $18,000 (two times cash) + $20,000 or $38,000.

51. (D) The Value Line index option has a multiple of 500 times the quoted value. 500 × $2.50 = $1,250.

52. (A) She breaks even where the $200 premium exactly offsets her loss on the stock. This occurs when CAI is at $43 since she bought it at $45. Note: The option strike price is irrelevant here.

53. (D) Her profit is $500 from stock which she bought at $45 and sold at $50 plus $200 of premium.

54. (B) Her loss is limited to $4,300. She loses $4,500 if the stock is worthless minus the $200 premium that she collected. Note: Her *potential profit* from owning the stock is unlimited and giving up this opportunity is *not a loss*.

55. (B) If a bond (par value $1,000) can be converted into common stock at $100 per share, then the conversion ratio is 10 shares to one bond.

56. (C) If they are at parity, then 10 shares must be worth $1,150 or each share $115.

57. (B) Only the shares which are issued (not including treasury stock) get dividends. Here 7,000,000 shares times $.75 per share = $5,250,000.

58. (B) The current yield is $3.00 ÷ $50.00 = 6%.

59. (D) The SEC responsibility is to determine that the statement contains all of the required information and not to pass judgment on the accuracy of the statement or advisability of the investment.

60. (C) The maximum possible profit would occur if ACI were at $45 where the 50 Puts would be worth $500 each and the 45 Puts would be worthless. Since the investor paid a *net* price of $300 for this opportunity for a net profit of $200 and there are two options, the maximum possible profit is two times $200 or $400.

61. (C) The maximum loss occurs if the investor loses all premiums, in this case ($350 − $50) times two. Note: There is no loss possible from exercise because the investor can exercise (at $50) if the option written is exercised (at $45).

62. (B) This investment breaks even if ACI is at $47 where being long a Put with a $50 strike earns $300, which is the net premium ($350 paid, $50 collected) paid.

63. (C) By definition. The current yield is the coupon rate divided by the market price as a percentage of par. The yield to maturity is a combination of the current and any additional yield positive (or negative) if the bond is selling at a discount (or premium).

64. (C) For United States treasuries, "regular way" is next business day payment and delivery.

65. (B) The investor collects $90 (9% of $1,000) and must add $10 each year for the ten years as additional interest since the bond purchased at $900 pays $1,000 at maturity. In the first year, $70 of the $90 goes to the previous owner, leaving the investor with $20 plus $10 = $30.

66. (C) The winning bid is the one that results in the lowest cost to the municipality.

67. (C) Legal opinions are the responsibility of bond attorneys.

68. (D) This does not include expenses generated in the normal course of business like business dinners, etc.

69. (C) Discretionary accounts of all kinds require written authorization.

70. (A) At $33, the $200 premium is offset by the $200 loss from having to buy 100 shares at $35 when their market value is $33.

71. (A) The maximum possible profit for someone who has written an option with no other position occurs if the investor keeps the entire premium, in this case $200.

72. (B) If CAI is at $25, the writer forced to buy at $35 loses $1,000 minus the $200 that he collected.

73. (D) The other statements are true. The fact that they mature quickly means that they have less principal risk than T-bonds.

74. (A) The yellow sheets have unlisted corporates and their market makers. Pink sheets are for securities, and the others are for municipal bonds.

75. (D) A dealer is not required to reveal the mark-up on a transaction but must list any commission that is charged.

76. (B) This act was the first major attempt to regulate the securities industries and focused primarily on the issuance of new securities.

77. (D) This act dealt with the secondary market and, in particular, the regulation of the exchanges. The cooling-off period refers to new issues and the time between the filing of a registration and its effective dates.

78. (A) Break-even occurs where the premium paid per share, $1.50, equals the amount realized per share on the stock position. Since it was sold short at $50, this occurs when ACI reads $48.50.

79. (A) The maximum possible profit would occur when the short position was most profitable. This naturally is at $0. Note: Any profits made by exercising the Call are lost on the short position.

80. (B) The maximum possible loss would occur if ACI were at $55: a loss of $1,000 on the short position plus a loss of $300 in premium for a total of $1,300.

81. (D) They are subject to all of these taxes. The GNMA pools of mortgages will include some mortgages which are refinanced when interest rates drop sharply. This is a return of capital.

82. (D) Earnings per share are net income divided by shares outstanding. In this case, three million dollars divided by one million dollars, since treasury stock is not part of outstanding shares.

83. (C) The profit margin on operations is operating profit divided by operating revenue (net sales here) or five million dollars divided by twenty million dollars.

84. (A) Times earned interest is earnings before interest and taxes, EBIT (the money available to pay interest with), divided by interest costs. In this case, five and a half million dollars divided by one million dollars or five and a half.

85. (C) The same class is all options of the same type (Put or Call) on the same security.

86. (B) An option "at the money" has no intrinsic value yet. It is at the point where it can begin to accumulate intrinsic value.

87. (C) A straddle is a Put and a Call on the same equity with the same strike. A long straddle is owning or buying a straddle.

88. (D) Commercial paper matures in 270 days or less. This allows issuers to avoid registration of these securities.

89. (A) A major tool in foreign trade. It allows traders to arrange payment in other countries at later dates.

90. (C) Repos are securities which are traded with an express agreement to repossess than at some specific future date.

91. (D) Joint tenants with rights of survivorship, choice A, means that the surviving tenant retains the deceased's interest.

92. (D) There is no such disclosure form.

93. (A) None of the other choices meet the requirements that the delivery be in round lots or units which make up single round lots. Choice A does since $4 \times 25 = 100$ and $5 \times 20 = 100$.

94. (D) The OCC is the issuer of all contracts. It is technically "on the other side" of each long or short.

95. (D) This is the rule except under extraordinary circumstances.

96. (B) By definition. Note: This is the requirement of the OCC, not the Federal Reserve.

97. (A) T-notes and T-bonds are issued in denominations of $1,000. The notes have maturity of one to ten years while bonds have maturities of ten to thirty years (or longer).

98. (C) These are non-negotiable and so would be useless to the broker if he held them as forfeit on a loan.

99. (D) As worded, choice D is correct since under cumulative voting he may cast up to 800 votes for a single director.

100. (B) If the employing firm acknowledges the fact of the account and does not want the confirms, the representative may proceed as with every other customer.

101. (B) No adjustments are made for cash dividends. All of the others result in a change in the number of shares represented. To keep the value constant, shares and strike prices are adjusted.

102. (D) The stock dividend changes 100 shares to 125 shares. The strike is adjusted so that $125 \times \$40$ (new strike) = $100 \times \$50$ (old strike).

103. (B) Trading for expiration month ends at 3:00 p.m. Central Time (4:00 p.m. Eastern Time). Other options trade for ten minutes longer.

104. (B) An income or adjustment bond promises to repay principal in full at maturity but pays interest only if earnings are sufficient to meet the payment.

105. (D) The investor is protected from the possibility of the bond being called during some time after issuance. Since the bond is called by the issuer only if that is good for him, and hence bad for the investor, call protection is valuable to the investor.

106. (B) If it trades to yield 10 and matures in one year, then the interest ($90)—plus appreciation—represent a 10% yield to maturity. Using the approximation (interest plus appreciation) divided by (average of current price and price at maturity). Choice B gives ($90 + $10) ÷ $995 or approximately 10%. None of the others is close to this value.

107. (A) Each of the others has at least a component that consists of productive wells.

108. (D) There is no change of status for such a limited partner.

109. (A) There are no dollar options, so to protect against a falling yen, one would buy Puts on the Japanese yen.

110. (A) He has collected $1,000 in premiums. He profits if exercise does not cost $1,000. Choice A is the only one where he loses more than $1,000 from exercise.

111. (B) The Put writer does not want to be exercised. He does not want D-marks to decline. Note: If United States interest rates rise (choice D), the dollar is more attractive and D-marks less attractive, which the writer does not want.

112. (C) Revenue bonds are usually awarded under competitive bidding and general obligation bonds are negotiated.

113. (C) This is not material to the investor's decision about the worth of the investment. It might steer him to a different broker.

114. (B) Writing a Call, one collects a premium which effectively lowers the cost of the underlying stock. This reduces possible loss but does not prevent major loss. Naturally, there is no advantage to limiting gain (choice A).

115. (A) A spread is being long and short a Call (or a Put) at different strike prices.

116. (A) Since annuities are a form of insurance, the securities are under the jurisdiction of state insurance commissions in any states where they are sold.

117. (A) Orders received before the sale get priority. Then sales for the benefit of the entire syndicate, then designated orders, and, finally, orders from members.

118. (A) The requirement is 15% of market value plus premium (less any out of the money). Here 15% of $5,000 plus $1,200 = $1,950. Since $1,200 has been collected in premiums, an additional $750 must be deposited.

119. (D) This agreement must be returned within 15 days of the beginning of trading. If it is not, trading is restricted to closing out exiting positions.

120. (C) With a fixed annuity payment, he assumes the risk that the purchasing power of that payment will be inadequate.

121. (B) A general obligation would be affected by the overall debt level relative to the base from which revenues (taxes) are generated. All of the other choices have specific revenues or another source of revenue.

122. (B) The $3,000 invested has purchased 20, 25, and 20 shares respectively. This gives an average cost of $3,000 divided by 65 or $46.15.

123. (B) Some of the payment is considered a return of capital, but the taxable portion is taxed as ordinary income.

124. (C) The 7.5% is based on the selling price. Here 7.5% of $50 = $3.75, which when subtracted from $50, yields the NAV of $46.25.

125. (A) A REIT is bought and sold on the market. As such, it resembles a closed-end fund which is not redeemed but rather is bought and sold in the market.

ANSWER EXPLANATIONS PART TWO

126. (D) A closed-end fund is sold on the market, and, hence, the seller receives the market price less any commission which is charged.

127. (C) The 15-year certain future guarantees a minimum payment to the annuitant or his estate. It does not affect the payment of a life annuity except that the existence of a minimum payment reduces the size of the payments.

128. (C) Municipals purchased in the market are treated as capital assets. If redeemed at face value, the investor realizes a $1,600 gain.

129. (D) Although it could help, it is not necessary to know the client's prior trading experience.

130. (B) No management fee, low sales charges, and a fixed portfolio of municipal or corporate bonds are the characteristics of a unit investment trust.

131. (A) Since municipal securities are exempt from the Securities Act of 1933, there is no requirement that an official statement be filed with the SEC.

132. (B) The Financial Guarantee and Insurance Company and the Municipal Bond Investors Assurance Company are two

companies that insure municipal bond investors. Two others are AMBAC Indemnity Corporation and Bond Investors Guaranty Insurance Corporation. Neither the FDIC nor the SIPC directly insures municipal bonds.

133. (C) The investor may deduct up to $3,000 of capital loss from ordinary income and carry the remainder forward. In this case, $3,000 for 1990, $11,000 for 1991, after netting out the $8,000 gain and $3,000 for 1992, exhausts the $17,000 capital loss.

134. (B) To avoid penalty or taxation, he must rollover this investment into another IRA within 60 days.

135. (D) No more than $2,000 may be deposited in a single account, but a $250 spousal deposit is allowed.

136. (A) The premium on this bond can be amortized over the life of the bond. Over five years, this would bring the price to $105 and hence a sale for $102.50 would represent a loss of $250.

137. (D) The equivalent yield is found by dividing the yield by 1 − tax bracket. Here 7½% divided by (1 − .33) = 11.19%.

138. (B) After a partial recall, the remaining bonds are more attractive since the total outstanding debt is now smaller and the likelihood of default is less.

139. (B) The depletion allowance refers to oil sold. The other choices are more directly applicable to real estate partnership except for choice D, which does not pertain to anything in particular.

140. (B) The size of a partnership does not directly or materially affect the suitability of the investment.

141. (D) To be considered an insider, one would have to own more than 10% of the stock.

142. (B) If the Federal Reserve caused interest rates to drop, the dollar would become less attractive as an investment vehicle for foreigners. They would sell dollars to invest in other countries.

143. (C) A passive investment cannot generate losses beyond the size of the investment.

Here the $30,000 loss is less than the total investment.

144. (A) Profits (and losses) are not distributed equally but rather in accordance with the percentage of participation by each investor.

145. (A) If he managed an adjacent property, he might be in a position to take advantage of that to the detriment of the partnership. The other choices do not inherently represent a conflict of interest.

146. (B) The settlement date would not be known. The bonds would trade on a when-issued basis. Such a letter is called a "release letter."

147. (C) The usual syndicate is set up for 30 days.

148. (D) The MSRB does not regulate institutional participation in the municipal bond market.

149. (A) The syndicate members get the takedown or discount from the offering price.

150. (D) All debt securities require an indenture and come under the provisions of the Trust Indenture Act of 1939.

151. (A) The NYSE has no direct enforcement responsibility for the MSRB.

152. (A) By definition. MSRB Rule 12.

153. (D) In general, all U.S. territories are triple exempt.

154. (D) Serial bonds are generally advertised on a yield to maturity basis. Term bonds are advertised on a dollar price basis.

155. (D) The most relevant factor would be the debt service coverage rather than the number of users since the latter does not specify anything about the rates that users pay.

156. (C) The number of shares in each option would be adjusted as would the exercise price. In this case, the exercise price would be 400 shares × $50/500 shares = $40.

157. (A) The premium would be 0.5 cents for each of 62,500 marks. This total is $312.50.

158. (D) Since Regulation T covers both cash and margin accounts, all of these come under it.

159. (A) Since the gift tax does not apply to the first $10,000 in any one year it is not a flat tax.

160. (D) All of them are empowered to grant extensions under appropriate circumstances.

161. (B) The existence of the backing is irrelevant since the investor is purchasing the options. The premium would be $^{16}/_{32}$ or $500 for each of the 4 options.

162. (B) An account that is "frozen" can only transact on the basis of payment or delivery in advance.

163. (C) By definition. Regulation U regulates credit by banks.

164. (B) The notes are negotiable and, hence, suitable. The EE's are not, and, of course, SMA funds are already in the account as part of equity so they do not represent an additional source of margin.

165. (A) The extent of coverage is limited and no additional coverage (choices B and D) is available. He does become a creditor of the firm.

166. (A) Ten days' grace is all that is allowed before the securities are bought back.

167. (C) By definition. Hypothecation is the pledging of his securities by the customer to the firm.

168. (C) Since the leasing arrangement provides a schedule of rent payments, the cash flow is most predictable.

169. (A) Foreign investment represents the purchase of U.S. goods even if they are capital goods. This decreases the balance of payments deficit.

170. (B) Keogh plans are specifically designed for self-employed individuals. All of the other choices apply to a more general population.

171. (B) These are part of the specialist's responsibility.

172. (C) Since each point is 1% of par, one point of a $1,000 bond is $10.

173. (A) While some firms do include the bond rating, MSRB rules do not require it. They do require a complete description of the bonds and the transaction including: coupon, call features, principal amount, accrued interest, and whether the firm acted as broker or agent.

174. (C) Recording his gains and losses is not required, nor are records of dividend payments required.

175. (B) There is no maximum; however, gifts of more than $10,000 per person per annum are subject to gift taxes.

176. (D) The order of priority of payouts would be in the partnership agreement.

177. (C) The acronym OBLOSS (open buy limit, open sell stop) describes orders that are automatically reduced.

178. (A) There is no appeal and all parties are subject to the findings.

179. (C) The bond counsel is responsible for the issue and not for the underwriters.

180. (C) Third party accounts are never permitted under NYSE rules.

181. (C) These do not represent ownership unless and until they have actually been converted.

182. (C) The primary market is the new issue market, the second is the over-the-counter, and the fourth is the one between institutional traders.

183. (C) There is no loan value on an option contract so such contracts cannot be used as collateral.

184. (A) Corporate earnings do not flow through to investors; they are taxed at the corporate level first.

185. (B) American Depository Receipts are negotiable receipts for specified numbers of shares of stock in foreign corporations.

186. (D) The stock dividend is treated as if the original purchase price was for all of the shares including those of the dividend. This effectively reduces the purchase price by 5%.

187. (D) Warrants usually can exist for some years. Rights typically expire in one year and options expire even sooner.

188. (C) Brokers are required to supply quarterly statements for inactive accounts.

189. (B) Arbitrage is the purchase and sale of the same security in two different markets in the hopes of being able to gain some price advantage.

190. (C) Some issue them more regularly.

191. (D) In general, the act regulates trading on the exchanges.

192. (D) In addition, the stock must have a minimum bid price of $5.

193. (D) The yield to the public would not be known until after a bid had been entered.

194. (B) Each share gets one right so that five rights are necessary to acquire one new share. The theoretical value is computed as the difference between a share "cum" rights and a share "ex" rights divided by the number of rights minus one. Here we have ($52 − $50) ÷ (5 − 1) = $.50.

195. (C) T-bills are always issued at a discount and the difference between purchase and sale prices is interest income.

196. (C) A tax rate of 1 mill represents $1 per $1,000 of assessed value. In this case, we have an assessed value of $12,500,000 and a rate of 10 mills or 10 × $12,500.

197. (B) Depletion is generally available from oil and gas programs.

198. (B) By definition.

199. (C) All of the others are sold through a prospectus and the rule does not apply.

200. (C) The nature of a limited partnership is that the risk is limited usually, although not always, to the amount invested.

201. (A) The primary market is the new issue market and does not appear on the tape.

202. (C) In fact, accounts payable is part of current liabilities.

203. (B) None of the other choices make much sense with respect to raw land. The investor hopes that the value of the land will increase.

204. (D) Regular way would settle on the 19th and accrued interest would be 16 days in June, 30 each for July and August, and 18 in September (up to but not including settlement day) for a total of 94 days.

205. (B) A special offer and a secondary distribution both appear beforehand, and the specialist block purchase does not appear at all. Only the exchange distribution is announced after the fact.

206. (C) A fund that invests in only one sector of the economy is subject to the risk that that sector or industry may falter.

207. (B) Growth stocks pay low dividends because they reinvest earnings. They are attractive and hence have high P/Es in spite of their low yields.

208. (D) An investment in money market instruments yields current income with little opportunity for capital loss or gain.

209. (D) By definition.

210. (D) The bond must have been sold at a discount to yield 8.5% on an 8% coupon. If it is called earlier *at par* then the yield would increase even more.

211. (D) Management fees are usually based on the amount managed and are some small percentage of that amount.

212. (B) Unless otherwise specified, any firm commitment to buy or sell is for 100 shares.

213. (D) This is not permitted. In providing this information to his clients, the accountant is, effectively, soliciting from the general public.

214. (A) The consequences are that they would be less attractive. When their price falls, their yield rises, which is what would be required to make them attractive again.

215. (C) The legal opinion does not guarantee interest payments.

216. (D) The investor can always take all cash dividends credited to the account.

217. (C) The breakout from this resistance area could be a signal to establish a long position.

218. (C) A municipal issue financed by a specific tax is called a special tax bond.

219. (A) The discount on original issue municipal bonds is considered part of the (nontaxable) interest that these bonds pay.

220. (D) All of the other costs would not be large if they existed at all in the first year.

221. (A) This is part of the broker's responsibility.

222. (C) As detailed in the act.

223. (B) In general, he would notify the client of any relationship which might represent a conflict of interest.

224. (A) Alternatively Baa.

225. (D) The rating would not exist yet.

226. (B) By definition.

227. (C) The size is the number of shares of the highest bid and the lowest offer.

228. (B) He would have to bid more than any of the customer bids.

229. (B) He would have to offer at a lower price than the customer offers. The stop offers would not be triggered by his action. Recall that his bid and offer may not trigger stops.

230. (C) By NYSE rules.

231. (B) All of the others (except the lump sum which has no monthly payment) have some fixed minimum. This forces the monthly payment to be lower than if it were not so encumbered.

232. (A) This is a regulation dealing with the registration of securities.

233. (B) Since there is no auction, but rather a negotiated market, there is no restriction on short sales.

234. (D) Also called "moral suasion." This is one way that the Fed attempts to reduce borrowing. It undertakes such an effort when rates are getting high. This is the only choice that fits the definition of disintermediation, the removal of money from banks to earn higher rates elsewhere.

235. (D) There is no direct link to the Dow even though payout is related to portfolio performance.

236. (B) These funds must be secure, and they represent advanced refunding of the original issue. Technically, the refunded bonds are no longer considered part of the municipalities' indebtedness. This process is also called defeasement.

237. (A) Different issuers is the safest way of avoiding wash sale rulings. Otherwise, the coupon and the maturity should be substantially different. The rating has least power to avoid a wash sale ruling.

238. (B) Choice D, maintenance funds come from gross revenues. The other funds come from net revenues. The order of disbursement would be: debt service, renewal, and then surplus, which might be used for redemption or for expanding the facility.

239. (B) This is a Regulation T requirement.

240. (D) Warrants have a long life and may even be perpetual. The calls and rights are both short lived and the Puts, of course, cannot be used to purchase stock.

241. (C) The point is that there are now two positions, one long and one short.

242. (A) By MSRB rules.

243. (D) Numbered accounts are allowed as long as the owner of the account has given written testimony that he is responsible for it.

244. (D) These are cash accounts. For margin accounts they would be required to get consent of (and to have duplicate copies of statements sent to) their employers.

245. (A) The definition of an abusive tax shelter. None of the other choices defines an abusive shelter.

246. (B) By definition. The rule states that orders for nine bonds or less must ordinarily be brought to the floor of the exchange.

247. (C)

248. (A) The total coverage for any one account has a maximum of $500,000 but only $100,000 of that can be for cash in the account.

249. (D) The conversion feature is a sweetener that allows them to be offered with a lower coupon.

250. (C) The efficient market hypothesis comes in three forms; weak, semi-strong, and strong. All of them say, with differing degrees of qualification, that one cannot trade markets profitably. The theory of random walk roughly states that future price movements are random in size and direction. Hence, one should not be able to predict the future direction of the market (or of any single security, for that matter).

Index

intrinsic value (options), 171
investment advisors, 74, 205
investment banker, 115
Investment Company Acts, 78, 82-84, 325
investment grade security, 34
IRAs, 107-09
issued stock, 10

joint accounts, 79, 204, 209

Keogh plans, 108
"Know Your Customer" rule, 202, 342, 348

leading indicators, 249
"legal list," 205, 328
legal opinion (bonds), 45, 126
letter of intent, 76-77
liabilities, 264
lien bonds, 24-25
LIFO (last in first out), 268
limit orders, on NYSE 149, 155; on OTC, 137; with odd lots, 157
limited partnership, 92-101
limited tax bond, 42
liquidity ratios, 270-71
listing on NYSE, 147, 345; of options, 183
"load," 75
loan value (margins), 217, 220-21
local lists (OTC), 139

maintenance calls, 226-29, 236
managed offerings, 95
management company, 70-71, 74, 83
manipulation, 321-22, 337
"mark to the market," 178, 235
market maker, 135
"market not held" order, 150
market orders, on NYSE, 149; on OTC, 137
"market out" clause, 118
market value, 10, 30
markup, 136, 139-40, 334, 349
matching orders, 321
member order, 126
membership, in NASD, 330-31; on NYSE, 146-47
MGIC, 47
mini-max underwriting, 117
minus tick, 236
monetary policies, 250-53
money supply, 251

Moody's Manual, 50
moral obligation bonds, 43
mortality risk, 101
mortgage bonds, 24-25
MSRB, see Municipal Securities Rulemaking Board
multiplier effect, 252
Municipal Guaranty Insurance Corp (MGIC), 47
Municipal Securities Rulemaking Board (MSRB), 345-46; rules, 346-50
Munifacts, 50, 125

NASDAQ, 138, 300; index, 257
National Assn. of Securities Dealers (NASD), 323-24, 329-30; regulations, 331-40
National Market System (NMS), 138-39
national list (OTC), 139
NAV, see net asset value
negotiated offering, 116
net asset value (NAV), 70-71, 75
new account form, 202-03
New Housing Authority bonds, 43
New York Stock Exchange (NYSE), 146-48; Index, 256; regulations, 340-45
nine-bond rule, 158
"no load," 75
nominal yield, 31
noncyclical industries, 260-61
nonmanaged offering, 95
nonrecourse financing, 94, 96
"not held" order, 150
numbered accounts, 208, 345
NYSE, see New York Stock Exchange

odd-lot theory, 258-59
odd lots, 156-57
"offer wanted," 137
offering circular, 319
Official Notice of Sale, 124, 125
official statement, 42-43
oil and gas programs, 93-94, 99-100
open end bond issues, 25
open end investment companies, 71, 80
"opening the books," 121
Options Clearing Corp. (OCC), 168; rules 181-83
Options Disclosure Document, 179, 180

order ticket, 209
overallot/oversell, 122
overlapping debt, 42, 52
owner bonds, 45

par value, 10, 30
parity price, 16, 28
part round lot, 157
participating preferred stock, 16
partnership accounts, 204, 209; see also limited partnerships
"pass-through" certificates, 39
passive income/losses, 92
penalty syndicate clause, 118-19
pension plans, 106-09
PHA bonds, 43
pink sheets, 139
plus-tick rule, 236, 321-22
points, on bonds, 31, 47
pollution control bonds, 44
portfolio policies, 276-77
position limits (options), 182-83, 193
preemptive rights, 14-15
preference items, 287-88
preferred stocks, 16
preliminary prospectus, 120, 314
premiums on options, 169, 171-72, 192
price-earnings ratio, 275
price spread (option strategy), 176
pricing, of bonds, 30-31; of investment company shares, 70-71, 74-75; of options, 181
primary offerings, 116, 313-15
prime rate, 253
priority, 148
private placements, 116, 315-16
"proceeds transactions," 140
profitability ratios, 272-73
prospectus for mutual funds, 84, 315; options, 179; stocks, 121, 314
protective convenants, 24, 45
proxies, 13, 323, 332
prudent man rule, 205, 327
public offering price (POP), 123
put (bonds), 29
puts (options), 168, 170, 178

qualified legal opinion, 45
quick ratio, 270